lonely p

D0248944

# Discover
# Scotland

Contents

Throughout this book, we use these icons to highlight special recommendations:

 **The Best...**
Lists for everything from bars to wildlife – to make sure you don't miss out

**Don't Miss**
A must-see – don't go home until you've been there

**Local Knowledge** Local experts reveal their top picks and secret highlights

**Detour**
Special places a little off the beaten track

**If you like...**
Lesser-known alternatives to world-famous attractions

These icons help you quickly identify reviews in the text and on the map:

**Sights**

**Eating**

**Drinking**

**Sleeping**

**Information**

**This edition written and researched by**
Neil Wilson,
Andy Symington

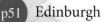

p233 Inverness &
the Highlands

p195

Skye & the Islands

p151 Stirling &
Northeast Scotland

Glasgow &
Loch Lomond  p111   p51 Edinburgh

# Contents

## Plan Your Trip | On the Road

# Contents

## On the Road

## Skye & the Islands · 195

## Inverness & the Highlands · 233

## In Focus

## Survival Guide

# This Is Scotland

Like a fine malt whisky, Scotland is a connoisseur's delight. It's an intoxicating blend of stunning scenery and sophisticated cities, of salt-tanged sea air and dark peaty waters, of wry humour and generous hospitality. It's a land with a rich, multilayered history that reveals its true depth and complex flavours only to those who savour it slowly.

Every corner of the Scottish landscape seems steeped in the past. A deserted croft on an island shore, a moor that was once a battlefield, a cave that once sheltered Bonnie Prince Charlie. History feels very close here, lurking over your shoulder as you explore the echoing halls of ancient castles, stately homes and royal palaces.

Scotland has made a contribution to Western civilization that's out of proportion to its size. The long list of influential Scottish scientists, philosophers, writers, explorers and inventors would fill a book – it was Scots who gave the world steamships, television, the telephone and countless other world-changing inventions. Oh, and golf, too. The country's museums and art galleries are richly rewarding.

The Highlands and islands are one of Europe's last great wildernesses. Their high peaks, wooded valleys and deep-sea lochs are a wildlife haven where you can see golden eagles soaring above the mountains and red deer foraging in the glens, spot otters frolicking along the kelp-fringed shores of Skye and watch minke whales breaching through shoals of mackerel off the coast of Mull.

Edinburgh, the festival city, is one of the world's favourite party towns, but it's also rich in history and culture. Glasgow offers stunning galleries, great pubs and a foot-stomping live-music scene, while Inverness combines a gorgeous riverside setting with superb dining. You could spend a whole lifetime savouring Scotland, but we've distilled it down to the quintessential experiences. Discover it your way.

> **"**
> *Scotland reveals its true depth only to those who savour it slowly*
> **"**

Bagpiper

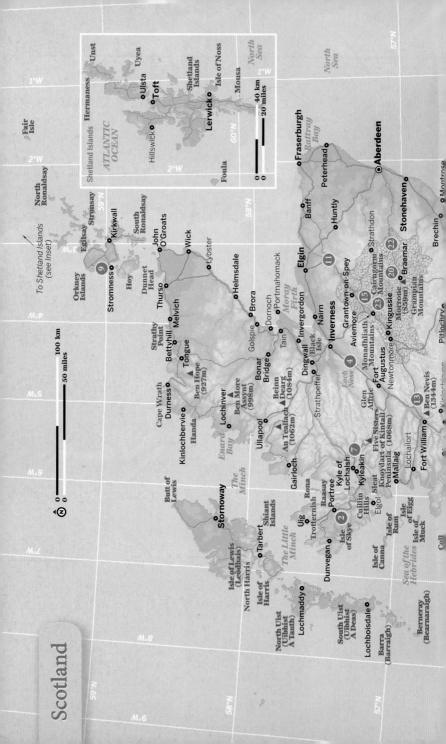

# Scotland

# 25 Top Experiences

| # | Experience |
|---|---|
| 1 | Edinburgh |
| 2 | Isle of Skye |
| 3 | Glasgow |
| 4 | Loch Ness |
| 5 | Walking |
| 6 | Golf |
| 7 | Castles |
| 8 | Perthshire |
| 9 | Ancient Sites |
| 10 | Rosslyn Chapel |
| 11 | Whisky |
| 12 | Glen Coe |
| 13 | Climbing Ben Nevis |
| 14 | Island Hopping |
| 15 | Wildlife |
| 16 | Loch Lomond |
| 17 | Stirling Castle |
| 18 | Isle of Iona |
| 19 | The Trossachs |
| 20 | Highland Games |
| 21 | Edinburgh Military Tattoo |
| 22 | Royal Deeside |
| 23 | Caledonian Pine Forest |
| 24 | Seafood |
| 25 | Fingal's Cave |

ELEVATION

1000m
700m
500m
300m
200m
100m
0

# 25 Scotland's Top Experiences

# Edinburgh

Scotland's capital (p51) may be famous for its festivals, but there's much more to it than that. Edinburgh is a city of many moods: see the Old Town silhouetted against a blue spring sky and a yellow haze of daffodils, or visit on a chill December morning with the fog snagging the spires of the Royal Mile, rain on the cobblestones and a warm glow beckoning from the window of a pub. The Royal Mile

1

JOHN SCOTT/ISTOCK ©

## ② Isle of Skye

In a country famous for stunning scenery, the Isle of Skye (p195) takes top prize. From the craggy peaks of the Cuillin Hills (p214) and the bizarre pinnacles of the Old Man of Storr (p218) and Quiraing (p218) to the spectacular sea cliffs of Neist Point, there's a photo opportunity at almost every turn. Walkers can share the landscape with red deer and golden eagles, and refuel in convivial pubs and top seafood restaurants. Sligachan, Isle of Skye

# Glasgow

Scotland's biggest city (p111) lacks Edinburgh's classical beauty, but makes up for it with a barrelful of things to do and a warmth and energy that leave every visitor impressed. Edgy and contemporary, it's a great spot to browse art galleries and – despite the deep-fried-Mars-bar reputation – it's Scotland's best place to eat. Add in what is perhaps Britain's best pub culture and one of the world's best live-music scenes, and the only thing to do is live it. Merchant City, Glasgow (p122)

## The Best...
## Places for Food

**GLASGOW**
Huge range of cuisines in the best food city in Scotland. (p135)

**EDINBURGH**
Sophisticated and atmospheric restaurants, some Michelin-starred. (p89)

**INVERNESS**
Has developed an excellent dining scene in recent years, with some outstanding restaurants. (p249)

**OBAN**
Probably has more top-notch seafood restaurants than any other town in Scotland. (p221)

**ISLE OF SKYE**
Funky cafes, fish restaurants, and fine dining at Three Chimneys. (p217)

## The Best...
## Hiking

**GLEN COE**
Scotland's spiritual home of hill-walking, with low-level hikes, too. (p264)

**ISLE OF SKYE**
A challenging destination for ambitious walkers, with long and technically demanding routes. (p208)

**THE CAIRNGORMS**
Everything from easy strolls around Loch Morlich to strenuous climbs onto the high tops. (p257)

**ROYAL DEESIDE**
Lovely, low-level walks on river banks and through native woods. (p188)

**BEN NEVIS**
Britain's highest peak; the ultimate for summit baggers. (p272)

## Loch Ness

**4**

In a land rich in legends, there are few that match the international reach of the Loch Ness monster, which is known the world over. While the monster legend may be what draws you to Loch Ness (p253) in the first place, once you're there you'll realise that it's a hauntingly beautiful place, rich in historic sites such as Urquhart Castle (p254) and Fort Augustus (p255), and close to some of Scotland's finest scenery in the shape of gorgeous Glen Affric (p263).
Urquhart Castle

## Walking

**5**

The best way to get inside Scotland's landscapes is to walk them. Despite the wind, midges and drizzle, walking here is a pleasure, with short- and long-distance trails, hills and mountains begging to be tramped. Top of the wish list for many hikers is the 95-mile West Highland Way (p145) from Milngavie (near Glasgow) to Fort William, a week-long walk through some of the country's finest scenery, finishing in the shadow of its highest peak, Ben Nevis. West Highland Way

## Golf

Scotland invented the game of golf and is revered as its spiritual home. Links courses are the classic experience here – bumpy coastal affairs where the rough is heather and machair and the main enemy is the wind, which can make a disaster of a promising round. St Andrews (p177), the historic Fife university town, is golf's headquarters, and an alluring place for anyone who loves the sport. Old Course, St Andrews (p180)

## Castles

Desolate stone fortresses looming in the mist (such as Eilean Donan, p211), majestic castles towering over historic towns, and luxurious palaces built on expansive grounds by lairds more concerned with pampering than with defence: Scotland has a full range of castles (p25) that reflect its turbulent history and tense relations with its southern neighbour. Most castles have a story (or 10) to tell of plots, intrigues, imprisonments and treachery – as well as a ghost rumoured to stalk their halls. Eilean Donan

# Perthshire

Blue-grey lochs shimmer, reflecting the changing moods of the weather; swathes of noble woodland clothe the hills; majestic glens scythe their way into remote wildernesses; and salmon leap upriver to the place of their birth. In Perthshire (p185), picturesque towns like Pitlochry bloom with flowers, distilleries emit tempting malty odours and sheep graze in impossibly green meadows. There's a feeling of the bounty of nature that no other place in Scotland can replicate.

# The Best...
## Museums

**NATIONAL MUSEUM OF SCOTLAND**
Its historic treasures include the famous Lewis chessmen. (p79)

**KELVINGROVE ART GALLERY & MUSEUM**
Offers everything from a Spitfire plane to an Egyptian sarcophagus. (p132)

**HIGHLAND FOLK MUSEUM**
An open-air museum of traditional rural buildings. (p263)

**SKYE MUSEUM OF ISLAND LIFE**
Turf-roofed crofters' cottages re-create farming life in the 1800s. (p218)

**ROYAL YACHT *BRITANNIA***
A floating museum of the royal family's former holiday yacht. (p87)

## The Best...
## Art Galleries

# Ancient Sites

When visiting ancient sites it can be difficult to feel a connection with the people who built them, but Scotland's superb prehistoric remains have an immediate impact. Few better glimpses of Stone Age life exist than Orkney's Skara Brae (p260); the incredible cairns and chambered tombs found across the islands are equally impressive. Mysterious standing stones, sturdy towers and richly symbolic Pictish stones make the distant past a constant presence. Skara Brae

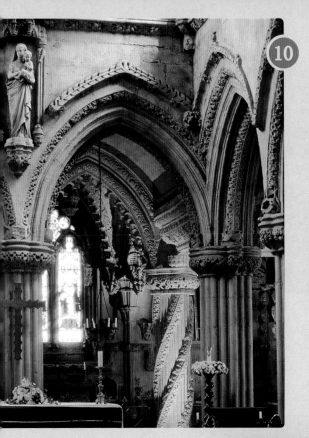

## Rosslyn Chapel

**10**

Made famous in the film version of Dan Brown's mystery novel *The Da Vinci Code*, Rosslyn Chapel (p91) is Scotland's most beautiful and enigmatic church. The ornately carved interior – at odds with the architectural fashion of its time – is a monument to the mason's art, rich in symbolic imagery. As well as flowers, vines, angels and biblical figures, the carved stones include many examples of the 'Green Man', an ancient pagan fertility symbol. Apprentice Pillar

## Whisky

Scotland's national drink – from the Gaelic *uisge bagh*, meaning 'water of life' – has been distilled here for more than 500 years. More than 100 distilleries are still in operation, producing hundreds of varieties of single malt; learning to distinguish the smoky, peaty whiskies of Islay from, say, the flowery, sherried malts of Speyside has become a hugely popular pastime. Many distilleries offer guided tours (p193), rounded off with a tasting session, and ticking off the local varieties is a great way to explore the whisky-making regions.

Speyside Cooperage (p193)

MAR PHOTOGRAPHICS/ALAMY ©

**11**

## Glen Coe

Scotland's most famous glen (p264) combines those two essential qualities of Highlands landscape: dramatic scenery and deep history. The peacefulness and beauty of this valley today belie the fact that it was the scene of a ruthless 17th-century massacre, when the local MacDonalds were murdered by soldiers of the Campbell clan. Some of the glen's finest walks – to the Lost Valley, for example – follow the routes used by the clanspeople trying to flee their attackers, and where many perished in the snow. Buachaille Etive Mor

## Climbing Ben Nevis

The allure of Britain's highest peak is strong – about 100,000 people a year set off up the summit trail, though not all make it to the top. But the highest Munro (a Scottish mountain over 3000ft high) of them all is within reach of anyone who's reasonably fit. Treat Ben Nevis (p272) with respect and your reward (weather permitting) will be a truly magnificent view. Walking enthusiasts can warm up by hiking the 95-mile West Highland Way (p145) first.

EOIN CLARKE/GETTY IMAGES ©

# Island Hopping

Much of western and northern Scotland's unique character comes from the more than 700 islands off the coast, of which almost 100 are inhabited. A network of ferry services links these islands to the mainland and each other; an Island Rover ticket (p309) – which offers unlimited ferry travel for 15 days – provides the best way to explore. Oban (p219), the 'gateway to the isles', has ferries to seven different islands. Oban

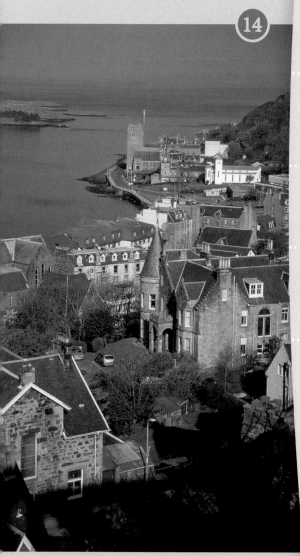

## The Best...
## Scenic Drives

**A939 COCKBRIDGE TO TOMINTOUL**
Swooping, whooping roller-coaster of a ride over the Grampian grouse moors. (p163)

**FORT WILLIAM TO MALLAIG**
The Road to the Isles provides classic views of Glenfinnan and offshore islands. (p271)

**TROTTERNISH PENINSULA (SKYE)**
Spectacular coastal panoramas take in islands, mountains and bizarre rock pinnacles. (p218)

**A82 GLASGOW TO FORT WILLIAM**
Includes Loch Lomond and Glen Coe, with the vast expanse of Rannoch Moor in between. (p39)

# The Best...
## Wildlife Watching

**ISLE OF MULL**
Eagles overhead and porpoises and whales in the waters below. (p225)

**LOCH GARTEN**
Get a close-up view of ospreys in the nest. (p263)

**ISLE OF SKYE**
An otter hotspot. (p195)

**MORAY FIRTH**
Home to Scotland's only resident pod of bottlenose dolphins. (p265)

**THE CAIRNGORMS**
Good chance of spotting red deer. (p257)

**HIGHLAND WILDLIFE PARK**
See rare species such as Scottish wildcat. (p262)

15

## Wildlife

Sparsely populated, and with large areas of wilderness, Scotland is an important sanctuary for all sorts of land- air- and sea-based creatures (see p298). Amazing birdwatching is on offer throughout the country, with the ospreys of Loch Garten and the white-tailed sea eagles of Skye and Mull the highlights. Capercaillie, corncrakes, golden eagles and red kites are other feathered drawcards. Meanwhile, red deer roam the heathered uplands, pine martens and wildcats stalk the forests, and dolphins, whales, otters and orcas splash about in the northern waters. Left: European otters, Isle of Mull; Above: Osprey

MARK HAMBLIN/GETTY IMAGES ©

MR ELLIOTT NEEP/GETTY IMAGES ©

## Loch Lomond

Despite being less than an hour's drive from the bustle and sprawl of Glasgow, the bonnie banks and bonnie braes of Loch Lomond (p145) – immortalised in the words of one of Scotland's best-known songs – comprise one of the most scenic parts of the country. At the heart of Scotland's first national park, the loch begins as a broad, island-peppered lake in the south, its shores clothed in bluebell woods, narrowing in the north to a fjord-like trench ringed by 900m-high mountains.

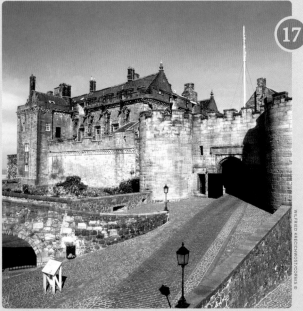

## Stirling Castle

For centuries Stirling sat astride the route taken by English armies invading from the south. Its crag-top castle commanded the crossing of the River Forth at Stirling Bridge – site of a famous victory for William Wallace in 1297 – and was a favourite residence of Kings James IV and James V. Stirling Castle (p154) is as much of a must-see as Edinburgh, along with the nearby historical attractions of Bannockburn battlefield and the National Wallace Monument (p169).

# Isle of Iona

Legend has it that when St Columba left Ireland in 563 to found a missionary outpost on Scotland's west coast, he kept sailing until he found a spot where he could no longer see his homeland on the southern horizon. That place was the little jewel of Iona (p228) – Scotland's most sacred island, and one of its most beautiful, with lush green pastures bordered by pink granite rocks, white shell-sand beaches, and shallow, turquoise waters. The Iona Community continues the island's spiritual calling in an abbey on the site of Columba's first chapel. Iona Abbey (p229)

## The Best...
## Castles

**STIRLING CASTLE**
Historic fortress with Great Hall and sumptuous Royal Palace. (p154)

**URQUHART CASTLE**
Wonderfully atmospheric ruins with a brilliant view over Loch Ness. (p254)

**EDINBURGH CASTLE**
The biggest and boldest, home to the Stone of Destiny and the Scottish crown jewels. (p65)

**EILEAN DONAN CASTLE**
Impossibly picturesque tower house perched on a sea-girt islet. (p211)

**BALMORAL CASTLE**
A profusion of Scottish Baronial turrets with that all-important royal connection. (p190)

## The Trossachs

The Trossachs (p173) is as famous for its literary links as it is for its picture-postcard scenery – it was here that Sir Walter Scott set his epic poem *The Lady in the Lake*, inspired by Loch Katrine, and his historic novel *Rob Roy*. While Loch Lomond is at its scenic best in spring and early summer, when bluebell woods and rhododendron blooms add colour to the scene, the Trossachs come alive in autumn, when the turning leaves bring a blaze of fire and gold to the native woods of oak, birch and ash.

Loch Katrine

DAVID C TOMLINSON/GETTY IMAGES ©

## The Best...
### Scenery

**GLEN AFFRIC**
Classic Highland scene of lochs, heather, high peaks and pine woods. (p263)

**THE TROSSACHS**
Compact and bijou combination of woods and water. (p173)

**ISLE OF SKYE**
Jagged peaks, wild waterfalls and expansive sea views. (p198)

**GLEN COE**
Steep cliffs and brooding mountains crowd around a glen of breathtaking beauty. (p264)

**ARISAIG**
Wide open vistas of sea and mountain, and superb sunsets over Eigg and Rum. (p273)

## Highland Games

**20**

The archetypal event of Scottish summer, the Highland Games – such as the Braemar Gathering (p191) – has its origins in after-battle celebratory dances and –trials of strength among warring clansmen. Today the traditional events – putting the shot, throwing the hammer and, of course, tossing the caber – have been joined by bagpipe playing and Highland dancing competitions, and more modern additions such as 100m sprints and hill-running races. But the atmosphere remains very much that of a family-friendly village fair, with strong local support and plenty to see and do.

ADINA TOVY/ROBERT HARDING WORLD IMAGERY/CORBIS ©

# Edinburgh Military Tattoo

Of all the events held in Edinburgh in August, few are as enduringly popular as the Military Tattoo (p101). It's an extravaganza of marching bands, dancers, motorcycle display teams, acrobats and military set pieces performed by service people from British, Commonwealth and other armed forces from around the world. Held annually on the castle esplanade since 1950, it regularly sells out, with more than 200,000 people attending each year.

# Royal Deeside

The valley of the River Dee stretches from the Cairngorms mountains to Aberdeen. Its picturesque upper reaches, ringed by rock-girt mountains and fringed with woods, has been known as Royal Deeside ever since Queen Victoria fell in love with Balmoral Castle (p190), which has been the royal family's summer retreat since the mid-19th century. Nearby is Ballater village, its shopfronts adorned with royal crests boasting their status as 'suppliers to her majesty'. Balmoral Castle

## Caledonian Pine Forest

In the wake of the last ice age, 10,000 years ago, much of the land that is now Scotland was covered in extensive forests of Scots pine, birch, oak and rowan. Known as the Caledonian Pine Forest, it has been mostly wiped out by thousands of years of human attrition – chopped down for fuel and timber. Only about 1% of the original forest remains, but what does is truly beautiful. The largest area of forest, at Rothiemurchus (p259) in the Cairngorms, harbours rare wildlife including capercaillie, crossbill and wildcat. Red deer stag

23

## The Best...
## Places to Stay

**WITCHERY BY THE CASTLE**
Divine decadence with a
Gothic touch. (p85)

**MONACHYLE MHOR**
Relaxed, luxurious Perth-
shire hideaway with superb
food. (p176)

**ROCPOOL RESERVE**
Boutique chic comes to
Inverness. (p247)

**AULD KIRK**
Atmospheric accommoda-
tion in a converted church
in Ballater. (p189)

**TORAVAIG HOUSE HOTEL**
Country house in Skye is
the quintessence of High-
land hospitality. (p212)

**LIME TREE**
More like an art gallery
with bedrooms. (p268)

# Seafood

One of the great pleasures of a visit to Scotland is the opportunity to indulge in the rich harvest of the sea. The cold, clear waters around the Scottish coast provide some of the most sought-after seafood in Europe, with much of it being whisked straight from the quayside to waiting restaurant tables from London to Lisbon. Fortunately there are plenty of places to sample this bounty right here, with Oban (p219) topping the list of towns with more than their fair share of seafood restaurants. A seafood platter at Tower restaurant (p90)

## The Best...
## Seafood Restaurants

**CAFÉ FISH**
Fresh shellfish straight off the boat and a view of Tobermory harbour. (p226)

**WATERFRONT FISHHOUSE RESTAURANT**
Their motto: 'From pier to pan as fast as we can'. (p221)

**LOCHBAY SEAFOOD RESTAURANT**
Cosy farmhouse kitchen-style restaurant overlooking a Skye sealoch. (p218)

**FISHERS BISTRO**
One of Edinburgh's oldest and best seafood places. (p95)

**SEAFOOD RESTAURANT**
Impeccable cuisine with a panoramic view of the West Sands. (p181)

**25**

# Fingal's Cave

The surge and echo of Atlantic waves in the dark recesses of Fingal's Cave (p230) on the Isle of Staffa inspired the composer Felix Mendehlsson to pen his enduringly popular *Hebrides Overture*. Since then, thousands of visitors have braved the step from a rocking boat onto Staffa's slippery landing place and clambered among the soaring basaltic columns that frame this impressive sea-filled cavern, to experience that same magical blend of sight and sound.

# Scotland's
# Top Itineraries

# Edinburgh to Glasgow

## 5 DAYS

## Three Historic Cities

*If you're short on time, this itinerary packs in Scotland's three most interesting and historic cities, allowing you to make the most of each town's attractions. It's easy to follow using only public transport.*

### ① Edinburgh (p51)

You'll need two days to do justice to the Scottish capital, taking in **Edinburgh Castle**, strolling down the **Royal Mile**, touring the halls of the **Palace of Holyroodhouse** and heading down to Leith to board the **Royal Yacht** *Britannia*. Put aside an afternoon to visit the beautiful and mysterious **Rosslyn Chapel**, made famous by the movie *The Da Vinci Code*. There's great shopping along Princes St and George St, and some of Scotland's best restaurants too.

**EDINBURGH ➡ STIRLING**

🚗 **45 minutes** Along the M9. 🚆 **One hour** From Edinburgh Waverley or Haymarket direct to Stirling.

### ② Stirling (p164)

One day will give you enough time to visit **Stirling Castle** – many people think this picturesque fortress is even more interesting and evocative than Edinburgh Castle – and **Bannockburn**, the battlefield where Robert the Bruce led the Scots to victory over the English in 1314. There's the **Wallace Monument** too, a tribute to the freedom fighter immortalised in the movie *Braveheart*. No need to stay overnight here – head on to Glasgow at the end of the day.

**STIRLING ➡ GLASGOW**

🚗 **45 minutes** Via the M80. 🚆 **40 minutes** Frequent services from Stirling to Glasgow Queen St.

### ③ Glasgow (p124)

Culture vultures will need two days to absorb all that Scotland's biggest city has to offer – **Kelvingrove Art Gallery & Museum** and the **Burrell Collection** are both world class and will occupy you for a full day. Then there's the **Hunterian Gallery** and the **Mackintosh House**, and the museums along the Clyde. But if one day of art appreciation is enough, you could spend your final day on a trip to the bonnie banks of **Loch Lomond**, less than an hour away by car or train.

---

Princes Street Gardens, below Edinburgh Castle (p65)

PHOTOGRAPHER: IAN CUMMING/GETTY IMAGES ©

**33**

## Edinburgh to Inverness
### Tayside to Speyside

*Another shortish route, this time forging north through the heart of the Highlands, taking in Blair Castle in the valley of the River Tay and Aviemore on the banks of the Spey before reaching the Highland capital, Inverness.*

## ① Edinburgh (p51)

As with the first itinerary, allow two days to make the most of Edinburgh and **Rosslyn Chapel**.

EDINBURGH ⊙ PITLOCHRY

🚗 **One hour 45 minutes** Via Forth Road Bridge, M90 and A9 via Scone Palace. 🚆 **One hour 50 minutes** Direct from Edinburgh Waverley or Haymarket.

## ② Pitlochry (p185)

If you're travelling by car, you can stop off at **Scone Palace** on your way north to visit the ancient coronation place of Scottish kings, and see the place where the **Stone of Destiny** (on display in Edinburgh Castle) was stolen in 1297 by the English King Edward. Plan to stay overnight at Pitlochry, giving yourself time to visit nearby sights such as **Blair Castle**, home to the Duke of Atholl and Britain's only private standing army, and **Killiecrankie**, site of an important battle during the 18th-century Jacobite rebellions; it's a name feted in many Scottish folk songs of the era.

PITLOCHRY ⊙ AVIEMORE

🚗 **One hour 20 minutes** Along the A9 via Newtonmore. 🚆 **One hour** Direct trains every two hours or so.

## ③ Aviemore (p258)

Day four sees you at Aviemore and ready to explore the **Cairngorms National Park**. You'll only have time for two or three sights – we recommend you head to **Loch Morlich** for a short hike, a visit to the **Cairngorm Reindeer Centre**, and (if the weather is clear) a trip on the **Cairngorm Mountain Railway** which will take you to the 1000m-high summit plateau. If you're driving, you can visit the **Highland Folk Museum** at Newtonmore on your way from Pitlochry.

AVIEMORE ⊙ INVERNESS

🚗 **40 minutes** Along the A9. 🚆 **40 minutes** Direct trains every two hours.

## ④ Inverness (p246)

It's only a short trip from Aviemore to the attractive Highland capital, Inverness. There are some excellent **restaurants** here where you can celebrate the end of your itinerary, but before you head for the dinner table be sure to take a monster-spotting cruise on **Loch Ness**.

European reindeer, Cairngorms National Park
PHOTOGRAPHER: BLICKWINKEL/ALAMY ©

# Edinburgh to Skye
## Over the Hills to Skye

*This is a more leisurely trip, leading to the beautiful Isle of Skye by way of St Andrews (home of golf), Royal Deeside, the Speyside whisky distilleries and Loch Ness.*

North Se

PORTREE    INVERNESS

SCOTLAND

DRUMNADROCHIT    BALLATER

ST ANDREWS

ATLANTIC
OCEAN

EDINBURGH

IRELAND

NORTHERN
IRELAND                    ENGLAND

## ① Edinburgh (p51)

Allow yourself two days to make the most of Edinburgh and **Rosslyn Chapel**.

**EDINBURGH ➲ ST ANDREWS**

🚗 **1½ hours** Via Forth Road Bridge and A92.
🚆🚆 **One hour** Direct trains from Edinburgh to Leuchars every 30 minutes; free connecting bus into St Andrews.

## ② St Andrews (p177)

History buffs can tour **St Andrews Castle** and the ruins of **St Andrews Cathedral**. Golf aficionados will want to play a round on the **Old Course**; alternatively, visit the **British Golf Museum**. Celebrate with a fancy dinner at the **Seafood Restaurant**.

**ST ANDREWS ➲ BALLATER**

🚗 **2½ hours** Tay Bridge to Dundee, then A90 and A928 to Glamis; A94 and A93 to Braemar and Ballater. 🚆🚆 **Four to five hours** Train Leuchars to Aberdeen, then bus Aberdeen to Ballater; both services hourly.

## ③ Ballater (p188)

Having your own wheels is an advantage on the next two legs, allowing you to travel through the heart of the mountains; public transport means a detour via Aberdeen. Call in at **Glamis Castle**, but leave time to visit **Balmoral Castle** too before over-nighting in the pretty Royal Deeside village of **Ballater**.

**BALLATER ➲ INVERNESS**

🚗 **Three hours** A939 and B-roads to Dufftown, then A941 and A96 via Elgin to Inverness.
🚆🚆 **4½ hours** Bus Ballater to Aberdeen, then train Aberdeen to Inverness.

## ④ Inverness (p246)

The A939 Cockbridge to Tominoul road is one of the finest drives in Britain, leading to the **whisky distilleries** of Speyside. Take a distillery tour before continuing to Inverness for a slap-up dinner at **Contrast**.

**INVERNESS ➲ DRUMNADROCHIT**

🚗 **20 minutes** on the A82; one hour each way for a detour to Glen Affric. 🚆 **30 minutes** Around six buses a day.

## ⑤ Drumnadrochit (p253)

Take a walk to Inverness' **Ness Islands** in the morning, then make the short trip to Drumnadrochit to visit the **Loch Ness Centre & Exhibition** and **Urquhart Cas-tle**, and take a cruise on the loch itself.

**DRUMNADROCHIT ➲ PORTREE**

🚗 **Three hours** Via A82, A887 and A87; add three or four hours for a detour to Glen Affric. 🚆 **Three hours** Two direct buses a day.

## ⑥ Portree (p213)

Take a whole day for the scenic drive from Loch Ness to Skye, starting with a side trip to beautiful **Glen Affric**. That leaves two whole days to explore the wonders of the **Isle of Skye**.

---

Glenfiddich Distillery, Dufftown, Speyside (p193)
PHOTOGRAPHER: ANDY STOTHERT/GETTY IMAGES ©

**10 DAYS**

# Glasgow to Inverness
## Island Hop to the Highlands

*Leading via the scenic treasures of Loch Lomond, Mull and Glenfinnan to the Highland delights of the Cairngorms, this route combines an island adventure with a journey through Scotland's highest mountains.*

North Sea

INVERNESS
6

FORT WILLIAM
4

5 AVIEMORE

TOBERMORY 3

2

SCOTLAND

ATLANTIC OCEAN

OBAN

1 GLASGOW

IRELAND

NORTHERN IRELAND

ENGLAND

## ① Glasgow (p124)

Spend a day in Glasgow to visit **Kelvingrove Art Gallery and Museum** and the **Burrell Collection**.

GLASGOW ⊙ OBAN

🚗 **2½ hours** A82 via Loch Lomond and A85.
🚌 **Three hours** Three direct buses daily.

## ② Oban (p219)

The road north leads past **Loch Lomond**, and there will be time for a break at **Loch Lomond Shores** or **Luss**. Oban, the 'gateway to the isles' awaits, with a choice of several top-notch **seafood restaurants**.

OBAN ⊙ TOBERMORY

🚗 **Two hours** Ferry from Oban to Craignure, then A849/848; detour to Iona takes at least four hours. 🚢🚌 **Two hours** Ferry to Craignure then connecting bus; Iona can be visited on an organised tour from Oban.

## ③ Tobermory (p224)

Be up in time for the first ferry to Mull, and head west to Fionnphort for a trip to the magical **Isle of Iona**. Plan to spend two nights in Tobermory so that you can explore the rest of Mull, including **Duart Castle** and the beach at **Calgary**.

TOBERMORY ⊙ FORT WILLIAM

🚗 **Three hours** Ferry to Kilchoan, then A861 and A830 via Glenfinnan; detour to Ardnamurchan Point adds one hour. 🚌 Not possible by public transport.

## ④ Fort William (p267)

Take the ferry from Tobermory to Kilchoan, and detour west to **Ardnamurchan Point**, the most westerly point on the British mainland. From here a magnificent scenic drive leads back east via **Glenfinnan** to Fort William. While you're there, make a trip to lovely **Glen Nevis**, and set aside the following day to climb **Ben Nevis**.

FORT WILLIAM ⊙ AVIEMORE

🚗 **1½ hours** Via A86 and A9. 🚌 Not possible by public transport.

## ⑤ Aviemore (p258)

You'll be weary after your climb, so plan a midday start and allow two nights in Aviemore and the **Cairngorms National Park**. As well as **Loch Morlich** and the **Cairngorm Mountain Railway**, visit the **Highland Wildlife Park** at nearby Kincraig and the osprey reserve at **Loch Garten**.

AVIEMORE ⊙ INVERNESS

🚗 **40 minutes** Along the A9. 🚌 **40 minutes** Direct trains every two hours.

## ⑥ Inverness (p246)

It's only a short trip from Aviemore to Inverness, allowing time for a visit to nearby **Culloden** and/or a monster-spotting cruise on **Loch Ness**.

# Edinburgh to Glasgow
## The Grand Highland Fling

*This two-week tour takes in as many of Scotland's highlights as possible without rushing things. It's possible using public transport but that would take a bit longer – a car really is necessary to make the most of this trip.*

### 1 Edinburgh (p51)

Allow yourself two days to make the most of Edinburgh and **Rosslyn Chapel**.

································

**EDINBURGH ⮕ ST ANDREWS**

🚗 **1½ hours** Via Forth Road Bridge and A92.
🚌🚆 **One hour** Direct trains from Edinburgh to Leuchars every 30 minutes; free connecting bus to St Andrews.

································

### 2 St Andrews (p177)

Tour **St Andrews Castle** and the ruins of **St Andrews Cathedral**, or play a round on the **Old Course**; alternatively, visit the **British Golf Museum**. Celebrate with a fancy dinner at the **Seafood Restaurant**.

································

**ST ANDREWS ⮕ BALLATER**

🚗 **2½ hours** Tay Bridge to Dundee, then A90 and A928 to Glamis; A94 and A93 to Braemar and Ballater. 🚌🚆 **Four to five hours** Train Leuchars to Aberdeen, then bus Aberdeen to Ballater; both services hourly.

································

### 3 Ballater (p188)

This leg goes through the heart of the mountains. Call in at **Glamis Castle**, but be sure to also stop by **Balmoral Castle** before overnighting in the pretty village of **Ballater**

································

**BALLATER ⮕ INVERNESS**

🚗 **Three hours** A939 and B-roads to Dufftown, then A941 and A96 via Elgin to Inverness. 🚌🚆 **4½ hours** Bus Ballater to Aberdeen, then train Aberdeen to Inverness.

································

### 4 Inverness (p246)

The A939 Cockbridge to Tomintoul road is one of the finest drives in Britain, leading to the **whisky distilleries** of Speyside. Take a distillery tour before continuing to Inverness for a slap-up dinner at one of its excellent **restaurants**.

································

**INVERNESS ⮕ PORTREE**

🚗 **3½ hours** Via A82, A887 and A87 via Drumnadrochit. 🚌 **Four hours** Two direct buses a day.

································

Loch Lomond (p145)
PHOTOGRAPHER: DAN TUCKER/ALAMY ©

## 6 **Fort William** (p267)

Heading south from Portree, turn right past Bradford on the road to **Armadale**, where you take the ferry to **Mallaig**; the drive from here to Fort William is on the scenic **Road to the Isles**. Spend two nights in **Fort William**, allowing time to visit lovely **Glen Nevis**, and perhaps even to climb **Ben Nevis**.

FORT WILLIAM ❍ OBAN

🚗 **1½ hours** Via A82 and A85; add one hour for a detour to Glen Coe. 🚌 **1½ hours** Direct buses twice a day.

## 7 **Oban** (p219)

Plan a day trip from Oban to **Iona** – you can take your own car on the ferry (Craignure to Fionnphort is only 35 miles, but allow 1½ hours each way) or take an organised tour.

OBAN ❍ GLASGOW

🚗 **2½ hours** A85 and A82 via Loch Lomond. 🚌 **Three hours** Three direct buses daily.

## 5 **Portree** (p213)

Allow a full day for the scenic drive from Inverness to Skye, stopping at Drumnadrochit to visit the **Loch Ness Centre & Exhibition**. Spend two nights in Portree, allowing time to visit **Dunvegan Castle** and the **Cuillin Hills**.

PORTREE ❍ FORT WILLIAM

🚗 **Four hours** Drive to Armadale, ferry to Mallaig, drive to Fort William via Glenfinnan. 🚌🚢🚆 **Four hours** Bus to Armadale, ferry to Mallaig, train to Fort William; connections twice daily.

## 8 **Glasgow** (p124)

The road south leads past **Loch Lomond**, and there will be time for a break at **Loch Lomond Shores** or **Luss**. That leaves two days to enjoy Glasgow's varied attractions.

# Scotland Month By Month

## January

The nation shakes off its Hogmanay hangover and gets back to work, but only until Burns Night comes along. It's still cold and dark, but the skiing can be good.

### Burns Night

Suppers all over the country (and the world for that matter) are held on 25 January to celebrate the anniversary of national poet Robert Burns, with much eating of haggis, drinking of whisky and reciting of poetry.

### Celtic Connections

Glasgow hosts the world's largest winter music festival, a celebration of Celtic music, dance and culture, with participants arriving from all over the globe. Held mid- to late January. See www.celticconnect ions.com.

### Up Helly Aa

Half of Shetland dresses up with horned helmets and battleaxes in this spectacular re-enactment of a Viking fire festival, with a torchlit procession leading the burning of a full-size Viking longship. Held in Lerwick on the last Tuesday in January. See www. uphellyaa.org.

## Top Events

- **Edinburgh Festival Fringe,** August
- **T in the Park,** July
- **West End Festival,** June
- **Celtic Connections,** January
- **Braemar Gathering,** September

## February

The coldest month of the year is usually the best for hill-walking, ice-climbing and skiing. The days are getting longer now, and snowdrops begin to bloom.

### Six Nations Rugby Tournament

Scotland, England, Wales, Ireland, France and Italy battle it out in this prestigious tournament, held February to March; home games are played at Murrayfield, Edinburgh. See www.rbs6nations.com.

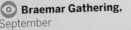

**(left) June** West End Festival, Glasgow
PHOTOGRAPHER: TRINITY MIRROR/MIRRORPIX/ALAMY ©

## Fort William Mountain Festival

The UK's Outdoor Capital celebrates the peak of the winter season with ski and snowboard learning workshops, talks by famous climbers, kids events and a festival of mountaineering films. See www.mountainfilmfestival.co.uk.

# April

The bluebell woods on the shores of Loch Lomond come into flower and ospreys arrive at their Loch Garten nests. Weather improving, though heavy showers are still common.

## Rugby Sevens

A series of weekend, seven-a-side rugby tournaments held in various towns throughout the Borders region in April and May, kicking off with Melrose in early April. Fast and furious rugby (sevens was invented here), crowded pubs and great craic. See www.melrose7s.com.

# May

Wildflowers on the Hebridean machair, hawthorn hedges in bloom and cherry blossom in city parks – Scottish weather is often at its best in May.

## Burns an' a' That

Ayrshire towns are the venues for performances of poetry and music, children's events, art exhibitions and more in celebrations of the Scottish bard. See www.burnsfestival.com.

## Spirit of Speyside

Based in the Moray town of Dufftown, this festival of whisky, food and music involves five days of distillery tours, knocking back the 'water of life', cooking, art and outdoor activities; held late April to early May in Moray and Speyside. See www.spiritofspeyside.com.

# June

Argyllshire is ablaze with pink rhododendron blooms as the long summer evenings stretch on till 11pm. Border towns are strung with bunting to mark gala days and Common Ridings.

## Common Ridings

Following the age-old tradition that commemorates the ancient conflict with England, horsemen and -women ride the old boundaries of common lands. There are also parades, marching bands and street parties. Held in various Border towns; Jedburgh (www.jethartcallantsfestival.com) is one of the biggest and best.

## Glasgow Festivals

June in Glasgow is equivalent to the 'festival month' of August in Edinburgh. The city hosts three major events – West End Festival (www.westendfestival.co.uk), Glasgow's biggest music and arts event; Glasgow International Jazz Festival (www.jazzfest.co.uk); and Glasgow Mela (www.glasgowmela.com), a celebration of the city's Asian community.

# July

School holidays begin, as does the busiest time of year for resort towns. High season for Shetland birdwatchers.

## T in the Park

Held annually since 1994, and headlined by world-class acts including The Who, REM, Eminem and Kasabian, this major music festival is Scotland's answer to Glastonbury. It's held over a mid-July weekend at Balado, by Kinross. See www.tinthepark.com.

# August

Festival time in Edinburgh and the city is crammed with visitors. On the west coast, this is the peak month for sighting minke whales and basking sharks.

### Edinburgh Festivals

You name it, Edinburgh has a festival event that covers it – books, art, theatre, music, comedy, dance, and the Military Tattoo (www.edintattoo.co.uk). The overlapping International Festival and Fringe keep the city jumping from the first week in August to the first week in September. See www.edinburghfestivals.co.uk.

# September

School holidays are over, midges are dying off, wild brambles are ripe for picking in the hedgerows, and the weather is often dry and mild – an excellent time of year for outdoor pursuits.

### Braemar Gathering

The biggest and most famous Highland Games in the Scottish calendar, traditionally attended by members of the royal family. Expect Highland dancing, bagpipe-playing and caber-tossing. Held early

**Below: January** Up Helly Aa; **Right: July** T in the Park

September in Braemar, Royal Deeside.
See www.braemargathering.org.

# December

Darkness falls mid-afternoon as the shortest day approaches. The often cold and wet weather is relieved by Christmas and New Year festivities.

## Hogmanay

Christmas celebrations in Edinburgh (www.edinburghschristmas.com) culminate in a huge street party on Hogmanay (31 December). The fishing town of Stonehaven echoes an ancient, pre-Christian tradition with its procession of fireball-swinging locals who parade to the harbour and fling their blazing orbs into the sea (www.stonehavenfireballs.co.uk).

# What's New

*For this new edition of Discover Scotland, our authors have hunted down the fresh, the transformed, the hot and the happening. These are some of our favourites. For up-to-the-minute recommendations, see lonelyplanet.com/scotland.*

## 1 RIVERSIDE MUSEUM
Glasgow's waterfront has been graced with a magnificent new home for the collections of the former Museum of Transport. Its sinuous metallic roof evokes waves, symbolising the city's historic link with shipbuilding. (p127)

## 2 NATIONAL MUSEUM OF SCOTLAND
Closed for two years, Edinburgh's leading museum reopened in 2011 after a major reconstruction that saw its exhibition space extended, and the Grand Gallery restored to its original Victorian splendour. (p79)

## 3 ROBERT BURNS BIRTHPLACE MUSEUM
Located in Burns' home village of Alloway, this new museum showcases an impressive collection of manuscripts and personal possessions, including the pistols Burns carried when he was employed as an excise man. (p147)

## 4 CASTLE TERRACE
TV chef Tom Kitchin has added to the success of his Leith restaurant by opening Castle Terrace in the shadow of Edinburgh Castle. Within a year of opening in 2010 it had garnered its first Michelin star. (p90)

## 5 SOUTH LOCH NESS TRAIL
The latest addition to Scotland's collection of waymarked hiking trails wends its way for 28 miles along the southern side of Loch Ness, allowing walkers and cyclists to explore this little-visited part of the country. For details, see www.visitlochness.com/south-loch-ness-trail.

## 6 RED ROOF CAFÉ
The Isle of Skye's newest (and most remote) eating place has proved a hit, serving lunch platters of fresh local produce (some grown just across the road) and hosting live music events. (p217)

## 7 ROYAL PALACE, STIRLING CASTLE
The Royal Palace's recent £12 million makeover has restored its six sumptuous apartments to how they would have appeared in the mid-16th century when they were the childhood home of Mary, Queen of Scots. (p164)

## 8 COMMONWEALTH GAMES 2014
In late July and early August of 2014, Glasgow will host the 20th Commonwealth Games (www.glasgow2014.com), involving athletes from some 70 countries. Expect some improvements to the public transport system; equally, expect some disruptions to services in the lead-up to the event.

# Get Inspired

##  Books

○ **Waverley** (1814; Sir Walter Scott) Historic derring-do by the master.

○ **A Scot's Quair** (1946; Lewis Grassic Gibbon) Vividly captures pre-war rural life in the northeast.

○ **The Prime of Miss Jean Brodie** (1962; Muriel Spark) Shrewd portrait of 1930s Edinburgh.

○ **The Crow Road** (1992; Iain Banks) Warm, witty and moving family saga.

○ **Exit Music** (2007; Ian Rankin) Crime novel exploring the darker side of modern Edinburgh.

## Films

○ **The 39 Steps** (1935; Alfred Hitchcock) Old-fashioned thriller.

○ **Whisky Galore!** (1949; Alexander Mackendrick) Gentle comedy.

○ **Gregory's Girl** (1981; Bill Forsyth) Teenage romance.

○ **Rob Roy** (1995; Michael Caton-Jones) Historic legend.

○ **Trainspotting** (1996; Danny Boyle) Gritty realism.

## Music

○ **The Crossing** (1983) Only Big Country could make guitars sound like bagpipes.

○ **This Is the Story** (1987) Debut album of folk-influenced, close-harmony pop from The Proclaimers.

○ **The Cutter and the Clan** (1987) Celtic folk-rock from Gaelic-speaking Skye band Runrig.

○ **Franz Ferdinand** (2004) Rousing guitar rock from Glasgow band Franz Ferdinand.

○ **This Is the Life** (2007) Best-selling pop from 18-year-old Amy Macdonald.

○ **Our Version of Events** (2012) Powerful soul and R&B from Aberdeenshire singer-songwriter Emeli Sandé.

## Websites

○ **VisitScotland** (www.visitscotland.com) Official Scottish Tourist Board site, online accommodation-booking service.

○ **Lonely Planet** (www.lonelyplanet.com) Destination information,

traveller forums, hotel bookings, guidebook shop.

○ **Scotland's People** (www.scotlandspeople.gov.uk) A comprehensive online resource for exploring your Scottish ancestry.

---

## Short on time?

This list will give you an instant insight into the country.

**Read** *Greenvoe* (1972), by George Mackay Brown, is a warm and poetic evocation of everyday life in an island community.

**Watch** *Local Hero* (1983), directed by Bill Forsyth, has it all: glorious scenery, wry wit and a streak of sentimentality.

**Listen** *Songs of Robert Burns* (2003) by Eddi Reader offers Burns' poetry and love songs by Scotland's finest vocalist.

**Log on** Internet Guide to Scotland (www.scotland-info.co.uk) is the best of several online tourist guides to Scotland.

Bagpiper at the Braemar Gathering (p191)
PHOTOGRAPHER: HANS-PETER MERTEN/GETTY IMAGES ©

# Need to Know

## Currency
Pounds Sterling (£)

## Language
English
Gaelic and Lallans

## ATMs
Widely available, except in remote areas and islands.

## Credit Cards
Widely accepted.

## Visas
Generally not needed for stays under six months. Not in the Schengen Zone.

## Mobile Phones
Mobile network uses GSM 900/1800. Local SIM cards can be used in European and Australian phones.

## Wi-Fi
Hot spots aplenty in cities, available in most hotels and many B&Bs.

## Internet Access
Internet cafes in most towns.

## Driving
A good way to get around. Cars drive on the left; steering wheel is on the right.

## Tipping
10–15% in restaurants (unless service charge already added); around 10% to taxi drivers in cities. Don't tip in pubs.

## When to Go

Cool to mild summers, cold winters

**Isle of Skye**
GO May, Jun & Sep

**Inverness**
• GO May–Sep

**The Cairngorms**
GO May–Sep

**Fort William**
GO May or Sep

**Edinburgh**
• GO Aug

### High Season
(Jul & Aug)
- Accommodations 10–20% more; pre-book for Edinburgh and popular resorts
- Warmest season, but often wet, too
- Midges worst in Highlands, islands
- Also applies to late December in Edinburgh

### Shoulder
(May, Jun & Sep)
- Wildflowers bloom May to June
- Best chance of dry weather; no midges
- Daylight till 11pm in June

### Low Season
(Oct–Apr)
- Many rural B&Bs and tourist attractions closed
- Snow on hills November to March at least
- December days get dark at 4pm
- Can be very cold and wet November to March

## Advance Planning

- **Six months before** Book Edinburgh accommodation for August festival period; reserve a table for Witchery at the Castle restaurant.
- **Two months before** Book hotel or B&B accommodation; reserve tables in top restaurants; book car hire.
- **One month before** Book train tickets, make reservations for wildlife tours and boat trips if timing is crucial.
- **Two weeks before** Confirm opening times for visitor attractions.

# Your Daily Budget

## Budget less than £30
- Dorm beds: £10–20
- Wild camping is free
- Cheap supermarkets for self-caterers
- Lots of free museums and galleries

## Midrange £30–100
- Double room in midrange B&B: £50–90
- B&Bs often better value than midrange hotels
- Bar lunch: £10; midrange restaurant dinner: £25
- Car hire: £30 a day
- Petrol costs: around 12p per mile

## Top End over £100
- Double room in top-end hotel: £120–250
- Dinner at top-end restaurant: £40–60
- Flights to islands: £60–120 each

# What to Bring
- **Travel insurance documents** Just in case.
- **Insect repellent** In summer – be prepared for those pesky midges.
- **Waterproof jacket** Any time of year – Scottish weather can go through four seasons in one day.
- **Hiking boots** You will want to wander off the highway and onto the soggy Scottish hillsides.
- **Binoculars** You'll wish you had them when you spot that otter/golden eagle/red deer/minke whale.
- **Small day-pack** To carry waterproofs, binoculars, insect repellent etc.

## Exchange Rates

| | | |
|---|---|---|
| **Australia** | A$1 | £0.63 |
| **Canada** | C$1 | £0.65 |
| **Euro zone** | €1 | £0.83 |
| **Japan** | ¥100 | £0.77 |
| **New Zealand** | NZ$1 | £0.49 |
| **USA** | US$1 | £0.64 |

For current exchange rates see www.xe.com.

# Arriving in Scotland

## Edinburgh Airport
**Buses** To Edinburgh city centre every 10 to 15 minutes from 4.30am to midnight (£3.50).

**Night buses** Every 30 minutes from 12.30am to 4am (£3.50).

**Taxis** £15–20; about 20 minutes to the city centre.

## Glasgow Airport
**Buses** To Glasgow city centre every 10 to 15 minutes from 6am to 11pm (£5).

**Night buses** Hourly 11pm to 4am, half-hourly 4am to 6pm (£5).

**Taxis** £20–25; about 30 minutes to city centre.

# Getting Around
- **Air** Can cut travel time significantly between Glasgow or Edinburgh and Inverness or the farther-flung islands (except Skye – nearest airport is Inverness).
- **Bus** Scottish Citylink coaches run frequent services between all the main tourist centres.
- **Train** Fast and comfortable for intercity travel, and scenic rail journeys to Oban, Mallaig and Kyle of Lochalsh.
- **Car** Having your own wheels is tops for speed and flexibility.

# Accommodation
- **Youth Hostels** The budget traveller's choice; good network in all the right places.
- **B&Bs and Guesthouses** Usually the best value for money, friendly, well equipped, and great breakfasts.
- **Hotels** Some great places in the cities, often average in the countryside; old Highland hotels are often full of character.

# Be Forewarned
- **School holidays** Roads, accommodation and tourist attractions are all busier during Easter, summer and Christmas vacations.
- **Traffic congestion** Can be a serious problem in and around the larger cities at rush hour.
- **Midges** Tiny biting flies can make life a misery in summer if you aren't prepared.

**49**

# Edinburgh

**Edinburgh is a city that just begs to be explored.** From the vaults and wynds that riddle the Old Town to the Georgian elegance of the New Town, it's filled with quirky, come-hither nooks that tempt you to walk just a little bit further. And every corner turned reveals sudden views and unexpected vistas – green, sunlit hills; a glimpse of rust-red crags; a blue flash of distant sea.

But there's more to Edinburgh than sightseeing – there are top shops, world-class restaurants and a bacchanalia of bars to enjoy. This is a city of pub crawls and impromptu music sessions; mad-for-it clubbing and all-night parties; overindulgence, late nights and wandering home through cobbled streets at dawn.

All these superlatives come together in August at festival time, when it seems as if half the world descends on Edinburgh for one enormous party. If you can possibly manage it, join in.

Edinburgh Castle and Old Town from Arthur's Seat **51**

National Museum of Scotland (p79)
MICHAEL DOOLITTLE/ALAMY ®

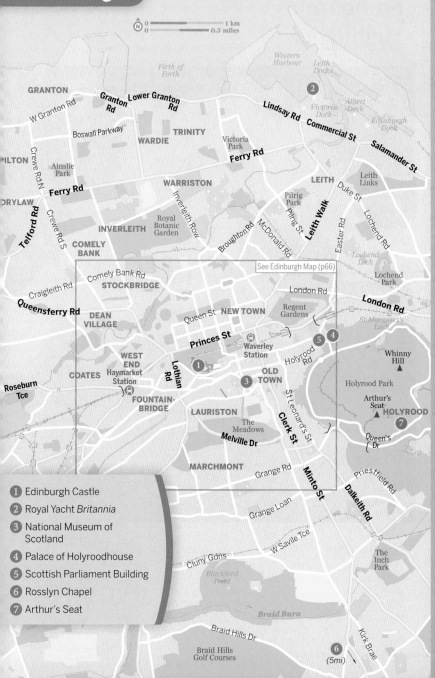

# Edinburgh

0 — 1 km
0 — 0.5 miles

GRANTON
W Granton Rd
Granton Rd
Lower Granton Rd
Lindsay Rd
Commercial St
Salamander St
Boswall Parkway
WARDIE
TRINITY
Victoria Park
PILTON
Crewe Rd N
Ainslie Park
Ferry Rd
Ferry Rd
WARRISTON
LEITH
Leith Links
DRYLAW
Telford Rd
Crewe Rd S
INVERLEITH
Royal Botanic Garden
Inverleith Row
Broughton Rd
McDonald Rd
Pilrig St
Leith Walk
Pilrig Park
Duke St
Easter Rd
Lochend Rd
Western Harbour
Leith Docks
Victoria Dock
Albert Dock
Edinburgh Dock

COMELY BANK
Craigleith Rd
Comely Bank Rd
STOCKBRIDGE
Queensferry Rd
DEAN VILLAGE
Queen St
NEW TOWN
London Rd
Regent Gardens
London Rd
Lochend Loch
Lochend Park

Roseburn Tce
COATES
Haymarket Station
WEST END
Lothian Rd
Princes St
Waverley Station
Holyrood Rd
OLD TOWN
Whinny Hill
Holyrood Park
St Margaret's Loch

FOUNTAIN-BRIDGE
LAURISTON
The Meadows
Melville Dr
St Leonard's St
Clerk St
Arthur's Seat
HOLYROOD
Queen's Dr

MARCHMONT
Grange Rd
Grange Loan
Minto St
Dalkeith Rd
Priestfield Rd
The Inch Park

Cluny Gdns
W Savile Tce
Blackford Pond
Braid Burn
Braid Hills Dr
Braid Hills Golf Courses
Kirk Brae

See Edinburgh Map (p66)

1 Edinburgh Castle
2 Royal Yacht *Britannia*
3 National Museum of Scotland
4 Palace of Holyroodhouse
5 Scottish Parliament Building
6 Rosslyn Chapel
7 Arthur's Seat

6 (5mi)

Firth of Forth

# Edinburgh's Highlights

## 1

## Edinburgh Castle

The brooding, black crags of Castle Rock are the very reason for Edinburgh's existence – it was the most easily defended hilltop on the invasion route from England. Crowning the crag with a profusion of battlements, Edinburgh Castle is now Scotland's most popular pay-to-enter tourist attraction. Top Right: Mons Meg; Below Right: Honours of Scotland

**Need to Know**
**BEST TIME TO GO** Noon (for the 1pm cannon) or two hours before closing. **TOP TIP** Buy tickets online to save time. **SECRET SPOT** The cemetery for officers' dogs! **For more, see p65.**

# Edinburgh Castle Don't Miss List

PETER YEOMAN, HISTORIC SCOTLAND'S
HEAD OF CULTURAL RESOURCES

### 1 HONOURS OF SCOTLAND

The Crown and Sceptre of Scotland and the Sword of State are glittering symbols of our nationhood. They were first used at the coronation of Mary, Queen of Scots in 1543 when she was only nine months old – Cardinal Beaton had to hold the crown to her tiny brow! The centuries-old regalia are displayed in the Royal Palace.

### 2 ST MARGARET'S CHAPEL

The oldest building in the castle is a wee gem, possibly part of a tower-keep built in the early 12th century to commemorate Scotland's royal saint, who died in the castle in 1093. The chapel's interior is delightfully decorated with fine Romanesque architecture; if you get a peaceful moment you can really connect with the medieval kings who carried out their private devotions here.

### 3 MONS MEG

Step outside the chapel to be confronted by the great bombard Mons Meg, gifted to James II in 1457. This is a great vantage point for the One O' Clock Gun, fired daily (except Sunday), causing many visitors to jump out of their skins! The views across the Georgian New Town to the Forth Estuary from here are truly magnificent.

### 4 DAVID'S TOWER

Deep beneath the Half Moon Battery lies David's Tower, built as a fancy residence for David II in 1371. Badly damaged in the siege of 1573, the tower became hidden in the foundations for the new battery, and was only rediscovered in 1912. The Honours of Scotland spent much of WWII here, hidden down a medieval loo!

### 5 CASTLE VAULTS

In 1720 21 pirates captured in Argyll were thrown into the castle dungeons. They had all sailed with one of the most infamous pirate captains of the Caribbean, 'Black Bart' Roberts. The following decades saw a busy time for this state prison, which was stuffed full of prisoners from the wars with America and France. The reconstructed cells allow you to experience something of the squalor!

## Royal Yacht *Britannia*

The *Britannia* served as the royal family's floating home during their foreign travels until it was decommissioned in 1997. Now permanently moored at Ocean Terminal in Leith, the ship offers an intriguing insight into the queen's private tastes. Below: Drawing Room

**Need to Know**

**ROYAL EDINBURGH TICKET** Admits to Britannia, Edinburgh Castle, Holyroodhouse and bus tours. **LOCATION** 25-min bus ride from city. **LUNCH** Fishers Bistro (p95) **For more: p87**

2

# Royal Yacht *Britannia*'s Don't Miss List

FIONA MAXWELL, BLUE BADGE TOUR GUIDE

### 1 ROYAL APARTMENTS

Don't expect a sumptuous royal residence – it's more like a comfortable country house, with simple furnishings and old-fashioned charm. Even the Queen's and Duke's private apartments are not at all elaborate, with basic, 3ft-wide single beds! The only double bed is in the honeymoon suite, where Bill and Hillary Clinton slept during a state visit.

### 2 STATE ROOMS

The State Rooms are slightly grander, but still understated. The **Drawing Room** has chintz chair covers and a grand piano (firmly bolted to the floor); Noël Coward once tickled its keys while entertaining the royal family. The **Dining Room** is adorned with treasures gifted to the Queen during her travels. Check out the place settings: it took over three hours to lay the table for a state banquet – the space between each piece of cutlery was meticulously measured with a ruler!

### 3 CREW QUARTERS

You'll get a shock when you see the cramped conditions below deck where the non-commissioned sailors, and even some of the officers, slept in narrow bunk beds three tiers high. There was no peace or privacy; the only officer who had en suite facilities was the admiral.

### 4 THE WOMBAT

There are some lovely reminders of traditions on the vessel, including that of the Wombat, still on view in the anteroom of the Wardroom – the officers would give the poor stuffed animal many a hammering during after-dinner batting games. And look for coins placed beneath the foot of each of the three masts, as payment to the angels for guiding the vessel safely at sea.

### 5 ROYAL DECK TEAROOM

During your visit you can enjoy delicious home-baked treats and tea served in bone china in the Royal Deck Tearoom while looking down on Prince Phillip's famous yacht *Bloodhound*, now lying alongside *Britannia*. On a clear day you'll have wonderful views across the Firth of Forth towards the hills of Fife.

# National Museum of Scotland

The National Museum of Scotland (p79) charts the history of the country from geological beginnings to the present day. Highlights include the Monymusk Reliquary, a tiny silver casket dating from 750 (said to have been carried into battle with Robert the Bruce at Bannockburn in 1314), and the Lewis Chessmen, a set of charming 12th-century chess pieces made from walrus ivory.

## Palace of Holyroodhouse

Mary, Queen of Scots spent six eventful years (1561–67) living at Holyroodhouse (p77), a 16th-century tower house that was extended to create a 17th-century royal palace, now Queen Elizabeth II's official residence in Scotland. Besides offering the chance to visit Mary's private bedchamber, the palace brims with fascinating antiques and artworks, and afterwards you'll have the opportunity to wander round Holyrood Park or climb Arthur's Seat.

## Scottish Parliament Building ⑤

Edinburgh's most spectacular and controversial building, officially opened in 2004, houses Scotland's devolved parliament (p75). The strange forms of the exterior are all symbolic, from the oddly shaped windows on the west wall to the ground plan of the whole complex, which represents a 'flower of democracy rooted in Scottish soil' (best seen looking down from Salisbury Crags).

## ⑥ Rosslyn Chapel

The success of Dan Brown's novel *The Da Vinci Code* and the subsequent Hollywood movie has seen a flood of visitors descend on Scotland's most beautiful and enigmatic church (p91). This 15th-century chapel, wreathed in ornate and mysterious stone carvings, has been the subject of Knights Templar and Holy Grail conspiracy theories for decades, and provides the setting for *The Da Vinci Code*'s dénouement.

## ⑦ Arthur's Seat

Hiking to the summit of this long-dormant volcano (p76) is an Edinburgh rite of passage, and you haven't really seen the city till you've done it. You'll be rewarded with a fantastic view that stretches from the Firth of Forth to the Pentland Hills, and the rocky summit makes a great spot for a picnic on one of those elusive sunny Scottish days.

# Edinburgh's Best...

## Wining & Dining

○ **Tower** (p90) Steaks and seafood in a chic setting with castle view

○ **Castle Terrace** (p90) Top modern Scottish cuisine from Michelin-starred chef

○ **Ondine** (p89) Elegant modern dining room specialising in superb seafood

○ **The Dogs** (p91) Bistro-style cuisine in one of Edinburgh's coolest restaurants

○ **Café Royal Oyster Bar** (p95) Classic seafood dishes amid magnificent 19th-century polished brass, marble and mahogany

## Viewpoints

○ **Edinburgh Castle** (p65) Grand views from Mills Mount Battery

○ **Camera Obscura** (p69) Outlook Tower offers a classic photo op for shots along Royal Mile rooftops

○ **Scott Monument** (p78) Lofty perch provides a stunning view across the gardens to Old Town skyline

○ **Nelson Monument** (p82) Picture-postcard scenes of Princes St, parliament building and Salisbury Crags

○ **Arthur's Seat** (p76) All-around city panorama from Firth of Forth to Pentland Hills

## Spooky Spots

○ **Real Mary King's Close** (p73) Remarkable 17th-century street preserved beneath 18th-century building

○ **Greyfriars Kirkyard** (p76) Edinburgh's spookiest graveyard, best visited on a night-time ghost tour

○ **South Bridge Vaults** (p85) Haunted stone cellars beneath Old Town streets

○ **Surgeons' Hall Museums** (p76) Grisly Burke and Hare exhibit includes pocketbook covered in human skin

## Historic Sites

○ **Palace of Holyroodhouse**
(p77) Mary, Queen of Scots'
bedchamber, where her
secretary (and lover?) was
murdered

○ **Edinburgh Castle** (p65)
Home to Scotland's crown
jewels and the Stone of
Destiny

○ **Greyfriars Kirk** (p76)
Where the National
Covenant was signed

○ **Grassmarket** (p76)Former
place of execution

○ **Heart of Midlothian** (p73)
Marks the spot of the Old
Tolbooth jail, made famous in
Walter Scott's novel

**Left:** Nelson Monument (p82);
**Above:** Towerrestaurant (p90)
(LEFT) JUSTIN CHEVALLIER/ALAMY ©;
(ABOVE) SCOTTISH VIEWPOINT/ALAMY ©

### ADVANCE PLANNING

○ **Six months before**
Book accommodation if
you plan to visit during
festival time (August) or
Hogmanay (New Year);
book tickets for the
Military Tattoo

○ **One month before**
Book accommodation
for any other time of
year; reserve a table
at the Tower or Ondine
restaurants

○ **Two weeks before**
Reserve a table at
any other fine-dining
restaurant

○ **One week before** Book
a tour of the Real Mary
King's Close

### RESOURCES

○ **Edinburgh & Lothians
Tourist Board** (www.
edinburgh.org) Official
tourism site, with listings
of accommodation, sights,
activities and events

○ **Edinburgh Museums
& Galleries** (www.
edinburghmuseums.org.
uk) Information on city-
owned museums and art
galleries

○ **Edinburgh Festivals**
(www.edinburghfestivals.
co.uk) Full details on
all of the city's official
festivals

○ **Edinburgh Bus Tours**
(www.edinburghtour.com)
Offers a range of tours
around the city; **Royal
Edinburgh Ticket** (adult/
child £40/20) gives two
days' unlimited travel on
sightseeing buses and
admission to Edinburgh
Castle, Palace of
Holyroodhouse and Royal
Yacht *Britannia*.

### GETTING AROUND

○ **From the Airport** Airlink
bus runs every 10 minutes
during the day, at least
hourly through the night;
30 minutes to the city
centre

○ **Bus** Good city bus
network; real-time bus
tracking info available on
free iPhone app (EdinBus)

○ **Car** Parking in the city
centre is difficult; best to
use public transport

○ **On Foot** The Old Town
is compact and easily
explored on foot; however,
be aware of steep hills and
flights of steps

○ **Train** Frequent trains
to Glasgow (every 15
minutes) and London
(every 30 minutes)

# ...rgh Walking Tour

*...makes Edinburgh's Old Town so fascinating is its maze of ...alleys. This walk explores a few of the many interesting nooks and crannies around the upper part of the Royal Mile.*

## WALK FACTS

- **Start** Castle Esplanade
- **Finish** High St, Royal Mile
- **Distance** 0.75 miles
- **Duration** One to two hours

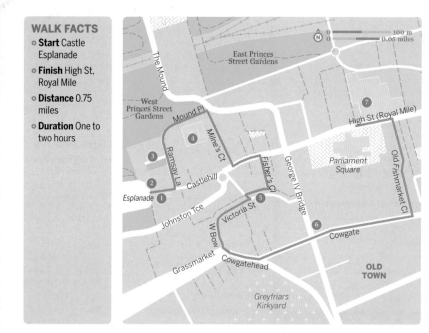

## 1 Cannonball House

Begin at the Castle Esplanade and walk downhill towards the Royal Mile. The 17th-century house on the right, above the steps of North Castle Wynd, is known as **Cannonball House** because of the iron ball lodged in the wall (look between, and slightly below, the two largest windows in the wall facing the castle). It was not fired in anger, but instead marks the gravitation height to which water would flow naturally from the city's first piped water supply.

## 2 Witches Well

The rectangular building across the street was originally the reservoir that held the Old Town's water supply. On its west wall is the **Witches Well**, where a modern bronze fountain commemorates around 4000 people (mostly women) who were burned or strangled in Edinburgh on suspicion of witchcraft between 1479 and 1722.

## 3 Ramsay Garden

Go past the reservoir, turn left down Ramsay Lane and take a look at **Ramsay Garden**, one of the most desirable addresses in Edinburgh, where late 19th-century apartments were built around the nucleus of the octagonal Ramsay Lodge, once home to poet Allan Ramsay.

## 4 New College

The cobbled street continues around to the right below student residences, to the twin towers of the **New College** – home to the University of Edinburgh's Faculty of Divinity. Nip into the courtyard to see the **statue of John Knox**.

## 5 Victoria Terrace

Turn right and climb up the stairs into Milne's Ct, a student residence. Exit onto Lawnmarket, cross the street (bearing left) and then turn right down Fisher's Close, which leads onto the delightful **Victoria Terrace**, poised above the cobbled curve of Victoria St. Wander right, enjoying the view, then descend the stairs at the foot of Upper Bow and continue downhill to the Grassmarket.

## 6 George IV Bridge

Turn left along the gloomy defile of the Cowgate. The first bridge you pass under is **George IV Bridge** (built 1829–34). Although you can see only one arch here, there are nine in total – one more is visible a block south at Merchant St, but the rest are hidden beneath and between the surrounding buildings, as are the haunted **vaults of South Bridge**, further west along Cowgate.

## 7 Real Mary King's Close

Beyond the bridge take the first left turn and climb up Old Fishmarket Close to emerge once more into the Royal Mile. Across the street to the left is the **Real Mary King's Close**. A guided tour of this historic building offers a fascinating look into 16th- and 17th-century Edinburgh life.

# Edinburgh in...

### TWO DAYS

Start by visiting **Edinburgh Castle,** then follow our walking tour of the Old Town. After lunch, continue down the Royal Mile to the **Scottish parliament building** and the **Palace of Holyroodhouse**. You can work up an appetite by climbing **Arthur's Seat**, then satisfy your hunger with dinner at the **Tower** restaurant while you watch the sun set behind the castle. On day two spend the morning visiting **Real Mary King's Close** or the **Royal Museum of Scotland**, then catch the bus to **Leith** for a visit to the **Royal Yacht** *Britannia*. In the evening have dinner at one of Leith's many excellent restaurants, or scare yourself silly on a guided ghost tour.

### FOUR DAYS

Two more days will give you time for a morning stroll around the **Royal Botanic Garden**, followed by a trip to the enigmatic and beautiful **Rosslyn Chapel**. Dinner at the **Café Royal Oyster Bar** could be had before or after your sunset walk to the summit of **Calton Hill**. On day four head out of town for a day trip to **Abbotsford**.

Café Royal Oyster Bar (p95)

- **Old Town** (p64) Medieval maze of towering tenements and ancient alleyways.

- **New Town** (p78) Classical grid of elegant Georgian townhouses.

- **Leith** (p82) Regenerated docklands emerging as desirable waterfront address.

## Sights

Edinburgh's main attractions are concentrated in the city centre – on and around the Old Town's Royal Mile between the castle and Holyrood, and in the New Town. A major exception is the Royal Yacht *Britannia,* which is in the redeveloped docklands district of Leith, 2 miles northeast of the centre.

If you tire of sightseeing, good areas for aimless wandering include the posh suburbs of Stockbridge and Morningside, the pretty riverside village of Cramond and the winding footpaths of Calton Hill and Arthur's Seat.

### Old Town

Edinburgh's Old Town stretches along a ridge to the east of the castle, and tumbles down Victoria St to the broad expanse of the Grassmarket. It's a jagged and jumbled maze of masonry riddled with closes (alleys) and wynds (narrow lanes), stairs and vaults, and cleft along its spine by the cobbled ravine of the Royal Mile.

Until the founding of the New Town in the 18th century, old Edinburgh was an overcrowded and insanitary hive of humanity squeezed between the boggy ground of the Nor' Loch (North Loch, now drained and occupied by Princes Street Gardens) to the north and the city walls to the south and east. The only way for the town to expand was upwards, and the five- and six-storey tenements that were raised along the Royal Mile in the 16th and 17th centuries were the skyscrapers of their day, remarked upon with wonder by visiting writers including Daniel Defoe.

Scottish National Portrait Gallery
EYE UBIQUITOUS/ALAMY ©

All classes of society, from beggars to magistrates, lived cheek by jowl in these urban ants' nests, the wealthy occupying the middle floors – high enough to be above the noise and stink of the streets, but not so high that climbing the stairs would be too tiring – while the poor squeezed into attics, basements, cellars and vaults amid the rats, rubbish and raw sewage.

The renovated Old Town tenements still support a thriving city-centre community, and today the street level is crammed with cafes, restaurants, bars, backpacker hostels and tacky souvenir shops. Few visitors wander beyond the main drag of the Royal Mile, but it's worth taking time to explore the countless closes that lead off the street into quiet courtyards, often with unexpected views of city, sea and hills (see the Walking Tour, p62).

## THE ROYAL MILE

This mile-long street earned its regal nickname in the 16th century when it was used by the king to travel between the castle and the Palace of Holyroodhouse. There are five sections (the Castle Esplanade, Castlehill, Lawnmarket, High St and Canongate), the names of which reflect their historical origins.

**EDINBURGH CASTLE** Castle
(Map p72; www.edinburghcastle.gov.uk; adult/child incl audioguide £16/9.20; ⊙9.30am-6pm Apr-Sep, to 5pm Oct-Mar, last admission 45min before closing) The brooding, black crags of Castle Rock, rising above the western end of Princes St, are the very reason for Edinburgh's existence. This rocky hill was the most easily defended hilltop on the invasion route between England and central Scotland, a route followed by countless armies from the Roman legions of the 1st and 2nd centuries AD to the Jacobite troops of Bonnie Prince Charlie in 1745.

Edinburgh Castle has played a pivotal role in Scottish history, both as a royal residence – King Malcolm Canmore (r 1058–93) and Queen Margaret made

## If You Like…
## Art Galleries

If the National Gallery has inspired in you an appreciation for all things artistic, there are several other top-quality galleries in the city.

### 1 SCOTTISH NATIONAL PORTRAIT GALLERY
(Map p80; www.nationalgalleries.org; 1 Queen St; ⊙10am-5pm Fri-Wed, to 7pm Thu) Illustrates Scottish history through paintings, photographs and sculptures, putting faces to famous names from Scotland's past and present. Portraits include Robert Burns, Mary, Queen of Scots, Bonnie Prince Charlie, Sean Connery, Billy Connolly and poet Jackie Kay.

### 2 FRUITMARKET GALLERY
(Map p72; www.fruitmarket.co.uk; 45 Market St; ⊙11am-6pm Mon-Sat, noon-5pm Sun) Showcases contemporary Scottish and international artists, and also has an excellent arts bookshop and cafe.

### 3 CITY ART CENTRE
(Map p72; www.edinburghmuseums.org.uk; 2 Market St; fee for temporary exhibitions; ⊙10am-5pm Mon-Sat, noon-5pm Sun) Six floors of exhibitions with a variety of themes, including an extensive collection of Scottish art.

### 4 SCOTTISH NATIONAL GALLERY OF MODERN ART
(Map p66; www.nationalgalleries.org; 75 Belford Rd; fee for special exhibitions; ⊙10am-5pm) The main collection, known as **Modern One**, concentrates on 20th-century art, with various European movements represented by the likes of Matisse, Picasso, Kirchner, Magritte, Miró, Mondrian and Giacometti. Directly across Belford Rd from Modern One is its annexe, **Modern Two**, which houses a large collection of sculpture and graphic art created by the Edinburgh-born artist Sir Eduardo Paolozzi.

their home here in the 11th century – and as a military stronghold. The castle last saw military action in 1745; from then until the 1920s it served as the British army's main base in Scotland. Today it is one of Scotland's most atmospheric,

# Edinburgh

EDINBURGH SIGHTS

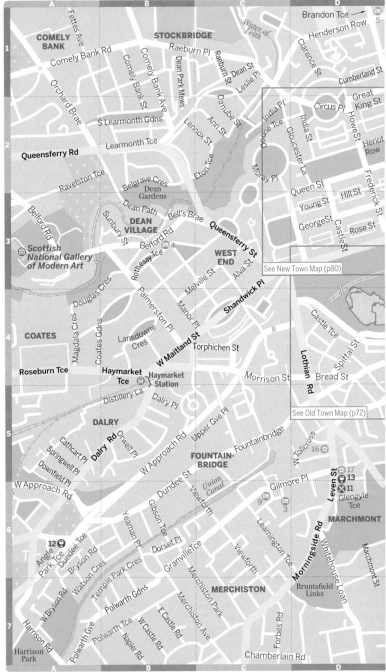

See New Town Map (p80)

See Old Town Map (p72)

Scottish National Gallery of Modern Art

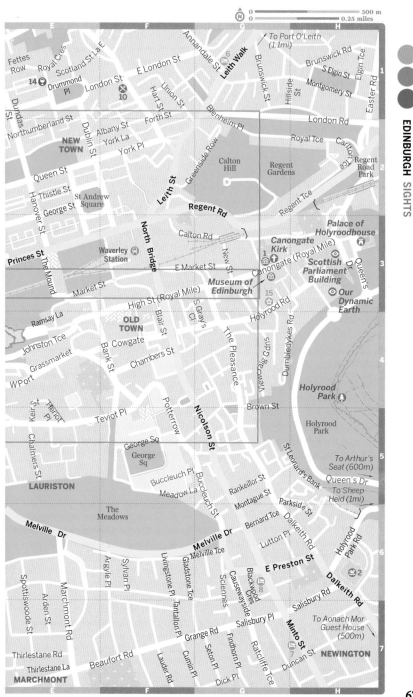

0   500 m
0   0.25 miles

Fettes Row
Royal Cres
Scotland St La E
14 Drummond Pl
London St
E London St
Annandale St
Leith Walk
6
To Port O'Leith (1.1mi)
Brunswick Rd
S Elgin St
Brunswick St
Hillside St
Montgomery St
Elgin Tce
Easter Rd
Dundas St
Northumberland St
Dublin St
Albany St
York La
York Pl
Union St
Hart St
Forth St
Greenside Row
Blenheim Pl
London Rd
Royal Tce
Carlton Tce
NEW TOWN
Queen St
Thistle St
George St
Hanover St
St Andrew Square
Leith St
Calton Hill
Regent Gardens
Regent Tce
Regent Road Park
Regent Rd
Princes St
The Mound
Waverley Station
North Bridge
Calton Rd
New St
E Market St
Palace of Holyroodhouse
Canongate Kirk
1
Canongate (Royal Mile)
15
Scottish Parliament Building
Queen's Dr
Our Dynamic Earth
Market St
High St (Royal Mile)
Museum of Edinburgh
Holyrood Rd
Ramsay La
Johnston Tce
Grassmarket
W Port
OLD TOWN
Bank St
Cowgate
Blair St
Chambers St
S Gray's Cl
The Pleasance
Viewcraig Gdns
Dumbledykes Rd
St Srey
Heriot Pl
Teviot Pl
Potterrow
Nicolson St
Brown St
Holyrood Park
Holyrood Park
Chalmers St
George Sq
George Sq
LAURISTON
Buccleuch Pl
Meadow La
The Meadows
Buccleuch St
Rankeillor St
Montague St
St Leonard's Bank
To Arthur's Seat (600m)
Queen's Dr
To Sheep Heid (1mi)
2
Melville Dr
Melville Dr
Melville Tce
Bernard Tce
Parkside St
Dalkeith Rd
Lutton Pl
Holyrood Park Rd
Dalkeith Rd
Spottiswoode St
Argyle Pl
Sylvan Pl
Livingstone Pl
Gladstone Tce
Tantallon Pl
Sciennes
Causewayside
Blackwood Cres
E Preston St
8
Salisbury Rd
To Aonach Mor Guest House (500m)
Marchmont Rd
Arden St
Thirlestane Rd
Thirlestane La
Beaufort Rd
Grange Rd
Lauder Rd
Salisbury Pl
Findhorn Pl
Seton Pl
Cumin Pl
Dick Pl
Ratcliffe Tce
Minto St
Duncan St
7
NEWINGTON
MARCHMONT

# Edinburgh

most popular – and most expensive – tourist attractions.

The **Entrance Gateway**, flanked by statues of Robert the Bruce and William Wallace, opens to a cobbled lane that leads up beneath the 16th-century **Portcullis Gate** to the cannons ranged along the Argyle and Mills Mount batteries. The battlements here have great views over New Town to the Firth of Forth.

At the far end of Mills Mount Battery is the famous **One O'Clock Gun**, where crowds gather to watch a gleaming WWII 25-pounder fire an ear-splitting time signal at exactly 1pm (every day except Sundays, Christmas Day and Good Friday).

South of Mills Mount, the road curls up leftwards through **Foog's Gate** to the highest part of Castle Rock, crowned by the tiny, Romanesque **St Margaret's Chapel**, the oldest surviving building in Edinburgh. It was probably built by David I or Alexander I in memory of their mother, Queen Margaret, sometime around 1130 (she was canonised in 1250). Beside the chapel stands **Mons Meg**, a giant 15th-century siege gun built at Mons (in what is now Belgium) in 1449.

The main group of buildings on the summit of Castle Rock are ranged around Crown Sq, dominated by the shrine of the **Scottish National War Memorial**. Opposite is the **Great Hall**, built for James IV (r 1488–1513) as a ceremonial hall and used as a meeting place for the Scottish parliament until 1639. Its most remarkable feature is the original, 16th-century hammer-beam roof.

The **Castle Vaults** beneath the Great Hall (entered from Crown Sq via the Prisons of War exhibit) were used variously as storerooms, bakeries and a prison. The vaults have been renovated to resemble 18th- and early 19th-century **prisons**, where graffiti carved by French and American prisoners can be seen on the ancient wooden doors.

On the eastern side of the square is the **Royal Palace**, built during the 15th and 16th centuries, where a series of historical tableaux leads to the highlight of the castle – a strongroom housing the **Honours of Scotland** (the Scottish crown jewels), the oldest surviving crown jewels in Europe. Locked away in a chest following the Act of Union in 1707, the crown (made in 1540 from the gold of Robert the Bruce's 14th-century coronet), sword and sceptre lay forgotten until they were unearthed at the instigation of the novelist Sir Walter Scott in 1818. Also on display here is the **Stone of Destiny**.

Among the neighbouring **Royal Apartments** is the bedchamber where Mary, Queen of Scots gave birth to her son James VI, who was to unite the crowns of Scotland and England in 1603.

## NATIONAL WAR MUSEUM
## OF SCOTLAND                              Museum

(Map p72; www.nms.ac.uk; admission incl in Edinburgh Castle ticket; ⏰9.45am-5.45pm Apr-Oct, to 4.45pm Nov-Mar) At the western end of the castle, to the left of the castle restaurant, a road leads down to the National War Museum of Scotland, which brings Scotland's military history vividly to life. The exhibits have been personalised by telling the stories of the original owners of the objects on display, making it easier to empathise with the experiences of war than any dry display of dusty weaponry ever could.

## SCOTCH WHISKY
## EXPERIENCE                              Exhibition

(Map p72; www.scotchwhiskyexperience.co.uk; 354 Castlehill; adult/child incl tour & tasting £12.50/6.50; ⏰10am-6.30pm Jun-Aug, to 6pm Sep-May; 📶) A former school houses this multimedia centre explaining the making of whisky from barley to bottle in a series of exhibits, demonstrations and tours that combine sight, sound and smell, including the world's largest collection of malt whiskies; look out for Peat the distillery cat! There's also a restaurant that serves traditional Scottish dishes with, where possible, a dash of whisky thrown in. It's a short distance downhill from the Castle Esplanade.

## CAMERA OBSCURA          Camera Obscura

(Map p72; www.camera-obscura.co.uk; Castlehill; adult/child £10.95/7.95; ⏰9.30am-9pm Jul & Aug, 9.30am-7pm Apr-Jun & Sep-Oct, 10am-6pm Nov-Mar) Edinburgh's camera obscura is a curious 19th-century device – in constant use since 1853 – that uses lenses and mirrors to throw a live image of the city onto a large horizontal screen. The accompanying commentary is entertaining and the whole experience has a quirky charm, complemented by an intriguing exhibition dedicated to illusions of all kinds. Stairs lead up through various displays to the **Outlook Tower**, which offers great views over the city.

## GLADSTONE'S LAND      Historic Building

(NTS; Map p72; www.nts.org.uk; 477 Lawnmarket; adult/child £6/5; ⏰10am-6.30pm Jul & Aug, to 5pm Apr-Jun & Sep-Oct) One of Edinburgh's most prominent 17th-century merchants was Thomas Gledstanes who, in 1617, purchased the tenement later known as Gladstone's Land. It contains fine

The Royal Mile

ANDY STOTHERT/GETTY IMAGES ©

# Royal Mile

## A Grand Day Out

Planning your own procession along the Royal Mile involves some tough decisions – it would be impossible to see everything in a single day, so it's wise to decide in advance what you don't want to miss and shape your visit around that. Remember to leave time for lunch, for exploring some of the Mile's countless side alleys and, during festival time, for enjoying the street theatre that is bound to be happening in High St.

The most pleasant way to reach the Castle Esplanade at the start of the Royal Mile is to hike up the zigzag path from the footbridge behind the Ross Bandstand in Princes Street Gardens (in springtime you'll be knee-deep in daffodils). Starting at **Edinburgh Castle** ❶ means that the rest of your walk is downhill. For a superb view up and down the length of the Mile, climb the **Camera Obscura's Outlook Tower** ❷ before visiting **Gladstone's Land** ❸ and **St Giles Cathedral** ❹. If history's your

### Royal Visits to the Royal Mile

**1561:** Mary, Queen of Scots arrives from France and holds an audience with John Knox.
**1745:** Bonnie Prince Charlie fails to capture Edinburgh Castle, and instead sets up court in Holyroodhouse.
**2004:** Queen Elizabeth II officially opens the Scottish Parliament building.

### Edinburgh Castle

If you're pushed for time, visit the Great Hall, the Honours of Scotland and the Prisons of War exhibit. Head for the Half Moon Battery for a photo looking down the length of the Royal Mile.

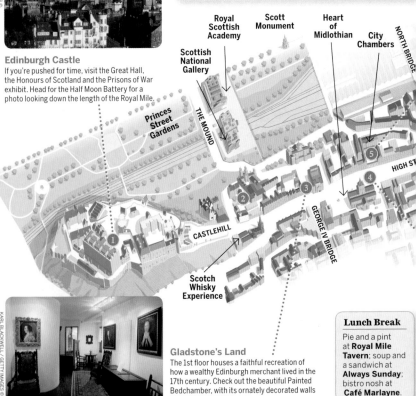

### Gladstone's Land

The 1st floor houses a faithful recreation of how a wealthy Edinburgh merchant lived in the 17th century. Check out the beautiful Painted Bedchamber, with its ornately decorated walls and wooden ceilings.

### Lunch Break

Pie and a pint at **Royal Mile Tavern**; soup and a sandwich at **Always Sunday**; bistro nosh at **Café Marlayne**.

thing, you'll want to add **Real Mary King's Close** ⑤, **John Knox House** ⑥ and the **Museum of Edinburgh** ⑦ to your must-see list.

At the foot of the mile, choose between modern and ancient seats of power – the **Scottish Parliament** ⑧ or the Palace of **Holyroodhouse** ⑨. Round off the day with an evening ascent of Arthur's Seat or, slightly less strenuously, Calton Hill. Both make great sunset viewpoints.

**TAKING YOUR TIME**

Minimum time needed for each attraction:

**Edinburgh Castle:** two hours

**Gladstone's Land:** 45 minutes

**St Giles Cathedral:** 30 minutes

**Real Mary King's Close:** one hour (tour)

**Scottish Parliament:** one hour (tour)

**Palace of Holyroodhouse:** one hour

**Real Mary King's Close**
The guided tour is heavy on ghost stories, but a highlight is standing in an original 17th-century room with tufts of horsehair poking from the crumbling plaster, and breathing in the ancient scent of stone, dust and history.

**Canongate Kirk**

CANONGATE

ST MARY'S ST

SOUTH BRIDGE

Tron Kirk

Our Dynamic Earth

**St Giles Cathedral**
Look out for the Burne-Jones stained-glass window (1873) at the west end, showing the crossing of the River Jordan, and the bronze memorial to Robert Louis Stevenson in the Moray Aisle.

**Scottish Parliament**
Don't have time for the guided tour? Pick up a 'Discover the Scottish Parliament Building' leaflet from reception and take a self-guided tour of the exterior, then hike up to Salisbury Crags for a great view of the complex.

**Palace of Holyroodhouse**
Find the secret staircase joining Mary, Queen of Scots' bedchamber with that of her husband, Lord Darnley, who restrained the queen while his henchmen stabbed to death her secretary (and possible lover), David Rizzio.

EDINBURGH SIGHTS

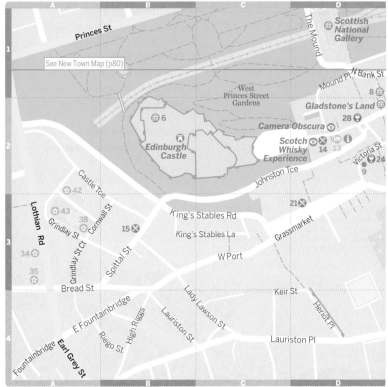

See New Town Map (p80)

painted ceilings, walls and beams, and some splendid furniture from the 17th and 18th centuries. The volunteer guides provide a detailed history with a wealth of anecdotes.

### FREE WRITERS' MUSEUM — Museum

(Map p72; www.edinburghmuseums.org.uk; Lady Stair's Close, Lawnmarket; ⏱10am-5pm Mon-Sat year-round, 2-5pm Sun Aug) Tucked down a close just east of Gladstone's Land you'll find Lady Stair's House (1622), home to this museum which contains manuscripts and memorabilia belonging to three of Scotland's most famous writers: Robert Burns, Sir Walter Scott and Robert Louis Stevenson.

### ST GILES CATHEDRAL — Church

(Map p72; www.stgilescathedral.org.uk; High St; suggested donation £3; ⏱9am-7pm Mon-Fri, to 5pm Sat, 1-5pm Sun May-Sep, 9am-5pm Mon-Sat, 1-5pm Sun Oct-Apr) Dominating the High St is the great grey bulk of St Giles Cathedral. Properly called the High Kirk of Edinburgh (it was only a true cathedral – the seat of a bishop – from 1633 to 1638 and from 1661 to 1689), St Giles Cathedral was named after the patron saint of cripples and beggars. A Norman-style church was built here in 1126 but was destroyed by English invaders in 1385; the only substantial remains are the central piers that support the tower.

The present church dates largely from the 15th century – the beautiful **crown spire** was completed in 1495 – but much of it was restored in the 19th century. The interior lacks grandeur but is rich in history: St Giles was at the heart of the Scottish Reformation, and John Knox

served as minister here from 1559 to 1572. One of the most interesting corners of the kirk is the **Thistle Chapel**, built in 1911 for the Knights of the Most Ancient & Most Noble Order of the Thistle. The elaborately carved Gothic-style stalls have canopies topped with the helms and arms of the 16 knights – look out for the bagpipe-playing angel amid the vaulting.

By the side of the street, outside the western door of St Giles, is the **Heart of Midlothian**, set into the cobblestone paving. This marks the site of the Tolbooth. Built in the 15th century and demolished in the early 19th century, the Tolbooth served variously as a meeting place for parliament, the town council and the General Assembly of the Reformed Kirk, before becoming law courts and, finally, a notorious prison and place of execution. Passers-by traditionally spit on the heart for luck (don't stand downwind!).

At the other end of St Giles is the **Mercat Cross**, a 19th-century copy of the 1365 original, where merchants and traders met to transact business and royal proclamations were read.

### REAL MARY KING'S
CLOSE    Historic Building
(Map p72; ☎0845 070 6244; www.realmarykings close.com; 2 Warriston's Close, High St; adult/child £12.95/7.45; ⏰10am-9pm Apr-Oct, to 11pm Aug, 10am-5pm Sun-Thu & to 9pm Fri & Sat Nov-Mar) Across from St Giles is the City Chambers, originally built by John Adam (brother of Robert) between 1753 and 1761 to serve as the Royal Exchange – a covered meeting place for city merchants. However, the merchants preferred their

# Old Town

old stamping ground in the street and the building became the city council offices in 1811.

Part of the Royal Exchange was built over the sealed-off remains of Mary King's Close, and the lower levels of this medieval Old Town alley have survived almost unchanged in the foundations of the City Chambers for 250 years. Now open to the public as the Real Mary King's Close, this spooky, subterranean labyrinth gives a fascinating insight into the daily life of 16th- and 17th-century Edinburgh. Costumed characters give tours through a 16th-century town house and the plague-stricken home of a 17th-century gravedigger. Advance booking recommended.

**JOHN KNOX HOUSE** Historic Building
(Map p72; www.scottishstorytellingcentre.co.uk; 43-45 High St; adult/child £4.25/1; ☺10am-6pm Mon-Sat year-round, noon-6pm Sun Jul & Aug) The Royal Mile narrows at the foot of High St beside the jutting facade of John Knox House. This is the oldest surviving tenement in Edinburgh, dating from around 1490. John Knox, an influential church reformer and leader of the Protestant Reformation in Scotland, is thought to have lived here from 1561 to 1572. The labyrinthine interior has some beautiful

painted-timber ceilings and an interesting display on Knox's life and work.

**FREE** PEOPLE'S STORY                Museum
(Map p66; www.edinburghmuseums.org.uk; 163 Canongate; ⊙10am-5pm Mon-Sat year-round, 2-5pm Sun Aug) One of the surviving symbols of Canongate's former independence is the **Canongate Tolbooth**. Built in 1591 it served successively as a collection point for tolls (taxes), a council house, a courtroom and a jail. With picturesque turrets and a projecting clock, it's an interesting example of 16th-century architecture. It now houses a fascinating museum called the People's Story, which covers the life, work and pastimes of ordinary Edinburgh folk from the 18th century to today.

**FREE** MUSEUM OF EDINBURGH Museum
(Map p66; www.edinburghmuseums.org.uk; 142 Canongate; ⊙10am-5pm Mon-Sat year-round, 2-5pm Sun Aug) You can't miss the colourful facade of Huntly House, newly renovated in bright red and yellow ochre, opposite

the Tolbooth clock. Built in 1570, it houses a museum covering Edinburgh from its prehistory to the present. Exhibits of national importance include an original copy of the National Covenant of 1638, but the big crowd-pleaser is the dog collar and feeding bowl that once belonged to **Greyfriars Bobby**, the city's most famous canine citizen.

CANONGATE KIRK                Church
(Map p66) Downhill from Huntly House is the attractive curved gable of the Canongate Kirk, built in 1688. The kirkyard contains the graves of several famous people, including the economist **Adam Smith**, author of *The Wealth of Nations;* Mrs Agnes MacLehose (the 'Clarinda' of Robert Burns' love poems); and the 18th-century poet **Robert Fergusson** (1750–74; there's a statue of him on the street outside the church). Fergusson was much admired by Robert Burns, who paid for the gravestone and penned the epitaph – take a look at the inscription on the back.

# Scottish Parliament Building

The **Scottish Parliament Building** (Map p66; ☏0131-348 5200; www.scottish.parliament. uk; admission free; ⊙9am-6.30pm Tue-Thu, 10am-5.30pm Mon & Fri in session, 10am-6pm Mon-Fri in recess Apr-Oct, 10am-4pm in recess Nov-Mar; 🛜), built on the site of a former brewery close to the Palace of Holyroodhouse, was officially opened by Queen Elizabeth II in October 2005.

The public areas of the building – the Main Hall, where there is an exhibition, shop and cafe; and the **public gallery** in the Debating Chamber – are open to visitors (tickets are needed for the public gallery – see website for details). You can also take a free, one-hour **guided tour** (advance booking recommended) that includes a visit to the Debating Chamber, a committee room, the Garden Lobby and, when possible, the office of an MSP (Member of the Scottish Parliament). If you want to see the **parliament in session**, check the website to see when it will be sitting – business days are normally Tuesday to Thursday year-round.

The **Main Hall**, inside the public entrance, has a low, triple-arched ceiling of polished concrete, like a cave, or cellar, or castle vault. It is a dimly lit space, the starting point for a metaphorical journey from this relative darkness up to the **Debating Chamber** (sitting directly above the Main Hall), which is, in contrast, a palace of light – the light of democracy. This magnificent chamber is the centrepiece of the parliament, designed not to glorify but to humble the politicians who sit within it.

(An information board just inside the gate lists famous graves and their locations.)

### OUR DYNAMIC EARTH — Exhibition

(Map p66; www.dynamicearth.co.uk; Holyrood Rd; adult/child £11.50/7.50; ⊙10am-6pm Jul & Aug, to 5.30pm Apr-Jun, Sep & Oct, 10am-5pm Wed-Sun Nov-Mar, last admission 90min before closing; ♿) The modernistic white marquee pitched beneath Salisbury Crags marks Our Dynamic Earth, billed as an interactive, multimedia journey of discovery through Earth's history from the Big Bang to the present day. Hugely popular with kids of all ages, it's a slick extravaganza of whiz-bang special effects and 3D movies cleverly designed to fire up young minds with curiosity about all things geological and environmental. Its true purpose, of course, is to disgorge you into a gift shop where you can buy model dinosaurs and souvenir T-shirts.

### HOLYROOD PARK — Park

(Map p66) In Holyrood Park, Edinburgh is blessed with a little bit of wilderness in the heart of the city. The former hunting ground of Scottish monarchs, the park covers 263 hectares of varied landscape, including crags, moorland and a loch. The highest point is the 251m summit of **Arthur's Seat** (p59), the deeply eroded remnant of a long-extinct volcano. Holyrood Park can be circumnavigated by car or bike along Queen's Dr, and you can hike from Holyrood to the summit in around 45 minutes.

## SOUTH OF THE ROYAL MILE

### FREE GREYFRIARS KIRK & KIRKYARD — Church

(Map p72; www.greyfriarskirk.com; Candlemaker Row; ⊙10.30am-4.30pm Mon-Fri & 11am-2pm Sat Apr-Oct, 1.30-3.30pm Thu only Nov-Mar) One of Edinburgh's most famous churches, Greyfriars Kirk was built on the site of a Franciscan friary and opened for worship on Christmas Day 1620. In 1638 the **National Covenant** was signed here, rejecting Charles I's attempts to impose episcopacy and a new English prayer book on the Scots, and affirming the independence of the Scottish Church. Many who signed were later executed at the Grassmarket and, in 1679, 1200 Covenanters were held prisoner in terrible conditions in the south-western corner of the kirkyard. There's a small exhibition inside the church.

Surrounding the church, hemmed in by high walls and overlooked by the brooding presence of the castle, **Greyfriars Kirkyard** is one of Edinburgh's most evocative cemeteries, a peaceful green oasis dotted with elaborate monuments. Many famous Edinburgh names are buried here, including the poet Allan Ramsay (1686–1758), architect William Adam (1689–1748) and William Smellie (1740–95), the editor of the first edition of the *Encyclopedia Britannica*.

If you want to experience the graveyard at its scariest – inside a burial vault, in the dark, at night – go on one of Black Hart Storytellers' (p83) guided tours.

### GREYFRIARS BOBBY STATUE — Monument

(Map p72) The memorials inside Greyfriars Kirkyard are interesting, but the one that draws the biggest crowds is outside, opposite the pub beside the kirkyard gate. It's the tiny statue of Greyfriars Bobby, a Skye terrier who, from 1858 to 1872, maintained a vigil over the grave of his master, an Edinburgh police officer. The story was immortalised in a novel by Eleanor Atkinson in 1912, and in 1963 was made into a movie by – who else? – Walt Disney. Bobby's own grave, marked by a small, pink granite stone, is just inside the entrance to the kirkyard. You can see his original collar and bowl in the **Museum of Edinburgh** (p75).

### SURGEONS' HALL MUSEUMS — Museum

(Map p72; www.museum.rcsed.ac.uk; Nicolson St; adult/child £5/3; ⊙noon-4pm Mon-Fri, plus Sat & Sun Apr-Oct) These fascinating museums take a look at surgery in Scotland from the 15th century – when barbers supplemented their income with bloodletting, amputations and other surgical procedures – to the present day. The highlight is the exhibit on **Burke and Hare**, which includes Burke's death mask and a pocketbook bound in his skin.

RIEGER BERTRAND/HEMIS.FR/GETTY IMAGES ©

# Don't Miss **Palace of Holyroodhouse**

This palace is the royal family's official residence in Scotland, but is more famous as the 16th-century home of the ill-fated Mary, Queen of Scots. The palace is closed to the public when the royal family is visiting and during state functions (usually in mid-May, and mid-June to early July; check the website for exact dates).

The self-guided audio tour leads you through a series of impressive royal apartments, ending in the **Great Gallery**. The 89 portraits of Scottish kings were commissioned by Charles II and supposedly record his unbroken lineage from Scota, the Egyptian pharaoh's daughter who discovered the infant Moses in a reed basket on the banks of the Nile.

But the highlight of the tour is **Mary, Queen of Scots' Bedchamber**, home to the unfortunate Mary from 1561 to 1567, and connected by a secret stairway to her husband's bedchamber. It was here that her jealous first husband, Lord Darnley, restrained the pregnant queen while his henchmen murdered her secretary – and favourite – Rizzio. A plaque in the neighbouring room marks the spot where he bled to death. The exit from the palace leads into the ruins of Holyrood Abbey. In summer you can join a guided tour of the ruins (included with your admission fee); the rest of the year you can explore them on your own. King David I founded the abbey here in the shadow of Salisbury Crags in 1128. It was probably named after a fragment of the True Cross (rood is an old Scots word for cross), said to have been brought to Scotland by his mother, St Margaret. Most of the surviving ruins date from the 12th and 13th centuries.

## NEED TO KNOW

Map p66; www.royalcollection.org.uk; adult/child £10.75/6.50; ☺9.30am-6pm Apr-Oct, to 4.30pm Nov-Mar

# New Town

Edinburgh's New Town lies north of the Old Town, on a ridge running parallel to the Royal Mile and separated from it by the valley of Princes Street Gardens. Its regular grid of elegant Georgian terraces is a complete contrast to the chaotic tangle of tenements and wynds that characterise the Old Town.

Between the end of the 14th century and the start of the 18th, the population of Edinburgh – still confined within the walls of the Old Town – increased from 2000 to 50,000. The tottering tenements were unsafe and occasionally collapsed, fire was an ever-present danger, and the overcrowding and squalor became unbearable.

When the Act of Union in 1707 brought the prospect of long-term stability, the upper classes were keen to find healthier, more spacious living quarters, and in 1766 the lord provost of Edinburgh announced an architectural competition to design an extension to the city. It was won by an unknown 23-year-old, James Craig, a self-taught architect whose simple and elegant plan envisaged a main axis along George St, with grand squares at either end, and with building restricted to one side only of Princes and Queen Sts so that the houses enjoyed views over the Firth of Forth to the north and to the castle and the Old Town to the south.

During the 18th and 19th centuries the New Town continued to sprout squares, circuses, parks and terraces, with some of its finest neoclassical architecture designed by Robert Adam. Today Edinburgh's New Town remains the world's most complete and unspoilt example of Georgian architecture and town planning. Along with the Old Town, it was declared a Unesco World Heritage Site in 1995.

## PRINCES STREET

Princes St is one of the world's most spectacular shopping streets. Built up on the north side only, it catches the sun in summer and allows expansive views across Princes Street Gardens to the castle and the crowded skyline of the Old Town.

**Princes Street Gardens** lie in a valley that was once occupied by the Nor' Loch, a boggy depression that was drained in the early 19th century. The gardens are split in the middle by **The Mound**, which was created from around two million cart-loads of earth excavated from the foundations of the New Town and dumped here to provide a road link across the valley to the Old Town. It was completed in 1830.

**SCOTT MONUMENT**                    Monument

(Map p80; www.edinburghmuseums.org.uk; East Princes Street Gardens; admission £3; ☺10am-7pm Mon-Sat Apr-Sep, 9am-4pm Mon-Sat Oct-Mar, 10am-6pm Sun year-round) The eastern half of Princes Street Gardens is dominated by the massive Gothic spire of the Scott Monument, built by public subscription in memory of the novelist Sir Walter Scott after his death in 1832. The exterior is decorated with carvings of characters from his novels; inside you can see an exhibition on Scott's life, and climb the 287 steps to the top for a superb view of the city.

**FREE** **SCOTTISH NATIONAL GALLERY**                    Gallery

(Map p72; www.nationalgalleries.org; The Mound; fee for special exhibitions; ☺10am-5pm Fri-Wed, to 7pm Thu; ☎) Designed by William Playfair, this imposing classical building with its Ionic porticoes dates from the 1850s. Its octagonal rooms, lit by skylights, have been restored to their original Victorian decor of deep-green carpets and dark-red walls.

The gallery houses an important collection of **European art** from the Renaissance to post-Impressionism, with works by Verrocchio (Leonardo da Vinci's teacher), Tintoretto, Titian, Holbein, Rubens, Van Dyck, Vermeer, El Greco, Poussin, Rembrandt, Gainsborough, Turner, Constable, Monet, Pissarro, Gauguin and Cézanne. Each year in January the gallery exhibits its collection of **Turner watercolours**, bequeathed by Henry Vaughan in 1900. Room X is graced by Antonio Canova's white marble sculpture, **The Three Graces**; it is owned

RIEGER BERTRAND/GETTY IMAGES ©

# Don't Miss National Museum of Scotland

Broad, elegant Chambers St is dominated by the long facade of the National Museum of Scotland. Its extensive collections are spread between two buildings, one modern, one Victorian. The museum reopened to the public in 2011 after two years of major renovation and reconstruction.

The golden stone and striking modern architecture of the museum's new building, opened in 1998, is one of the city's most distinctive landmarks. The five floors of the museum trace the history of Scotland from geological beginnings to the 1990s, with many imaginative and stimulating exhibits – audio guides are available in several languages.

Highlights include the Monymusk Reliquary, a tiny silver casket dating from AD 750, which is said to have been carried into battle with Robert the Bruce at Bannockburn in 1314; and some of the Lewis Chessmen, a set of charming 12th-century chess pieces carved from walrus ivory.

The new building connects with the original Victorian museum, dating from 1861, the stolid, grey exterior of which gives way to a bright and airy, glass-roofed hall. The museum houses an eclectic collection covering natural history, archaeology, scientific and industrial technology, and the decorative arts of ancient Egypt, Islam, China, Japan, Korea and the West.

### NEED TO KNOW

Map p72; www.nms.ac.uk; Chambers St; fee for special exhibitions; ⊙10am-5pm

jointly with London's Victoria & Albert Museum.

The upstairs galleries house portraits by Sir Joshua Reynolds and Sir Henry Raeburn, and a clutch of **Impressionist** paintings, including Monet's luminous *Haystacks*, Van Gogh's demonic *Olive Trees* and Gauguin's hallucinatory *Vision After the Sermon*. But the painting that really catches your eye is the gorgeous

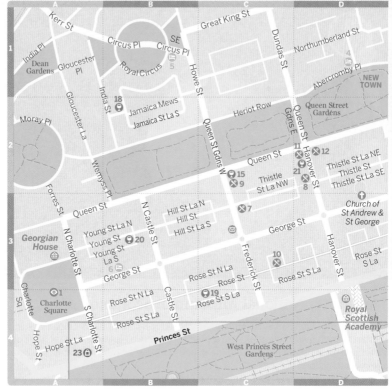

portrait of *Lady Agnew of Lochnaw* by John Singer Sargent.

The basement galleries dedicated to **Scottish art** include glowing portraits by Allan Ramsay and Sir Henry Raeburn, rural scenes by Sir David Wilkie and impressionistic landscapes by William MacTaggart. Look out for Raeburn's iconic *Reverend Robert Walker Skating on Duddingston Loch,* and Sir George Harvey's hugely entertaining *A Schule Skailin* (A School Emptying) – a stern dominie (teacher) looks on as the boys stampede for the classroom door, one reaching for a spinning top that was confiscated earlier. Kids will love the fantasy paintings of Sir Joseph Noel Paton in Room B5; the incredibly detailed canvases are crammed with hundreds of tiny fairies, goblins and elves.

**FREE** ROYAL SCOTTISH
ACADEMY                          Gallery
(Map p80; www.royalscottishacademy.org; The Mound; fee for special exhibitions; ⏲10am-5pm Mon-Sat, 2-5pm Sun; 🛜) The distinguished Greek Doric temple at the corner of The Mound and Princes St, its northern pediment crowned by a seated figure of Queen Victoria, is the home of the Royal Scottish Academy (RSA). Designed by William Playfair and built between 1823 and 1836, it was originally called the Royal Institution; the RSA took over the building in 1910. The galleries display a collection of paintings, sculptures and architectural drawings by academy members dating from 1831, and they also host temporary exhibitions throughout the year.

The RSA and the Scottish National Gallery are linked via an underground

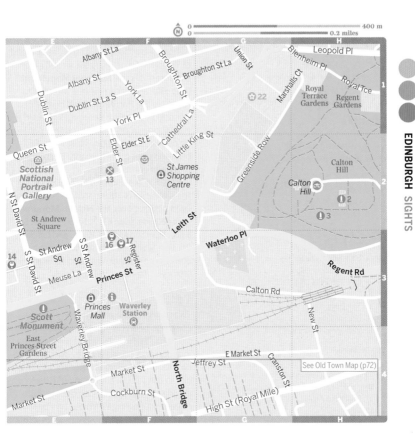

mall – the **Weston Link** – which gives them twice the temporary exhibition space of the Prado in Madrid and three times that of the Royal Academy in London, as well as housing cloakrooms, a lecture theatre and a restaurant.

## GEORGE STREET & CHARLOTTE SQUARE

Until the 1990s George St – the major axis of New Town – was the centre of Edinburgh's financial industry and Scotland's equivalent of Wall St. Today the big financial firms have moved to premises in the Exchange office district west of Lothian Rd, and George St's former banks and offices house upmarket shops, pubs and restaurants.

At the western end of George St is **Charlotte Square** (Map p80; ☐ all Princes St buses), the architectural jewel of New Town, designed by Robert Adam shortly before his death in 1791. The northern side of the square is Adam's masterpiece and one of the finest examples of Georgian architecture anywhere. **Bute House**, in the centre at No 6, is the official residence of Scotland's first minister, the equivalent of London's 10 Downing St.

**GEORGIAN HOUSE**   Historic Building
(NTS; Map p80; 7 Charlotte Sq; adult/child £6/5; ☺10am-6pm Jul & Aug, to 5pm Apr-Jun & Sep-Oct, 11am-4pm Mar, to 3pm Nov) The National Trust for Scotland's Georgian House has been beautifully restored and furnished to show how Edinburgh's wealthy elite lived at the end of the 18th century. The walls are decorated with paintings by Allan Ramsay, Sir Henry Raeburn and Sir Joshua Reynolds.

81

## New Town

**◎ Top Sights**

**◎ Sights**

**◉ Sleeping**

**✖ Eating**

**◉ Drinking**

**◉ Entertainment**

**◉ Shopping**

### CALTON HILL

Calton Hill (100m), rising dramatically above the eastern end of Princes St, is Edinburgh's acropolis, its summit scattered with grandiose memorials dating mostly from the first half of the 19th century. It is also one of the best viewpoints in Edinburgh, with a panorama that takes in the castle, Holyrood, Arthur's Seat, the Firth of Forth, the New Town and the full length of Princes St.

You can reach the summit of Calton Hill via the road beside the Royal High School or by the stairs at the eastern end of Waterloo Pl. The largest structure on the summit is the **National Monument (Map p80)**, an overambitious attempt to replicate the Parthenon in Athens and intended to honour Scotland's dead in the Napoleonic Wars. Construction – paid for by public subscription – began in 1822, but funds ran dry when only 12 columns had been completed.

Looking like an upturned telescope – the similarity is intentional – and offering even better views, the **Nelson Monument (Map p80; admission £3; ⊙10am-7pm Mon-Sat & noon-5pm Sun Apr-Sep, 10am-3pm Mon-Sat Oct-Mar; ☐all Leith St buses)** was built to commemorate Admiral Lord Nelson's victory at Trafalgar in 1805.

## Leith

Two miles northeast of the city centre, Leith has been Edinburgh's seaport since the 14th century and remained an independent burgh with its own town council until it was incorporated by the city in the 1920s. Like many of Britain's dockland areas, it fell into decay in the decades following WWII but has been undergoing a revival since the late 1980s. Old warehouses have been turned into luxury flats, and a lush crop of trendy bars and restaurants has sprouted along the waterfront. The area was given an additional boost in the late 1990s when the Scottish Executive (a government department) moved to a new building on the Leith docks.

The city council has formulated a major redevelopment plan for the entire Edinburgh waterfront from Leith to Granton, the first phase of which is **Ocean Terminal** (☎555 8888; www.oceanterminal. com; Ocean Dr; ⊙10am-8pm Mon-Fri, to 7pm Sat, 11am-6pm Sun; ☐1, 11, 22, 34, 35 or 36), a shopping and leisure complex that includes the former Royal Yacht *Britannia* and a berth for visiting cruise liners. Parts of Leith are still a bit rough but it's a distinctive corner of the city and well worth exploring.

**Tours**

## Bus Tours

Tickets for the following tours are valid for 24 hours.

### CITY SIGHTSEEING
Bus Tours
(www.edinburghtour.com; adult/child £12/5)
Bright-red, open-top buses depart every 20 minutes from Waverley Bridge.

### MAJESTIC TOUR
Bus Tours
(www.edinburghtour.com; adult/child £12/5)
Runs every 30 minutes (every 20 minutes in July and August) from Waverley Bridge to the Royal Yacht *Britannia* at Ocean Terminal via the New Town, Royal Botanic Garden and Newhaven, returning via Leith Walk, Holyrood and the Royal Mile.

## Walking Tours

### BLACK HART
### STORYTELLERS
Walking Tours
(www.blackhart.uk.com; adult/concession £10/5)
Not suitable for young children. The 'City of the Dead' tour of Greyfriars Kirkyard is probably the scariest of Edinburgh's 'ghost' tours. Many people have reported encounters with the 'McKenzie Poltergeist'.

### CADIES & WITCHERY
### TOURS
Walking Tours
(Map p72; www.witcherytours.com; adult/child £8.50/6) The becloaked and pasty-faced Adam Lyal (deceased) leads a 'Murder & Mystery' tour of the Old Town's darker corners. These tours are famous for their 'jumper-ooters' – costumed actors who 'jump oot' when you least expect it.

### EDINBURGH LITERARY
### PUB TOUR
Walking Tours
(www.edinburghliterarypubtour.co.uk; adult/student £10/8) An enlightening trawl through Edinburgh's literary history – and its associated howffs (pubs) – in the entertaining company of Messrs Clart and McBrain. One of the city's best walking tours.

### MERCAT TOURS
Walking Tours
(Map p72; www.mercattours.com; adult/child £10/5) Mercat offers a wide range of

# The Stone of Destiny

On St Andrew's Day 1996 a block of sandstone – 26.5 inches by 16.5 inches by 11 inches in size, with rusted iron hoops at either end – was installed with much pomp and ceremony in Edinburgh Castle. For the previous 700 years it had lain in London, beneath the Coronation Chair in Westminster Abbey. Almost all English, and later British monarchs from Edward II in 1307 to Elizabeth II in 1953 have parked their backsides firmly over this stone during their coronation ceremony.

The legendary Stone of Destiny – said to have originated in the Holy Land, and on which Scottish kings placed their feet during their coronation – was stolen from Scone Abbey near Perth by King Edward I of England in 1296. It was taken to London and there it remained for seven centuries – except for a brief removal to Gloucester during WWII air raids, and a three-month sojourn in Scotland after it was stolen by Scottish Nationalist students at Christmas in 1950 – as an enduring symbol of Scotland's subjugation by England.

The Stone of Destiny returned to the political limelight in 1996, when the then Scottish secretary and Conservative Party MP Michael Forsyth arranged for the return of the sandstone block to Scotland. A blatant attempt to boost the flagging popularity of the Conservative Party in Scotland prior to a general election, Forsyth's publicity stunt failed. The Scots said thanks for the stone and then, in May 1997, voted every Conservative MP in Scotland into oblivion.

fascinating tours, including history walks in the Old Town and Leith, 'Ghosts & Ghouls' tours and visits to haunted underground vaults.

# 🛏 Sleeping

A boom in hotel building saw Edinburgh's tourist capacity swell significantly since 2000, but you can guarantee the city will still be packed to the gills during the festival period (August) and over Hogmanay (New Year). If you want a room during these periods, book as far in advance as possible – a year ahead if you can. In general, it's best to book at least a few months ahead for accommodation at Easter and from mid-May to mid-September.

Hotels and hostels are found throughout the Old and New Towns; midrange B&Bs and guesthouses are concentrated outside the centre in the suburbs of Tollcross, Bruntsfield, Newington and Pilrig.

If you're driving, don't even think about staying in the city centre unless your hotel has its own private car park – parking in the centre is a nightmare. Instead, look for somewhere in a suburb like Newington, where there's a chance of finding free on-street parking (even then, don't bet on getting a parking space outside the front door). Alternatively, stay outside the city and travel in by bus or train.

## Accommodation Agencies

If you arrive in Edinburgh without a room, the Edinburgh Information Centre (p106) booking service will try to find a room to suit you (and will charge a £5 fee if successful). If you have the time, pick up the tourist office's accommodation brochure and ring around yourself.

You can also try VisitScotland's **booking hotline** ( 📞 0845 859 1006), which has a £3 surcharge; or search for accommodation on the Edinburgh & Lothians Tourist Board (p106) website.

## Old Town

Most of the interesting accommodation in the Old Town is either backpacker hostels or expensive hotels. For midrange options you'll have to resort to chain hotels – check the websites of Travelodge, Ibis etc.

**HOTEL MISSONI**
Boutique Hotel £££
(Map p72; 📞 0131-220 6666; www.hotelmissoni.com; 1 George IV Bridge; r £90-225; 📶) The Italian fashion house has established a style icon in the heart of the medieval Old Town with this bold statement of a hotel – modernistic architecture, black-and-white decor with well-judged splashes of colour, impeccably mannered

Debating Chamber, Scottish Parliament Building (p75)
KATHY COLLINS/GETTY IMAGES ©

# Underground Edinburgh

As Edinburgh expanded in the late 18th and early 19th centuries, many old tenements were demolished and new bridges were built to link the Old Town to the newly built areas to its north and south. South Bridge (built between 1785 and 1788) and George IV Bridge (built between 1829 and 1834) lead south from the Royal Mile over the deep valley of Cowgate, but so many buildings have been constructed around them you can hardly tell they are bridges – George IV Bridge has a total of nine arches but only two are visible; South Bridge has no less than 18 hidden arches.

These **subterranean vaults** were originally used as storerooms, workshops and drinking dens. But as Edinburgh's population swelled in the early 19th century with an influx of penniless Highlanders who were cleared from their lands, and Irish refugees from the potato famine, the dark, dripping chambers were given over to slum accommodation and abandoned to poverty, filth and crime.

The vaults were eventually cleared in the late 19th century, then lay forgotten until 1994 when the **South Bridge vaults** were opened to guided tours. Certain chambers are said to be haunted and one particular vault was investigated by paranormal researchers in 2001.

staff and, most importantly, very comfortable bedrooms and bathrooms with lots of nice little touches, from fresh milk in the minibar to plush bathrobes.

**WITCHERY BY THE CASTLE**  B&B ££

(Map p72; ☎ 0131-225 5613; www.thewitchery. com; Castlehill, Royal Mile; ste £325-350) Set in a 16th-century Old Town house in the shadow of Edinburgh Castle, the Witchery's eight lavish Gothic suites are extravagantly furnished with antiques, oak panelling, tapestries, open fires, four-poster beds and roll-top baths, and supplied with flowers, chocolates and complimentary champagne. Overwhelmingly popular – book several months in advance to be sure of getting a room.

**TEN HILL PLACE**  Hotel ££

(Map p72; ☎ 0131-662 2080; www.tenhillplace. com; 10 Hill Pl; r from £110; ☎) This attractive modern hotel offers good-value accommodation close to the city centre. The standard bedrooms are comfortable and stylish with a sober but sophisticated colour scheme in rich browns, purples and tweedy greens, and appealing modern

bathrooms. For a special weekend, ask for one of the four 'skyline' rooms on the top floor, with king-size beds and panoramic views of Salisbury Crags.

## New Town & Around

**SHERIDAN GUEST HOUSE**  B&B ££

( ☎ 0131-554 4107; www.sheridanedinburgh. co.uk; 1 Bonnington Tce, Newhaven Rd; s/d from £55/70; ☎) Flowerpots filled with blooms line the steps of this little haven hidden away to the north of the New Town. The eight bedrooms (all with en suites) blend crisp colours with contemporary furniture, stylish lighting and colourful paintings, which complement the house's clean-cut Georgian lines, while the breakfast menu adds omelettes, pancakes with maple syrup, and scrambled eggs with smoked salmon to the usual offerings. Take bus 11 from the city centre.

**ONE ROYAL CIRCUS**  B&B £££

(Map p80; ☎ 0131-625 6669; www.oneroyalcir cus.com; 1 Royal Circus; r £180-260; ☎ ⛹) Live the New Town dream at this incredibly chic Georgian mansion where genuine antiques and parquet floors sit comfortably alongside slate bathrooms and Philippe

Starck furniture. Bedrooms are kitted out with Egyptian cotton sheets, iPod docks and Arran Aromatics toiletries, and there are babyfoot and pool tables in the drawing room.

### GERALD'S PLACE                    B&B ££

(Map p80; ☑ 0131-558 7017; www.geraldsplace. com; 21b Abercromby Pl; d £119-149; @ 🛜) Gerald is an unfailingly charming and helpful host, and his lovely Georgian garden flat (just two guest bedrooms) has a great location across from a peaceful park, an easy stroll from the city centre.

### TIGERLILY              Boutique Hotel £££

(Map p80; ☑ 0131-225 5005; www.tigerlily edinburgh.co.uk; 125 George St; r from £175; 🛜) Georgian meets gorgeous at this glamorous, glittering boutique hotel (complete with its own nightclub) decked out in mirror mosaics, beaded curtains, swirling Timorous Beasties textiles and wall coverings and atmospheric pink uplighting. Book the Georgian Suite (from £310) for a truly special romantic getaway.

### B+B EDINBURGH                   Hotel ££

(Map p66; ☑ 0131-225 5084; www.bb-edinburgh. com; 3 Rothesay Tce; s/d £99/140; 🛜) Built in 1883 as a grand home for the proprietor of the *Scotsman* newspaper, this Victorian extravaganza of carved oak, parquet floors, stained glass and elaborate fireplaces was given a designer makeover in 2011 to create a striking contemporary hotel. Rooms on the 2nd floor are the most spacious, but the smaller top-floor rooms enjoy the finest views – those at the front can see Edinburgh Castle, those at the back look across the Water of Leith to the Firth of Forth.

### DENE GUEST HOUSE               B&B ££

(Map p66; ☑ 0131-556 2700; www.deneguest house.com; 7 Eyre Pl; per person £25-50; 👶) The Dene is a friendly and informal place, set in a charming Georgian town house, with a welcoming owner and spacious bedrooms. The inexpensive single rooms make it ideal for solo travellers; children under 10 staying in their parents' room pay half price.

# South Edinburgh

There are lots of guest houses in the South Edinburgh suburbs of Tollcross, Morningside, Marchmont and Newington, especially on and around Minto St and Mayfield Gardens (the continuation of North Bridge and Nicolson St) in Newington. This is the main traffic artery from the south and a main bus route into the city centre.

### SOUTHSIDE GUEST HOUSE         B&B ££

(Map p66; ☑ 0131-668 4422; www.south sideguesthouse.co.uk; 8 Newington Rd; s/d £70/90; 🛜) Though set in a typical Victorian terrace, the Southside transcends the traditional guesthouse category and feels more like a modern boutique hotel. Its eight stylish rooms ooze interior design, standing out from other Newington B&Bs through the clever use of bold colours and modern furniture.

### PRESTONFIELD HOUSE
### HOTEL                 Boutique Hotel £££

(☑ 0131-668 3346; www.prestonfield.com; Priestfield Rd; r/ste from £221/274; P 🛜) If the blonde wood, brown leather and brushed steel of modern boutique hotels leave you cold, then this is the place for you. A 17th-century mansion set in 8 hectares of parkland (complete with peacocks and Highland cattle), Prestonfield House is draped in damask, packed with antiques and decorated in red, black and gold – look out for original tapestries, 17th-century embossed-leather panels, and £500-a-roll hand-painted wallpaper. The hotel's rooms are supplied with all mod cons, including Bose sound systems, DVD players and plasma-screen TVs. The hotel is southeast of the city centre, east of Dalkeith Rd.

### 45 GILMOUR RD                   B&B ££

(☑ 0131-667 3536; www.edinburghbedbreakfast. com; 45 Gilmour Rd; s/d £70/140) A peaceful setting, large garden and friendly owners contribute to the appeal of this Victorian terraced house, which overlooks the local bowling green. The decor is a blend of 19th- and 20th-century influences, with bold Victorian reds, a period fireplace and pine floors in the lounge, a rocking horse

CORBIS NOMAD/ALAMY ©

## Don't Miss **Royal Yacht** *Britannia*

One of Scotland's biggest tourist attractions is the former Royal Yacht *Britannia*. She was the British royal family's floating home during their foreign travels from the time of her launch in 1953 until her decommissioning in 1997, and is now moored permanently in front of Ocean Terminal.

The tour, which you take at your own pace with an audio guide (available in 20 languages), gives an intriguing insight into the Queen's private tastes – *Britannia* was one of the few places where the royal family could enjoy true privacy. The entire ship (including the sitting room, pictured above) is a monument to 1950s decor and technology, and the accommodation reveals Her Majesty's preference for simple, unfussy surroundings – the Queen's own bed is surprisingly tiny and plain.

There was nothing simple or unfussy, however, about the running of the ship. When the Queen travelled, along with her went 45 members of the royal household, five tons of luggage and a Rolls-Royce that was carefully squeezed into a specially built garage on the deck. The ship's company consisted of an admiral, 20 officers and 220 yachtsmen. The decks (made of Burmese teak) were scrubbed daily, but all work near the royal accommodation was carried out in complete silence and had to be finished by 8am. A thermometer was kept in the Queen's bathroom to make sure the water was the correct temperature, and when in harbour one yachtsman was charged with ensuring that the angle of the gangway never exceeded 12 degrees. Note the mahogany windbreak that was added to the balcony deck in front of the bridge; it was put there to stop wayward breezes from blowing up skirts and inadvertently revealing the royal undies.

### NEED TO KNOW

www.royalyachtbritannia.co.uk; Ocean Terminal; adult/child £11.75/7.50; ⊗ 9.30am-4.30pm Jul-Sep, to 4pm Apr-Jun & Oct, 10am-3.30pm Nov-Mar, last admission 90min before closing; 📶

and art-nouveau lamp in the hallway, and a 1930s vibe in the three spacious bedrooms. Located 1 mile southeast of the city centre.

**AONACH MOR GUEST HOUSE**  B&B ££
( 0131-667 8694; www.aonachmor.com; 14 Kilmaurs Tce; r per person £33-70; @ ) This elegant Victorian terraced house is located on a quiet backstreet and has seven bedrooms, beautifully decorated, with many original period features. Our favourite is the four-poster bedroom with polished mahogany furniture and period fireplace. Located 1 mile southeast of the city centre.

**SHERWOOD GUEST HOUSE**  B&B ££
(Map p66; 0131-667 1200; www.sherwood-edin burgh.com; 42 Minto St; s £65-85, d £75-100; P ) One of the most attractive guesthouses on Minto St's B&B strip, the Sherwood is a refurbished Georgian

terraced house decked out with hanging baskets and shrubs. Inside are six en suite rooms that combine Regency-style striped wallpaper with modern fabrics and pine furniture.

**TOWN HOUSE**  B&B ££
(Map p66; 0131-229 1985; www.thetownhouse. com; 65 Gilmore Pl; per person £45-60; P ) The five-room Town House is a plush little place, offering the sort of quality and comfort you might expect from a much larger and more expensive hotel. It's an elegant Victorian terraced house with big bay windows, spacious bedrooms (all with en suites) and a breakfast menu that includes salmon fishcakes and kippers alongside the more usual offerings.

**AMARYLLIS GUEST HOUSE**  B&B ££
(Map p66; 0131-229 3293; www.amaryllis guesthouse.com; 21 Upper Gilmore Pl; s/d £60/80; ) The Amaryllis is a cute little

# Edinburgh for Kids

Edinburgh has a multitude of attractions for children, and most things to see and do are child-friendly. Kids under five travel for free on Edinburgh buses, and five- to 15-year-olds pay a flat fare of 70p.

The Edinburgh Information Centre (p106) has lots of info on children's events, and the handy guidebook **Edinburgh for Under Fives** (www. edinburghforunderfives.co.uk) can be found in most bookshops. The List (p106) magazine has a special kids' section listing children's activities and events in and around Edinburgh. The week-long **Imaginate Festival** (www.imaginate.org.uk) of children's theatre, dance and puppetry takes place each year in late May/early June.

Ideas for outdoor activities include exploring the **Royal Botanic Garden** (www. rbge.org.uk; 20a Inverleith Row; admission to glasshouses £4.50; 10am-6pm Mar-Sep, to 5pm Feb & Oct, to 4pm Nov-Jan), going to see the animals at Edinburgh Zoo (p89), visiting the statue of Greyfriars Bobby (p76) and feeding the swans and playing on the beach at **Cramond**. During the Edinburgh and Fringe Festivals there is also plenty of **street theatre** for kids, especially on the High St and at the foot of The Mound, and in December there's an open-air ice rink and fairground rides in Princes Street Gardens.

If it's raining, you can visit the Discovery Centre, a hands-on activity zone on level 3 of the National Museum of Scotland (p79), play on the flumes at the **Royal Commonwealth Pool** (Map p66; www.thecommiepool.co.uk; 21 Dalkeith Rd; adult/ child £5.50/2.80; 5.30am-9.30pm Mon-Fri, to 5pm Sat, 7.30am-5pm Sun), try out the earthquake simulator at **Our Dynamic Earth** (p76), or take a tour of the haunted **Real Mary King's Close** (p73).

Georgian town house on a quiet back-street. There are five bedrooms, including a spacious family room that can take two adults and up to four kids. Princes St is only 10 minutes' walk away.

## Leith Walk & Pilrig Street

Northeast of the New Town, the area around Leith Walk and Pilrig St has lots of guesthouses, all within about a mile of the centre. To get there, take bus 11 from Princes St.

**MILLERS 64**  B&B **££**

(☏0131-454 3666; www.millers64.com; 64 Pilrig St; s from £80, d £90-150; 🛜) Luxury textiles, colourful cushions, stylish bathrooms and fresh flowers added to a warm Edinburgh welcome make this Victorian town house a highly desirable address. There are just two bedrooms (and a minimum three-night stay during festival periods) so book well in advance.

**ARDMOR HOUSE**  B&B **££**

(☏0131-554 4944; www.ardmorhouse.com; 74 Pilrig St; s £60-85, d £85-170; 🛜) The 'gay-owned, straight-friendly' Ardmor is a stylishly renovated Victorian house with five en suite bedrooms, and all those little touches that make a place special – an open fire, thick towels, crisp white bed linen and free newspapers at breakfast.

**EDINBURGH CENTRAL YOUTH HOSTEL**  Hostel **£**

(SYHA; Map p66; ☏0131-524 2090; www.edinburghcentral.org; 9 Haddington Pl, Leith Walk; dm/s/tw £25/49/74; @🛜🚻) This modern, purpose-built hostel, about a half-mile north of Waverley train station, is a big (300 beds), flashy, five-star establishment with its own cafe-bistro as well as self-catering kitchen, smart and comfortable eight-bed dorms and private rooms, and mod cons including keycard entry and plasma-screen TVs.

 **Eating**

Edinburgh has more restaurants per head of population than any other UK city. Eating out has become a commonplace

## Detour:
## Edinburgh Zoo

Opened in 1913, **Edinburgh Zoo** (www.edinburghzoo.org.uk; 134 Corstorphine Rd; adult/child £15.50/11; ⊙9am-6pm Apr-Sep, to 5pm Oct & Mar, to 4.30pm Nov-Feb) is one of the world's leading conservation zoos. Edinburgh's captive breeding programme has helped save many endangered species, including Siberian tigers, pygmy hippos and red pandas. The main attractions are the penguin parade (the zoo's penguins go for a walk every day at 2.15pm), the sea lion training session (daily at 11.15am), and the two giant pandas, Tian Tian and Yang Guang, who arrived in December 2011.

The zoo is 2.5 miles west of the city centre; take Lothian Bus 12, 26 or 31, First Bus 16, 18, 80 or 86, or the Airlink Bus 100 westbound from Princes St.

event rather than something reserved for special occasions, and the choice of eateries ranges from stylish but inexpensive bistros and cafes to Michelin-starred gourmet restaurants.

## Old Town & Around

**ONDINE**  Seafood **£££**

(Map p72; ☏0131-226 1888; www.ondinerestaurant.co.uk; 2 George IV Bridge; mains £15-25) Ondine is one of Edinburgh's finest seafood restaurants, with a menu based on sustainably sourced fish. Take an octopus-inspired seat at the curved Crustacean Bar and tuck into oysters Kilpatrick, lobster thermidor, a roast shellfish platter, or just good old haddock and chips (with minted pea purée, just to keep things posh). The two-course lunch (noon to 2.30pm) and pretheatre (5pm to 6.30pm) menu costs £17.

## TOWER
Scottish £££

(Map p72; ☎0131-225 3003; www.tower -restaurant.com; National Museum of Scotland, Chambers St; mains £16-30; ⏲noon-11pm) Chic and sleek, with a great view of the castle, Tower is perched in a turret atop the National Museum of Scotland building. A star-studded guest list of celebrities has enjoyed its menu of quality Scottish food, simply prepared – try half a dozen oysters followed by roast partridge with chestnut stuffing. A two-/three-course pre-theatre menu (£16/22) is available from 5pm to 6.30pm, and afternoon tea (£16) is served from 3pm to 5pm.

## PORTO & FI
Cafe £

(Map p72; www.portofi.com; 9 North Bank St; mains £4-8; ⏲10am-11pm Mon-Sat, to 9pm Sun) With its designer decor, a prime location overlooking The Mound, and a suprisingly sophisticated menu built around quality Scottish produce, this cafe is hard to beat for a breakfast of eggs Benedict or Stornoway black pudding (served till noon, all day Sunday), or lunch of smoked salmon cannelloni or roast fig and asparagus salad.

## CASTLE TERRACE
Modern Scottish £££

(Map p72; ☎0131-229 1222; www.castleterrace restaurant.com; 33-35 Castle Tce; mains £25-28, 3-course lunch £24; ⏲lunch & dinner Tue-Sat) It was little more than a year after opening in 2010 that TV chef Tom Kitchin's second Edinburgh restaurant was awarded a Michelin star. The menu is seasonal and applies sharply whetted Parisian skills to the finest of local produce, be it Ayrshire pork, Aberdeenshire lamb or Newhaven crab – even the cheese in the sauces is Scottish.

## LEVEN'S
Fusion ££

(Map p66; ☎0131-229 8988; 30-32 Leven St; mains £12-19; ⏲lunch & dinner Sun-Thu, noon-10.30pm Fri & Sat) From the spectacular chandeliers and slowly pulsing blue/purple mood lighting to the designer colour palette and Villeroy and Boch tableware, everything about this restaurant oozes style. The food lives up to the surroundings, with clever and unexpected combinations of flavours, colours and textures

in dishes such as beef sirloin Panang curry, with peanuts and lime leaves.

## MUMS
Cafe £

(Map p72; www.monstermashcafe.co.uk; 4a Forrest Rd; mains £6-9; ⏲9am-10pm Mon-Sat, 10am-10pm Sun) This nostalgia-fuelled cafe serves up classic British comfort food that wouldn't look out of place on a 1950s menu – bacon and eggs, bangers and mash, shepherd's pie, fish and chips. But there's a twist – the food is all top-quality nosh freshly prepared from local produce, including Crombie's gourmet sausages. There's even a wine list, though we prefer the real ales and Scottish-brewed cider.

## PASSEPARTOUT
International £

(Map p72; ☎0131-629 0252; 7 Old Fishmarket Close; platters for two £12-13) Hidden down a steep cobbled alley off the Royal Mile, with three indoor seating areas (including a 'cinema room' screening old movies) and a lovely little sun-trap of an outdoor terrace, this French-owned, Indian-inspired bistro offers an eclectic menu of dishes – from lobster with mussels to chickpea curry to kebabs – served as sharing platters for two, which you eat with your fingers. Good fun, and good value.

## MOTHER INDIA
Indian ££

(Map p72; ☎0131-524 9801; www.motherindia glasgow.co.uk; 3-5 Infirmary St; tapas £4-5; ⏲lunch & dinner Mon-Thu, noon-10pm Fri-Sun) A simple concept pioneered in Glasgow has captured hearts and minds – and stomachs – in Edinburgh: Indian food served in tapas-size portions, so that you can sample a greater variety of different dishes without busting your gut. Hugely popular, so book a table to avoid disappointment.

## AMBER
Scottish ££

(Map p72; ☎0131-477 8477; www.amber -restaurant.co.uk; 354 Castlehill; mains £10-25; ⏲lunch daily, dinner Tue-Sat) You've got to love a place where the waiter greets you with the words, 'My name is Craig, and I'll be your whisky adviser for this evening'. Located inside the Scotch Whisky Experience (p69), this whisky-themed restaurant manages to avoid the tourist clichés

RICCARDO SPILA/SIME/4CORNERS ©

## Don't Miss **Rosslyn Chapel**

The success of Dan Brown's novel *The Da Vinci Code* and the subsequent Hollywood film has seen a flood of visitors descend on Scotland's most beautiful and enigmatic church – **Rosslyn Chapel**. The chapel was built in the mid-15th century for William St Clair, third earl of Orkney, and the ornately carved interior – at odds with the architectural fashion of its time – is a monument to the mason's art, rich in symbolic imagery. As well as flowers, vines, angels and biblical figures, the carved stones include many examples of the pagan 'Green Man'; other figures are associated with Freemasonry and the Knights Templar. Intriguingly, there are also carvings of plants from the Americas that predate Columbus' voyage of discovery. The symbolism of these images has led some researchers to conclude that Rosslyn is some kind of secret Templar repository, and it has been claimed that hidden vaults beneath the chapel could conceal anything from the Holy Grail or the head of John the Baptist to the body of Christ himself. The chapel is owned by the Episcopal Church of Scotland and services are still held here on Sunday mornings.

The chapel is on the eastern edge of the village of Roslin, 7 miles south of Edinburgh's centre. Lothian Bus 15 (not 15A) runs from the west end of Princes St in Edinburgh to Roslin (£1.20, 30 minutes, departs every 30 minutes).

### NEED TO KNOW

Collegiate Church of St Matthew; www.rosslynchapel.org.uk; adult/child £9/free; ☺9.30am-6pm Mon-Sat, noon-4.45pm Sun

and creates genuinely interesting and flavoursome dishes such as mussels in a cream, leek and Islay-whisky sauce, and sirloin steak with thyme-roasted potatoes and whisky butter.

## New Town

**THE DOGS**                    British ££

(Map p80; ☏0131-220 1208; www.thedogsonline.co.uk; 110 Hanover St; mains £9-13; ☺noon-4pm & 5-10pm) One of the coolest tables in

# Rosslyn Chapel

## Deciphering Rosslyn

Rosslyn Chapel is a small building, but the density of decoration inside can be overwhelming. It's well worth buying the official guidebook by the Earl of Rosslyn first; find a bench in the gardens and have a skim through before going into the chapel – the background information will make your visit all the more interesting. The book also offers a useful self-guided tour of the chapel, and explains the legend of the Master Mason and the Apprentice.

Entrance is through the **north door** ❶. Take a pew and sit for a while to allow your eyes to adjust to the dim interior; then look up at the ceiling vault, decorated with engraved roses, lilies and stars (can you spot the sun and the moon?). Walk left along the north aisle to reach the Lady Chapel, separated from the rest of the church by the **Mason's Pillar** ❷ and the **Apprentice Pillar** ❸. Here you'll find carvings of **Lucifer** ❹, the Fallen Angel, and the **Green Man** ❺. Nearby are **carvings** ❻ that appear to resemble Indian corn (maize). Finally, go to the western end and look up at the wall – in the left corner is the head of the **Apprentice** ❼; to the right is the (rather worn) head of the **Master Mason** ❽.

### ROSSLYN CHAPEL & THE DA VINCI CODE

Dan Brown was referencing Rosslyn Chapel's alleged links to the Knights Templar and the Freemasons – unusual symbols found among the carvings, and the fact that a descendant of its founder, William St Clair, was a Grand Master Mason – when he chose it as the setting for his novel's denouement. Rosslyn is indeed a coded work, written in stone, but its meaning depends on your point of view. See *The Rosslyn Hoax?* by Robert LD Cooper (www.rosslynhoax.com) for an alternative interpretation of the chapel's symbolism.

SANDRO VANNINI/CORBIS ©

### Explore Some More

After visiting the chapel, head downhill to see the spectacularly sited ruins of Roslin Castle, then take a walk along leafy Roslin Glen.

**Lucifer, the Fallen Angel**
At head height, to the left of the second window from the left, is an upside-down angel bound with rope, a symbol often associated with Freemasonry. The arch above is decorated with the Dance of Death.

**The Apprentice**
High in the corner, beneath an empty statue niche, is the head of the murdered Apprentice, with a deep wound in his forehead above the right eye. Legend says the Apprentice was murdered in a jealous rage by the Master Mason. The worn head on the side wall to the left of the Apprentice is that of his mother.

Nu
Doo

**The Master Mason**
❽

Baptistery

### Practical Tips

Buy your tickets in advance through the chapel's website (except in August, when no bookings are taken). No photography is allowed inside the chapel.

### Green Man
On a boss at the base of the arch between the second and third windows from the left is the finest example of more than a hundred 'green man' carvings in the chapel, pagan symbols of spring, fertility and rebirth.

SANDRO VANNINI/CORBIS ©

Sacristy

(2) Mason's Pillar

(4)

(5) Lady Chapel

(3)

North Aisle

Altar

Choir

South Aisle

(6)

(7)

### The Apprentice Pillar
This is perhaps the chapel's most beautiful carving. Four vines spiral up the pillar, issuing from the mouths of eight dragons at its base. At the top is Isaac, son of Abraham, lying bound upon the altar.

TRAVEL DIVISION IMAGES/ALAMY ©

### Indian Corn
The frieze around the second window on the south wall is said to represent Indian corn (maize), but it predates Columbus' discovery of the New World in 1492. Other carvings seem to resemble aloe vera.

JOHN HESELTINE/ALAMY ©

**Below:** An Edinburgh pub; **Right:** Valvona & Crolla Vincaffè
(BELOW) IZZET KERIBAR/GETTY IMAGES ©; (RIGHT) LONELY PLANET/GETTY IMAGES ©

town, this bistro-style place uses cheaper cuts of meat and less well-known, more sustainable species of fish to create hearty, no-nonsense dishes such as lamb sweetbreads on toast, baked coley with *skirlie* (fried oatmeal and onion), and devilled liver with bacon and onions.

**CAFÉ MARLAYNE** French ££
(Map p80; ☎0131-226 2230; www.cafemarlayne.com; 76 Thistle St; mains £12-15; ⏲noon-10pm) All weathered wood and candlelit tables, Café Marlayne is a cosy nook offering French farmhouse cooking – *brandade de morue* (salt cod) with green salad, slow-roast rack of lamb, *boudin noir* (black pudding) with scallops and sautéed potato – at very reasonable prices. Booking recommended.

**L 'ESCARGOT BLEU** French ££
(Map p66; ☎0131-556 1600; www.lescargotbleu.co.uk; 56 Broughton St; mains £13-18; ⏲lunch & dinner Mon-Sat) As with its sister restaurant,

l'Escargot Blanc on Queensferry St, this cute little bistro is as Gallic as garlic but makes fine use of quality Scottish produce – the French-speaking staff will lead you knowledgeably through a menu that includes authentic Savoyard *tartiflette*, *quenelle* of pike with lobster sauce, and pigs' cheeks braised in red wine with roasted winter vegetables.

**VALVONA & CROLLA VINCAFFÈ** Italian ££
(Map p80; ☎0131-557 0088; www.valvonacrolla.co.uk; 11 Multrees Walk, St Andrew Sq; mains £9-17; ⏲8am-11pm Mon-Sat, noon-5pm Sun; 🛜) Foodie colours dominate the decor at this delightful Italian bistro – bottle-green pillars and banquettes, chocolate-and-cream-coloured walls, espresso-black tables – a perfect backdrop for VinCaffè's superb antipasto (£17.50 for two), washed down with a bottle of pink Pinot Grigio.

**🍴 MUSSEL INN** Seafood ££
(Map p80; www.mussel-inn.com; 61-65 Rose St; mains £9-23; ⏲noon-10pm; 👪) Owned by

west-coast shellfish farmers, the Mussel Inn provides a direct outlet for fresh Scottish seafood. The busy restaurant, decorated with bright beechwood indoors, spills out onto the pavement in summer. A 1kg pot of mussels with a choice of sauces – try leek, Dijon mustard and cream – costs £12.20.

**CAFÉ ROYAL OYSTER BAR** Seafood £££
(Map p80; ✆0131-556 4124; www.caferoyal. org.uk; 17a West Register St; mains £11-28)
Pass through the revolving doors on the corner of West Register St and you're transported back to Victorian times – a palace of glinting mahogany, polished brass, marble floors, stained glass, Doulton tiles, gilded cornices and starched table linen so thick it creaks when you fold it. The menu is mostly classic seafood, from oysters on ice to scallops with chorizo, to lobster with Café Royal sauce, augmented by a handful of beef and lamb dishes.

## Leith

**FISHERS BISTRO** Seafood ££
(✆0131-554 5666; www.fishersbistros.co.uk; 1 The Shore; mains £10-23; ⏱noon-10.30pm Mon-Sat, 12.30-10pm Sun) This cosy little restaurant, tucked beneath a 17th-century signal tower, is one of the city's best seafood places. The menu ranges widely in price, from cheaper dishes such as classic fishcakes with lemon and chive mayonnaise, to more expensive delights such as North Berwick lobster thermidor.

**PLUMED HORSE** Modern Scottish £££
(✆0131-554 5556; www.plumedhorse.co.uk; 50-54 Henderson St; 3-course dinner £49; ⏱lunch & dinner Tue-Sat) Smartly suited and booted staff welcome you to this quiet corner of understated elegance, where the muted decor of pale blues and greens, cream leather chairs and crisp white linen place the focus firmly on the exquisitely prepared and presented food. An eight-course tasting menu is £65, plus £45 for matching wines.

# Top Three Vegetarian Restaurants

Many Edinburgh restaurants offer vegetarian options on the menu, some good, some bad, some indifferent. The places listed here are all 100% veggie and fall into the 'good' category.

**David Bann** (Map p72; 0131-556 5888; www.davidbann.com; 56-58 St Mary's St; mains £9-13; noon-10pm Mon-Fri, 11am-10pm Sat & Sun; ) If you want to convince a carnivorous friend that cuisine à la veg can be as tasty and inventive as a meat-muncher's menu, take them to David Bann's stylish restaurant – dishes such as beetroot, apple and Dunsyre blue-cheese pudding, and Thai fritter of spiced broccoli and smoked tofu, are guaranteed to win converts.

**Kalpna** (Map p72; 0131-667 9890; www.kalpnarestaurant.com; 2-3 St Patrick Sq; mains £6-11; lunch & dinner Mon-Sat year-round, plus dinner Sun May-Sep; ) A long-standing Edinburgh favourite, Kalpna is one of the best Indian restaurants in the country, vegetarian or otherwise. The cuisine is mostly Gujarati, with a smattering of dishes from other parts of India. The all-you-can-eat lunch buffet (£8) is superb value.

**Henderson's** (Map p80; 0131-225 2131; www.hendersonsofedinburgh.co.uk; 94 Hanover St; mains £6-8; 8am-10pm Mon-Sat year-round, 11am-4pm Sun Aug & Dec; ) Established in 1962, Henderson's is the grandmother of Edinburgh's vegetarian restaurants. The food is mostly organic, guaranteed GM-free, and special dietary requirements can be catered for. The place still has a 1970s feel to it (in a good way), and the daily salads and hot dishes are as popular as ever. Two-course set lunch is £8.95.

**DINER 7** Cafe ££
(www.diner7.co.uk; 7 Commercial St; mains £7-12; 4-11pm Mon-Sat, 11am-11pm Sun) A neat local eatery with rust-coloured leather booths and banquettes, black and copper tables, and local art on the walls, this diner has a menu of succulent Aberdeen Angus steaks and homemade burgers, but also offers more unusual fare such as chicken and chorizo kebabs, or smoked haddock with black-pudding stovies.

## Drinking

Edinburgh has more than 700 bars, which are as varied as the population – you'll find everything from Victorian palaces to rough-and-ready drinking dens, and from bearded, real-ale howffs (meeting places) to trendy cocktail bars.

## Old Town

The pubs in the Grassmarket have outdoor tables on sunny summer afternoons, but in the evenings are favoured by boozed-up lads on the pull, so steer clear if that's not your thing. The Cowgate – the Grassmarket's extension to the east – is Edinburgh's clubland.

**BOW BAR** Pub
(Map p72; 80 West Bow) One of the city's best traditional-style pubs (it's not as old as it looks), serving a range of excellent real ales and a vast selection of malt whiskies, the Bow Bar often has standing-room only on Friday and Saturday evenings.

**JOLLY JUDGE** Pub
(Map p72; www.jollyjudge.co.uk; 7a James Ct; ) A snug little howff tucked away down a close, the Jolly Judge exudes a cosy 17th-century atmosphere (it features low,

timber-beamed painted ceilings) and has the added attraction of a cheering open fire in cold weather. There's no music or gaming machines, just the buzz of conversation.

### BREWDOG
Bar

(Map p72; www.brewdog.com; 143 Cowgate; 📶) A new bar from Scotland's self-styled 'punk brewery', BrewDog stands out among the grimy, sticky-floored dives that line the Cowgate, with its cool, industrial-chic designer look. As well as its own highly rated beers, there's a choice of four guest real ales.

### ECCO VINO
Wine Bar

(Map p72; www.eccovinoedinburgh.com; 19 Cockburn St; 📶) With outdoor tables on sunny afternoons, and cosy candlelit intimacy in the evenings, this comfortably cramped Tuscan-style wine bar offers a tempting range of Italian wines, though not all are available by the glass – best to share a bottle.

### VILLAGER
Bar

(Map p72; www.villagerbar.com; 49-50 George IV Bridge; 📶) A cross between a traditional pub and a pre-club bar, Villager has a comfortable, laid-back vibe. It can be standing-room only in the main bar in the evenings (the cocktails are excellent), but the side room, with its brown leather sofas and subtropical pot plants, comes into its own for a lazy Sunday afternoon with the papers.

### ROYAL MILE TAVERN
Pub

(Map p72; www.royalmiletavern.com; 127 High St) An elegant, traditional bar lined with polished wood, mirrors and brass, Royal Mile serves real ale (Deuchars IPA and Caledonian 80/-), good wines and decent pub grub – fish and chips, steak and Guinness pie, sausage and mash etc.

### HOLYROOD 9A
Pub

(Map p72; www.fullerthomson.com; 9a Holyrood Rd; 📶) Candlelight flickering off hectares of polished wood creates an atmospheric setting for this superb real-ale bar, with no fewer than 20 taps pouring craft beers from all corners of the country. If you're peckish, they serve excellent gourmet burgers, too.

## New Town

Rose St (between Princes St and George St) was once a famous pub crawl, where

Leith (p82)

generations of students, sailors and rugby fans would try to visit every pub on the street (around 17 of them) and down a pint of beer in each one.

### OXFORD BAR
Pub

(Map p80; www.oxfordbar.co.uk; 8 Young St) The Oxford is that rarest of things these days: a real pub for real people, with no 'theme', no music, no frills and no pretensions. 'The Ox' has been immortalised by Ian Rankin, author of the Inspector Rebus novels, whose fictional detective is a regular here.

### CUMBERLAND BAR
Pub

(Map p66; www.cumberlandbar.co.uk; 1-3 Cumberland St; 🛜) Immortalised as the stereotypical New Town pub in Alexander McCall Smith's serialised novel *44 Scotland Street,* the Cumberland has an authentic, traditional wood-brass-and-mirrors look (despite being relatively new) and serves well looked-after, cask-conditioned ales and a wide range of malt whiskies. There's also a pleasant little beer garden outside.

### GUILDFORD ARMS
Pub

(Map p80; www.guildfordarms.com; 1 West Register St) Located next door to the Café Royal Circle Bar, the Guildford is another classic Victorian pub full of polished mahogany, brass and ornate cornices. The range of real ales is excellent – try to get a table in the unusual upstairs gallery, with a view of the sea of drinkers down below.

### BRAMBLE
Cocktail Bar

(Map p80; www.bramblebar.co.uk; 16a Queen St) One of those places that easily earns the sobriquet 'best-kept secret', Bramble is an unmarked cellar bar where a maze of stone and brick hideaways conceals what is arguably the city's best cocktail bar. No beer taps, no fuss, just expertly mixed drinks.

### KENILWORTH
Pub

(Map p80; 152-154 Rose St) A gorgeous, Edwardian drinking palace, complete with original fittings – from the tile floors, mahogany circle bar and gantry, to the ornate mirrors and gas lamps – the Kenilworth was Edinburgh's original gay bar back in the 1970s. Today it attracts a mixed crowd of all ages, and serves a good range of real ales and malt whiskies.

### UNDERDOGS
Cocktail Bar

(Map p80; 104 Hanover St; 🛜) A cellar furnished with stone-slab floors and a fire sale of mismatched sofas makes an unlikely setting for one of Edinburgh's best cocktail bars, but the relaxed atmosphere and friendly welcome can't be beaten. Excellent mixed drinks and some unusual bottled beers, but no brews on tap.

### KAY'S BAR
Pub

(Map p80; www.kaysbar.co.uk; 39 Jamaica St) Housed in a former wine-merchant's office, tiny Kay's Bar is a cosy haven with a coal fire and a fine range of

Bow Bar (p96)
KARL BLACKWELL/GETTY IMAGES ©

# Top Three Lunch Spots

**Urban Angel** (Map p80; ☏ 0131-225 6215; www.urban-angel.co.uk; 121 Hanover St; mains £8-14; ⏱ 9am-10pm Mon-Sat, 10am-5pm Sun; 🖊🚹) A wholesome deli that puts the emphasis on fair-trade, organic and locally sourced produce, Urban Angel is also a delightfully informal cafe-bistro that serves all-day brunch (porridge with honey, French toast, eggs Benedict), tapas and a wide range of light, snacky meals.

**La P'tite Folie** (Map p80; ☏ 0131-225 7983; www.laptitefolie.co.uk; 61 Frederick St; mains £16-25) This is a delightful little restaurant with a Breton owner whose menu includes French classics – onion soup, *moules marinières* – alongside steaks, seafood and a range of *plats du jour*. The two-course lunch is a bargain at £9.95.

**Petit Paris** (Map p72; ☏ 0131-226 2442; www.petitparis-restaurant.co.uk; 38-40 Grassmarket; mains £14-18; ⏱ noon-3pm & 5.30-11pm, closed Mon Oct-Mar) Like the name says, this is a little piece of Paris, complete with checked tablecloths, friendly waiters and good-value grub – the *moules-frîtes* (mussels and chips) are excellent. There's a lunch/pre-theatre deal (noon to 3pm and 5.30pm to 7pm) offering the *plat du jour* and a coffee for £7.90; add a starter and it's £11.90.

real ales. Good food is served in the back room at lunchtime, but you'll have to book a table – Kay's is a popular spot.

## Leith

### ROSELEAF
Cafe-Bar

(www.roseleaf.co.uk; 23-24 Sandport Pl; ⏱ 10am-1am; 📶) Cute and quaint and verging on chintzy, the Roseleaf could hardly be further from the average Leith bar. Decked out in flowered wallpaper, old furniture and rose-patterned china (cocktails are served in teapots), the real ales and bottled beers are complemented by a range of specialty teas, coffees and fruit drinks (including rose lemonade) and well above-average pub grub (served 10am to 10pm).

### TEUCHTER'S LANDING
Pub

(www.aroomin.co.uk; 1 Dock Pl; 📶) A cosy warren of timber-lined nooks and crannies housed in a single-storey red-brick building (once a waiting room for ferries across the Firth of Forth), this real-ale and malt-whisky bar also has outdoor tables on a floating terrace in the dock.

### PORT O'LEITH
Pub

(www.portoleithpub.com; 58 Constitution St) This is a good, old-fashioned, friendly local boozer, swathed with flags and cap bands left behind by visiting sailors – the Leith docks are just down the road. Pop in for a pint and you'll probably stay until closing time.

##  Entertainment

Edinburgh has a number of fine theatres and concert halls, and there are independent art-house cinemas as well as mainstream movie theatres. Many pubs offer entertainment ranging from live Scottish folk music to pop, rock and jazz as well as karaoke and quiz nights, while a range of stylish modern bars purvey house, dance and hip-hop to the pre-clubbing crowd.

The comprehensive source for what's-on info is *The List* (www.list.co.uk), an excellent listings magazine covering both Edinburgh and Glasgow. It's available

# Top Five Traditional Pubs

Edinburgh is blessed with a large number of traditional 19th- and early 20th-century pubs, which have preserved much of their original Victorian or Edwardian decoration and serve cask-conditioned real ales and a staggering range of malt whiskies.

**Athletic Arms** (Diggers; Map p66; 1-3 Angle Park Tce) Nicknamed after the cemetery across the street – the gravediggers used to nip in and slake their thirst after a hard day's interring – the Diggers dates from the 1890s. It's still staunchly traditional – the decor has barely changed in 100 years – and has recently revived its reputation as a real-ale drinker's mecca by serving locally brewed Diggers' 80-shilling ale. Packed to the gills with football and rugby fans on match days.

**Abbotsford** (Map p80; www.theabbotsford.com; 3 Rose St) One of the few pubs in Rose St that has retained its Edwardian splendour, the Abbotsford has long been a hang-out for writers, actors, journalists and media people, and has many loyal regulars. Dating from 1902, and named after Sir Walter Scott's country house, the pub's centrepiece is a splendid mahogany island bar. Good selection of Scottish and English real ales.

**Bennet's Bar** (Map p66; 8 Leven St) Situated beside the King's Theatre, Bennet's has managed to hang on to almost all of its beautiful Victorian fittings, from the leaded stained-glass windows and ornate mirrors to the wooden gantry and the brass water taps on the bar (for your whisky – there are over 100 malts to choose from).

**Café Royal Circle Bar** (Map p80; www.caferoyal.org.uk; 17 West Register St) Perhaps *the* classic Edinburgh bar, the Café Royal's main claims to fame are its magnificent oval bar and the series of Doulton tile portraits of famous Victorian inventors. Check out the bottles on the gantry – staff line them up to look like there's a mirror there, and many a drink-befuddled customer has been seen squinting and wondering why he can't see his reflection.

**Sheep Heid** (www.sheepheid.co.uk; 43-45 The Causeway) Possibly the oldest inn in Edinburgh (with a licence dating back to 1360) the Sheep Heid feels more like a country pub than an Edinburgh bar. Set in the semirural shadow of Arthur's Seat, it's famous for its 19th-century skittles alley and the lovely little beer garden.

from most newsagents, and is published fortnightly on a Thursday.

## Live Music

Check out the *List* and the *Gig Guide* (www.gigguide.co.uk), a free email newsletter and listings website, to see who's playing where.

## Jazz, Blues & Rock

### BANNERMAN'S
Live Music

(Map p72; www.bannermanslive.co.uk; 212 Cowgate) A long-established favourite – it seems like every Edinburgh student for the last four decades spent half their youth here – Bannerman's straggles through a warren of old vaults beneath South Bridge. It pulls in crowds of students, locals and backpackers alike with live rock, punk and indie bands.

### HENRY'S CELLAR
Live Music

(Map p72; www.musicglue.com/theraft; 8a Morrison St) One of Edinburgh's most eclectic live-music venues, Henry's has something going on most nights of the week, from rock and indie to 'Balkan-inspired folk', funk to hip-hop to hardcore, staging both local bands and acts from around the world. Open till 3am at weekends.

### WHISTLE BINKIE'S
Live Music

(Map p72; www.whistlebinkies.com; 4-6 South Bridge) This crowded cellar bar, just off the Royal Mile, has live music every night till 3am, from rock and blues to folk and jazz. Open-mic night on Monday and breaking bands on Tuesday are showcases for new talent.

### JAZZ BAR
Jazz

(Map p72; www.thejazzbar.co.uk; 1a Chambers St; 🛜) This atmospheric cellar bar, with its polished parquet floors, bare stone walls, candlelit tables and stylish steel-framed chairs, is owned and operated by jazz musicians. There's live music every night from 9pm to 3am, and on Saturday from 3pm.

### LIQUID ROOM
Club, Live Music

(Map p72; www.liquidroom.com; 9c Victoria St) Set in a subterranean vault deep beneath Victoria St, the Liquid Room is a superb club venue with a thundering sound system. There are regular club nights Wednesday to Saturday as well as live bands.

## Traditional

The capital is a great place to hear traditional Scottish (and Irish) folk music, with a mix of regular spots and impromptu sessions.

### SANDY BELL'S
Traditional Music

(Map p72; 25 Forrest Rd) This unassuming pub is a stalwart of the traditional music scene (the founder's wife sang with The Corries). There's music almost every evening at 9pm, and from 3pm Saturday and Sunday, plus lots of impromptu sessions.

### ROYAL OAK
Traditional Music

(Map p72; www.royal-oak-folk.com; 1 Infirmary St) This popular folk pub is tiny, so get there early (9pm start weekdays, 2.30pm Saturday) if you want to be sure of a place. Sundays from 4pm to 7pm is open session – bring your own instruments (or a good singing voice).

## Nightclubs

Edinburgh's club scene has some fine DJ talent and is well worth exploring; there are club-night listings in the *List*. Most of the venues are concentrated in and around the twin sumps of Cowgate and Calton Rd – so it's downhill all the way...

### BONGO CLUB
Multi-Arts Venue

(Map p66; www.thebongoclub.co.uk; Moray House, Paterson's Land, 37 Holyrood Rd) The weird and wonderful Bongo Club boasts a long history of hosting everything from wild club nights to performance art to kids' comedy shows, and is open as a cafe and exhibition space during the day. The

# Edinburgh Military Tattoo

August kicks off with the **Edinburgh Military Tattoo** (📞 0131-225 1188; www.edintattoo.co.uk; Tattoo Office, 32 Market St), a spectacular display of military marching bands, massed pipes and drums, acrobats, cheerleaders and motorcycle display teams, all played out in front of the magnificent backdrop of the floodlit castle. Each show traditionally finishes with a lone piper, dramatically lit, playing a lament on the battlements. The Tattoo takes place over the first three weeks of August (from a Friday to a Saturday); there's one show at 9pm Monday to Friday and two (at 7.30pm and 10.30pm) on Saturday, but no performance on Sunday.

**Below:** Edinburgh Festival Theatre; **Right:** Musicians at Sandy Bell's (p101)

(BELOW) JASON FRIEND PHOTOGRAPHY LTD/ALAMY ©; (RIGHT) ILPO MUSTO/ALAMY ©

club may shift to new premises in 2013 – check the website for the latest news.

**CABARET VOLTAIRE**     Club, Live Music
(Map p72; www.thecabaretvoltaire.com; 36 Blair St) An atmospheric warren of stone-lined vaults houses Edinburgh's most 'alternative' club, which eschews huge dance floors and egotistical DJ worship in favour of a 'creative crucible' hosting an eclectic mix of DJs, live acts, comedy, theatre, visual arts and the spoken word. Well worth a look.

**LULU**     Club
(Map p80; www.luluedinburgh.co.uk; 125 George St) Lush leather sofas, red satin cushions, fetishistic steel-mesh curtains and dim red lighting all help to create a decadent atmosphere in this drop-dead gorgeous club venue beneath the Tigerlily boutique hotel. Resident and guest DJs show a bit more originality than your average club.

## Cinemas

Film buffs will find plenty to keep them happy in Edinburgh's art-house cinemas, while popcorn munchers can choose from a range of multiplexes.

**FILMHOUSE**     Cinema
(Map p72; www.filmhousecinema.com; 88 Lothian Rd; 📶) The Filmhouse is the main venue for the annual Edinburgh International Film Festival and screens a full program of art-house, classic, foreign and second-run films, with lots of themes, retrospectives and 70mm screenings. It has wheelchair access to all three screens.

**CAMEO**     Cinema
(Map p66; www.picturehouses.co.uk; 38 Home St) The three-screen, independently owned Cameo is a good, old-fashioned cinema showing an imaginative mix of mainstream and art-house movies. There is a good program of midnight mov-

ies and Sunday matinees, and the seats in Screen one are big enough to get lost in.

## Classical Music, Opera & Ballet

The following are the main venues for classical music.

### EDINBURGH FESTIVAL THEATRE
Ballet, Opera

(Map p72; www.edtheatres.com/festival; 13-29 Nicolson St; ☻box office 10am-6pm Mon-Sat, to 8pm show nights, 4pm-showtime Sun) A beautifully restored art-deco theatre with a modern frontage, the Festival is the city's main venue for opera, dance and ballet, but also stages musicals, concerts, drama and children's shows.

### USHER HALL
Classical Music

(Map p72; www.usherhall.co.uk; Lothian Rd; ☻box office 10.30am-5.30pm, to 8pm show nights) The architecturally impressive Usher Hall hosts concerts by the Royal Scottish National Orchestra and performances of popular music.

### ST GILES CATHEDRAL
Classical Music

(Map p72; www.stgilescathedral.org.uk; High St) The big kirk on the Royal Mile plays host to a regular and varied program of classical music, including popular lunchtime and evening concerts and organ recitals. The cathedral choir sings at the 10am and 11.30am Sunday services.

## Theatre, Musicals & Comedy

### ROYAL LYCEUM THEATRE
Drama, Musicals

(Map p72; www.lyceum.org.uk; 30b Grindlay St; ☻box office 10am-6pm Mon-Sat, to 8pm show nights; 🚻) A grand Victorian theatre located beside the Usher Hall, the Lyceum stages drama, concerts, musicals and ballet.

### TRAVERSE THEATRE
Drama, Dance

(Map p72; www.traverse.co.uk; 10 Cambridge St; ☻box office 10am-6pm Mon-Sat, to 8pm show nights) The Traverse is the main focus for new Scottish writing and stages an adventurous program of contemporary

# Festival City

August in Edinburgh sees a frenzy of festivals, with half-a-dozen world-class events running at the same time.

## EDINBURGH INTERNATIONAL FESTIVAL

First held in 1947 to mark a return to peace after the ordeal of WWII, the **Edinburgh International Festival** (📞0131-473 2099; www.eif.co.uk) is festooned with superlatives – the oldest, the biggest, the most famous, the best in the world. The original was a modest affair, but today hundreds of the world's top musicians and performers congregate in Edinburgh for three weeks of diverse and inspirational music, opera, theatre and dance.

The festival takes place over the three weeks ending on the first Saturday in September; the program is usually available from April. Tickets for popular events – especially music and opera – sell out quickly, so it's best to book as far in advance as possible. You can buy tickets in person at the **Hub** (📞01131-473 2000; www.thehub-edinburgh.com; Castlehill; admission free; ⊙ticket centre 10am-5pm Mon-Sat), or by phone or internet.

## EDINBURGH FESTIVAL FRINGE

When the first Edinburgh Festival was held in 1947, there were eight theatre companies who didn't make it onto the main programme. Undeterred, they grouped together and held their own mini-festival, on the fringe, and an Edinburgh institution was born. Today the **Edinburgh Festival Fringe** (📞0131-226 0026; www.edfringe.com; 180 High St) is the biggest festival of the performing arts anywhere in the world.

The Fringe takes place over 3½ weeks, the last two weeks overlapping with the first two of the Edinburgh International Festival.

drama and dance. The box office is only open on Sunday (from 4pm) when there's a show on.

**KING'S THEATRE** Drama, Musicals
(Map p66; www.edtheatres.com/kings; 2 Leven St; ⊙box office open 1hr before show) King's is a traditional theatre with a program of musicals, drama, comedy and its famous Christmas pantomimes.

**EDINBURGH PLAYHOUSE** Musicals
(Map p80; www.edinburgh-playhouse.co.uk; 18-22 Greenside Pl; ⊙box office 10am-6pm Mon-Sat, to 8pm show nights) This restored theatre at the top of Leith Walk stages Broadway musicals, dance shows, opera and popular-music concerts.

# 🔒 Shopping

Princes St is Edinburgh's principal shopping street, lined with all the big high-street stores, with many smaller shops along pedestrianised Rose St, and more expensive designer boutiques on George St. There are also two big shopping centres in the New Town – **Princes Mall**, at the eastern end of Princes St, and the nearby **St James Centre** at the top of Leith St, plus **Multrees Walk**, a designer shopping complex with a flagship Harvey Nichols store on the eastern side of St Andrew Sq. The huge **Ocean Terminal** in Leith is the biggest shopping centre in the city.

For more off-beat shopping – including fashion, music, crafts, giftware and jewellery – head for the cobbled lanes of Cockburn, Victoria and St Mary's Sts, all near the Royal Mile in the Old Town; William St in the western part of the New Town; and the Stockbridge district, immediately north of the New Town.

## Cashmere & Wool

Woollen textiles and knitwear are one of Scotland's classic exports. Scottish cashmere – a fine, soft wool from young goats and lambs – provides the most luxurious and expensive knitwear and has been seen gracing the torsos of pop star Robbie Williams and English footballer David Beckham.

**KINROSS CASHMERE**    Fashion
(Map p72; 2 St Giles St) Wide range of traditional and modern knitwear.

**JOYCE FORSYTH DESIGNER KNITWEAR**    Fashion
(Map p72; www.joyceforsyth.co.uk; 42 Candlemaker Row; ☺Tue-Sat) Colourful designs

that will drag your ideas about woollens firmly into the 21st century.

**EDINBURGH WOOLLEN MILL**    Fashion
(Map p80; www.ewm.co.uk; 139 Princes St) An old stalwart of the tourist trade, with a good selection of traditional jerseys, cardigans, scarves, shawls and rugs.

## Tartan & Highland Dress

There are dozens of shops along the Royal Mile and Princes St where you can buy kilts and tartan goods.

**KINLOCH ANDERSON**    Fashion
(www.kinlochanderson.com; 4 Dock St, Leith) One of the best, this was founded in 1868 and is still family run. Kinloch Anderson is a supplier of kilts and Highland dress to the royal family.

**GEOFFREY (TAILOR) INC**    Fashion
(Map p72; www.geoffreykilts.co.uk; 57-59 High St) Can fit you out in traditional Highland dress, or run up a kilt in your own clan tartan. Its offshoot, 21st Century Kilts, offers modern fashion kilts in a variety of fabrics.

EDINBURGH SHOPPING

Princes Mall

JOEFOX/ALAMY ©

# ℹ Information

## Internet Resources

**Edinburgh & Lothians Tourist Board** (www.edinburgh.org) Official tourist-board site, with listings of accommodation, sights, activities and events.

**Edinburgh Architecture** (www.edinburgharchitecture.co.uk) Informative site dedicated to the city's modern architecture.

**Edinburgh Festival Guide** (www.edinburghfestivals.co.uk) Everything you need to know about Edinburgh's many festivals.

**Events Edinburgh** (www.eventsedinburgh.org.uk) The city council's official events guide.

**The List** (www.list.co.uk) Listings of restaurants, pubs, clubs and nightlife.

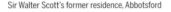

## Medical Services

For urgent medical advice you can call the **NHS 24 Helpline** (☎08454 24 24 24; www.nhs24.com). Chemists (pharmacists) can advise you on minor ailments. At least one local chemist remains open round the clock – its location will be displayed in the windows of other chemists.

For urgent dental treatment you can visit the walk-in **Chalmers Dental Centre** (3 Chalmers St; ⊙9am-4.45pm Mon-Thu, to 4.15pm Fri). In the case of a dental emergency in the evenings or at weekends, call **Lothian Dental Advice Line** (☎0131-536 4800).

**Royal Hospital for Sick Children** (☎0131-536 0000; www.nhslothian.scot.nhs.uk; 9 Sciennes Rd) Casualty department for children aged under 13 years; located in Marchmont.

**Royal Infirmary of Edinburgh** (☎0131-536 1000; www.nhslothian.scot.nhs.uk; 51 Little France Cres, Old Dalkeith Rd) Edinburgh's main general hospital; has 24-hour accident and emergency department.

**Western General Hospital** (☎0131-537 1330; www.nhslothian.scot.nhs.uk; Crewe Rd South; ⊙9am-9pm) For non-life-threatening injuries and ailments, you can attend the Minor Injuries Unit without having to make an appointment.

## Tourist Information

**Edinburgh Information Centre** (☎0131-473 3868; www.edinburgh.org; Princes Mall, 3 Princes St; ⊙9am-9pm Mon-Sat, 10am-8pm Sun Jul & Aug, 9am-7pm Mon-Sat, 10am-7pm Sun May-Jun & Sep, 9am-5pm Mon-Wed, to 6pm Thu-Sun Oct-Apr) Includes an accommodation booking

Sir Walter Scott's former residence, Abbotsford

service, currency exchange, gift and bookshop, internet access and counters selling tickets for Edinburgh city tours and Scottish Citylink bus services.

## ℹ Getting There & Away

### Air

**Edinburgh Airport** (☏0131-333 1000; www.edinburghairport.com) Edinburgh Airport, 8 miles west of the city, has numerous flights to other parts of Scotland and the UK, Ireland and mainland Europe. **FlyBe/Loganair** (☏0871 700 2000; www.loganair.co.uk) operates daily flights to Inverness, Wick, Orkney, Shetland and Stornoway.

### Bus

Edinburgh Bus Station is at the northeast corner of St Andrew Sq, with pedestrian entrances from the square and from Elder St. For timetable information, contact **Traveline** (☏0871 200 22 33; www.travelinescotland.com).

**Scottish Citylink** (☏0871 266 3333; www.citylink.co.uk) buses connect Edinburgh with all of Scotland's cities and major towns. The following are sample one-way fares departing from Edinburgh.

| DESTINATION | FARE |
| --- | --- |
| Aberdeen | £28 |
| Dundee | £15 |
| Fort William | £33 |
| Glasgow | £6.80 |
| Inverness | £28 |
| Portree | £47 |
| Stirling | £7.50 |

It's also worth checking with **Megabus** (☏0900 160 0900; www.megabus.com) for cheap intercity bus fares (from as little as £5) from Edinburgh to Aberdeen, Dundee, Glasgow, Inverness and Perth.

There are various buses to Edinburgh from London and the rest of the UK.

### Car & Motorcycle

Arriving in or leaving Edinburgh by car during the morning and evening rush hours (7.30am to 9.30am and 4.30pm to 6.30pm Monday to Friday)

## Detour:
# Abbotsford

Fans of Sir Walter Scott should visit the writer's former residence, **Abbotsford** (www.scottsabbotsford.co.uk; admission to house adult/child £8/4; admission to visitor centre free; ☉9.30am-5pm Mon-Sat year-round, 9.30am-5pm Sun Jun-Sep, 11am-4pm Sun Mar-Oct). The inspiration he drew from the surrounding 'wild' countryside influenced many of his most famous works. The house is closed for renovations until July 2013, but a new visitor centre and interpretive display is open, feautring an exhibition on the writer's life.

The mansion is about 2 miles west of Melrose between the River Tweed and the B6360. Frequent buses run between Galashiels and Melrose; alight at the Tweed bank roundabout and follow the signposts (it's a 15-minute walk). You can also walk from Melrose to Abbotsford in an hour along the southern bank of the Tweed.

is an experience you can live without. Try to time your journey to avoid these periods.

### Train

The main terminus in Edinburgh is Waverley train station, located in the heart of the city. Trains arriving from, and departing for the west also stop at Haymarket station, which is more convenient for the West End.

You can buy tickets, make reservations and get travel information at the **Edinburgh Rail Travel Centre** (☉4.45am-12.30am Mon-Sat, 7am-12.30am Sun) in Waverley station. For fare and timetable information, phone the **National Rail Enquiry Service** (☏08457 48 49 50; www.nationalrail.co.uk) or use the Journey Planner on the website.

First ScotRail (☎08457 55 00 33; www. scotrail.co.uk) operates a regular shuttle service between Edinburgh and Glasgow (£12.90, 50 minutes, every 15 minutes), and frequent daily services to all Scottish cities, including Aberdeen (£45, 2½ hours), Dundee (£23, 1¼ hours) and Inverness (£40, 3½ hours).

# ℹ️ Getting Around

## To/From the Airport

The Lothian Buses Airlink (www.flybybus.com) service 100 runs from Waverley Bridge, outside the train station, to the airport (£3.50/6 one way/return, 30 minutes, every 10 to 15 minutes) via the West End and Haymarket.

An airport taxi to the city centre costs around £16 and takes about 20 minutes. Both buses and taxis depart from outside the arrivals hall; go out through the main doors and turn left.

## Car & Motorcycle

Though useful for day trips beyond the city, a car in central Edinburgh is more of a liability than a convenience. The streets have been in chaos for years as the city's controversial tram system gets built. There is restricted access on Princes St, George St and Charlotte Sq, many streets are one

way and finding a parking place in the city centre is like striking gold. Queen's Dr around Holyrood Park is closed to motorised traffic on Sunday.

## Car Rental

All the big, international car-rental agencies have offices in Edinburgh.

There are many smaller, local agencies that offer better rates. Arnold Clark (☎0131-657 9120; www.arnoldclarkrental.co.uk; 20 Seafield Rd East) near Portobello, charges from £30 a day, or £180 a week for a small car, including VAT and insurance.

## Parking

There's no parking on main roads into the city from 7.30am to 6.30pm Monday to Saturday. Also, parking in the city centre can be a nightmare. **On-street parking** is controlled by self-service ticket machines from 8.30am to 6.30pm Monday to Saturday, and costs £1 to £2 per hour, with a 30-minute to four-hour maximum. If you break the rules, you'll get a fine, often within minutes of your ticket expiring – Edinburgh's parking wardens are both numerous and notorious. The fine is £60, reduced to £30 if you pay up within 14 days. Cars parked illegally will be towed away. There are large, long-stay car parks at the St James Centre, Greenside Pl, New St, Castle Tce and Morrison

The Royal Mile (p65)

St. Motorcycles can be parked free at designated areas in the city centre.

## Public Transport

For the moment, Edinburgh's public-transport system consists entirely of buses (a tram network is under construction, due to come into operation in 2014). The main operators are Lothian Buses (www.lothianbuses.com) and First (☎0131-663 9233; www.firstedinburgh.co.uk); for timetable information contact Traveline (p107).

Bus timetables, route maps and fare guides are posted at all main bus stops, and you can pick up a copy of the free *Lothian Buses Route Map* from **Lothian Buses Travelshops**.

Adult **fares** are £1.40; purchase from the driver. Children aged under five travel free and those aged five to 15 pay a flat fare of 70p. On Lothian Buses you must pay the driver the exact fare, but First buses will give change. Lothian Bus drivers also sell a Daysaver ticket (£3.50) that gives unlimited travel (on Lothian Buses only, excluding night buses) for a day. **Night-service buses** (www.nightbuses.com), which run hourly between midnight and 5am, charge a flat fare of £3.

You can also buy a **Ridacard** (from Travelshops; not available from bus drivers) that gives unlimited travel for one week for £17.

The Lothian Buses lost-property office is in the Hanover St Travelshop.

Lothian Buses Travelshops:

Hanover St (27 Hanover St; ⊙9am-6pm Mon-Fri, 10am-6pm Sat)

Shandwick Pl (7 Shandwick Pl; ⊙9am-6pm Mon-Fri, 10am-6pm Sat)

Waverley Bridge (31 Waverley Bridge; ⊙9am-6pm Mon-Fri, 10am-6pm Sat, 10am-5.15pm Sun)

## Taxi

Edinburgh's black taxis can be hailed in the street, ordered by phone (extra 80p charge), or picked up at one of the many central ranks.

Central Taxis (☎0131-229 2468)

City Cabs (☎0131-228 1211)

ComCab (☎0131-272 8000)

# Glasgow & Loch Lomond

**Regenerating and evolving at a dizzying pace, Glasgow is edgy, modish and downright ballsy.** Its Victorian architectural legacy is now swamped with stylish bars, top-notch restaurants to tickle your taste buds and a hedonistic club culture that will bring out your nocturnal instincts. Glasgow's pounding live-music scene is one of the best in Britain, and accessible through countless venues dedicated to home-grown beats.

Yet nightlife is only the beginning. Top-drawer museums and galleries abound, where the city's proud industrial and artistic heritage is innovatively displayed. Charles Rennie Mackintosh's sublime works dot the town, and the River Clyde, traditionally associated with Glasgow's earthier side, is now a symbol of the city's renaissance.

If that's not enough, one of Glasgow's biggest selling points is that it sits on the doorstep of some of Scotland's finest scenery – Loch Lomond, part of the country's first national park, is just 20 miles away.

A busy Glasgow bar

# Glasgow & Loch Lomond

Jordanhill

To Milngavie
(8mi)

**2** 15 mi

Great Western Rd

**KELVINSIDE**

A81

*Firhill Basin*

Hyndland

Botanic Gardens

River Kelvin

Garscube Rd

*Victoria Park*

**BROOMHILL**

Hyndland Rd

A82

A814

Clydeside Expressway

Partick

Dumbarton Rd

Byres Rd

**6**

**HILLHEAD**

River Clyde

**KELVINGROVE**

**1**

**GARNETHILL**

Charing Cross

Exhibition Centre

A814

**ANDERSTON**

Anderston

**GOVAN**

West Quay

Argyle St

To Glasgow International Airport (3mi)

**IBROX**

See West End Map (p130)

Edmiston Dr

Paisley Rd West

**KINNING PARK**

M8

M8

Scotland St

Eglinton St

Paisley Rd West

A737

**Bellahouston Park**

Dumbreck

Mosspark Blvd

M77

**POLLOKSHIELDS**

Pollokshields East

Pollokshields West

**GOVANHILL**

Dumbreck Rd

Maxwell Park

Queens Park

M77

**Pollok Country Park**

*White Cart Water*

**4**

Crossmyloof

Pollokshaws Rd

To Alloway (30mi); Glasgow Prestwick Airport (30mi);

**7** 44mi

Shawlands

A77

**POLLOKSHAWS**

Pollokshaws East

Mount Florida

B767

Pollokshaws West

# Glasgow & Loch Lomond's Highlights

## ① Kelvingrove Art Gallery & Museum

A grand Victorian cathedral of culture, Kelvingrove is the most visited museum in the UK outside London. Exhibits range from natural history and evolution to arms and armour (as well as a WWII Spitfire fighter aircraft), and from Glasgow history to Charles Rennie Mackintosh's designs.

**Need to Know**

**BEST TIME TO GO** On a weekday, to avoid weekend crowds. **GOOD NEWS** Admission is free. **TOP TIP** Don't try to see everything – focus on what interests you most. **For more, see p132.**

# Kelvingrove Don't Miss List

DR NEIL BALLANTYNE, MUSEUM
MANAGER, KELVINGROVE

### 1 SALVADOR DALÍ'S CHRIST OF ST JOHN OF THE CROSS

One of our most controversial purchases ever, Christ of St John of the Cross has become as iconic as Kelvingrove itself. The painting was proclaimed an outrageous waste of money and in its time has been attacked twice. It is now one of our most valued treasures.

### 2 CHARLES RENNIE MACKINTOSH AND THE GLASGOW STYLE

The 'Glasgow Style' describes the distinctive form of decorative art produced by Glasgow designers between 1890 and 1920. This gallery contains some fabulous jewellery, stained glass and furniture. My favourite object is the Wassail, a large gesso wall frieze from the Ingram Street Tearooms, designed by Charles Rennie Mackintosh.

### 3 THE PEMBROKE ARMOUR

Dating back to 1557, this is the only complete set of Greenwich armour for man and horse in existence. The rarity of this magnificent exhibit demonstrates the passion of the man behind the collection – RL Scott built up one of the finest collections of European arms and armour in the world. A little-known fact is that he preferred to collect equipment that had actually been used in battle, rather than merely decorative armour or display pieces.

### 4 THE SARCOPHAGUS OF PA-BA-SA

This granite sarcophagus from around 650 BC holds great mystery and intrigue for visitors of all ages. Perhaps it's a good thing that the occupant is long gone considering the items that visitors have 'posted' through the gap over the years: ticket stubs from past exhibitions and a 1970s *Playboy* magazine, to name just a few.

### 5 SCOTTISH IDENTITY IN ART

Paintings of historic heroes such as William Wallace, together with the rugged landscapes and majestic stags beloved by Victorian artists, have all been used to define 'Scottishness'. More controversially, there's an image of Robert Burns as Che Guevara, and a caricature of the modern, kilt-wearing Scotsman with a can of beer and a football for a head.

# Loch Lomond

Loch Lomond is the largest lake in mainland Britain and, after Loch Ness, the most famous of Scotland's lochs. Renowned for its scenery, the loch straddles the Highland border – the southern part is broad and island-studded, fringed by bluebell woods and meadows, while the northern part occupies a deep trench gouged out by glaciers, with 900m mountains crowding in on either side.

**Need to Know**

**BEST TIME TO GO** May, to see bluebells at their best. **BEST PHOTO OP** View of Ben Lomond from Loch Lomond Shores. **COFFEE STOP** The Coach House (p149). **For more, see p145.**

# Loch Lomond Don't Miss List

JASON MCINALLY, OWNER CANYOU
EXPERIENCE & OUTDOOR ACTIVITY
ENTHUSIAST

### 1 INCHCAILLOCH

A visit to Inchcailloch by kayak, canoe or local ferry is a must. The tree-clad island is covered in bluebells in spring, and has a lot of historical interest including an old burial ground; the views from the summit over the loch and surrounding area are breathtaking.

### 2 LOCH LOMOND SHORES

Loch Lomond Shores (p147) is a top visitor attraction with a beautiful setting beside the loch. The magnificent Drumkinnon Tower offers the most spectacular views towards domineering Ben Lomond. The complex also hosts regular events and outdoor leisure pursuits with walks, a play park, fairground rides and water activities.

### 3 ISLAND HOPPING

Take a guided canoe trip or boat cruise (p145) around Loch Lomond's many islands, which have a wealth of history, including clan strongholds, religious sites and wildlife – even wallabies! These marsupials were introduced to the island of Inchconnachan in the 1940s by Lady Arran, and have managed to create a viable population.

### 4 BEN LOMOND

Ben Lomond (p145) is the most southerly Munro (Scottish mountain over 3000ft in height) and dominates the skyline of the national park. It's a very accessible climb, made by around 30,000 visitors each year. Starting from the car park at Rowardennan, two footpaths provide the option of a circular hike. Whatever your route the reward is simple... stunning 360-degree views of Loch Lomond and beyond.

### 5 CYCLE CRUISES

There are many ways to explore the loch but one of the best is to take a 'cycle cruise'. Starting at Loch Lomond Shores (bike hire available), the West Loch Lomond Cycle Path allows mainly traffic-free lochside riding all the way to Tarbet where a scheduled cruise provides an 'on the loch' perspective with historical commentary. Loch Lomond from every angle!

# Experiencing Glasgow's Pubs

Some of Scotland's best nightlife is to be found in the din and roar of Glasgow's crowded pubs and bars. There are as many different styles of bar as there are patrons who drink in them, ranging from the classic Victorian polished brass and mirrors of the Horse Shoe (p14C to the hip decadence of baroque Artà (p140). A month of solid drinking wouldn't get you pas the halfway mark.

## Burrell Collection

Wealthy industrialist Sir William Burrell bequeathed his magnificent art collectio (p136), comprising more than 8000 objects, to the city of Glasgow in 1944. Bu it wasn't until 1983 that this splendid building was constructed in leafy Pollo Park to display everything from Chines porcelain and medieval furniture to Islamic art and paintings by Renoir and Cézanne. The most famous piece is Rodin's iconic sculpture, *The Thinker*.

## Glasgow Cathedral

The only cathedral on the Scottish mainland to survive the destructive period of the Reformation intact, Glasgow Cathedral (p125) is a superb example of Scottish Gothic architecture, almost all of it dating from the 15th century. The most atmospheric part is the forest of pillars around St Mungo's tomb, but no visit is complete without a stroll through the neighbouring Necropolis, one of the most impressive and picturesque cemeteries in Scotland.

## Mackintosh House

The house where Glasgow architect and designer Charles Rennie Mackintosh lived with his wife from 1906 to 1914 was demolished due to subsidence in 1963. But it has risen from the rubble in this faithful reconstruction (p135) by Glasgow University – closely following period drawings and photographs, furnished as much as possible with Mackintosh's original furniture and fittings and decorated as it was when he lived there.

## Culzean Castle

This stunning stately home (p148) – considered by many to be Scotland's finest – is the work of the Scottish architect Robert Adam, best known for his show-stopping neoclassical designs. Its famous features include a superb oval staircase leading to an opulent circular drawing room with views of the Isle of Arran and Ailsa Craig. Everywhere you look there are classical friezes and roundels in delicate 18th-century plasterwork.

# Glasgow & Loch Lomond's Best...

## Wining & Dining

○ **Café Gandolfi** (p137)
Classic Glasgow eatery
offering everything from
breakfast to seafood dinners

○ **The Ubiquitous Chip**
(p138) A local institution
and the original champion of
fresh Scottish produce

○ **Mother India** (p138)
The epitome of the famous
Glasgow curry restaurant

○ **Stravaigin** (p138) Cool
and contemporary, a serious
foodie's delight

○ **Oak Tree Inn** (p149) Great
lochside lunch spot serving
excellent Cullen skink

## Pubs & Bars

○ **Horse Shoe** (p140)
Legendary Glasgow drinking
den with original Victorian
decor

○ **Babbity Bowster** (p141)
Charming bar in a quiet
corner of trendy Merchant
City

○ **Òran Mór** (p141)
Converted church now home
to a buzzing bar

○ **Artà** (p140) Cocktail bar
draped in an extravaganza of
baroque decadence

○ **Drover's Inn** (p148)
Atmospheric Loch Lomond
pub with kilted bar staff

## Museums & Galleries

○ **Kelvingrove Art Gallery
& Museum** (p132) Grand
Victorian cathedral of culture,
one of Scotland's best

○ **Burrell Collection** (p136)
Famous art collection
bequeathed to the city, in a
lovely parkland setting

○ **Riverside Museum** (p127)
Striking modern museum
of transport with a 19th-
century sailing ship moored
outside

○ **Robert Burns Birthplace
Museum** (p147) Dedicated
to Scotland's best-known
poet; includes his birthplace
cottage

# Need to Know

## Beauty Spots

- **Botanic Gardens** (p130) Perfect summer picnic spot on the banks of River Kelvin in Glasgow's West End

- **Culzean Castle & Country Park** (p148) Gorgeous castle grounds with views to the Isle of Arran

- **Loch Lomond Shores** (p147) Top of Drumkinnon Tower affords a classic view along the loch to Ben Lomond

- **Millarochy Bay** (p149) Picnic area with gravel beach and a glorious view across the loch to Luss Hills

## ADVANCE PLANNING

- **One month before** Book accommodation in central Glasgow and Loch Lomond if visiting in summer

- **Two weeks before** Reserve a table at top Glasgow restaurants, especially for weekend evenings

- **One week before** Make bookings for boat trips on Loch Lomond

## RESOURCES

- **Glasgow: Scotland with Style** (www.seeglasgow.com) Official convention-bureau site with accommodation booking, sights, activities and events

- **Glasgow Museums** (www.glasgowmuseums.com) Information on city-owned museums and art galleries

- **Clyde Waterfront** (www.clydewaterfront.com) Latest developments on Glasgow's redeveloped waterfront, including the new Riverside Museum

- **SPT** (www.spt.co.uk) Comprehensive public-transport information for Glasgow and surrounding area

- **Loch Lomond & the Trossachs National Park** (www.lochlomond-trossachs.org) Information on wildlife, activities, things to see and public transport

- **Ayrshire & Arran Tourist Board** (www.ayrshire-arran.com) Tourist information for Culzean Castle and Robert Burns country

## GETTING AROUND

- **From the airport** Bus runs every 10 or so minutes from Glasgow International to Buchanan St bus station

- **Bus** Good city bus network operated by **First Glasgow** (www.firstglasgow.com)

- **Car** Confusing one-way-streets system, and parking in the city centre is difficult; best to use public transport

- **On foot** City centre easily explored on foot; West End, however, will need public transport

- **Subway** Circular underground railway links the city centre with the West End; trains run every four to 12 minutes

**Left:** Riverside Museum (p127; Architect: Zaha Hadid); **Above:** Botanic Gardens (p130)

# Glasgow Walking Tour

*Central Glasgow is famous for its grand Victorian architecture, a legacy of its rich trading history. This stroll takes you to Glasgow Cathedral via trendy Merchant City, once the headquarters for Glasgow industrialists.*

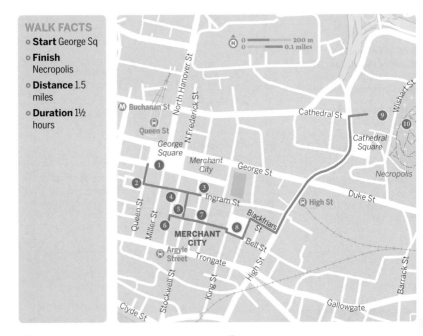

## 1 George Square

The square is surrounded by imposing Victorian architecture: the old post office, the Bank of Scotland and the grandiose **City Chambers**. Statues include those of Robert Burns, James Watt and, atop a 24m-high Doric column, Sir Walter Scott.

## 2 Gallery of Modern Art

Walk one block south down Queen St to the Gallery of Modern Art. This striking colonnaded building, built in 1827, was once the Royal Exchange and now hosts some of the country's best contemporary art displays.

## 3 Hutcheson's Hall

The gallery faces Ingram St, which you should cross and then follow east four blocks to Hutcheson's Hall. Built in 1805, this elegant building is now maintained by the National Trust for Scotland (NTS).

## 4 Corinthian Bar

Retrace your steps one block and duck into the former Court House cells that now house the ornate Corinthian Bar for a glimpse of the extravagant interior (and perhaps a pint!).

### ⑤ Trades Hall

Continue south down Glassford St past Trades Hall, designed by Robert Adam in 1791 to house the trades guild and the only surviving building in Glasgow by this famous Scottish architect. The exterior is best viewed from Garth St.

### ⑥ Tobacco Exchange

Turn right into Wilson St and take the first left along Virginia St, which is lined with the old warehouses of the Tobacco Lords (Glasgow merchants who grew rich from the tobacco trade); many of these have been converted into posh flats. The Tobacco Exchange became the Sugar Exchange in 1820.

### ⑦ Sheriff Court

Head back to Wilson St, where you'll find the bulky Sheriff Court, which fills a whole block. This arresting building was originally Glasgow's town hall but has been developed as luxury apartments.

### ⑧ Merchant Square

Continue east on Wilson St past Ingram Sq, another warehouse development, to Merchant Sq, a covered courtyard that was once the city's fruit market but now bustles with cafes and bars.

### ⑨ Glasgow Cathedral

Head up Albion St, then take the first right into Blackfriars St. Emerging onto High St, turn left and follow it up to the cathedral.

### ⑩ Necropolis

Behind the cathedral, wind your way up through the noble, crumbling tombs of the Necropolis, which offers great city views.

## Glasgow in...

### ONE DAY

Glasgow deserves more time than this, but if you're squeezed, hit the East End for **Glasgow Cathedral**, **St Mungo's Museum** and a wander through the hillside **Necropolis**. In the afternoon take on one of the city's top museums, either the **Burrell Collection** or **Kelvingrove**. As evening falls, head to trendy **Merchant City** for a stroll and dinner – **Café Gandolfi** perhaps, or the latest trendy newcomer. Head to **Artá** for a pre- or post-meal drink.

### TWO DAYS

Follow the walking tour, opposite, then visit whichever museum you missed yesterday. Then it's Mackintosh time: **Glasgow School of Art** is his finest work, or there's the reproduction **Mackintosh House** to admire. Later, head for the **River Clyde** and the **Glasgow Science Centre**. Hungry? Thirsty? Down a pint at the **Horse Shoe Bar**, then choose somewhere for dinner – perhaps a curry house such as **Mother India**. To round off the evening, check out one of Glasgow's excellent live-music venues.

Necropolis (p125)

# Discover Glasgow & Loch Lomond

## GLASGOW

###  Sights

Glasgow's major sights are fairly evenly dispersed, with many found along the Clyde (the focus of a long-term regeneration program), the leafy cathedral precinct in the East End and the museum-rich south side. Many museums are free. The centre also contains a variety of attractions, particularly Mackintoshania. The trendy West End swarms with students during term time.

### City Centre

The grid layout and pedestrian streets of the city centre make it easy to get around, and there are many cafes and pubs that make good pit stops between attractions.

**GLASGOW SCHOOL OF ART** Mackintosh Building
(Map p126; ☏ 0141-353 4526; www.gsa.ac.uk/tours; 167 Renfrew St; adult/child/family £8.75/7/24; ⊙9.30am-6.30pm Apr-Sep, 10.30am-5pm Oct-Mar) Mackintosh's greatest building, the Glasgow School of Art, still fulfils its original function, so just follow the steady stream of eclectically dressed students up the hill to find it. It's hard not to be impressed by the thoroughness of the design; the architect's pencil seems to have shaped everything inside and outside the building. The interior design is strikingly austere, with simple colour combinations (often just black and cream) and the uncomfortable-looking high-backed chairs for which Mackintosh is famous. The library, designed as an addition in 1907, is a masterpiece. The visitor

Glasgow School of Art
ATLANTIDE S.N.C./GETTY IMAGES ©

entrance is at the side of the building on Dalhousie St; here you'll find a shop with a small but useful interpretative display. Excellent hour-long guided tours (roughly hourly in summer; 11am, 1pm and 3pm in winter) run by architecture students leave from here; this is the only way (apart from enrolling) you can visit the building's interior. They're worth booking by phone at busy times. Multilingual translations are available.

FREE **GALLERY OF MODERN ART**    Gallery
(GoMA; Map p126; www.glasgowmuseums.com; Royal Exchange Sq; ⏰10am-5pm Mon-Wed & Sat, to 8pm Thu, 11am-5pm Fri & Sun; @ 📶) Scotland's most popular contemporary art gallery features modern works from international artists in a graceful neoclassical building. The original interior is used to make a daring, inventive art display. Social issues are a focal point of the museum but it's not all heavy going: there's a big effort made to keep the kids entertained.

**CITY CHAMBERS**    Town Hall
(Map p126; www.glasgow.gov.uk; George Sq) The grand City Chambers, the seat of local government, were built in the 1880s at the high point of the city's wealth. The interior is even more extravagant than the exterior, and the chambers have sometimes been used as a movie location to represent the Kremlin or the Vatican. Free guided tours are held at 10.30am and 2.30pm Monday to Friday.

## East End

The oldest part of the city, given a facelift in the 1990s, is concentrated around Glasgow Cathedral, to the east of the modern centre. It takes 15 minutes to walk from George Sq, but numerous buses pass nearby, including buses 11, 12, 36, 37, 38 and 42.

**GLASGOW CATHEDRAL**    Cathedral
(HS; Map p126; www.historic-scotland.gov.uk; Cathedral Sq; ⏰9.30am-5.30pm Mon-Sat, 1-5pm Sun Apr-Sep, closes 4.30pm Oct-Mar) Glasgow's 15th-century cathedral is a shining example of Gothic architecture and, unlike most of Scotland's cathedrals, survived the turmoil of the Reformation almost intact. The **nave** is hung with regimental colours, while the four stained-glass panels of the east window, depicting the four Apostles, are particularly evocative. The lower church, the most interesting part of the cathedral, is a forest of pillars clustered around **St Mungo's tomb** (St Mungo founded a monastic community here in the 5th century), the focus of a famous medieval pilgrimage.

Behind the cathedral, the **Necropolis** spreads picturesquely across a green hill. The elaborate Victorian tombs of the city's wealthy industrialists make for an intriguing stroll, great views and a vaguely Gothic thrill.

FREE **ST MUNGO'S MUSEUM OF RELIGIOUS LIFE & ART**    Museum
(Map p126; www.glasgowmuseums.com; 2 Castle St; admission free; ⏰10am-5pm Tue-Thu & Sat, 11am-5pm Fri & Sun) A startling achievement, this museum, set in a reconstruction of the bishop's palace that once stood here in the cathedral forecourt, is an audacious attempt to capture the world's major religions in an artistic nutshell, while presenting the similarities and differences in how they approach common themes such as birth, marriage and death. The result is commendable. The attraction is twofold: firstly, impressive art that blurs the lines between religion and culture; and secondly, the opportunity to delve into different faiths, an experience that can be as deep or shallow as you wish. There are three galleries, representing religion as art, religious life and, on the top floor, religion in Scotland. A Zen garden is outside.

FREE **PROVAND'S LORDSHIP**    Historic House
(Map p126; www.glasgowmuseums.com; 3 Castle St; ⏰10am-5pm Tue-Thu & Sat, 11am-5pm Fri & Sun) Near the cathedral is Provand's Lordship, the oldest house in Glasgow. A rare example of 15th-century domestic Scottish architecture, it was built in 1471 as a manse for the chaplain of St Nicholas Hospital. The ceilings and doorways are

GLASGOW SIGHTS

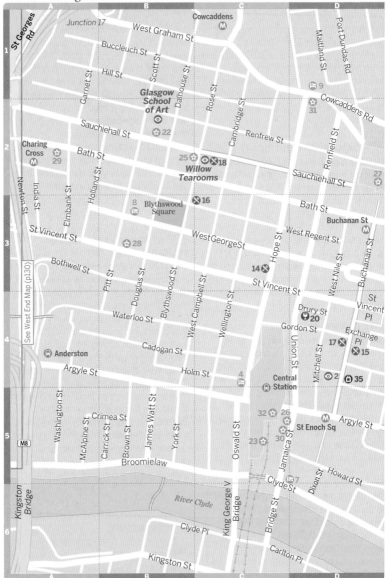

low, and the rooms are sparsely furnished with period artefacts, except for an upstairs room, which has been furnished to reflect the living space of an early 16th-century chaplain. The building's best feature is its authentic feel – if you ignore the tacky imitation-stone linoleum covering the ground floor.

## The Clyde

Once a thriving shipbuilding area, the Clyde sank into dereliction but is being

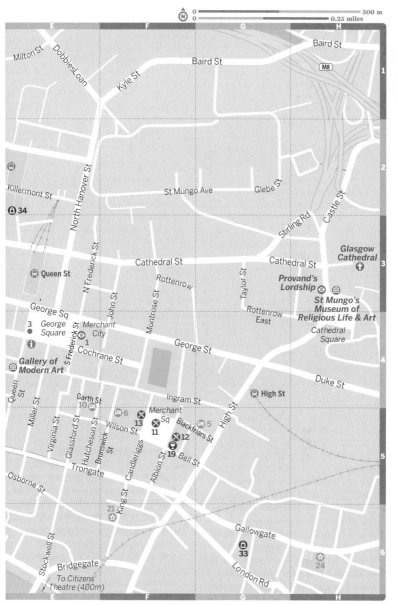

Milton St

Dobbies Loan

Baird St

Baird St

M8

Kyle St

Killermont St

34

North Hanover St

St Mungo Ave

Glebe St

Stirling Rd

Castle St

Queen St

Cathedral St

Cathedral St

**Glasgow
Cathedral**

N Frederick St

Rottenrow

Taylor St

**Provand's
Lordship**

George Sq

John St

Montrose St

Rottenrow
East

**St Mungo's
Museum of
Religious Life & Art**

3   George
    Square

Frederick St

Merchant
City

Cochrane St

George St

*Cathedral
Square*

**Gallery of
Modern Art**

Queen St

Miller St

Garth St
10

Virginia St

Glassford St

Hutcheson St

Wilson St

Brunswick St

6

13

Merchant
Sq

11

12

Blackfriars St

5

High St

Ingram St

High St

Duke St

19

Bell St

Candleriggs

Albion St

Trongate

Osborne St

King St

21

Gallowgate

Stockwell St

Bridgegate

33

24

London Rd

To Citizens'
Theatre (400m)

rejuvenated. A major campaign to
redevelop Glasgow Harbour, involving
the conversion of former docklands into
shops and public areas, is under way – to
find out more about this project see www.
glasgowharbour.com.

**FREE** **RIVERSIDE MUSEUM**    Museum
(www.glasgowmuseums.com; 100 Pointhouse
Pl; ☺10am-5pm Mon-Thu & Sat, 11am-5pm Fri
& Sun; 🛜) The latest development along
the Clyde is the building of this visually

# Central Glasgow

GLASGOW SIGHTS

## Top Sights

| | |
|---|---|
| Gallery of Modern Art | E4 |
| Glasgow Cathedral | H3 |
| Glasgow School of Art | B2 |
| Provand's Lordship | H3 |
| St Mungo's Museum of Religious Life & Art | H3 |
| Willow Tearooms | C2 |

## Sights
| | | |
|---|---|---|
| 1 | City Chambers | E4 |
| 2 | Lighthouse | D4 |

## Activities, Courses & Tours
| | | |
|---|---|---|
| 3 | City Sightseeing | E4 |

## Sleeping
| | | |
|---|---|---|
| 4 | Artto | C4 |
| 5 | Babbity Bowster | G5 |
| 6 | Brunswick Hotel | F5 |
| 7 | Euro Hostel | D5 |
| 8 | Malmaison | B3 |
| 9 | Pipers Tryst Hotel | D1 |
| 10 | Rab Ha's | E4 |

## Eating
| | | |
|---|---|---|
| 11 | Arisaig | F5 |
| | Brutti Ma Buoni | (see 6) |
| 12 | Café Gandolfi | F5 |
| 13 | Dakhin | F5 |
| 14 | Mussel Inn | C3 |
| 15 | The Chippy Doon The Lane | D4 |
| 16 | Where the Monkey Sleeps | C3 |
| 17 | Willow Tearooms | D4 |
| 18 | Willow Tearooms | C2 |

## Drinking
| | | |
|---|---|---|
| 19 | Artà | F5 |
| | Babbity Bowster | (see 5) |
| 20 | Horse Shoe | D4 |

## Entertainment
| | | |
|---|---|---|
| 21 | 13th Note Café | F6 |
| 22 | ABC | B2 |
| 23 | Arches | C5 |
| 24 | Barrowland | H6 |
| 25 | Brunswick Cellars | B2 |
| 26 | Classic Grand | C5 |
| 27 | Glasgow Royal Concert Hall | D2 |
| 28 | King Tut's Wah Wah Hut | B3 |
| 29 | King's Theatre | A2 |
| 30 | Sub Club | C5 |
| 31 | Theatre Royal | D2 |
| 32 | Tickets Scotland | C5 |

## Shopping
| | | |
|---|---|---|
| 33 | Barras | G6 |
| 34 | Buchanan Galleries | E2 |
| 35 | Princes Square | D4 |

impressive new museum; its striking curved facades are the work of Iraqi architect Zaha Hadid. The main part of the collection is a transport museum, with an excellent series of cars made in Scotland, plus assorted railway locos, trams, bikes (including the world's first pedal-powered bicycle from 1847) and model Clyde-built ships. An atmospheric re-creation of a Glasgow shopping street from the early 20th century puts the vintage vehicles into a social context. The magnificent **Tall Ship Glenlee** (www.thetallship.com; adult/child £5/3; ☺10am-5pm Mar-Oct, till 4pm Nov-Feb), a beautiful three-master launched in 1896, is berthed alongside the museum. On board are displays about her history, restoration and shipboard life during its heyday. The Riverside is west of the centre at Glasgow Harbour; you can reach it on bus 100 from the north side of George

Sq, or via the Clyde Clippers boat service. There's also a cafe here.

**GLASGOW SCIENCE CENTRE**  Museum
(Map p130; ☏0141-420 5000; www.gsc.org.uk; 50 Pacific Quay; Science Mall adult/child £9.95/7.95, IMAX, tower or planetarium £2.50; ☺10am-5pm Wed-Sun) Scotland's flagship millennium project, the superb, ultramodern Glasgow Science Centre will keep the kids entertained for hours (that's middle-aged kids, too!). It brings science and technology alive through hundreds of interactive exhibits on four floors. Look out for the illusions (like rearranging your features through a 3D headscan) and the cloud chamber, showing tracks of natural radiation. The museum consists of an egg-shaped titanium-covered **IMAX theatre** (phone for current screenings) and an interactive **Science Mall** with floor-to-ceiling windows – a bounty of discovery

for young, inquisitive minds. There's also a rotating **observation tower**, 127m high. And check out the planetarium, where the **Scottish Power Space Theatre** brings the night sky to life and a **Virtual Science Theatre** treats visitors to a 3D molecular journey. To get here take Arriva bus 24 from Renfield St or First Glasgow bus 89 or 90 from Union St. It closes earlier in winter, and doesn't open Monday or Tuesday.

## West End

With its expectant buzz, trendy bars and cafes and nonchalant swagger, the West End is probably the most engaging area of Glasgow – it's great for people-watching, and is as close as Glasgow gets to bohemian. From the centre, buses 9, 16 and 23 run towards Kelvingrove, 8, 11, and 16 to the university, and 20, 44 and 66 to Byres Rd (among others).

FREE **HUNTERIAN MUSEUM**    Museum
(Map p130; www.hunterian.gla.ac.uk; University Ave; ☺10am-5pm Tue-Sat, 11am-4pm Sun)
Housed in the glorious sandstone main building of the university, which is in itself reason enough to pay a visit, this quirky museum contains the collection of renowned one-time student of the university, William Hunter (1718–83). Hunter was primarily an anatomist and physician but, as one of those gloriously well-rounded Enlightenment figures, he interested himself in everything the world had to offer. Pickled organs in glass jars take their place alongside geological phenomena, potsherds gleaned from ancient brochs, dinosaur skeletons and a creepy case of deformed animals. The main halls of the exhibition, with their high vaulted roofs, are magnificent in themselves. A highlight is the 1674 'Map of the Whole World' in the World Culture section.

FREE **HUNTERIAN ART GALLERY**    Gallery, Museum
(Map p130; www.hunterian.gla.ac.uk; 82 Hillhead St; ☺10am-5pm Tue-Sat, 11am-4pm Sun)
Across the road from the Hunterian Museum, the bold tones of the Scottish Colourists (Samuel Peploe, Francis Cadell, JD Fergusson) are well represented in this gallery, which also forms part of Hunter's bequest to the university. There are also Sir William MacTaggart's impressionistic Scottish landscapes and a gem by

Glasgow Science Centre, and Scottish Exhibition and Conference Centre designed by Foster and Partners

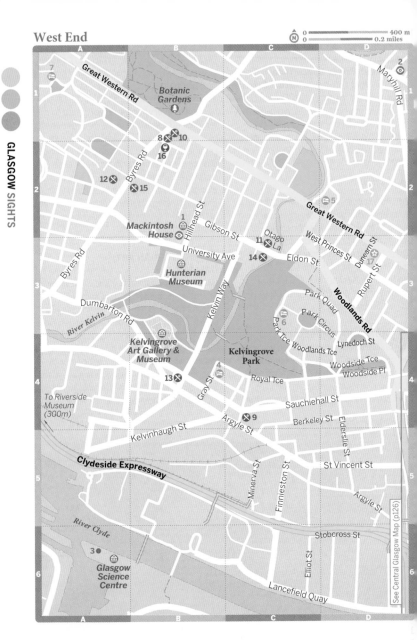

Thomas Millie Dow. There's a special collection of James McNeill Whistler's limpid prints, drawings and paintings. Upstairs, in a section devoted to late 19th-century Scottish art, you can see works by several of the Glasgow Boys.

**BOTANIC GARDENS** Park
(Map p130; 730 Great Western Rd; ⏱7am-dusk, glasshouse 10am-6pm summer, to 4.15pm winter) A marvellous thing about walking into these beautiful gardens is the way the noise of Great Western Rd suddenly

## West End

recedes into the background. Amazingly, the lush grounds don't seem that popular with locals (except on sunny weekends) and you may just about have the place to yourself. The wooded gardens follow the riverbank of the River Kelvin and there are plenty of tropical species to discover. **Kibble Palace**, an impressive Victorian iron and glass structure dating from 1873, is one of the largest glasshouses in Britain; check out the herb garden, too, with its medicinal species. The gorgeous hilly grounds make the perfect place for a picnic. There are also organised walks and concerts in summer – look at the noticeboard near the entrance to see what's on.

## South Side

The south side is a tangled web of busy roads with a few oases giving relief from the urban congestion. It does, however, contain the excellent Burrell Collection (p136).

 **Tours**

**CITY SIGHTSEEING**  Bus Tour
(Map p126; ☎0141-204 0444; www.citysight seeingglasgow.co.uk; adult/child £11/5) These double-decker tourist buses run a circuit along the main sightseeing routes, starting near the tourist office on George Sq. You get on and off as you wish. A ticket, bought from the driver or in the tourist office, is valid for two consecutive days. All buses have wheelchair access and multilingual commentary.

**GLASGOW TAXIS CITY TOUR**  Taxi Tour
(☎0141-429 7070; www.glasgowtaxis.co.uk) If you're confident you can understand the driver's accent, a taxi tour is a good way to get a feel of the city and its sights. The 60-minute tour takes you around all the centre's important landmarks, with commentary. The standard tour costs £35 for up to five people.

**LOCH LOMOND SEAPLANES**  Scenic Flights
(Map p130; ☎0143-667 5030; www.lochlomond seaplanes.com; Clyde River, Glasgow Science Centre; flights from £129) This set-up uses the Clyde as its runway and will take you on scenic flights over Glasgow and Loch Lomond, or even run you up to Oban.

**WAVERLEY**  Boat Trips
(Map p130; www.waverleyexcursions.co.uk; Clyde River, near Glasgow Science Centre; tickets £15-40; ☺Apr-Sep) The world's last ocean-going paddle steamer (built in 1947) cruises the Firth of Clyde from April to September; the website details days of departure. It serves several towns and the islands of Bute, Great Cumbrae and Arran. It departs from Glasgow Science Centre, among other places near Glasgow.

PATRICK DIEUDONNE/GETTY IMAGES ©

# Don't Miss **Kelvingrove Art Gallery & Museum**

A magnificent stone building, this grand Victorian cathedral of culture has been revamped into a fascinating and unusual museum, with a bewildering variety of exhibits. You'll find fine art alongside stuffed animals, and Micronesian shark-tooth swords alongside a Spitfire plane, but it's not mix 'n' match: rooms are carefully and thoughtfully themed, and the collection is a manageable size. There's an excellent room of Scottish art, a room of fine French Impressionist works, and quality Renaissance paintings from Italy and Flanders. Salvador Dalí's superb *Christ of St John of the Cross* is also here. Best of all, nearly everything – including the paintings – has an easy-reading paragraph of interpretation next to it. You can learn a lot about art and more here, and it's excellent for children, with plenty for them to do and displays aimed at a variety of ages. There are free hour-long guided tours beginning at 11am and 2.30pm. Bus 17, among many others, runs here from Renfield St.

## NEED TO KNOW

Map p130; www.glasgowmuseums.com; Argyle St; admission free; ⊙10am-5pm Mon-Thu & Sat, 11am-5pm Fri & Sun; @ ♿

 **Sleeping**

The city centre gets very rowdy at weekends, and accommodation options fill up fast, mostly with groups who will probably roll in boisterously some time after 3am. If you prefer an earlier appointment with your bed, you'll be better off in a smaller,

quieter lodging or in the West End. Booking ahead is essential anywhere at weekends and in July and August.

## City Centre

**BRUNSWICK HOTEL**    Hotel ££
(Map p126; ☑0141-552 0001; www.brunswick hotel.co.uk; 106 Brunswick St; d £50-95; 🛜 🍽)
Some places have dour owners threaten-

ing lockouts if you break curfew. Then there's the Brunswick, which every now and then converts the whole hotel into a party venue, with DJs in the lifts and art installations in the rooms. You couldn't ask for a more relaxed and friendly Merchant City base. The rooms are all stylish with a mixture of minimalism and rich, sexy colours. Compact and standard doubles will do if you're here for a night out, but king-size rooms are well worth the £10 upgrade. There's an excellent restaurant downstairs and occasional nightclub in the basement.

### MALMAISON — Hotel £££
(Map p126; ☎0141-572 1000; www.malmaison. com; 278 West George St; r/ste £160/345; ☎🎮) Heavenly Malmaison is the ultimate in seductive urban accommodation. Cutting-edge but decadent and plush living at its best, this sassy sister of hospitality is super slinky and a cornerstone of faith in Glaswegian accommodation. Stylish rooms with mood lighting have a dark, brooding tone, opulent furnishings and a designer touch. It's best to book online, as it's cheaper, and various suite offers can be mighty tempting.

### RAB HA'S — Inn ££
(Map p126; ☎0141-572 0400; www.rabhas.com; 83 Hutcheson St; r £69-89; ☎) This Merchant City favourite is an atmospheric pub-restaurant with four stylish upstairs rooms. They are all quite distinct and colourful. Room 1 is the best and largest, but all are comfortable, and the location is great. The personal touches like fresh flowers, iPod docks, a big welcome and any-time breakfast make you feel special.

### ARTTO — Hotel ££
(Map p126; ☎0141-248 2480; www.arttohotel. com; 37 Hope St; s/d £75/90; ☎) Right by the train station, this modish but affordable hotel has soft white, fawn, and burgundy tones in its compact but attractive rooms above a popular bar and eatery. Large windows make staying at the front appealing but, though the double glazing does a good job of subduing the street noise, light sleepers will be happier in the

rear. Rates vary widely by the day, and there are room-only prices available.

### 🌿 PIPERS TRYST HOTEL — Hotel ££
(Map p126; ☎0141-353 5551; www.thepiping centre.co.uk; 30-34 McPhater St; s/d £50/65; ☎) The name is no strategy to lure tartan tourists; this intimate, cosy hotel is in a noble building actually run by the adjacent bagpiping centre, with all profits going to maintain it. Cheery staff, great value and a prime city-centre location make this a cut above other places. Of the eight well-appointed rooms, Nos 6 and 7 are our faves; you won't have far to migrate after a night of Celtic music and fine single malts in the snug bar-restaurant downstairs.

### EURO HOSTEL — Hostel £
(Map p126; ☎0141-222 2828; www.euro-hostels. co.uk; 318 Clyde St; dm £17-20, s £29-40, d £36-52; @☎) With hundreds of beds, this mammoth hostel is handily close to the station and centre. While it feels a bit institutional, it has excellent facilities, with en suite dorms with lockers, internet access, a compact kitchen, breakfast available, and a laundry. Dorms range in size from four to 14 beds, and price varies on a daily basis. It's very popular with groups and has an instant social life, with snooker, pool, and a great downstairs bar on-site.

### BABBITY BOWSTER — Inn £
(Map p126; ☎0141-552 5055; www.babbity bowster.com; 16-18 Blackfriars St; s/d £45/60; 🅿) Smack bang in the heart of the trendy Merchant City, this lively, pleasant pub has simple rooms with sleek furnishings and a minimalist design (No 3 is a good one). Staying here is an excellent Glaswegian experience – the building's design is attributed to Robert Adam. Unusually, room rates do not include breakfast – but that helps keep prices down.

## West End

### GLASGOW SYHA — Hostel £
(Map p130; ☎0141-332 3004; www.syha.org. uk; 8 Park Tce; dm/tw £23/62; @☎) Perched on a hill overlooking Kelvingrove Park in a

charming town house, this place is simply fabulous and one of Scotland's best official hostels. Dorms are mostly four to six beds with padlock lockers and all have their own en suite – very posh. The common rooms are spacious, plush and good for lounging about. There's no curfew, a good kitchen, and meals are available. The prices mentioned here reflect maximums and are usually cheaper.

**ALAMO GUEST HOUSE**   B&B ££
(Map p130; ☎0141-339 2395; www.alamoguest house.com; 46 Gray St; d/superior d £95/145, s/d without bathroom £55/74; @ ☎) The Alamo may not sound like a quiet, peaceful spot – the city centre and West End are within walking distance – but that's exactly what this great little place is. Opposite Kelvingrove Park, it feels miles from

the hustle of the city, but several of the best museums and restaurants in town are close by. The decor is an enchanting mixture of antique furnishings and modern design, with excellent bathrooms, and the breezy owners will make you very welcome. All rooms have DVD players and there's an extensive collection to borrow from. Breakfast is abundant but there's no full Scottish option.

**KIRKLEE HOTEL**   Hotel ££
(Map p130; ☎0141-334 5555; www.kirkleehotel. co.uk; 11 Kensington Gate; s/d £65/80; ☎) Want to spoil someone special? In a leafy neighbourhood, Kirklee is a quiet little gem that combines the luxury of a classy hotel with the warmth of staying in someone's home. The rooms are simply gorgeous, beautifully furnished and

# The Genius of Charles Rennie Mackintosh

Great cities have great artists, designers and architects contributing to the cultural and historical roots of their urban environment while expressing its soul and individuality. Charles Rennie Mackintosh was all of these. His quirky, linear and geometric designs have had almost as much influence on the city as have Gaudí's on Barcelona. Many of the buildings Mackintosh designed in Glasgow are open to the public, and you'll see his tall, thin, art nouveau typeface repeatedly reproduced.

Born in 1868, Mackintosh studied at the Glasgow School of Art. It was there that he met the also influential artist and designer Margaret Macdonald, whom he married; they collaborated on many projects and were major influences on each others' work. In 1896, when he was aged only 27, he won a competition for his design of the School of Art's new building. The first section was opened in 1899 and is considered to be the earliest example of art nouveau in Britain, as well as Mackintosh's supreme architectural achievement. This building demonstrates his skill in combining function and style.

Although Mackintosh's genius was quickly recognised on the Continent, he did not receive the same encouragement in Scotland. His architectural career here lasted only until 1914, when he moved to England to concentrate on furniture design. He died in 1928, and it is only since the last decades of the 20th century that Mackintosh's genius has been widely recognised. For more about the man and his work, contact the **Charles Rennie Mackintosh Society** (☎0141-946 6600; www.crmsociety.com; 870 Garscube Rd, Mackintosh Church). Check its website for special events.

If you're planning to go CRM crazy, the **Mackintosh Trail ticket** (£16), available at the tourist office or any Mackintosh building, gives you a day's admission to all his creations as well as unlimited bus and subway travel.

ALBERT KNAPP/ALAMY ©

# Don't Miss **Mackintosh House**

Attached to the Hunterian Art Gallery, this is a reconstruction of the first home that Charles Rennie Mackintosh bought with his wife, noted artist Mary Macdonald. It's fair to say that interior decoration was one of their strong points; the Mackintosh House is startling even today. The quiet elegance of the hall and dining room on the ground floor give way to a stunning drawing room. There's something otherworldly about the very mannered style of the beaten silver panels, the long-backed chairs and the surface decorations echoing Celtic manuscript illuminations. You wouldn't have wanted to be the guest that spilled a glass of red on this carpet.

mostly have a view onto lush gardens. For families there is an excellent downstairs room with enormous en suite. This could be Glasgow's most beautiful street.

**AMADEUS GUEST HOUSE**   B&B £
(Map p130; ✆0141-339 8257; www.amadeus guesthouse.co.uk; 411 North Woodside Rd; s £26-36, d £48-60; ☞) Just off the bustle of Great Western Road, a minute's walk from the subway but on a quiet street by the riverside pathway, this B&B has compact bright rooms with cheerful cushions on

the comfortable beds. There's a variety of room types, but prices are very good for all of them. Breakfast is continental.

 **Eating**

Glasgow is the best place to eat in Scotland, with an excellent range of eateries. The West End is the culinary centre of the city, with Merchant City also boasting an incredible concentration of quality restaurants and cafes. Many Glasgow

# Don't Miss **Burrell Collection**

One of Glasgow's top attractions is the Burrell Collection. Amassed by wealthy industrialist Sir William Burrell before being donated to the city, it is housed in an outstanding museum 3 miles south of the city centre. This idiosyncratic collection includes everything from Chinese porcelain and medieval furniture to paintings by Degas and Cézanne, but it's not so big as to be overwhelming.

Visitors will find their own favourite part of this museum, but the exquisite tapestry galleries are outstanding. Intricate stories capturing life in Europe are woven into staggering wall-size pieces dating from the 13th to 16th centuries.

Within the spectacular interior, carved-stone Romanesque doorways are incorporated into the structure so you actually walk through them. Floor-to-ceiling windows admit a flood of light, and enable the surrounding landscape outside to enhance the effect of the exhibits. It feels as if you're wandering in a huge tranquil greenhouse.

In springtime, it's worth making a full day of your trip here and spending some time wandering in the beautiful park, studded with flowers. Once part of the estates of **Pollok House**, which can be visited, the grounds have numerous enticing picnic spots; if you're not heading further north, here's the place to see shaggy Highland cattle, as well as heavy horses.

Many buses pass the park gates (including buses 45, 47, 48 and 57 from the city centre), and there's a twice-hourly bus service between the gallery and the gates (a pleasant 10-minute walk). Alternatively catch a train to Pollokshaws West from Central station (four per hour; you want the second station on the line for East Kilbride or Kilmarnock).

## NEED TO KNOW

www.glasgowmuseums.com; Pollok Country Park; ☺10am-5pm Mon-Thu & Sat, 11am-5pm Fri & Sun

restaurants post offers on the internet (changing daily) at www.5pm.co.uk. Note also that pubs and bars are always a good lunchtime option.

## City Centre

**CAFÉ GANDOLFI**  Cafe, Bistro ££
(Map p126; 0141-552 6813; 64 Albion St; mains £11-15; 9am-11.30pm) In the fashionable Merchant City, this cafe was once part of the old cheese market. It's been pulling in the punters for years and packs an interesting mix of clientele: die-hard Gandolfers, the upwardly mobile and tourists. It's an excellent, friendly bistro and upmarket coffee shop. Book a Tim Stead-designed, medieval-looking table in advance for well-prepared Scottish and Continental food. There's an expansion, specialising in fish, next door.

**BRUTTI MA BUONI**  Mediterranean £
(Map p126; 0141-552 0001; www.brunswickhotel.co.uk; 106 Brunswick St; mains £7-11; 11am-10pm; ) If you like dining in a place that has a sense of fun, Brutti delivers – it's the antithesis of some of the pretentious places around the Merchant City. With dishes such as 'ugly but good' pizza and 'angry or peaceful' prawns, Brutti's menu draws a smile for its quirkiness and its prices. The Italian and Spanish influences give rise to tapas-like servings or full-blown meals, which are imaginative, fresh and frankly delicious.

**MUSSEL INN**  Seafood ££
(Map p126; 0141-572 1405; www.mussel-inn.com; 157 Hope St; mains £10-18) Airy and easy-going, this two-level eatery – a longtime Rose St favourite in Edinburgh – has recently opened in Scotland's largest city. It specialises in sustainable scallops, oysters, and mussels at affordable prices, served with a smile in a comfortable atmosphere.

**DAKHIN**  Indian ££
(Map p126; 0141-553 2585; www.dakhin.com; 89 Candleriggs; mains £7-19) This south Indian restaurant breathes some fresh air into the city's curry scene. Dishes are from all over the south, and include dosas – thin rice-based crêpes – and a yummy variety of fragrant coconut-based curries. If you're really hungry, try a thali: an assortment of Indian 'tapas'.

**ARISAIG**  Scottish ££
(Map p126; 0141-553 1010; www.arisaig restaurant.co.uk; 1 Merchant Sq; mains £12-20) Located in the Merchant Square building, a historical location converted into an echoing food court, Arisaig offers a good chance to try well-prepared Scottish cuisine at a fair price, with friendly service to boot. Candlelight and crisp linen makes for atmosphere despite the artificial situation, with both terrace and indoor seating.

**THE CHIPPY DOON THE LANE**  Fish & Chips £
(Map p126; www.thechippyglasgow.com; McCormick Lane, 84 Buchanan St; meals £6-11; noon-9.30pm) Don't be put off by this down-at-heel alleyway off the shopping precinct, for this is a cut above your average chip shop. Sustainable seafood is served in a rather chic space, all old-time brick, metal archways and jazz. Otherwise, chow down on your takeaway at the wooden tables in the lane or out on Buchanan St itself.

**WHERE THE MONKEY SLEEPS**  Cafe £
(Map p126; www.monkeysleeps.com; 182 West Regent St; dishes £4-7; 7am-5pm Mon-Fri) This funky little number in the middle of the business district is just what you need to get away from the ubiquitous coffee chains. Laid-back and a little hippy, the bagels and paninis, with names like Burn the Witch or Meathammer, are highlights, as are some very inventive dishes, such as the 'nuclear' beans, dripping with cayenne and Tabasco.

**WILLOW TEAROOMS**  Cafe £
(www.willowtearooms.co.uk; light meals £4-8; 9am-5pm Mon-Sat, 11am-5pm Sun) Buchanan St (Map p126; 97 Buchanan St) Sauchiehall St (Map p126; 217 Sauchiehall St). These re-creations of tearooms designed by Charles Rennie Mackintosh in 1904 back up the design with excellent bagels, pastries or, more splendidly, champagne

# If You Like...
## Charles Rennie Mackintosh

If the Glasgow School of Art has fired your enthusiasm for all things Mackintosh, the city has several more delights in store.

1 **WILLOW TEAROOMS**
(Map p126; www.willowtearooms.co.uk; 217 Sauchiehall St; ⊙9am-5pm Mon-Sat, 11am-5pm Sun) An authentic reconstruction of tearooms Mackintosh designed and furnished in the early 20th century for restaurateur Kate Cranston.

2 **LIGHTHOUSE**
(Map p126; ☎0141-221 6362; www.thelighthouse.co.uk; 11 Mitchell Lane; ⊙10.30am-5pm Mon-Sat, noon-5pm Sun) Mackintosh's first building, designed in 1893, now serves as Scotland's Centre for Architecture & Design.

3 **SCOTLAND STREET SCHOOL MUSEUM**
(www.glasgowmuseums.com; 225 Scotland St; ⊙10am-5pm Tue-Thu & Sat, 11am-5pm Fri & Sun) Worth a visit for its stunning facade and interesting museum of education that occupies the interior.

4 **HOUSE FOR AN ART LOVER**
(☎0141-353 4770; www.houseforanartlover.co.uk; Bellahouston Park, Dumbreck Rd; adult/child £4.50/3; ⊙10am-4pm Mon-Wed, to 1pm Thu-Sun) Although designed in 1901, this house was not built until the 1990s. Mackintosh worked closely with his wife on the design and her influence is evident, especially in the rose motif.

5 **MACKINTOSH CHURCH**
(Map p130; www.crmsociety.com; 870 Garscube Rd; adult/child £4/free; ⊙10am-5pm Mon, Wed & Fri Apr-Oct, till 4pm Nov-Mar) The only one of Mackintosh's church designs to be built.

afternoon teas (£20). At busy times the queues for a table can be long.

## West End

There are numerous excellent restaurants in the West End. They cluster along Byres Rd and, just off it, on Ashton Lane and Ruthven Lane. Gibson St and Great Western Rd also have plenty to offer.

**THE UBIQUITOUS CHIP** Scottish £££
(Map p130; ☎0141-334 5007; www.ubiquitous chip.co.uk; 12 Ashton Lane; 2-/3-course dinner £35/40, brasserie mains lunch £7-12, dinner £12-15) The original champion of Scottish produce, The Ubiquitous Chip has won lots of awards for its unparalleled Scottish cuisine, and for its lengthy wine list. Named to poke fun at Scotland's perceived lack of finer cuisine, it offers a French touch but resolutely Scottish ingredients, carefully selected and following sustainable principles. The elegant courtyard space offers some of Glasgow's highest-quality dining, while above and in the atmospheric pub, the cheaper brasserie menu doesn't skimp on quality but keeps things affordable. The cute 'Wee Pub' down the side alley offers plenty of drinking pleasure. There's always something going on at the Chip - check the website for upcoming events.

**STRAVAIGIN** Scottish ££
(Map p130; ☎0141-334 2665; www.stravai gin.co.uk; 28 Gibson St; mains £10-18; ⊙9am-11pm) Stravaigin is a serious foodie's delight, with a menu constantly pushing the boundaries of originality and offering creative culinary excellence. The cool contemporary dining space in the basement has booth seating and helpful, laid-back waiting-staff to assist in deciphering the audacious menu. Entry-level has a buzzing two-level bar; you can also eat here. There are always plenty of menu deals and special culinary nights.

**MOTHER INDIA** Indian ££
(Map p130; ☎0141-221 1663; www.motherindia.co.uk; 28 Westminster Tce, Sauchiehall St; mains £8-14; ⊙lunch Fri-Sun, dinner daily; ☑👬) Glasgow curry buffs are forever debating the merits of the city's numerous excellent south Asian restaurants, and Mother

India features in every discussion. It may lack the trendiness of some of the up-and-comers but it's been a stalwart for years, and the quality and innovation on show is superb. It also makes a real effort for kids, with a separate menu.

### THE BUTCHERSHOP    Steakhouse £££
(Map p130; www.butchershopglasgow.com; 1055 Sauchiehall St; steaks £16-30; ⊘noon-10pm) Offering several different cuts of traceably sourced, properly aged beef, this is just about the best spot in Glasgow for a tasty, served-as-you-want-it steak; a perfect lunch venue after the Kelvingrove Museum. There are seats out the front if the weather happens to be fine. There's also seafood on the menu, and decently mixed cocktails.

### 🍽 THE LEFT BANK    Bistro ££
(Map p130; ☏0141-339 5969; www.theleftbank. co.uk; 33 Gibson St; mains £12-18; ⊘9am-10pm Mon-Fri, 10am-10pm Sat & Sun; 🍴👶) Huge windows fronting the street greet patrons to this outstanding eatery specialising in gastronomic delights and lazy afternoons. There are lots of little spaces filled with couches and chunky tables, reflecting a sense of intimacy. The large starter-menu can be treated like tapas, making it good for sharing plates. There are lots of delightful creations that use seasonal and local produce, with an eclectic variety of influences.

### HEART BUCHANAN    Cafe, Deli £
(Map p130; www.heartbuchanan.co.uk; 380 Byres Rd; light meals £6-10; ⊘9am-4pm Mon-Sat, 10am-6pm Sun) The famous West End deli – give your nose a treat and drop in – has a small cafe space next door. Break any or all of the 10 commandments to bag a table, then enjoy some of Glasgow's best breakfasts, all made with produce of exquisite quality. Or try a refreshing juice or milkshake, or one of the regularly changing light-lunch options. If you failed in the table quest, remember the deli also does some of these meals to take away.

### 🍽 STRAVAIGIN II    Scottish ££
(Map p130; ☏0141-334 7165; www.stravaigin2. com; 8 Ruthven Lane; lunch mains £7-13, dinner £10-16; ⊘noon-11pm) Top service makes all feel welcome at this relaxed eatery just off Byres Rd. The menu changes regularly but always features a few surprises from around the globe. Slow-cooking features prominently in the preparation of both meat and vegetables, so expect those flavours to burst out at you. It's also got a legendary reputation for its burgers, fish 'n' chips and haggis, so there's something here for any appetite.

### ÒRAN MÓR BRASSERIE    Scottish ££
(Map p130; ☏0141-357 6226; www.oran-mor. co.uk; 731 Great Western Rd; mains £12-20; ⊘noon-9pm Sun-Wed, to 10pm Thu-Sat) This temple to Scottish dining and drinking is

Willow Tearooms (p137)

**Below:** Kibble Palace, Botanic Gardens (p130); **Right:** Burns National Heritage Park, Alloway (p147)

(BELOW) VISITBRITAIN/BRITAIN ON VIEW/GETTY IMAGES © ; (RIGHT) JOHN PETER PHOTOGRAPHY/ALAMY ©

a superb venue in an old church. Giving new meaning to the word 'conversion', the brasserie pumps out high-quality meals in a dark, Mackintosh-inspired space. The menu runs from burgers to more elaborate mains and, at the time of research, there was a great-value two-course special for £13 from 4pm until close.

# Drinking

Glasgow's pubs and bars are the raucous embodiment of the city's character – loud, garrulous, convivial and dedicated to the pursuit of good *craic*.

## City Centre

### ARTÀ                                          Bar
(Map p126; www.arta.co.uk; 13-19 Walls St; ⏰5pm-3am Thu-Sat) This extraordinary place is so baroque that when you hear a Mozart concerto over the sound system, it wouldn't surprise you to see the man himself at the other end of the bar. Set in a former cheese market, it really does have to be seen to be believed. As its door slides open, Artà's opulent, cavernous candle-lit interior is unveiled, with its floor-to-ceiling red velvet curtains revealing a staircase to the tapas bar and restaurant above in a show of decadence that the Romans would have appreciated. Despite the luxury, it's got a relaxed, chilled vibe and a mixed crowd. The big cocktails are great.

### HORSE SHOE                                  Pub
(Map p126; www.horseshoebar.co.uk; 17 Drury St) This legendary city pub and popular meeting place dates from the late 19th century and is largely unchanged. It's a picturesque spot, with the longest continuous bar in the UK, but its main attraction is what's served over it – real ale and good cheer. Upstairs in the lounge is some of the best value pub food (3-course lunch £4.25) in town.

### BABBITY BOWSTER
Pub

(Map p126; 16-18 Blackfriars St) In a quiet corner of Merchant City, this handsome spot is perfect for a tranquil daytime drink, particularly in the adjoining beer garden. Service is attentive, and the smell of sausages may tempt you to lunch; there's also accommodation. This is one of the centre's most charming pubs, in one of its noblest buildings.

## West End

### HILLHEAD BOOKCLUB
Bar

(Map p130; www.hillheadbookclub.com; 17 Vinicombe St) Atmosphere in spades is the call sign of this easygoing West End bar. An ornate wooden ceiling overlooks two levels of well-mixed cocktails, seriously cheap drinks, comfort food and numerous intriguing decorative touches. There's even a ping-pong table in a cage.

### ÒRAN MÓR
Bar

(Map p130; www.oran-mor.co.uk; 731 Great Western Rd) Now some may be a little uncomfortable with the thought of drinking in a church. But we say: the Lord giveth. Praise be and let's give thanks – a converted church, and an almighty one at that, is now a bar, restaurant and club venue. The bar feels like it's been here for years – all wood and thick, exposed stone giving it warmth and a celestial air. There's an excellent array of whiskies. The only thing missing is holy water on your way in.

### BREL
Bar

(Map p130; www.brelbarrestaurant.com; 39 Ashton Lane) Perhaps the best on Ashton Lane, this bar can seem tightly packed, but there's a conservatory out the back so you can pretend you're sitting outside when it's raining, and when the sun does peek through there's a beer garden. They've got a huge range of Belgian beers, and they also do mussels and other Lowlands favourites.

141

# ⭐ Entertainment

Glasgow is Scotland's entertainment city, from classical music, fine theatres and ballet to cracking nightclubs pumping out state-of-the-art hip-hop, electro, or techno, to cheesy chart tunes and contemporary Scottish bands at the cutting edge of modern music.

To tap into your scene, check out *The List* (www.list.co.uk), an invaluable fortnightly events-guide available at newsagents and bookshops.

For theatre tickets, book directly with the venue. For concerts, a useful booking centre is **Tickets Scotland** (Map p126; ☎0141-204 5151; www.tickets-scotland.com; 237 Argyle St).

## Nightclubs

Glasgow has one of Britain's biggest and best clubbing scenes, attracting devotees from afar. Glaswegians usually hit clubs after the pubs have closed, so many clubs offer discounted admission and cheaper drinks if you go before 10.30pm. Entry costs £5 to £10 (up to £25 for big events),

although bars often hand out free passes. By law, clubs shut at 3am, so keep your ear to the ground to find out where the after-parties are at.

**SUB CLUB**                                Club

(Map p126; www.subclub.co.uk; 22 Jamaica St) Saturdays at the Sub Club are one of Glasgow's legendary nights, offering serious clubbing with a sound system that aficionados usually rate as the city's best. The claustrophobic, last-one-in vibe is not for those faint of heart.

**ARCHES**                                  Club

(Map p126; www.thearches.co.uk; 253 Argyle St) R-e-s-p-e-c-t is the mantra at the Arches. The Godfather of Glaswegian clubs, it has a design based around hundreds of arches slammed together, and is a must for funk and hip-hop freaks. It is one of the city's biggest clubs pulling top DJs, and you'll also hear some of the UK's up-and-coming turntable spinners. It's off Jamaica St.

## Live Music

Glasgow is the king of Scotland's live-music scene. Year after year, touring musicians, artists and travellers alike

Gallery of Modern Art (p125)

name Glasgow one of their favourite cities in the world to enjoy live music. As much of Glasgow's character is encapsulated within the soul and humour of its inhabitants, the main reason for the city's musical success lies within its audience and the musical community it has bred and nurtured for years.

There are so many venues it's impossible to keep track of them all. Pick up a copy of the **Gig Guide** (www.gigguide.co.uk), available free in most pubs and venues, for the latest listings.

One of the city's premier live-music pub venues, the excellent **King Tut's Wah Wah Hut** (Map p126; ☎0141-221 5279; www.kingtuts.co.uk; 272a St Vincent St) hosts bands every night of the week. Oasis were signed after playing here.

Two bars to see the best, and worst, of Glasgow's newest bands are **Brunswick Cellars** (Map p126; 239 Sauchiehall St) and **Classic Grand** (Map p126; www.classicgrand.com; 18 Jamaica St).

**13TH NOTE CAFÉ**    Live Music, Cafe
(Map p126; www.13thnote.co.uk; 50-60 King St) Also does decent vegetarian food.

**ABC**    Club, Live Music
(O2 ABC; Map p126; www.o2abcglasgow.co.uk; 300 Sauchiehall St) Both nightclub and venue, this star of Sauchiehall has two large concert spaces and several attractive bars. It's a good all-rounder, with a variety of DJs playing every Thursday to Saturday. Punters scrub up fairly well here.

**BARROWLAND**    Concert Venue
(Map p126; www.glasgow-barrowland.com; 244 Gallowgate) An exceptional old dancehall catering for some of the larger acts that visit the city.

**THE CAPTAIN'S**    Live Music
(Map p130; www.captainsrest.co.uk; 185 Great Western Rd) Variety of indie bands. Gigs nearly every night, and a Monday open-mic session.

## Theatres & Concert Halls

**THEATRE ROYAL**    Opera/Ballet/Theatre
(Map p126; ☎0844 871 7627; www.atgtickets.com; 282 Hope St) This is the home of Scot-tish Opera, and the Scottish Ballet often has performances here. For advance bookings in person, head to the King's Theatre.

**GLASGOW ROYAL CONCERT HALL**    Concert Venue
(Map p126; ☎0141-353 8000; www.glasgowconcerthalls.com; 2 Sauchiehall St) A feast of classical music is showcased at this concert hall, the modern home of the Royal Scottish National Orchestra.

**KING'S THEATRE**    Theatre
(Map p126; ☎0844 871 7627; www.atgtickets.com; 297 Bath St) King's Theatre hosts mainly musicals; on rare occasions there are variety shows, pantomimes and comedies.

**CITIZENS' THEATRE**    Theatre
(☎0141-429 0022; www.citz.co.uk; 119 Gorbals St) This is one of the top theatres in Scotland and it's well worth trying to catch a performance here.

# Shopping

Boasting the UK's largest retail phalanx outside London, Glasgow is a shopaholic's paradise. The 'Style Mile' around Buchanan St, Argyle St and Merchant City (particularly upmarket Ingram St) is a fashion hub, while the West End has quirkier, more bohemian shopping options: Byres Rd is great for vintage clothing.

**BARRAS**    Flea Market
(Map p126; www.glasgow-barrowland.com; btwn Gallowgate & London Rd; ⏱10am-5pm Sat & Sun) Glasgow's flea market, the Barras on Gallowgate, is the living, breathing heart of this city in many respects. It has almost a thousand stalls and people come here just for a wander as much as for their shopping, which gives the place a holiday air. The Barras is notorious for selling designer frauds, so be cautious. Watch your wallet, too.

**BUCHANAN GALLERIES**    Shopping Centre
(Map p126; www.buchanangalleries.co.uk; Royal Exchange Sq) Huge number of contemporary clothing retailers.

**PRINCES SQUARE** Fashion
(Map p126; www.princessquare.co.uk; Buchanan
St) Set in a magnificent 1841 renovated
square. Beauty and fashion outlets including Vivienne Westwood.

## ℹ Information

### Medical Services

To see a doctor, visit the outpatients department
at any general hospital.

**Glasgow Dental Hospital** (☎0141-211 9600;
www.nhsggc.org.uk; 378 Sauchiehall St)

**Glasgow Royal Infirmary** (☎0141-211 4000;
www.nhsggc.org.uk; 84 Castle St) Medical
emergencies and outpatients facilities.

**Western Infirmary** (☎0141-211 2000; www.
nhsggc.org.uk; Dumbarton Rd)

### Tourist Information

**Glasgow Information Centre** (☎0141-204
4400; www.seeglasgow.com; 11 George Sq;
⊙9am-5pm Mon-Sat) Excellent tourist office;
makes local and national accommodation
bookings (£4). Closes later and opens Sundays
from July to August.

**Airport Tourist Office** (☎0141-848 4440;
Glasgow International Airport; ⊙7.30am-5pm
Mon-Sat, to 3.30pm Sun)

## ℹ Getting There & Away

### Air

Ten miles west of the city, **Glasgow International
Airport** (GLA; www.glasgowairport.com) handles
domestic traffic and international flights. **Glasgow
Prestwick Airport** (PIK; www.glasgowprestwick.
com), 30 miles southwest of Glasgow, is used
by **Ryanair** (www.ryanair.com) and some other
budget airlines, with many connections to the rest
of Britain and Europe.

### Bus

All long-distance buses arrive at and depart from
**Buchanan bus station** (☎0141-333 3708; www.
spt.co.uk; Killermont St), which has pricey lockers,
ATMs, and a cafe with wi-fi.

Your first port of call if you're looking for
the cheapest fare should be **Megabus** (www.
megabus.com), which offers very cheap demand-
dependent prices on many major bus routes,
including Edinburgh and London. The fare to
London can be as little as £12 if you're lucky.

**Scottish Citylink** (☎0871 266 3333; www.
citylink.co.uk) has buses to most major towns
in Scotland, including:

**Edinburgh** (£6.80, 1¼ hours, every 15
minutes)

**Stirling** (£7.30, 45 minutes, at
least hourly)

**Perth** (£11.20, 1½ hours,
hourly)

**Inverness** (£27.50, 3½
hours, eight daily)

**Aberdeen** (£28.80, 2½ to
three hours, hourly)

**Oban** (£17.50, three hours,
four direct daily)

**Fort William** (£22, three
hours, seven daily)

**Portree, Isle of Skye**
(£39.40, 6¼ to seven hours,
three daily)

Glasgow School of Art (p124)

## Car & Motorcyle

There are numerous car-rental companies; the big names have offices at Glasgow and Prestwick airports. Companies include the following:

**Arnold Clark** ( ☎0141-423 9559; www. arnoldclarkrental.com; 43 Allison St)

**Avis** ( ☎0844 544 6064; www.avis.co.uk; 70 Lancefield St)

**Europcar** ( ☎0141-204 1072; www.europcar. co.uk; 1 Waterloo St)

## Train

As a general rule, **Glasgow Central station** serves southern Scotland, England and Wales, and **Queen St station** serves the north and east. There are buses every 10 minutes between the two stations. There are direct trains from London's Euston station; they're much quicker (advance purchase single £28 to £105, full fare £162, 4½ hours, more than hourly) and more comfortable than the bus.

**Scotrail** ( ☎08457 55 00 33; www.scotrail. co.uk) runs Scottish trains. Destinations include: Edinburgh (£12.90, 50 minutes, every 15 minutes), Oban (£21.60, three hours, three to four daily), Fort William (£26.30, 3¾ hours, four to five daily), Dundee (£25.30, 1½ hours, hourly), Aberdeen (£45.20, 2½ hours, hourly) and Inverness (£79, 3½ hours, 10 daily, four on Sunday).

## ⓘ Getting Around

## Public Transport

**Bus** City bus services, mostly run by **First Glasgow** ( ☎0141-423 6600; www.firstglasgow. com), are frequent. You can buy tickets when you board buses but on most you must have the exact change.

**Train & Underground** There's an extensive suburban network of trains in and around Glasgow; tickets should be bought before travel if the station is staffed, or from the conductor if it isn't. There's also an underground line, the Subway, that serves 15 stations in the centre, west and south of the city.

## Taxi

You can pay by credit card with **Glasgow Taxis** ( ☎0141-429 7070; www.glasgowtaxis.co.uk) if you order by phone; most of its taxis are wheelchair accessible.

# LOCH LOMOND & AROUND

The 'bonnie banks' and 'bonnie braes' of Loch Lomond have long been Glasgow's rural retreat – a scenic region of hills, lochs and healthy fresh air within easy reach of Scotland's largest city (Loch Lomond is within an hour's drive of 70% of Scotland's population). Since the 1930s Glaswegians have made a regular weekend exodus to the hills – by car, by bike and on foot – and today the loch's popularity shows no sign of decreasing.

The importance of the Loch Lomond region was recognised when it became the heart of **Loch Lomond & the Trossachs National Park** (www.lochlomond -trossachs.org) – Scotland's first national park, created in 2002.

 **Activities**

## Walking

The big walk around here is the **West Highland Way** (www.west-highland-way.co.uk), which runs along the eastern shore of the loch. There are shorter lochside walks at Firkin Point on the western shore and at several other places around the loch. You can get further information on local walks from the national park informa-tion centres at Loch Lomond Shores and Balmaha.

Rowardennan is the starting point for an ascent of **Ben Lomond** (974m), a popular and relatively straighforward (if strenuous) five- to six-hour round trip. The route starts at the car park just past the Rowardennan Hotel.

## Boat Trips

**SWEENEY'S CRUISES**          Boat Tours
( ☎01389-752376; www.sweeneyscruises.com; Balloch Rd, Balloch) The main centre for boat trips is Balloch, where Sweeney's Cruises offers a range of trips including a one-hour cruise to Inchmurrin and back (adult/child £8.50/5, five times daily), and a two-hour cruise (£15/8 departs

**145**

1pm and 3pm) around the islands. The quay is directly opposite Balloch train station, beside the tourist office.

**CRUISE LOCH LOMOND**     Boat Tour
(www.cruiselochlomond.co.uk; Tarbet) Cruise Loch Lomond is based in Tarbet and offers two-hour trips to Inversnaid, Arklet Falls and Rob Roy MacGregor's Cave (adult/child £12.50/7.50). You can also be dropped off at Rowardennan to climb Ben Lomond (£14.50/7.50), getting picked up at Rowardennan seven hours later, or get picked up at Inversnaid after a 9-mile hike along the West Highland Way (£14.50/7.50).

**BALMAHA BOATYARD**     Boat Trips
(www.balmahaboatyard.co.uk; Balmaha) The mailboat, run by Balmaha Boatyard, cruises from Balmaha to the loch's four inhabited islands, departing at 11.30am and returning at 2pm, with a one-hour stop on Inchmurrin (adult/child £9/4.50). Trips depart daily (except Sunday) in July and August; on Monday, Thursday and Saturday in May, June and September; and Monday and Thursday only October to April.

### Other Activities

The mostly traffic-free **Clyde and Loch Lomond Cycle Way** links Glasgow to Balloch (20 miles), where it links with the **West Loch Lomond Cycle Path**, which continues along the loch shore to Tarbet (10 miles).

You can rent **rowing boats** at Balmaha Boatyard (see above) for £10/40 per hour/day (or £20/60 for a boat with outboard motor). **Lomond Adventure** (01360-870218; www.lomondadventure. co.uk; Balmaha), also in Balmaha, rents out Canadian **canoes** (£30 per day) and **sea kayaks** (£25).

**CanYou Experience** (01389-756251; www.canyouexperience.com; Loch Lomond Shores, Balloch) rent out canoes (£12/17 per half-/full hour) and bicycles (£13/17 per three hours/full day), and offer a full-day **guided canoe safari** on the loch (adult/child £65/55).

## Information

**Balloch Tourist Office** (0870 720 0607; Balloch Rd, Balloch; 9.30am-6pm Jun-Aug, 10am-6pm Apr & Sep)

**Balmaha National Park Centre** (01389-722100; Balmaha; 9.30am-4.15pm Apr-Sep)

**National Park Gateway Centre** (01389-751035; www.lochlomondshores.com; Loch Lomond Shores, Balloch; 10am-6pm Apr-Sep, to 5pm Oct-Mar; @ )

**Tarbet Tourist Office** (0870-720 0623; Tarbet; 10am-6pm Jul & Aug, to 5pm Easter-Jun, Sep & Oct) At the junction of the A82 and the A83.

## Getting There & Away

### Bus

**First Glasgow** (0141-423 6600; www. firstglasgow.com) buses 204 and 215 run from Argyle St in central Glasgow to Balloch and Loch Lomond Shores (1½ hours, at least two per hour).

**Scottish Citylink** (www.citylink.co.uk) coaches from Glasgow to Oban and Fort William stop at Luss (£8.20, 55 minutes, six daily), Tarbet (£8.20, 65 minutes) and Ardlui (£14.30, 1¼ hours).

### Train

**Glasgow to Balloch** £4.70, 45 minutes, every 30 minutes

**Glasgow to Arrochar & Tarbet** £11, 1¼ hours, three or four daily

**Glasgow to Ardlui** £14, 1½ hours, three or four daily, continuing to Oban and Fort William

## Getting Around

Pick up the useful **public transport booklet** (free), which lists timetables for all bus, train and ferry services in Loch Lomond and the Trossachs National Park, available from any tourist office or park information centre.

### Bus

**McColl's Coaches** (www.mccolls.org.uk) bus 309 runs from Balloch to Balmaha (25 minutes, every two hours). An **SPT Daytripper ticket** (www. spt.co.uk/tickets) gives a family group unlimited travel for a day on most bus and train services in the Glasgow, Loch Lomond and Helensburgh

# Detour:
## Alloway

The pretty town of Alloway (38 miles south of Glasgow) should be on the itinerary of every Robert Burns fan – he was born here on 25 January 1759.

The impressive new **Robert Burns Birthplace Museum,** part of **Burns National Heritage Park** (NTS; www.nts.org.uk; adult/child £8/6; ⊙10am-5pm Oct-Mar, to 5.30pm Apr-Sep; [♿]), has collected a solid range of Burns memorabilia, including manuscripts and possessions of the poet, like the pistols he packed in order to carry out his daily work as a tax man.

The admission fee also covers the atmospheric Burns Cottage, connected via a walkway to the Birthplace Museum. Born in the little box-bed in this cramped thatched dwelling, the poet spent the first seven years of his life here. It's an attractive display which gives you a context for reading plenty of his verse. Much-needed translations of some of the more obscure Scots farming terms he loved to use decorate the walls.

Near the Birthplace Museum are the ruins of **Alloway Auld Kirk**, the setting for part of 'Tam o' Shanter'. Burns' father, William Burnes (his son dropped the 'e' from his name), is buried in the kirkyard; read the poem on the back of the gravestone.

area. Buy the ticket (£10.70 for one adult and one or two children, £19 for two adults and up to four children) from any train station or the main Glasgow bus station.

### Boat

From April to October a network of passenger ferries criss-crosses Loch Lomond, allowing you to explore the loch's hiking and biking trails using public transport (there are train services to Balloch, Arrochar and Tarbet and Ardlui, and buses to Luss and Balmaha). A Loch Lomond Water Bus (www.lochlomond-trossachs.org/waterbus) timetable is available from tourist offices, national park centres and online. Fares quoted are one-way.

## Western Shore

The town of **Balloch**, which straddles the River Leven where it flows from the southern end of Loch Lomond, is the loch's main population centre and transport hub. A Victorian resort once thronged by day-trippers transferring between the train station and the steamer quay, it is now a 'gateway centre' for Loch Lomond and the Trossachs National Park.

**Loch Lomond Shores** (www. lochlomondshores.com), a major tourism development a half-mile north of Balloch, sports a national park information centre plus various visitor attractions, outdoor activities and boat trips. In keeping with the times, the heart of the development is a large shopping mall. It's also home to the **Loch Lomond Aquarium** (www. sealife.co.uk; per person £13.20; ⊙10am-5pm), which has displays on the wildlife of Loch Lomond, an otter enclosure (housing short-clawed Asian otters, not Scottish ones), and a host of sea-life exhibits ranging from sharks to sea turtles.

The vintage paddle steamer **Maid of the Loch** (www.maidoftheloch.com; admission free; ⊙11am-4pm Sat & 2-4pm Sun Easter-Aug), built in 1953, is moored here while undergoing restoration – you can nip aboard for a look around. It is hoped that her steam engines will be restored to working order in 2013.

Unless it's raining, give Loch Lomond Shores a miss and head for the little picture-postcard village of **Luss**. Stroll among the pretty cottages with roses around their doors (the cottages were built by the local laird in the 19th century for the workers on his estate), then pop

## Detour:
# Culzean Castle

Magnificent **Culzean Castle** (NTS; ☎01655-884400; www.culzeanexperience.org; adult/child/family £15/11/36, park only adult/child £9.50/7; ⏲castle 10.30am-5pm Apr-Oct, park 9.30am-sunset year-round) is one of the most impressive of Scotland's great stately homes. Designed by Robert Adam, the most influential architect of his time, this 18th-century mansion is perched dramatically on the edge of the cliffs.

The beautiful oval staircase here is regarded as one of Adam's finest achievements. On the 1st floor, the opulence of the circular saloon contrasts violently with the views of the wild sea below. Lord Cassillis' bedroom is said to be haunted by a lady in green, mourning for a lost baby. Even the bathrooms are palatial, the dressing room beside the state bedroom being equipped with a Victorian state-of-the-art shower.

There are also two ice houses, a swan pond, a pagoda, a re-creation of a Victorian vinery, an orangery, a deer park and an aviary. Wildlife in the area includes otters.

If you really want to experience the magic of this place, it's possible to stay in the **castle** (s/d from £140/225, Eisenhower ste s/d £250/375; Ｐ 🛜) from April to October.

Culzean is 49 miles south of Glasgow; Maybole is the nearest train station, but since it's 4 miles away it's best to come by bus from Ayr (30 minutes, 11 daily, Monday to Saturday); there are frequent trains from Glasgow to Ayr. Buses pass the park gates, from where it's a 20-minute walk through the grounds to the castle.

into the **Clan Colquhoun Visitor Centre** (☎01436-860814; Shore Cottage, Luss; adult/child £1/free; ⏲10.30am-6pm Easter-Oct) for some background history before enjoying a cup of tea at the Coach House Coffee Shop.

## 🛏 Sleeping & Eating

### DROVER'S INN                    Inn ££
(☎01301-704234; www.thedroversinn.co.uk; bar meals £7-12; ⏲lunch & dinner) This is one howff (drinking den) you shouldn't miss – a low-ceilinged place with smoke-blackened stone, bare wooden floors spotted with candle wax, barmen in kilts, and walls festooned with moth-eaten stags' heads and stuffed birds. There's even a stuffed bear and the desiccated husk of a basking shark.

The bar serves hearty hill-walking fuel such as steak-and-Guinness pie with mustard mash, and hosts live folk music on Friday and Saturday nights. We recommend this inn more as an atmospheric place to eat and drink than somewhere to stay – accommodation varies from eccentric, old-fashioned and rather run-down rooms in the old building (including a ghost in room 6), to more comfortable rooms (with en suite bathrooms) in the modern annexe across the road. Ask to see your room before taking it.

### LOCH LOMOND SYHA          Hostel £
(☎01389-850226; www.syha.org.uk; dm £19; ⏲Mar-Oct; Ｐ@🛜) Forget about roughing it, this is one of the most impressive hostels in the country – an imposing 19th-century country house set in beautiful grounds overlooking the loch. It's 2 miles north of Balloch and very popular, so book in advance in summer. And yes, it *is* haunted.

**COACH HOUSE COFFEE SHOP** Cafe **£**
(mains £6-11; ⌚10am-5pm; 📶 👤 😺) With its
chunky pine furniture and deep, deep sofa
in front of a rustic fireplace, the Coach
House is one of the cosiest places to eat
on Loch Lomond. The menu includes coffee and tea, home-baked cakes, scones,
ciabattas and more substantial offerings
such as smoked salmon and prawns with
Marie Rose sauce, and haggis with neeps
and tatties (mashed potatoes and turnip).

## Eastern Shore

The road along the loch's eastern shore
passes through the attractive village of
**Balmaha**, where you can hire boats or
take a cruise on the mailboat. A short
but steep climb from the village car park
leads to the summit of **Conic Hill** (361m),
a superb viewpoint (2.5 miles round trip,
allow two to three hours).

There are several picnic areas along
the lochside; the most attractive is
at **Millarochy Bay** (1.5 miles north of
Balmaha), which has a nice gravel beach
and superb views across the loch to the
Luss hills.

The road ends at **Rowardennan**, but
the West Highland Way (p145) hiking trail
continues north along the shore of the
loch. It's 7 miles to **Inversnaid**, which can
be reached by road from the Trossachs,
and 15 miles to **Inverarnan** on the main
A82 road at the northern end of the loch.

# 🛌 Sleeping & Eating

From March to October, camping outside
designated campsites is banned on the
eastern shore of Loch Lomond between
Drymen and Ptarmigan Lodge. There
are campsites at Millarochy, Cashel and
Sallochy.

**PASSFOOT COTTAGE** B&B **££**
( ☎01360-870324; www.passfoot.com;
Balmaha; per person £37.50; ⌚Apr-Sep; 📶)
Passfoot is a pretty little whitewashed
cottage decked out with colourful flower
baskets, with a lovely location overlooking
Balmaha Bay. The bright bedrooms have
a homely feel, and there's a cosy lounge
with a wood-burning stove and loch view.

**OAK TREE INN** Inn **££**
( ☎01360-870357; www.oak-tree-inn.co.uk;
Balmaha; dm/s/d £30/60/75; 🅿 📶 👤) An
attractive traditional inn built in slate
and timber, the Oak Tree offers luxurious
guest bedrooms for pampered hikers,
and two four-bed bunkrooms for hardier
souls. The rustic restaurant dishes up
hearty lunches and dinners (mains £9 to
£12), such as steak-and-mushroom pie,
and roast Arctic char with lime and chive
butter, and cooks up an excellent bowl
of Cullen skink (soup made with smoked
haddock, potato, onion and milk).

# Stirling & Northeast Scotland

**Many visitors pass by this corner of the country in their headlong rush to the tourist honey-pots of Loch Ness and Skye.** But they're missing out on a region that's as beautiful and diverse as the more obvious attractions of the western Highlands and islands.

Stirling and the northeast is the historic and cultural heartland of Scotland. Iconic sites that chronicle the country's turbulent history pepper the landscape, from the battlefields of Bannockburn and Killiecrankie to the castles of Stirling and Glamis, and the ancient coronation place of Scottish kings at Scone.

Here too is St Andrews, the home of golf; Balmoral Castle, the holiday retreat of British monarchs since Victorian times; and glorious Speyside, dotted with dozens of whisky distilleries. All set in a landscape that increases in drama from the picturesque lochs and woods of the Trossachs to the full-blown grandeur of the Grampian mountains.

Callander, the Trossachs (p173)
DENNIS BARNES/GETTY IMAGES ©

A golfer at St Andrews (p177)

# Stirling & Northeast Scotland

1 Stirling Castle
2 Speyside Whisky Trail
3 The Trossachs
4 Royal Deeside
5 Scone Palace
6 St Andrews
7 Blair Castle

North Sea

Moray Firth

Lossiemouth
Cullen  Portsoy
Findhorn  Elgin  Fochabers  Banff  A98
Forres  Keith  Aberchirder
Nairn  Lossie  Speyside  Turriff
Macallan  Cooperage  Deveron
Glenfarclas  Dufftown  Huntly
Grantown-on-Spey  A95  A96
A9  Rhynie
Monadhliath  Gadie Burn
Mountains  Tomintoul  Kintore
Cairngorm  Allt Tulleach  Alford
Mountains
Spey
Ben Macdui  Gairn  Balmoral  Aboyne  Banchory
(1309m)  Castle  Ballater
Braemar  Dee
Inverey  Muick
Dee  Lochnagar
A86  (1154m)  North Esk
Grampian  A93  Clova  Laurencekirk
A9  Mountains  Spittal of  Edzell
Garry  Glenshee  Brechin  A90
ort  Blair  Montrose
illiam  Castle  7  Blair Atholl
Kinloch  Killiecrankie  South Esk
Rannoch  Tay  Pitlochry
Glencoe  Forest  Forfar
Gaur  Park  Glamis
Glen Lyon  Tay  Castle
A82  Lyon  Aberfeldy  Blairgowrie  Arbroath
Fortingall  Kenmore  Dunkeld  Isla
Loch  A9
Tay  Almond
Tyndrum  Killin  Dundee  Broughty
A85  Crianlarich  Loch Lomond &  Comrie  A85  Firth  Ferry
Trossachs  Crieff  Perth  of Tay
National Park  Balquhidder  5  Newburgh
The  Auchterarder  Cupar  St Andrews
Loch  Trossachs  Earn  Eden  3
Katrine  6  A84  Callander  Falkland  Crail
A83  Tarbet  Loch  A907  St Monans  Anstruther
Achray  Dunblane  Kinross  Earlsferry  Pittenweem
Aberfoyle  Teith  Dollar  Elie
Argyll  Queen  Devon  Loch Leven
Forest Park  Elizabeth  1  Stirling  Ore  Kirkcaldy
Forest Park  Culross  Dunfermline  Firth
The Campsies  M80  Rosyth  of Forth
Dumbarton  Strathblane  Falkirk  Aberdour
Dunoon  Kelvin  A90  Edinburgh  Tyne
Glasgow

N  0  ____ 50 km
     0  ____ 25 miles

# Stirling & Northeast Scotland's Highlights

## ① Stirling Castle

Edinburgh Castle tops the visitor stakes, but in terms of history and heritage its sister fortress at Stirling is arguably more rewarding. This sturdy bastion has played a pivotal role in many key events of Scottish history, and was once a residence of the Stuart monarchs.

**Need to Know**
**BEST TIME TO GO** Two hours before closing (to avoid crowds). **COFFEE STOP** Darnley Coffee House (p172). **BEST PHOTO OP** View over River Forth. **For more, see p164.**

# Stirling Castle Don't Miss List

PETER YEOMAN, HISTORIC
SCOTLAND'S HEAD OF CULTURAL
RESOURCES

### 1 GREAT HALL

The largest medieval banqueting hall ever built in Scotland (pictured far left), created by James IV around 1503 as a spectacular setting for great state occasions. Recently restored to its former glory with the only new hammerbeam oak roof built in Britain since medieval times. Now a venue for concerts and dinners.

### 2 ROYAL PALACE

A sumptuous suite of apartments created by the young James V for his aristocratic French bride, Mary of Guise. Re-created interiors feature period furniture, fittings, textiles and decoration, but the king's lodgings are left bare as they would have been after his untimely death in 1542. These magnificent rooms are enlivened by the carved replicas of oak roundels known as the Stirling Heads, and by a spectacular new tapestry series in the Queen's Lodgings.

### 3 MUSICAL HEAD

During restoration, John Donaldson, the talented carver who copied all 36 Stirling Heads for the replica ceiling, discovered musical notation secreted in the border of one of the heads. The lady depicted in the portrait even seems to have her lips parted in song. This beautiful harp tune, perhaps created for James V, will be playing in a new permanent exhibition, 'Image-Makers to the King'.

### 4 PALACE VAULTS

The castle's 'below-stairs' life in the time of James V and Mary of Guise is explored in a series of family-friendly displays on the trades essential to court life. Follow the work of the painters, tailors, musicians, carvers and jesters to explore everyday life at Stirling in the 1540s.

### 5 BRAVEHEART!

The castle overlooks two great battlefields, Stirling Bridge (1297) and Bannockburn (1314), both fought and won by the Scots against the English over possession of Stirling Castle. William Wallace's decisive victory at Stirling Bridge is powerfully commemorated in the National Wallace Monument (pictured left).

# Speyside Whisky Trail

No trip to Scotland is complete without visiting a whisky distillery, and the Speyside region is the heartland of Scotch whisky with no fewer than 50 distilleries. Dufftown lies at the middle of it all, within easy reach of seven distilleries, and sporting its own whisky museum.

Below Right: Glenfiddich Distillery (p193)

**Need to Know**

**TOP TIP** Book distillery tours in advance. **BEST TIME TO GO** May or September, for the Spirit of Speyside festivals. **BEST PHOTO OP** Casks at Speyside Cooperage. For more, see p193.

# Speyside Don't Miss List

IAN LOGAN, BRAND AMBASSADOR, CHIVAS BROTHERS

### 1 THE GLENLIVET DISTILLERY
The home of the most iconic single malt whisky in the world, the Glenlivet (www.theglenlivet.com; at Ballindalloch, 10 miles west of Dufftown), offers a great mix of old and new, and a chance to see how modern technology has been adapted to work alongside traditional techniques. If you are a whisky connoisseur, join me on my weekly tour and discover behind-the-scenes secrets.

### 2 SPEYSIDE COOPERAGE
The Speyside Cooperage (p193; pictured far left and above left) gives you a chance to watch a craft that has changed little over the centuries – the quality of the cask is one of the biggest contributing factors to the flavour of a single malt. The team here supply barrels to distilleries all over the world and share with the distillers the passion of creating the finest whiskies in the world.

### 3 GORDON & MACPHAIL
The most famous whisky shop in the world, Gordon & MacPhail (www.gordonandmacphail.com; 58-60 South St, Elgin) is home to some of the oldest whiskies, including a 70-year-old Mortlach. The Urquhart family (owners) have played an important part in making single malt whisky what it is today, bottling these whiskies long before the distillers ever did.

### 4 CORGARFF CASTLE
The impressive and remote Corgarff Castle (near Cockbridge, 30 miles south of Dufftown on the road to Ballater) was once home to the redcoats whose job it was to chase down illegal distillers in the early 19th century.

### 5 GROUSE INN
Set deep in the heart of the old smuggling country, this remote pub at Cabrach, in the hills 10 miles south of Dufftown, has nearly 250 single malts on offer, with many many more on display around the bar – a collection that is home to several rare and unique bottlings.

# The Trossachs

Made famous by Sir Walter Scott's writings in the early 19th century during the first flush of Scottish tourism, the Trossachs (p173) is a region of scenic lochs ringed by craggy, wooded hills often described as 'the Highlands in miniature'. At its heart is Loch Katrine (p175), where a classic steamboat cruises the waters among remote hills that were once the territory of the outlaw Rob Roy MacGregor. Loch Katrine

③

# Royal Deeside

④

The valley of the River Dee – often called Royal Deeside because of the royal family's long association with the area – is famed for its salmon fishing, forest walks and grandiose castles, including the queen's holiday home at Balmoral Castle (p190). Other charms include the pretty village of Ballater, and the remote outpost of Braemar, home to Scotland's most famous Highland games. Balmoral Castle

## Scone Palace

This sumptuous stately home (p177) near Perth exudes history from every corniced nook and cranny. Kenneth MacAilpin, the first king of a united Scotland, was crowned on this site in AD 838, and Scone became the traditional coronation site of Scottish kings. The famous Stone of Destiny was stolen from here by the English King Edward I in 1296; it subsequently became a powerful symbol of Scottish nationhood.

## St Andrews

Scotland is the home of golf, and the Old Course (p180) at St Andrews – the world's oldest golf course – is on every golfer's wish list. But there's more to the place than golf. This was once Scotland's religious capital, and the remains of its castle and cathedral are well worth visiting. And don't miss the magnificent West Sands, where scenes from the movie *Chariots of Fire* were filmed.

## Blair Castle

The ancient seat of the dukes and earls of Atholl, Blair Castle (p187) controls the main route north to Inverness along the valley of the River Tay. Its long and illustrious history is displayed in sumptuous suites and grand drawing rooms, where visitors also learn about the Atholl Highlanders, Europe's only private standing army. Nearby is Killiecrankie, a key battlefield in the Jacobite rebellion of the 18th century.

# Stirling & Northeast Scotland's Best...

## Castles

○ **Stirling Castle** (p164) Hilltop fortress that has played a crucial role in Scottish history

○ **Glamis Castle** (p183) Regal, turreted childhood home of the late Queen Mother

○ **Balmoral Castle** (p190) The queen's holiday home, built in classic Scottish Baronial style

○ **St Andrews Castle** (p179) Historic ruin with coastal views and a warren of former siege tunnels

## Museums

○ **British Golf Museum** (p179) The history of golf chronicled in the home of golf

○ **Scottish Fisheries Museum** (p184) Everything you need to know about the fishing industry, including restored wooden boats afloat in the harbour

○ **Angus Folk Museum** (p183) A fascinating insight into rural life in Scotland in the 18th and 19th centuries

○ **Whisky Museum** (p192) Whisky distilling, distilled (as it were)

## Cultural Experiences

○ **Braemar Gathering** (p191) The most famous Highland games in the country, favoured by royalty

○ **Spirit of Speyside** (p193) Twice-yearly festival of whisky, with tastings, food stalls and traditional music

○ **St Andrews Festival** A rip-roaring celebration of all things Scottish, from haggis to Highland dancing

○ **Pitlochry Festival Theatre** (p186) Since its founding in 1951, the 'Theatre in the Hills' has become a national cultural institution

## Historic Sites

o **Bannockburn** (p170) The battlefield where Robert the Bruce won independence for Scotland in 1314

o **Scone Palace** (p177) Ancient crowning place of Scottish kings, once home to the Stone of Destiny

o **Balquhidder** (p175) The former stamping ground (and last resting place) of outlaw Rob Roy MacGregor, romanticised in novel and film

o **Killiecrankie** (p186) Scenic beauty spot and site of pivotal battle in the 18th-century Jacobite rebellion

**Left:** Drawing room, Glamis Castle;
**Above:** A Highland gathering

# Need to Know

## ADVANCE PLANNING

o **Six months before** Reserve a tee time for playing golf on St Andrews Old Course

o **Two weeks before** Book accommodation if visiting in summer

o **One week before** Make bookings for Speyside distillery tours and Trossachs boat trips

## RESOURCES

o **Scottish Heartlands** (www.visitscottishheartlands.com) Tourist information for Stirling and the Trossachs

o **Aberdeen & Grampian** (www.aberdeen-grampian.com) Tourist information for Royal Deeside

o **Highlands of Scotland** (www.visithighlands.com) Tourist information for Speyside

o **Loch Lomond & The Trossachs National Park** (www.lochlomond-trossachs.org) Wildlife, activities, things to see, public transport

o **Visit Fife** (www.visitfife.com) Tourist information for St Andrews and the East Neuk of Fife

o **Whisky Trail** (www.maltwhiskytrail.com) Places to visit near Dufftown in Speyside

## GETTING AROUND

o **Bus** Good network of intercity and local buses

o **Car** The most time-efficient way to get around this region

o **Train** OK for reaching major centres from Edinburgh or Glasgow, but less useful for day-to-day getting around – the railway lines skirt the region to east and west

## BE FOREWARNED

o **Open Golf Championship** Check to see if it's being staged in St Andrews before you go – if so, accommodation will be impossible to find, and the roads approaching town will be clogged with traffic.

# Stirling & Northeast Scotland Itineraries

*These routes cover the heartland of Scottish history and nationhood, from Bannockburn battlefield and Stirling Castle to the whisky capital of Speyside.*

**3 DAYS**

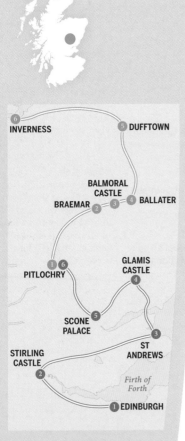

EDINBURGH TO PITLOCHRY

## The History Trail

It's little more than a 30-minute drive along the M9 from **(1) Edinburgh** to the imposing fortress of **(2) Stirling Castle** – approaching this way, along the ancient invasion route from England, it's easy to see how Stirling controls the road to the north. Visiting the castle and the nearby Bannockburn and Wallace Monument will take the best part of the day, before you head east on the A91 to **(3) St Andrews**.

Allow a day for this old ecclesiastical capital, taking in the ruined cathedral, the castle and perhaps a game of golf on a world-famous course. Cross the Tay Bridge and head for **(4) Glamis Castle**, an imposing turreted pile famous for resident ghosts and royal connections; don't forget the Angus Folk Museum near the entrance. The A94 leads back west to **(5) Scone Palace**, the ancient crowning place of Scottish kings and the original resting place of the Stone of Destiny.

A final 35-mile stretch north along the fast A9 road will bring you to **(6) Pitlochry** and nearby Blair Castle, seat of the Duke of Atholl who heads Britain's only private army.

**Top Left:** Loch Tummel, Pitlochry (p185);
**Top Right:** Glenfiddich Distillery (p193)
(TOP LEFT) DAVID ROBERTSON/ALAMY ©; (TOP RIGHT) MARKUS KELLER/IMAGEBROKER ©

**2**
*DAYS*

# Castles & Whisky

From **(1) Pitlochry** the day starts with a two-hour scenic drive across the hills on the A924 and B950 to reach the A93. Follow this north over the high pass of Glenshee and down to the classic Highland village of **(2) Braemar**, a good place to stop for lunch.

After a look at Braemar Castle or a walk up Creag Choinnich, a short drive east on the Aberdeen road will bring you to **(3) Balmoral Castle**, the royal family's holiday home (they usually visit in August). Allow at least two hours for exploring this fascinating royal estate before continuing to the pretty village of **(4) Ballater** for an overnight stop.

Another scenic drive awaits on the following morning, on the famous A939 Cockbridge to Tomintoul road, usually the first to be blocked with snow at the onset of winter. From Tomintoul a B-road leads north to Bridge of Avon on the A95, which runs along the Spey valley with whisky distilleries on every side, to reach **(5) Dufftown**, the whisky capital. From here, it's a 90-minute drive via Elgin to **(6) Inverness**.

# Discover Stirling & Northeast Scotland

Whisky barrels, Speyside
TIM WRIGHT/ALAMY ©

## STIRLING

POP 32,673

With an utterly impregnable position atop a mighty wooded crag (the plug of an extinct volcano), Stirling's beautifully preserved Old Town is a treasure trove of noble buildings and cobbled streets winding up to the ramparts of its dominant castle, which offer views for miles around. Clearly visible is the brooding Wallace Monument, a strange Victorian Gothic creation honouring the legendary freedom fighter of *Braveheart* fame. Nearby is Bannockburn, the scene of Robert the Bruce's major triumph over the English.

The castle makes a fascinating visit, but make sure you also spend time exploring the Old Town and the picturesque path that encircles it. Below the Old Town, retail-minded modern Stirling doesn't offer the same appeal; stick to the high ground as much as possible and you'll love the place.

## ◉ Sights

**STIRLING CASTLE**   Castle
(HS; Map p165; www.historic-scot land.gov.uk; adult/child £13/6.50; ⏱9.30am-6pm Apr-Sep, to 5pm Oct-Mar) Hold Stirling and you control Scotland. This maxim has ensured that a fortress of some kind has existed here since prehistoric times. You cannot help drawing parallels with Edinburgh Castle, but many find Stirling's fortress more atmospheric – the location, architecture, historical significance and utterly commanding views combine to make it a grand and memorable sight. This means it draws plenty of visitors, so it's advisable to visit in the afternoon; many tourists

# Stirling

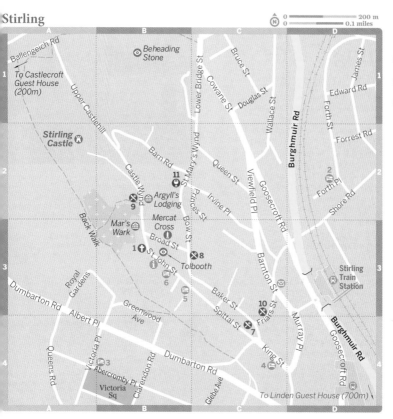

come on day trips, so you may have the castle to yourself by about 4pm.

The current castle dates from the late 14th to the 16th century, when it was a residence of the Stuart monarchs. The undisputed highlight of a visit is the fabulous, recently restored **Royal Palace**. The idea was that it should look brand new, just as when it was constructed by French masons under the orders of James V in the mid-16th century with the aim of impressing his new (also French) bride and other crowned heads of Europe. The suite of six rooms – three for the king, three for the queen – is a sumptuous riot of colour. Particularly notable are the fine fireplaces, the re-created painted oak discs in the ceiling of the king's audience chamber, and the fabulous series of **tapestries** that have

# Stirling Castle

## Planning Your Attack

Stirling's a sizeable fortress, but not so huge that you'll have to decide what to leave out – there's time to see it all. Unless you've got a working knowledge of Scottish monarchs, head to the **Castle Exhibition** ① first: it'll help you sort one James from another. That done, take on the sights at leisure. First, stop and look around you from the **ramparts** ②; the views high over this flat valley, a key strategic point in Scotland's history, are magnificent.

Next, head through to the back of the castle to the **Tapestry Studio** ③, which is open for shorter hours; seeing these skilful weavers at work is a highlight. Track back towards the citadel's heart, stopping for a quick tour through the **Great Kitchens** ④; looking at all that fake food might make you seriously hungry, though. Then enter the main courtyard. Around you are the principal castle buildings. During summer there are events (such as Renaissance dancing) in the **Great Hall** ⑤ – get details at the entrance. The Museum of the Argyll & Sutherland **Highlanders** ⑥ is a treasure trove if you're interested in regimental history, but missable if you're not. Leave the best for last – crowds thin in the afternoon – and enter the sumptuous Royal **Palace** ⑦.

## The Way Up & Down

If you have time, take the atmospheric Back Walk, a peaceful, shady stroll around the Old Town's fortifications and up to the castle's imposing crag-top position. Afterwards, wander down through the Old Town to admire its facades.

### TOP TIPS

**Admission** Entrance is free for Historic Scotland members. If you'll be visiting several Scottish castles and ruins, a membership will save you plenty.

**Vital Statistics** First constructed: before 1110. Number of sieges: at least 9. Last besieger: Bonnie Prince Charlie (unsuccessful). Cost of refurbishing the Royal Palace: £12 million.

DAVID ROBERTSON/ALAMY ©

### Museum of the Argyll & Sutherland Highlanders
The history of one of Scotland's legendary regiments – now subsumed into the Royal Regiment of Scotland – is on display here, featuring memorabilia, weapons and uniforms.

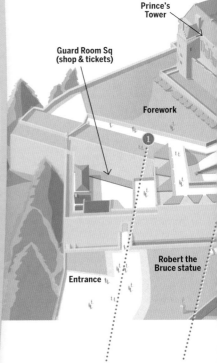

Prince's Tower

Guard Room Sq (shop & tickets)

Forework

Robert the Bruce statue

Entrance

### Castle Exhibition
A great overview of the Stewart dynasty here will get your facts straight, and also offers the latest archaeological titbits from the ongoing excavations under the citadel. Analysis of skeletons has revealed surprising amounts of biographical data.

### Royal Palace
The impressive new highlight of a visit to the castle is this recreation of the royal lodgings originally built by James V. The finely worked ceiling, ornate furniture and sumptuous unicorn tapestries dazzle.

## Great Hall & Chapel Royal

Creations of James IV and VI, respectively, these elegant spaces around the central courtyard have been faithfully restored. The vast Great Hall, with its imposing beamed roof, was the largest medieval hall in Scotland.

**King's Old Building**

**Nether Bailey**

**Grand Battery**

## Tapestry Studio (until late 2013)

An exquisite series of tapestries depicting a unicorn hunt, full of themes with Christian undertones, is being painstakingly reproduced here: each tapestry takes four years to make. It's fascinating to watch the weavers at work.

## Ramparts

Perched on the walls you can appreciate the utter dominance of the castle's position atop this lofty volcanic crag. The view includes the site of Robert the Bruce's victory at Bannockburn and the monument to William Wallace.

## Great Kitchens

Dive into this original display that brings home the massive enterprise of organising, preparing and cooking a feast fit for a Renaissance king. Your stomach may rumble at the lifelike haunches of meat, loaves of bread, fowl and fishes.

been painstakingly woven over many years. Based on originals in New York's Metropolitan Museum of Art, they depict the hunting of a unicorn – an event ripe with Christian metaphor – and are utterly beautiful. Don't miss the palace exterior, studded with beautiful sculptures, or the **Stirling Heads Gallery** above the royal chambers. This has the original oak roundels – a real rogue's gallery of royals, courtiers and classical personalities. In the vaults beneath the palace is a kid-friendly **exhibition** on various aspects of castle life.

The other buildings surrounding the main castle courtyard are the vast **Great Hall**, built by James IV; the **Royal Chapel**, remodelled in the early 17th century by James VI and with the colourful original mural painting intact; and the King's Old Building. This is now home to the **Museum of the Argyll & Sutherland Highlanders** (donations appreciated), which traces the history of this famous regiment from 1794, including its famous defensive action in the Battle of Balaclava in 1854. Make sure you read the moving letters from the World Wars.

Until the last tapestry is completed, probably in late 2013, you can watch the weavers at work in the **Tapestry Studio** at the far end of the castle. It's fascinating to see. Other displays include the **Great Kitchens**, bringing to life the bustle and scale of the enterprise of cooking for the king and, near the entrance, the **Castle Exhibition**, which gives good background information on the Stuart kings and updates on current archaeological investigations. The magnificent vistas from the **ramparts** are stirring.

Admission includes an audioguide, and free guided tours leave regularly from near the entrance. Tours (£2 extra, free for HS members) also run to **Argyll's Lodging**, at the top of Castle Wynd. Complete with turrets, this spectacular lodge is Scotland's most impressive 17th-century town house. It's the former home of William Alexander, Earl of Stirling and noted literary figure. It has been tastefully restored and gives an insight into lavish, 17th-century aristocratic life. There are four or five tours daily (you can't enter by other means).

**OLD TOWN**                     Historic District

Below the castle, the steep Old Town has a remarkably different feel to modern Stirling, its cobblestone streets packed with 15th- to 17th-century architectural

## William Wallace, Scottish Patriot

William Wallace is one of Scotland's greatest heroes, a patriot whose exploits helped revive interest in Scottish history. Born in 1270, he was catapulted into fame and a place in history as a highly successful guerrilla commander who harassed the English invaders for many years.

In the wake of his victory over the English at Stirling Bridge in 1297, Wallace was knighted by Robert the Bruce and proclaimed Guardian of Scotland. However, it was only a short time before English military superiority and the fickle nature of the nobility's loyalties would turn against the defender of Scottish independence.

Disaster struck in July 1298 when King Edward's force defeated the Scots at the Battle of Falkirk. Wallace went into hiding and travelled throughout Europe to drum up support for the Scottish cause. Many of the Scottish nobility were prepared to side with Edward, and Wallace was betrayed after his return to Scotland in 1305, tried for treason at Westminster and hanged, beheaded and disembowelled at Smithfield, London.

DAVID ROBERTSON/PHOTOSHOT ©

## Don't Miss **National Wallace Monument**

Towering over Scotland's narrow waist, this nationalist memorial is so Victorian Gothic it deserves circling bats and ravens. It commemorates the bid for Scottish independence depicted in the film *Braveheart*. From the visitor centre below, walk or shuttle-bus up the hill to the building itself. Once there, break the climb up the narrow staircase inside to admire Wallace's 66 inches of broadsword and see the man himself re-created in a 3D audiovisual display. More staid is the marble pantheon of lugubrious Scottish heroes, but the view from the top over the flat, green gorgeousness of the Forth Valley, including the site of Wallace's 1297 victory over the English at Stirling Bridge, almost justifies the steep entry fee.

Buses 62 and 63 run from Murray Pl in Stirling to the tourist office, otherwise it's a half-hour walk from central Stirling. There's a cafe here.

### NEED TO KNOW

www.nationalwallacemonument.com; adult/child £8.25/5.25; ◷10am-5pm Apr-Jun, Sep & Oct, to 6pm Jul & Aug, 10.30am-4pm Nov-Mar

gems. Its growth began when Stirling became a royal burgh (about 1124), and in the 15th and 16th centuries rich merchants built their houses here.

Stirling has the best surviving **town wall** in Scotland. It was built around 1547 when Henry VIII of England began the 'Rough Wooing' – attacking the town in order to force Mary, Queen of Scots to marry his son so the two kingdoms could be united. The wall can be explored on the **Back Walk**, which follows the line of the wall from Dumbarton Rd to the castle. You pass the town cemeteries (check out the **Star Pyramid**, an outsized affirmation of Reformation values dating from 1863), then the path continues around the back of the castle to Gowan Hill, where you can see the **Beheading Stone**, now encased in iron bars to prevent contemporary use.

169

View of St Andrews from St Rule's Tower (p179)

BOISVIEUX CHRISTOPHE/HEMIS.FR/GETTY IMAGES ©

**Mar's Wark**, on Castle Wynd at the head of the Old Town, is the ornate facade of a Renaissance town house commissioned in 1569 by the wealthy Earl of Mar, regent of Scotland during James VI's minority.

The **Church of the Holy Rude** (Map p165; www.holyrude.org; St John St; admission free; ⏰11am-4pm May-Sep) has been the town's parish church for 600 years and James VI was crowned here in 1567. The nave and tower date from 1456, and the church has one of the few surviving medieval open-timber roofs. Stunning stained-glass windows and huge stone pillars create a powerful effect.

**BANNOCKBURN**　　　　Historic Site

Though Wallace's heroics were significant, it was Robert the Bruce's defeat of the English on 24 June 1314 at Bannockburn, just outside Stirling, that eventually established lasting Scottish nationhood. Exploiting the marshy ground, Bruce won a great tactical victory against a much larger and better-equipped force, and sent Edward II 'homeward, tae think again', as the song 'Flower of Scotland' commemorates.

The **Bannockburn Heritage Centre** (NTS; www.nts.org.uk) is due to reopen after a big refurbishment in spring 2014, in time for the 700th anniversary of the battle.

The battlefield itself (which never closes) will hopefully receive a bit of work too; at present, apart from a statue of the victor astride his horse and a misbegotten flag memorial, there's nothing to see. Bannockburn is 2 miles south of Stirling; you can reach it on bus 51 from Murray Pl in the centre.

 **Sleeping**

There's also a string of B&Bs along Causewayhead Rd, between the centre and the Wallace Monument.

**CASTLECROFT GUEST HOUSE**　B&B ££ (📞01786-474933; www.castlecroft-uk.com; Ballengeich Rd; s/d £50/65; P @ 🛜) Nestling into the hillside under the back of the castle, this great hideaway feels like a rural retreat but is a short, spectacular walk from the heart of historic Stirling. The fabulous lounge and deck area boast extravagant views over green fields to the hills that gird the town, the rooms have excellent modern bathrooms and the welcome couldn't be more hospitable. Breakfast features homemade bread, among other delights.

### NEIDPATH
B&B £

( ☎ 01786-469017; www.neidpath-stirling.co.uk; 24 Linden Ave; s/d £40/58; P 🛜) Offering excellent value and a genuine welcome, this is a fine choice and easily accessed by car. A particularly appealing front room is one of three excellent modernised chambers with fridges and good bathrooms. The owners also run various self-catering options around town; details via the website. It's next to Linden Guest House.

### LINDEN GUEST HOUSE
B&B ££

( ☎ 01786-448850; www.lindenguesthouse.co.uk; 22 Linden Ave; d £60-80; P @ 🛜 👬) The warm welcome and easy parking here offer understandable appeal. The rooms, two of which are great for families, have fridges and posh TVs with DVD players and iPod docks, and the gleaming bathrooms could feature in ads for cleaning products. Breakfast features fresh fruit and kippers, among other choices.

### STIRLING SYHA
Hostel £

(Map p165; ☎ 01786-473442; www.syha.org.uk; St John St; dm/tw £18.75/48; P @ 🛜) Right in the Old Town, this hostel has an unbeatable location and great facilities. Though its facade is that of a former church, the interior is modern and efficient. The dorms are compact but comfortable with lockers and en suite bathrooms; other highlights include a pool table, bike shed and, at busy times, cheap meals on offer. Lack of atmosphere can be the only problem.

### SRUIGHLEA
B&B ££

(Map p165; ☎ 01786-471082; www.sruighlea. com; 27 King St; s/d £40/60; 🛜) This place feels like a secret hideaway – there's no sign – but it's conveniently located smack bang in the centre of town. You'll feel like a local staying here, and there are eating and drinking places practically on the doorstep. It's a B&B that welcomes guests with the kind of warmth that keeps them returning.

### GARFIELD GUESTHOUSE
B&B ££

(Map p165; ☎ 01786-473730; www.garfieldgh. com; 12 Victoria Sq; d small/large £65/70) Though close to the centre of town, Victoria Sq is a quiet oasis, with noble Victorian buildings surrounding a verdant swathe of lawn. The Garfield's huge rooms, bay windows, ceiling roses and other period features make it a winner. There's a great family room, and some rooms have views to the castle towering above.

### FORTH GUEST HOUSE
B&B ££

(Map p165; ☎ 01786-471020; www.forthguesthouse.co.uk; 23 Forth Pl; s/d £50/60; P 🛜) Just a couple of minutes' walk from town, on the other side of the railway, this noble Georgian terrace offers attractive and stylish accommodation at a fair price. The rooms are very commodious, particularly the cute garret rooms with their coombed ceilings and good modern bathrooms. Substantially cheaper in low season.

### STIRLING HIGHLAND HOTEL
Hotel £££

(Map p165; ☎ 01786-272722; www.pumahotels. co.uk; Spittal St; r £130-190; P @ 🛜 ☒) The unusual Stirling Highland Hotel is a sympathetic refurbishment of the old high school. The curious place still feels institutional in parts, but has great facilities that include pool, spa, gym, sauna and squash courts. It's very convenient for the castle and Old Town, service is helpful and the comfortably refitted rooms have decent beds, though they vary widely in size. Deluxe rooms offer the best views but aren't really worth the £50 upgrade. Prices are often lower than listed here.

## ✖ Eating & Drinking

### THE KITCHEN
Bistro ££

(Map p165; ☎ 01786-448833; www.thekitchenstirling.co.uk; 3 Friars St; mains £11-15) Likeable and laid-back on a central pedestrian street, this Stirling newcomer is doing things right. The small slate-floored dining area offers – in particular – excellent fish and seafood options with willing if slow service. It's worth booking ahead at weekends.

# Rob Roy

Nicknamed Red ('*ruadh*' in Gaelic, anglicised to 'roy') for his ginger locks, Robert MacGregor (1671–1734) was the wild leader of the wildest of Scotland's clans. Although they had rights to the lands the clan occupied, these estates stood between powerful neighbours who had the MacGregors outlawed, hence their sobriquet, Children of the Mist. Incognito, Rob became a prosperous livestock trader, before a dodgy deal led to a warrant for his arrest.

A legendary swordsman, the fugitive from justice then became notorious for his daring raids into the Lowlands to carry off cattle and sheep. He was forever hiding from potential captors; he was twice imprisoned, but escaped on both occasions. He finally turned himself in and received his liberty and a pardon from the king. He lies buried in the churchyard at Balquhidder; his uncompromising epitaph reads 'MacGregor despite them'. His life has been glorified over the years due to Walter Scott's novel and the 1995 film. Many Scots see his life as a symbol of the struggle of the common folk against the inequitable ownership of vast tracts of the country by landed aristocrats.

**PORTCULLIS** Pub ££
(Map p165; 01786-472290; www.theportcullis hotel.com; Castle Wynd; bar meals £8-12) Built in stone as solid as the castle that it stands below, this former school is just the spot for a pint and a pub lunch after your castle visit. With bar meals that would have had even William Wallace loosening his belt a couple of notches, a little beer garden and a cosy buzz indoors, it's well worth a visit; there are also rooms here (single/double £69/89).

**BREÁ** Cafe £
(Map p165; www.breastirling.co.uk; 5 Baker St; mains £7-13; 10am-9.30pm Tue-Sun) Bringing a bohemian touch to central Stirling, this has pared-back contemporary decor and a short menu showcasing carefully sourced Scottish produce. Best in show is perhaps the pork burger with apple and black pudding – a huge thing with homemade bread.

**DARNLEY COFFEE HOUSE** Cafe £
(Map p165; 01786-474468; www.darnley. connectfree.co.uk; 18 Bow St; snacks £4-7; breakfast & lunch) Just down the hill from the castle, beyond the end of Broad St, this is a good pit stop for home baking and speciality coffees during a walk around the Old Town. The cafe is in the vaulted cellars of a 16th-century house where Darnley, lover and later husband of Mary, Queen of Scots, once stayed while visiting her.

**SETTLE INN** Pub
(Map p165; 01786-474609; 91 St Mary's Wynd; ) A warm welcome is guaranteed at Stirling's oldest pub (1733), a spot redolent with atmosphere, what with its log fire, vaulted back room and low-slung ceilings. Guest ales, atmospheric nooks for settling in for the night and a blend of local characters make it a classic of its kind.

## Information

**Stirling Community Hospital** (01786-434000; Livilands Rd) South of the town centre.

**Stirling Information Centre** (01786-475019; www.visitscottishheartlands.com; St John St; 10am-5pm; @) At the entrance to the Old Town Jail below the castle.

## Getting There & Away

### Bus

The **bus station** (01786-446474) is on Goosecroft Rd. **Citylink** (0871 266 33 33;

www.citylink.co.uk) offers a number of services to/from Stirling:

**Edinburgh** £7.50, one hour, hourly

**Glasgow** £7, 40 minutes, hourly

Some buses continue to Aberdeen, Inverness and Fort William; more frequently a change will be required.

### Train

First ScotRail (www.scotrail.co.uk) has services to/from a number of destinations, including the following:

**Edinburgh** £7.70, 55 minutes, twice hourly Monday to Saturday, hourly Sunday

**Glasgow** £8, 40 minutes, twice hourly Monday to Saturday, hourly Sunday

# THE TROSSACHS

The Trossachs region has long been a favourite weekend getaway, offering outstanding natural beauty and excellent walking and cycling routes within easy reach of the southern population centres. With thickly forested hills, romantic lochs and an increasingly interesting selection of places to stay and eat, its popularity is sure to continue, protected by its national-park status.

The Trossachs first gained popularity as a tourist destination in the early 19th century, when curious visitors came from all over Britain, drawn by the romantic language of Walter Scott's poem *Lady of the Lake*, inspired by Loch Katrine, and his novel *Rob Roy*, about the derring-do of the region's most famous son.

In summer the Trossachs can be overburdened with people on coach tours, but many of these are day trippers – peaceful, long evenings gazing at the reflections in the

nearest loch are still possible. It's worth timing your visit not to coincide with a weekend.

## Callander

POP 2754

Callander has been pulling in the tourists for over 150 years, and has a laid-back ambience along its main thoroughfare that quickly lulls visitors into lazy pottering. There's also an excellent array of accommodation options here.

## Sights & Activities

The impressive **Bracklinn Falls** are reached by track and footpath from Bracklinn Rd (30 minutes each way from the car park). Also off Bracklinn Rd, a woodland trail leads up to **Callander Crags**, with great views over the surroundings; a return trip from the car park is about 4 miles.

The Trossachs is a lovely area to cycle around. On a cycle route, the excellent

Bracklinn Falls
JOHN MCKENNA/ALAMY ©

**Wheels Cycling Centre** (☎01877-331100; www.wheelscyclingcentre.com) has a wide range of hire bikes starting from £12/18 per half-/full day. To get there, take Bridge St off Main St, then turn right onto Invertrossachs Rd and continue for a mile.

# 🛏 Sleeping

### ROMAN CAMP HOTEL                     Hotel ££

(☎01877-330003; www.romancamphotel.co.uk; Main St; s/d/superior £100/155/195; P 🛜 🐾) Callander's best hotel is centrally located but feels rural, set by the river in its own beautiful grounds, with birdsong the only sound. Its endearing features include a lounge with blazing fire and a library with a tiny secret chapel. Reassuringly, the name refers not to toga parties but to a ruin in the adjacent fields.

### ABBOTSFORD LODGE                      B&B ££

(☎01877-330066; www.abbotsfordlodge. com; Stirling Rd; s/d £50/85; 🕐mid-Feb–mid-Dec; P 🛜) This friendly Victorian house offers something different to the norm, with tartan and florals consigned to the bonfire, replaced by stylish, comfortable contemporary design that enhances the building's original features. Ruffled fabrics and ceramic vases with flower arrangements characterise the renovated rooms. It's on the main road on the eastern side of town.

### ROSLIN COTTAGE                        B&B ££

(☎01877-339787; www.roslincottage.co.uk; Stirling Rd; s £40-50, d £60-70; P 🛜) A characterful cottage that's a haven of good hospitality holds three snug en suite rooms that make an enticing Trossachs base. They all have charm: we love the Kirtle room with the original 17th-century wall exposed. It's on the right as you enter Callander from the east, before the petrol station.

### ARDEN HOUSE                           B&B ££

(☎01877-330235; www.ardenhouse.org.uk; Bracklinn Rd; s/d £45/75; P 🛜) This elegant home has a woodsy, hillside location close to the centre but far from the crowds. The commodious rooms include a suite (£90) with great views. New owners will be in place by the time you read this, but it should definitely still be worth a look.

Loch Katrine

# Eating & Drinking

**CALLANDER MEADOWS**   Scottish ££
(☎ 01877-330181; www.callandermeadows.co.uk; 24 Main St; lunch £8.95, mains £11-18; ☺ Thu-Sun) Informal but smart, this well-loved restaurant in the centre of Callander occupies the two front rooms of a house on the main street. There's a contemporary flair for presentation and unusual flavour combinations, but a solidly British base underpins the cuisine, with things like mackerel, red cabbage, salmon and duck making regular and welcome appearances. There's a great daytime beer/coffee garden out the back, and the restaurant is also open on Mondays from April to September, and daily in high summer.

**MHOR FISH**   Seafood ££
(☎ 01877-330213; www.mhor.net; 75 Main St; fish supper £6, mains £8-14; ☺ noon-9pm Tue-Sun) Both chip shop and fish restaurant, but wholly different, this endearing black-and-white-tiled cafe displays the day's fresh catch. You can choose how you want it cooked, whether pan-seared and accompanied by one of many good wines, or fried and wrapped in paper with chips to take away.

**LADE INN**   Pub
(www.theladeinn.com; Kilmahog; 🚻) Callander's best pub isn't in Callander – it's a mile west of town. They pull a good pint here (the real ales here are brewed to a house recipe), and next door, the owners run a shop with a dazzling selection of Scottish beers.

## ⓘ Information

**Loch Lomond & the Trossachs National Park Visitor Centre** (☎ 01389-722600; www.lochlomond-trossachs.org; 52 Main St; ☺ 9.30am-3.30pm Mon & Wed-Thu, 9.30am-4.30pm Tue & Fri) This place is a useful centre for specific information on the park. Closes half an hour for lunch.

**Rob Roy & Trossachs Information Centre** (☎ 01877-330342; www.visitscottishheartlands.com; Ancaster Sq; ☺ 10am-5pm Apr-Oct, to 4pm Nov-Mar; @) This centre has heaps of info on the area. There's a 20-minute film on Rob Roy that costs £1.50.

## ⓘ Getting There & Away

**First** (☎ 0871 200 2233; www.firstgroup.com) operates buses from Stirling (45 minutes, hourly Monday to Saturday, every two hours Sunday), while **Kingshouse** (☎ 01877-384768; www.kingshousetravel.com) buses run from Killin (45 minutes, two to six daily). For Aberfoyle, get off a Stirling-bound bus at Blair Drummond safari park and cross the road. There are also **Citylink** (www.citylink.co.uk) buses from Edinburgh to Oban or Fort William via Callander (£15.60, 1¾ hours, two daily).

## Loch Katrine

This rugged area, 6 miles north of Aberfoyle and 10 miles west of Callander, is the heart of the Trossachs. From April to October two **boats** (☎ 01877-376315; www.lochkatrine.com; Trossachs Pier; 1hr cruise adult/child £12/8) run cruises from Trossachs Pier at the eastern tip of Loch Katrine. One of these is the fabulous centenarian steamship *Sir Walter Scott*; check the website to see which boats depart when, as it's worth going on the veteran if you can. They run various one-hour afternoon sailings, and at 10.30am (and 2pm from June to August) there's a departure to Stronachlachar at the other end of the loch before returning (single/return adult £13/15.50, child £8/9.50, two hours return). From Stronachlachar (also accessible by car via Aberfoyle), you can reach the eastern shore of Loch Lomond at isolated Inversnaid.

## Balquhidder & Around

North of Callander, you'll skirt past the shores of gorgeous Loch Lubnaig. Not as famous as some of its cousins, it's still well worth a stop for its sublime views of forested hills. In the small village of **Balquhidder** (ball-whidder), 9 miles north of Callander off the A84, there's a churchyard with **Rob Roy's grave**. It's an appropriately beautiful spot in a deep, winding glen in big-sky country.

**Monachyle Mhor** (☎ 01877-384622; www.mhor.net; d £195-265; ☺ Feb-Dec; 🅿 📶 🚻 🐾),

4 miles on, is a luxury hideaway in a fantastically peaceful location overlooking two lochs. It's a great fusion of country Scotland and contemporary attitudes to design and food. The rooms are superb and feature quirkily original decor, and the restaurant serves à-la-carte lunches and five-course dinners (£50) which are high in quality, sustainably sourced, and deliciously innovative. Enchantment lies in its successful combination of top-class hospitality with a relaxed rural atmosphere; dogs and kids happily romp on the lawns, and no-one looks askance if you come in flushed and muddy after a day's fishing or walking.

Local buses between Callander and Killin stop at the main road turn-off to Balquhidder, as do daily **Citylink** (www.citylink.co.uk) buses between Edinburgh and Oban/Fort William.

# Killin

POP 666

A fine base for the Trossachs or Perthshire, this lovely village sits at the western end of Loch Tay and has a spread-out, relaxed sort of feel, particularly around the scenic **Falls of Dochart**, which tumble through the centre. On a sunny day people sprawl over the rocks by the bridge with a pint or a picnic. Killin offers some fine walking around the town, and mighty mountains and glens close at hand.

 **Sleeping & Eating**

### FAIRVIEW HOUSE
B&B ££

(📞01567-820667; www.fairview-killin.co.uk; Main St; s £32, d £60-70; P 📶) Very cosy rooms, all with en suite or private bathroom, and very fair prices characterise this handsome and cordial central guest house. There's a pleasant guest lounge, drying room and bike shed. The name doesn't lie; there are lovely perspectives over the surrounding hills from many of the rooms.

### FALLS OF DOCHART INN
Pub ££

(📞01567-820270; www.falls-of-dochart-inn.co.uk; mains £10-13; 📶) In a prime position overlooking the falls, this is a terrific pub, a snug, atmospheric space with a roaring fire, personable service and really satisfying, great-value food, ranging from light meals to tasty, tender steaks and a couple

Scone Palace

DEA/W. BUSS/GETTY IMAGES ©

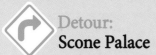

# Detour:
## Scone Palace

'So thanks to all at once and to each one, whom we invite to see us crowned at Scone.' This line from *Macbeth* indicates the importance of this place (pronounced 'skoon'), 2 miles north of Perth. **Scone Palace** (www.scone-palace.co.uk; adult/child/family £10/7/30; ☺9.30am-5pm Apr-Oct, closes 4.30pm Sat) itself was built in 1580 on the site where, in 838, Kenneth MacAlpin became the first king of a united Scotland and brought the Stone of Destiny (p83), on which Scottish kings were ceremonially invested, to Moot Hill. In 1296 Edward I of England carted the talisman off to Westminster Abbey, where it remained for 700 years before being returned to Scotland. These days, Scone doesn't really conjure up hoary days of bearded warrior-kings swearing oaths in the mist, however, as the palace, rebuilt in the early 19th century, is a Georgian mansion of extreme elegance and luxury.

The visit takes you through a succession of sumptuous **rooms** filled with fine French furniture and noble artworks. There's an astonishing collection of porcelain and fine portraits, as well as a series of exquisite Vernis Martin papier-mâché. Scone has belonged for centuries to the Murray family, earls of Mansfield, and many of the objects have a fascinating history (friendly guides are on hand to elaborate). Each room has comprehensive multilingual information; there are also panels relating histories of some of the Scottish kings crowned at Scone over the centuries.

Outside, peacocks – all named after a monarch – strut around the magnificent **grounds**, which incorporate woods, a butterfly garden, and a maze.

of more advanced creations. The rooms (single/double from £60/80) are handsome but a few glitches like poor heating let some of them down.

## ⓘ Getting There & Away

Two daily Citylink (www.citylink.co.uk) buses between Edinburgh and Oban/Fort William stop here; two buses from Dundee to Oban also pass through. These buses stop in Crianlarich among other places. Kingshouse (☏01877-384768; www.kingshousetravel.com) runs buses to Callander, where you can change to a Stirling service.

# ST ANDREWS
POP 14,209

For a small place, St Andrews made a big name for itself, firstly as religious centre, then as Scotland's oldest university town. But its status as the home of golf has propelled it to even greater fame, and today's pilgrims arrive with a set of clubs. But it's a lovely place to visit even if you've no interest in the game, with impressive medieval ruins, stately university buildings, idyllic white sands and excellent accommodation and eating options.

## History

St Andrews is said to have been founded by St Regulus, who arrived from Greece in the 4th century bringing the bones of St Andrew, Scotland's patron saint. The town soon grew into a major pilgrimage centre and St Andrews developed into the ecclesiastical capital of the country. The university, the first in Scotland, was founded in 1410.

Golf has been played here for more than 600 years; the game's governing body was founded here in 1754 and the imposing Royal & Ancient clubhouse was built 100 years later.

##  Sights

**ST ANDREWS CATHEDRAL**              Ruin
(HS; Map p178; www.historic-scotland.gov.uk; The Pends; adult/child £4.50/2.70, incl castle

177

# St Andrews

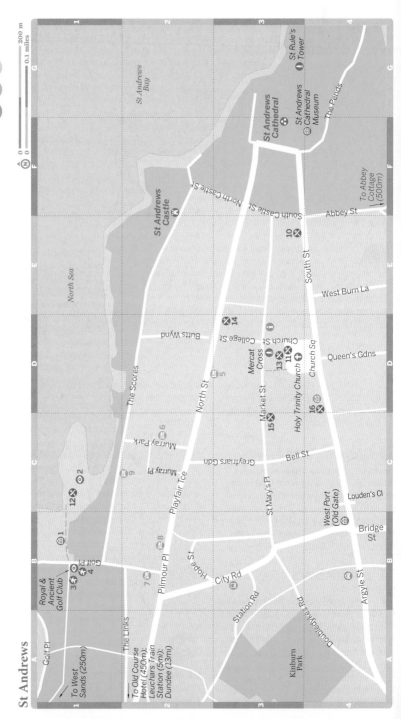

# St Andrews

£7.60/4.60; ⊘9.30am-5.30pm Apr-Sep, to 4.30pm Oct-Mar) The ruins of this cathedral are all that's left of one of Britain's most magnificent medieval buildings. You can appreciate the scale and majesty of the edifice from the small sections that remain standing. Although founded in 1160, it was not consecrated until 1318, but stood as the focus of this important pilgrimage centre until 1559, when it was pillaged during the Reformation.

St Andrew's supposed bones lie under the altar; until the cathedral was built, they had been enshrined in the nearby Church of St Regulus (Rule). All that remains of this church is **St Rule's Tower**, worth the climb for the view across St Andrews. There's also a **museum** with a collection of Celtic crosses and gravestones found on the site. The entrance fee only applies for the tower and museum; you can wander freely around the ruins, a fine picnic spot.

**ST ANDREWS CASTLE**　Castle
(HS; Map p178; www.historic-scotland.gov.uk; The Scores; adult/child £5.50/3.30, incl cathedral

£7.60/4.60; ⊘9.30am-5.30pm Apr-Sep, to 4.30pm Oct-Mar) With dramatic coastline views, the castle is mainly in ruins, but the site itself is evocative. It was founded about 1200 as the bishop's fortified home. After the execution of Protestant reformers in 1545, other reformers retaliated by murdering Cardinal Beaton and taking over the castle. They spent almost a year holed up, during which they and their attackers dug a complex of **siege tunnels**; you can walk along their damp mossy lengths. A tourist office gives an audiovisual introduction and has a collection of Pictish stones.

**THE SCORES**　Street
From the castle, the Scores follows the coast west down to the first tee at the Old Course. Family-friendly **St Andrews Aquarium** (Map p178; www.standrewsaquarium.co.uk; adult/child £8/6; ⊘10am-5pm Mar-Oct, to 4.30pm Nov-Feb; ⊞) has a seal pool, rays and sharks from Scottish waters and exotic tropical favourites. Once introduced to our finny friends, you can snack on them with chips in the cafe.

Nearby, the **British Golf Museum** (Map p178; www.britishgolfmuseum.co.uk; Bruce Embankment; adult/child £6/3; ⊘9.30am-5pm Mon-Sat, 10am-5pm Sun Apr-Oct, 10am-4pm Nov-Mar) has an extraordinarily comprehensive overview of the history and development of the game and the role of St Andrews in it. Favourite fact: bad players were formerly known as 'foozlers'.

Opposite the museum is the **Royal & Ancient Golf Club**, which stands proudly at the head of the Old Course (p180). Beside it stretches **West Sands** beach, made famous by the film *Chariots of Fire*.

# 🛏 Sleeping

St Andrews' accommodation is overpriced and often heavily booked (especially in summer), so reserve in advance. Almost every house on super-central Murray Park and Murray Pl is a guest house.

**ABBEY COTTAGE**　B&B ££
(☎01334-473727; coull@lineone.net; Abbey Walk; s £45, d £65-70; ℗☞) You know you've

# Playing the Old Course

Golf has been played at St Andrews since the 15th century. By 1457 it was so popular that James II placed a ban on it because it interfered with his troops' archery practice. Although it lies beside the exclusive, all-male-membership Royal & Ancient Golf Club, the **Old Course** (Map p178; ☎01334-466666; www. standrews.org.uk; Reservations Office, St Andrews Links Trust) is public.

You'll need to book in advance to play via **St Andrews Links Trust** (☎01334-466666; www.standrews.org.uk). Reservations open on the first Wednesday in September the year before you wish to play. No bookings are taken for Saturdays or the month of September.

Unless you've booked months in advance, getting a tee-off time is literally a lottery; enter the ballot at the **caddie office** (Map p178; ☎01334-466666) before 2pm two days before you wish to play (there's no Sunday play). Be warned that applications by ballot are normally heavily oversubscribed, and green fees are £150 in summer. Singles are not accepted in the ballot and should start queuing as early as possible on the day – 5am is good – in the hope of joining a group. You'll need a handicap certificate (24/36 for men/women).

**Guided walks** (£2.50) of the Old Course run Tuesday to Sunday in July and August, and hit famous landmarks such as the Swilcan Bridge and the Road Hole bunker. They run from outside the shop by the 18th green at 11am and 1.30pm and last 50 minutes. On Sunday, a three-hour walk (£5) takes you around the whole course.

strayed from B&B mainstream when your charming host's hobby is photographing tigers in the wild – don't leave without browsing her albums. This engaging spot sits below the town, surrounded by stone walls that enclose a rambling garden; it feels like you're staying in the country. There are three excellent rooms, all different, with patchwork quilts, sheepskins and antique furniture.

**FAIRWAYS OF ST ANDREWS**   B&B ££
(Map p178; ☎01334-479513; www.fairwaysof standrews.co.uk; 8a Golf Pl; s £80-120, d £90-150; ☎) Just around the corner from golf's most famous 18th green, this is more of a boutique hotel than a B&B. There are just three super-stylish rooms; the best on the top floor is huge and has its own balcony with views over the Old Course.

**OLD COURSE HOTEL**   Hotel £££
(☎01334-474371; www.oldcoursehotel.co.uk; Old Station Rd; d with/without view £460/410, ste £745; P@☎☎) A byword for golfing luxury, this hotel is right alongside the famous 17th hole and has huge rooms, excellent service and a raft of facilities, including a spa complex. Fork out the extra £50 or so for a view over the Old Course. You can usually find better deals online than the rack rates we list here.

**HAZELBANK HOTEL**   Hotel ££
(Map p178; ☎01334-472466; www.hazelbank. com; 28 The Scores; s £69-89, d £99-151; @☎) Offering a genuine welcome, the family-run Hazelbank is the most likeable of the pleasingly old-fashioned hotels along the Scores. The front rooms have marvellous views along the beach and out to sea; those at the back are cheaper. Prices drop significantly outside the height of summer.

**FIVE PILMOUR PLACE**   B&B ££
(Map p178; ☎01334-478665; ww.5pilmourplace. com; 5 Pilmour Pl; s £78, d £120-160; @☎) Just around the corner from the Old Course, this luxurious and intimate spot offers stylish, compact rooms with an eclectic

range of styles as well as modern conveniences such as flatscreen TVs and DVD players. The king-size beds are especially comfortable, and the lounge area is a stylish treat.

## ASLAR HOUSE
B&B ££

(Map p178; 📞01334-473460; www.aslar.com; 120 North St; s/d/ste £50/96/100; ⊙Feb–mid-Nov; 🛜) The rooms are so impeccable at this place that it's frightening to imagine how much work goes on behind the scenes. The modern comforts don't detract from the house's historical features (including a whimsical turret room) but certainly add value. IPod docks, hair straighteners and DVD players in every room are complemented by fabulous new bathrooms. The master suite is very spacious and a good extra investment. No under-16s.

## CAMERON HOUSE
B&B ££

(Map p178; 📞01334-472306; www.cameron house-sta.co.uk; 11 Murray Park; s/d £45/90; 🛜) Beautifully decorated rooms and warm, cheerful hosts make this a real home away from home on this guest house–filled street. The two single rooms share

a bathroom. Prices drop £10 per person outside high season.

# 🍴 Eating

## VINE LEAF
Scottish £££

(Map p178; 📞01334-477497; www.vineleafstand rews.co.uk; 131 South St; 2-course dinner £26.50; ⊙dinner Tue-Sat; 🍴) Classy, comfortable and well-established, the friendly Vine Leaf offers a changing menu of sumptuous Scottish seafood, game and vegetarian dishes. There's a huge selection within the set-price menu, all well presented, and an interesting, mostly old-world wine list. It's down a close off South St.

## 🐟 SEAFOOD RESTAURANT
Seafood £££

(Map p178; 📞01334-479475; www.theseafoodres taurant.com; The Scores; lunch/dinner £22/45) The Seafood Restaurant occupies a stylish glass-walled room, built out over the sea, with plush navy carpet, crisp white linen, an open kitchen and panoramic views of St Andrews Bay. It offers top seafood and an excellent wine list. Look out for its special winter deals.

Scottish seafood

### DOLL'S HOUSE                    Scottish ££

(Map p178; 📞 01334-477422; www.dolls-house.co.uk; 3 Church Sq; mains £13-15) With its high-backed chairs, bright colours and creaky wooden floor, the Doll's House blends a Victorian child's bedroom with modern stylings. The result is a surprising warmth and no pretensions. The menu makes the most of local fish and other Scottish produce, and the £6.95 two-course lunch is unbeatable value. The early evening two-course deal for £12.95 isn't bad, either.

### THE GLASS HOUSE    Italian, Scottish ££

(Map p178; www.glasshouse-restaurant.co.uk; 80 North St; mains £7-15; 🕙noon-9pm) Casual but comfortable, this restaurant offers plenty of light in its split-level, open-kitchen dining area. The menu is basically Italian, with attractively presented pizzas and pastas popular with students. But a handful of daily specials offer more Scottish meat and game choices of notable quality.

### THE CAFÉ IN THE SQUARE        Cafe £

(Map p178; 4 Church Sq; light meals £4-7; 🕙10.30am-4.30pm Mon-Sat) Hidden away down the side of the library, this upbeat wee coffee stop also makes a good venue for a light lunch, with sandwiches, panini and salads and a couple of secluded picnic tables out the back.

### 🖉 THE TAILEND               Seafood £

(Map p178; www.tailendfishbar.co.uk; 130 Market St; takeaway/eat in £6/10.50; 🕙11.30am-10pm) Delicious fresh fish sourced from Arbroath, just up the coast, puts this a class above most chippies. It fries to order and it's worth the wait. The array of exquisite smoked delicacies at the counter will have you planning a picnic or fighting for a table in the licensed cafe out the back.

### B JANNETTA                  Ice Cream £

(Map p178; 📞 01334-473285; www.jannettas.co.uk; 31 South St; 1/2 scoop cone £1.40/2; 🕙Mon-Sat) B Jannetta is a St Andrews institution, offering 52 varieties of ice cream, from the weird (Irn-Bru sorbet) to the decadent (strawberries-and-champagne).

## 🛈 Information

**St Andrews Community Hospital** ( 📞 01334-465656; www.nhsfife.org; Largo Rd)

River Tummel, Pitlochry (p185)

# Detour:
## Glamis Castle & Village

Looking every inch the Scottish Baronial castle, with its roofline sprouting a forest of pointed turrets and battlements, **Glamis Castle** (www.glamis-castle.co.uk; adult/child £9.75/7.25; ⊙10am-6pm Mar-Oct, 10.30am-4.30pm Nov & Dec, closed Jan-Feb) claims to be the legendary setting for Shakespeare's *Macbeth*. A royal residence since 1372, it is the family home of the earls of Strathmore and Kinghorne – the Queen Mother (born Elizabeth Bowes-Lyon; 1900–2002) spent her childhood at Glamis (pronounced 'glams') and Princess Margaret (the queen's sister; 1930–2002) was born here.

Hour-long guided tours depart every 15 minutes (last tour at 4.30pm, or 3.30pm in winter).

The **Angus Folk Museum** (NTS; Kirkwynd; adult/child £6/5; ⊙10.30am-4.30pm Thu-Mon Jul & Aug, 11.30am-4.30pm Sat-Mon Apr-Jun, Sep & Oct), in a row of 18th-century cottages just off the flower-bedecked square in Glamis village, houses a fine collection of domestic and agricultural relics.

Glamis Castle is 12 miles north of Dundee. There are two to four buses a day from Dundee (35 minutes) to Glamis; some continue to Kirriemuir.

**St Andrews Information Centre** (☎01334-472021; www.visit-standrews.co.uk; 70 Market St; ⊙9.15am-6pm Mon-Sat, 10am-5pm Sun Jul & Aug, 9.15am-5pm Mon-Sat Sep-Jun, plus 11am-4pm Sun Apr-Jun, Sep & Oct; @) Helpful staff with good knowledge of St Andrews and Fife.

## ℹ Getting There & Away

### Bus

All buses leave from the bus station on Station Rd. There are frequent services to the following:

**Anstruther** 40 minutes, regularly

**Crail** 30 minutes, regularly

**Edinburgh** £9.50, two hours, hourly

**Glasgow** £9.95, 2½ hours, hourly

**Stirling** £7.45, two hours, every two hours Monday to Saturday

### Train

There is no train station in St Andrews itself, but you can take a train from Edinburgh to Leuchars (£12.60, one hour, hourly), 5 miles to the northwest. From here, buses leave regularly for St Andrews.

## ℹ Getting Around

To order a cab, call **Golf City Taxis** (☎01334-477788). A taxi between Leuchars train station and the town centre costs around £12.

**Spokes** (☎01334-477835; www.spokescycles.com; 37 South St; per half-/full day/week £8.50/13.50/60; ⊙9am-5.30pm Mon-Sat) hires out mountain bikes.

# EAST NEUK OF FIFE

This charming stretch of coast runs south from St Andrews to the point at Fife Ness, then west to Leven. Neuk is an old Scots word for corner, and it's an appealing nook to investigate, with picturesque fishing villages and coastal walks; the Fife Coastal Path's most scenic stretches are in this area. It's easily visited from St Andrews, but also makes a pleasant place to stay.

## Crail
POP 1695

Pretty and peaceful, little Crail has a much-photographed stone-sheltered harbour surrounded by wee cottages with red-tiled roofs. You can buy lobster and crab from a **kiosk** (⊙lunch Sat & Sun) there. The benches in the nearby grassed area are perfectly placed for eating while admiring the view across to the Isle of May.

The village's history and involvement with the fishing industry is outlined in the **Crail Museum** (www.crailmuseum.org.uk; 62 Marketgate; admission free; ⏱10am-1pm & 2-5pm Mon-Sat, 2-5pm Sun Jun-Sep, Sat & Sun only Apr & May), which also offers tourist information.

Crail is 10 miles southeast of St Andrews. **Stagecoach** (www.stagecoachbus.com) bus 95 between Leven, Anstruther, Crail and St Andrews passes through Crail hourly every day (30 minutes to St Andrews).

## Anstruther
POP 3442

Once among Scotland's busiest ports, cheery Anstruther has ridden the tribulations of the declining fishing industry better than some, and now has a very pleasant mixture of bobbing boats, historic streets and visitors ambling around the harbour grazing on fish and chips or contemplating a trip to the Isle of May.

## ◉ Sights

The displays at the excellent **Scottish Fisheries Museum** (www.scotfishmuseum.org; adult/child £6/free; ⏱10am-5.30pm Mon-Sat, 11am-5pm Sun Apr-Sep, 10am-4.30pm Mon-Sat, noon-4.30pm Sun Oct-Mar) include the **Zulu Gallery**, which houses the huge, partly restored hull of a traditional Zulu-class fishing boat, redolent with the scent of tar and timber. Afloat in the harbour outside the museum lies the *Reaper*, a fully restored Fifie-class fishing boat built in 1902.

## 🛏 Sleeping & Eating

**THE SPINDRIFT**   B&B ££
(☎01333-310573; www.thespindrift.co.uk; Pittenweem Rd; s/d £60/80; P 🛜 🐾) Arriving from the west, there's no need to go further than Anstruther's first house on the left, a redoubt of Scottish cheer and warm hospitality. The rooms are elegant, classy and extremely comfortable – some have views across to Edinburgh and one is like a ship's cabin, courtesy of the sea captain who once owned the house.

**THE BANK**   Inn ££
(☎01333-310189; www.thebank-anstruther.co.uk; 23 High St; s/d £50/100; 🛜) Refitted rooms at this modernised central pub offer loads of space, big beds and great bathrooms. The building itself backs onto the river mouth, meaning pleasant views from many of the chambers. The bar is enticing, with tables out the back, though its proximity means you might be better off in the lower rooms (7 and 8) at weekends. Prices are usually substantially lower than we list here.

The *Reaper*, Scottish Fisheries Museum
PHIL SEALE/ALAMY ©

## CRICHTON HOUSE

B&B ££

(☎ 01333-310219; www.crichtonhouse.com; High St W; d £70-80; P 🛜) You'll spot this B&B on the right as you approach the centre of town from the west. Sparklingly clean rooms with fresh fruit and slate-floored bathrooms are complemented by a cheery host and plenty of breakfast options. Enter via the wooden stairs at the side of the house.

## CELLAR RESTAURANT

Seafood £££

(☎ 01333-310378; www.cellaranstruther.co.uk; 24 East Green; 2-/3-course set dinner £35/40; ⏱ lunch Fri & Sat, dinner Tue-Sat) Tucked away in an alley behind the museum, the Cellar is famous for its seafood and fine wines. Try the local crab, lobster or whatever delicacies they've brought in that day. Inside it's elegant and upmarket. Advance bookings are essential.

## 🏷 WEE CHIPPY

Fish & Chips £

(4 Shore St; fish supper £5.50) The Anstruther Fish Bar is one of Britain's best chippies, but we – and plenty of locals – reckon this one might be even better. The fish is of a very high quality and there's less of a queue too. Eat your catch by the water.

## ⓘ Information

Anstruther Information Centre (☎ 01333-311073; www.visitfife.com; Harbourhead; ⏱ 10am-5pm Mon-Sat, 11am-4pm Sun Apr-Oct) The best tourist office in East Neuk.

## ⓘ Getting There & Away

Stagecoach (www.stagecoachbus.com) bus 95 runs daily from Leven (more departures from St Monans) to Anstruther and on to St Andrews (40 minutes, hourly) via Crail.

# PERTHSHIRE

## Pitlochry

POP 2564

Pitlochry, with its air smelling of the Highlands, is a popular stop on the way north and a convenient base for exploring northern central Scotland. On a quiet

## Detour:
# Gleneagles

Deep in rural Perthshire, near the town of Auchterarder, one of Scotland's most famous lodgings can be found: the **Gleneagles Hotel** (☎ 01764-662231; www.gleneagles. com; d £435-535; P @ 🛜 ⛱ 🛝). Not your typical B&B, this is a no-holds-barred luxury spot with three championship golf courses, Andrew Fairlie at Gleneagles – often referred to as Scotland's best restaurant (open for dinner Tuesday to Saturday) – and a variety of extravagantly elegant rooms and suites designed to cope with anything from a serious romantic splash-out to a royal family in exile. Despite the imposing building and kilted staff snapping to attention, it's welcoming to non-VIPs and it's family-friendly to boot, with lots of activities available. There's Gleneagles train station if you wish to arrive sustainably; if not, limousine transfers are available. Check the website for deals. Gleneagles is the venue for the 2014 Ryder Cup.

spring evening it's a pretty place with salmon jumping in the Tummel and good things brewing at the Moulin Hotel. In summer the main street can be a conga line of tour groups, but get away from that and it'll still charm you.

## ⊙ Sights

One of Pitlochry's attractions is its beautiful **riverside**; the River Tummel is dammed here, and you can watch salmon swimming (not jumping) up a **fish ladder** to the loch above.

### BELL'S BLAIR ATHOL DISTILLERY · Distillery

(☏01796-482003; www.discovering-distilleries.com; Perth Rd; tour £6; ⏰daily Apr-Oct, Mon-Fri Nov-Mar) One of two distilleries around Pitlochry, this one is at the southern end of town. Tours focus on whisky making and blending. More detailed private tours give you greater insights and superior tastings.

## 🛏 Sleeping & Eating

### CRAIGATIN HOUSE · Guest House ££

(☏01796-472478; www.craigatinhouse.co.uk; 165 Atholl Rd; s £75, d standard/deluxe £85/95; ⏰mid-Jan-Oct; P@🛜) Several times more tasteful than the average Pitlochry lodging, this noble house and garden is set back from the main road. Chic contemporary fabrics covering expansive beds offer a standard of comfort above and beyond the reasonable price; the rooms in the converted stable block are particularly

---

## Pass of Killiecrankie

Drop into the **Killiecrankie visitor centre** (NTS; ☏01796-473233; www.nts.org.uk; admission free, parking £2; ⏰10am-5.30pm Apr-Oct) in this beautiful, rugged gorge, 3.5 miles north of Pitlochry. It has great interactive displays on the Jacobite rebellion and local flora and fauna. There's plenty to touch, pull and open – great for kids. There are some stunning walks into the wooded gorge, too; keep an eye out for red squirrels. Also here, **Highland Fling** (☏0845 366 5844; www.bungeejumpscotland.co.uk; £70, repeat jumps £30) offers breathtaking 40m jumps off the bridge over the gorge at weekends, plus Wednesday and Friday in summer.

Buses run between Pitlochry and Blair Atholl via Killie-crankie (10 minutes, three to seven daily).

---

inviting. A fabulous breakfast and lounge area gives perspectives over the lush garden. Breakfast choices include whisky-laced porridge, smoked-fish omelettes and apple pancakes. Kids not allowed.

### MOULIN HOTEL · Pub ££

(☏01796-472196; www.moulinhotel.co.uk; bar mains £9-12) A mile away but a world apart, this atmospheric hotel was trading centuries before the tartan tack came to Pitlochry. With its romantic low ceilings, ageing wood and booth seating, the inn is a great spot for a house-brewed ale or a portion of Highland comfort food: try the filling haggis or venison stew. The best way to get here from Pitlochry is walking: it's a pretty uphill stroll through green fields, and an easy roll down the slope afterwards.

### ASHLEIGH · B&B £

(☏01796-470316; www.realbandbpitlochry.co.uk; 120 Atholl Rd; s/d £30/50; 🛜) Genuine welcomes don't come much better than Nancy's, and her place on the main street makes a top Pitlochry pit stop. Three comfortable rooms share an excellent bathroom, and there's an open kitchen stocked with goodies where you make your own breakfast. A home away from home and a standout budget choice. She also has a good self-catering apartment with great views, available by the night.

### KNOCKENDARROCH HOUSE · Hotel ££

(☏01796-473473; www.knockendarroch.co.uk; Higher Oakfield; d dinner, bed & breakfast £188; P🛜👪) Top of the town and boasting the best views, this genteel, well-run hotel has a range of luxurious rooms with huge windows that take advantage of the Highland light. The standard rooms have better views than the larger, slightly pricier superior ones. A couple of rooms have great little balconies, perfect for a sundowner. Meals are highly commended here.

## ⭐ Entertainment

### PITLOCHRY FESTIVAL THEATRE · Theatre

(☏01796-484626; www.pitlochry.org.uk; Foss Rd; tickets £26-35) This well-known and loved theatre has a summer season of

GÜNTER LENZ/IMAGEBROKER ©

## Don't Miss **Blair Castle**

One of the most popular tourist attractions in Scotland, magnificent Blair Castle and the 108 square miles it sits on, is the seat of the Duke of Atholl, head of the Murray clan. It's an impressive white building set beneath forested slopes above the River Garry.

The original tower was built in 1269, but the castle has undergone significant remodelling since. Thirty rooms are open to the public and they present a wonderful picture of upper-class Highland life from the 16th century on. The dining room is sumptuous – check out the nine-pint wine glasses – and the ballroom is a vaulted chamber that's a virtual stag cemetery.

The current duke visits the castle every May to review the Atholl Highlanders, Britain's only private army.

Blair Atholl is 6 miles northwest of Pitlochry, and the castle a further mile beyond it. Local buses run between Pitlochry and Blair Atholl (25 minutes, three to seven daily). Four buses a day (Monday to Saturday) go directly to the castle. There's a train station in the village, but not all trains stop here.

### NEED TO KNOW

☎ 01796-481207; www.blair-castle.co.uk; adult/child/family £9.50/5.70/25.75; ⏰ 9.30am-5.30pm Apr-Oct, 10am-4pm Sat & Sun Nov-Mar

---

several different plays daily except Sunday, from May to mid-October.

## ℹ Information

**Pitlochry Information Centre** ( ☎ 01796-472215; www.perthshire.co.uk; 22 Atholl Rd;

⏰ daily Mar-Oct, Mon-Sat Nov-Feb; @ ) Good information on local walks.

## ℹ Getting There & Away

**Citylink** (www.citylink.co.uk) buses run roughly hourly to Inverness (£15.50, two hours), Perth

(£10, 40 minutes), Edinburgh (£15.50, two to 2½ hours) and Glasgow (£15.70, 2¼ hours). Megabus (☎0871 266 3333; www.megabus.com) discount services also run these routes.

Stagecoach (www.stagecoachbus.com) runs to Aberfeldy (30 minutes, hourly Monday to Saturday, three Sunday), Dunkeld (25 minutes, up to 10 daily Monday to Saturday) and Perth (one hour, up to 10 daily Monday to Saturday).

Pitlochry is on the main railway from Perth (£12.30, 30 minutes, nine daily Monday to Saturday, five on Sunday) to Inverness.

# ROYAL DEESIDE

The valley of the **River Dee** – often called **Royal Deeside** because of the royal family's long association with the area – stretches west from Aberdeen to Braemar, closely paralleled by the A93 road. From Deeside north to Strathdon is serious castle country – there are more examples of fanciful Scottish Baronial architecture here than anywhere else in Scotland.

# Ballater
POP 1450

The attractive little village of Ballater owes its 18th-century origins to the curative waters of nearby Pannanich Springs (now bottled commercially as Deeside Natural Mineral Water) and its prosperity to nearby Balmoral Castle.

The **tourist office** (☎01339-755306; Station Sq; ⏰9am-6pm Jul & Aug, 10am-5pm Sep-Jun) is in the Old Royal Station.

## 🎯 Sights & Activities

When Queen Victoria travelled to Balmoral Castle she would alight from the royal train at Ballater's **Old Royal Station** (☎01339-755306; Station Sq; admission £2; ⏰9am-6pm Jul & Aug, 10am-5pm Sep-Jun). The station has been beautifully restored and now houses the tourist office, a cafe

and a museum with a replica of Victoria's royal coach. Note the crests on the shop fronts along the main street proclaiming 'By Royal Appointment' – the village is a major supplier of provisions to Balmoral.

As you approach Ballater from the east the hills start to close in, and there are many pleasant walks in the surrounding area. The steep woodland walk up Craigendarroch (400m) takes just over one hour. Morven (871m) is a more serious prospect, taking about six hours, but offers good views from the top; ask at the tourist office for more info.

## 🛏 Sleeping & Eating

**AULD KIRK**                                          Hotel **££**
( ☎ 01339-755762; www.theauldkirk.com; Braemar Rd; s/d from £73/110; **P** 🛜) Here's something a little out of the ordinary – a six-bedroom 'restaurant with rooms' housed in a converted 19th-century church. The interior blends original

features with sleek modern decor, and the stylish Scottish restaurant (two-/three-course dinner £29/36) serves local lamb, venison and seafood.

**GREEN INN**                                          B&B **££**
( ☎ 01339-755701; www.green-inn.com; 9 Victoria Rd; B&B per person from £40; **P**) This lovely old house dotted with plush armchairs and sofas has three comfortable en suite bedrooms, but the accent is on fine dining. The menu includes French-influenced dishes such as roast quail with crayfish, truffle and wild mushrooms. A three-course dinner costs £43, served from 7pm till 9pm Tuesday to Saturday.

**HABITAT**                                            Hostel **£**
( ☎ 013397-53752; www.habitat-at-ballater.com; Bridge Sq; dm/tw £20/45; 🚻) Tucked up a lane near the bridge over the River Dee, Habitat is an attractive and eco-friendly hostel with three eight-bed bunk rooms (with personal lockers and reading lamps), and a comfortable lounge with big, soft sofas and a wood-burning stove.

**189**

PATRICIA HOFMEESTER/SHUTTERSTOCK ©

## Don't Miss **Balmoral Castle**

Eight miles west of Ballater lies Balmoral Castle, the queen's Highland holiday home, screened from the road by a thick curtain of trees. Built for Queen Victoria in 1855 as a private residence for the royal family, it kicked off the revival of the Scottish Baronial style of architecture that characterises so many of Scotland's 19th-century country houses.

The admission fee includes an interesting and well thought-out audioguide, but the tour is very much an outdoor one through garden and grounds; as for the castle itself, only the ballroom, which displays a collection of Landseer paintings and royal silver, is open to the public. Don't expect to see the queen's private quarters! The main attraction is learning about Highland estate management, rather than royal revelations. Guided tours are available on Saturdays from October to December – check the website for details.

### NEED TO KNOW
☎ 01339-742334; www.balmoralcastle.com; adult/child £9/5; ⊙ 10am-5pm Apr-Jul, last admission 4pm

---

**🖋 OLD STATION CAFE**  Cafe ££
(☎ 01339-755050; Station Sq; mains £9-15; ⊙ 10am-5pm daily, plus 6.30-8.30pm Thu-Sat) The former waiting room at Queen Victoria's train station is now an attractive dining area with black-and-white floor tiles, basketwork chairs, and a marble fireplace and table tops. Daily specials make good use of local produce, from salmon to venison, and good coffee and home-baked goods are available all day.

**ℹ Getting There & Away**

Bus 201 runs from Aberdeen to Ballater (£9.60, 1¾ hours, hourly Monday to Saturday, six on Sunday) via Crathes Castle, and continues to Braemar (30 minutes) every two hours.

## Braemar
POP 400

Braemar is a pretty little village with a grand location on a broad plain ringed by mountains where the Dee valley and Glen Clunie meet. In winter this is one of the coldest places in the country – temperatures as low as -29°C have been recorded here – and during spells of severe cold, hungry deer wander the streets looking for a bite to eat.

The **tourist office** ( 01399-741600; The Mews, Mar Rd; 9am-6pm Aug, 9am-5pm Jun, Jul, Sep & Oct, 10am-1.30pm & 2-5pm Mon-Sat, 2-5pm Sun Nov-May), opposite the Fife Arms Hotel, has lots of useful info on walks in the area.

## Sights & Activities

Just north of the village, turreted **Braemar Castle** (www.braemarcastle.co.uk; adult/child £6/3; 10am-4pm Sat & Sun Easter-Oct, also Wed Jul–mid-Sep) dates from 1628 and served as a government garrison after the 1745 Jacobite rebellion. It was taken over by the local community in 2007, and now offers guided tours of the historic castle apartments.

An easy walk from Braemar is up **Creag Choinnich** (538m), a hill to the east of the village above the A93. The route is waymarked and takes about 1½ hours.

You can hire mountain bikes from **Braemar Mountain Sports** ( 01339-741242; www.braemarmountainsports.com; 5 Invercauld Rd; 9am-6pm) for £16 for 24 hours. They also rent skiing and mountaineering equipment.

## Sleeping & Eating

**CLUNIE LODGE GUESTHOUSE**    B&B ££
( 01339-741330; www.clunielodge.com; Cluniebank Rd; r per person from £32; P ) A spacious Victorian villa set in beautiful gardens, the Clunie is a great place to relax after a hard day's hiking, with its comfortable residents lounge, bedrooms with views of the hills and red squirrels scampering through the neighbouring woods. There's a drying room and secure storage for bicycles.

**CRAIGLEA**    B&B ££
( 01339-741641; www.craigleabraemar.com; Hillside Dr; d £72; P ) Craiglea is a homely B&B set in a pretty stone cottage with three en suite bedrooms. Vegetarian breakfasts are available and the owners can give advice on local walks.

**BRAEMAR LODGE HOTEL**    Hotel, Bunkhouse ££
( 01339-741627; www.braemarlodge.co.uk; Glenshee Rd; dm from £12, s/d £75/120; P ) This Victorian shooting lodge on the southern outskirts of Braemar has bags of character, not least in the wood-panelled Malt Room bar, which is as well stocked with mounted deer heads as it is with single-malt whiskies. There's a good

## Braemar Gathering

There are Highland games in many Scottish towns and villages throughout the summer, but the best known is the **Braemar Gathering** ( 01339-755377; www.braemargathering.org; adult/child from £10/2), which takes place on the first Saturday in September. It's a major occasion, organised every year since 1817 by the Braemar Royal Highland Society. Events include Highland dancing, pipers, tug-of-war, a hill race up Morrone, tossing the caber, hammer- and stone-throwing and the long jump. International athletes are among those who take part.

These kinds of events took place informally in the Highlands for many centuries as tests of skill and strength, but they were formalised around 1820 as part of the rise of Highland romanticism initiated by Sir Walter Scott and King George IV. Queen Victoria attended the Braemar Gathering in 1848, starting a tradition of royal patronage that continues to this day.

# If You Like...
## Castles

The royal connection means that Balmoral is the name everyone knows, but there are many other castles in and around Royal Deeside.

### 1 CRATHES CASTLE
(NTS; ☎ 01330-844525; adult/child £10.50/7.50; ⊙10.30am-5pm Jun-Aug, to 4.30pm Sat-Thu Apr, May, Sep & Oct, to 3.45pm Sat & Sun Nov-Mar; 🚻) Famous for its Jacobean painted ceilings, magnificently carved canopied beds, and the 'Horn of Leys', presented to the Burnett family by Robert the Bruce in the 14th century; 16 miles west of Aberdeen.

### 2 CRAIGIEVAR CASTLE
(NTS; adult/child £11.50/8.50; ⊙11am-5.30pm daily Jul & Aug, Fri-Tue only Apr-Jun & Sep) A superb example of the original Scottish Baronial style, Craigievar has managed to survive pretty much unchanged since its completion in the 17th century; 15 miles north of Ballater.

### 3 FYVIE CASTLE
(NTS; adult/child £11/8; ⊙11am-5pm Jul & Aug, noon-5pm Sat-Tue Apr-Jun, Sep & Oct) A magnificent example of Scottish Baronial architecture, probably more famous for its ghosts, which include a phantom trumpeter and the mysterious Green Lady; 25 miles north of Aberdeen.

### 4 CASTLE FRASER
(NTS; adult/child £9.50/7; ⊙11am-5pm Jul & Aug, noon-5pm Thu-Sun Apr-Jun, Sep & Oct) The impressive 16th-century ancestral home of the Fraser family. The largely Victorian interior includes the great hall (with a hidden opening where the laird could eavesdrop on his guests); 16 miles west of Aberdeen.

restaurant with hill views, plus a 12-berth hikers' bunkhouse in the hotel grounds.

**GATHERING PLACE**　　　　　Bistro ££
(☎ 01339-741234; www.the-gathering-place. co.uk; 9 Invercauld Rd; mains £15-19; ⊙dinner Tue-Sat) This bright and breezy bistro is an unexpected corner of culinary excellence, with a welcoming dining room and sunny conservatory, tucked below the main road junction at the entrance to Braemar village.

## ❶ Getting There & Away

Bus 201 runs from Aberdeen to Braemar (£9.60, 2¼ hours, eight daily Monday to Saturday, five on Sunday). The 50-mile drive from Perth to Braemar is beautiful, but there's no public transport on this route.

# SPEYSIDE

## Dufftown
POP 1450

Rome may be built on seven hills, but Dufftown's built on seven stills, say the locals. Founded in 1817 by James Duff, 4th Earl of Fife, Dufftown is 17 miles south of Elgin and lies at the heart of the Speyside whisky-distilling region.

The **tourist office** (☎ 01340-820501; ⊙10am-1pm & 2-5.30pm Mon-Sat, 11am-3pm Sun Easter-Oct) is in the clock tower in the main square; the adjoining museum contains some interesting local items.

## ◉ Sights & Activities

**WHISKY MUSEUM**　　　　　Museum
(☎ 01340-821097; www.dufftown.co.uk; 12 Conval St; ⊙1-4pm Mon-Fri May-Sep) As well as housing a selection of distillery memorabilia (try saying that after a few drams), the Whisky Museum holds 'nosing and tasting evenings' where you can learn what to look for in a fine single malt (£10 per person; 8pm Wednesday in July and August).

You can then test your new-found skills at the nearby **Whisky Shop** (☎ 01340-821097; www.whiskyshopdufftown.co.uk; 1 Fife St), which stocks hundreds of single malts.

# Blaze Your Own Whisky Trail

Visiting a distillery can be memorable, but only hardcore malthounds will want to go to more than two or three. Some are great to visit; others are depressingly corporate. The following are some recommendations.

**Aberlour** (☎01340-881249; www.aberlour.com; tours £12; ☺10am & 2pm daily Apr-Oct, by appointment Mon-Fri Nov-Mar) Has an excellent, detailed tour with a proper tasting session. It's on the main street in Aberlour.

**Glenfarclas** (☎01807-500257; www.glenfarclas.co.uk; admission £5; ☺10am-4pm Mon-Fri Oct-Mar, to 5pm Mon-Fri Apr-Sep, plus to 4pm Sat Jul-Sep) Small, friendly and independent, Glenfarclas is 5 miles south of Aberlour on the Grantown road. The last tour leaves 90 minutes before closing. The in-depth Connoisseur's Tour (Fridays only July to September) is £20.

**Glenfiddich** (www.glenfiddich.com; admission free; ☺9.30am-4.30pm daily year-round, closed Christmas & New Year) It's big and busy, but handiest for Dufftown and foreign languages are available. The standard tour starts with an overblown video, but it's fun, informative and free. An in-depth Connoisseur's Tour (£20) must be prebooked. Glenfiddich kept single malt alive during the dark years.

**Macallan** (☎01340-872280; www.themacallan.com; ☺9.30am-4.30pm Mon-Sat Easter-Oct, 11am-3pm Mon-Fri Nov-Mar) Excellent sherry-casked malt. Several small-group tours are available (last tour at 3.30pm), including an expert one (£20); all should be prebooked. Lovely location 2 miles northwest of Craigellachie.

**Speyside Cooperage** (☎01340-871108; www.speysidecooperage.co.uk; adult/child £3.50/2; ☺9am-4pm Mon-Fri) Here you can see the fascinating art of barrel-making in action. It's a mile from Craigellachie on the Dufftown road.

**Spirit of Speyside** (www.spiritofspeyside.com) This biannual whisky festival in Dufftown has a number of great events. It takes place in early May and late September; both accommodation and events should be booked well ahead.

## 🛏 Sleeping & Eating

**DAVAAR B&B**      B&B ££
(☎01340-820464; www.davaardufftown.co.uk; 17 Church St; s/d from £40/60) Just along the street opposite the tourist office, this Victorian villa has three smallish but comfy rooms; the breakfast menu is superb, offering the option of Portsoy kippers instead of the traditional fry-up (which uses eggs from the owners' own chickens).

**LA FAISANDERIE**      Scottish £££
(☎01340-821273; The Square; mains £19-23; ☺noon-1.30pm & 5.30-8.30pm) This is a great place to eat, run by a local chef who shoots much of his own game. The interior is decorated in French *auberge* style with a cheerful mural and pheasants hiding in every corner. The three-course early-bird dinner menu (£19.50, from 5.30pm to 7pm) won't disappoint, but you can order à la carte as well.

## ℹ Getting There & Away

Buses link Dufftown to Elgin (50 minutes, hourly), Huntly, Aberdeen and Inverness.

On summer weekends, you can take a train from Aberdeen or Inverness to Keith, and then ride the Keith and Dufftown Railway to Dufftown.

# Skye &
# the Islands

**Skye epitomises the romantic image of Scotland.** The jagged peaks of the Cuillin tear through the mist, and the ghosts of Bonnie Prince Charlie and Flora MacDonald haunt the hallways of Dunvegan Castle. Weather permitting, Skye is also a paradise for walkers and wildlife enthusiasts; its rugged hills, lonely lochs and scenic coastlines are home to golden eagles, red deer, otters and seals.

To the south, the bustling port of Oban is the 'gateway to the isles', with regular ferries to the peaceful backwaters of Kerrera and Lismore, the dramatic landscapes of Mull and the wild, windswept beaches of Coll and Tiree.

Mull can lay claim to some of the finest and most varied scenery in the Scottish islands. Add in two impressive castles, a narrow-gauge railway and the sacred island of Iona and you can see why it's sometimes impossible to find a spare bed on the island.

Sunset at Elgol beach (p213)

Neist Point lighthouse, Duirinish Peninsula (p217)

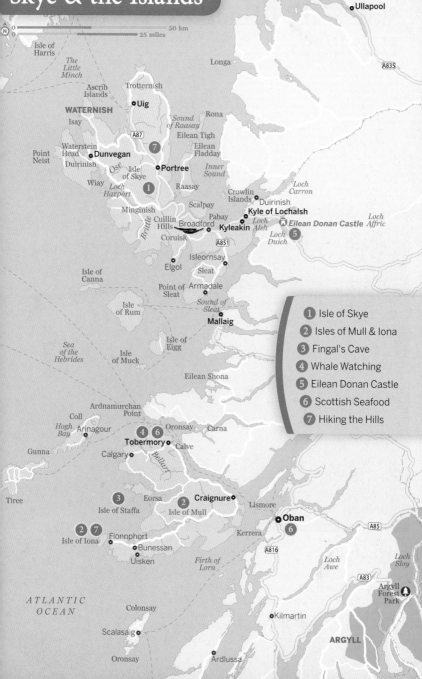

# Skye & the Islands

50 km
25 miles

Isle of Harris

*The Little Minch*

Longa

Ullapool

A835

Ascrib Islands

Trotternish

Uig

WATERNISH

Isay

Rona

Waterstein Head

Dunvegan

Point Neist

Duirinish

Isle of Skye

*Sound of Raasay*

Eilean Tigh

Eilean Fladday

**7**

A87

Wiay

Loch Harport

**1**

Portree

*Inner Sound*

Raasay

Scalpay

Minginish

Cuillin Hills

Brittle

Broadford

Coruisk

Isle of Canna

Elgol

Isleornsay

Sleat

Pabay

Kyleakin

Crowlin Islands

Duirinish

Kyle of Lochalsh

Loch Alsh

Loch Carron

Eilean Donan Castle

Loch Affric

Loch Duich

**5**

A851

Point of Sleat

Armadale

*Sound of Sleat*

Isle of Rum

Mallaig

*Sea of the Hebrides*

Isle of Eigg

Isle of Muck

Eilean Shona

Coll

Hogh Bay

Arinagour

Ardnamurchan Point

Oronsay

Carna

**4** **6**

Tobermory

Calve

Gunna

Calgary

Bellart

Tiree

**3**

Eorsa

Isle of Staffa

**2**

Isle of Mull

Craignure

Lismore

Oban

**6**

A85

Kerrera

A816

**2** **7**

Isle of Iona

Fionnphort

Bunessan

Uisken

*Firth of Lorn*

Loch Awe

Loch Sloy

A83

*ATLANTIC OCEAN*

Colonsay

Kilmartin

Argyll Forest Park

Scalasaig

Oronsay

Ardlussa

**ARGYLL**

**1** Isle of Skye
**2** Isles of Mull & Iona
**3** Fingal's Cave
**4** Whale Watching
**5** Eilean Donan Castle
**6** Scottish Seafood
**7** Hiking the Hills

# Skye & the Islands' Highlights

## ① Isle of Skye

Travellers and tourists have been going 'over the sea to Skye' for centuries, although these days the journey is rather more straightforward thanks to a controversial modern road bridge. But Skye remains as alluring as ever, boasting some of the most beautiful and dramatic landscapes in Europe. Bottom Right: Skye Museum of Island Life

**Need to Know**

BEST TIME TO GO May and September (best chance of dry weather).
BEST PHOTO OP In fine weather, almost anywhere!
TOP TIP Bring midge repellent. **For more, see p208.**

# Isle of Skye Don't Miss List

SUU RAMSAY, RABBIE'S
TRAILBURNERS DRIVER/GUIDE

## 1 CUILLIN HILLS

Rising from the ground in a dramatic skyline of black volcanic gabbro, these serrated pinnacles (p213) will test hikers and climbers alike; the aptly named Inaccessible Pinnacle is the pièce de résistance. For those looking for a more leisurely option, superb boat trips operate from Elgol to Coruisk, where the Cuillin rise spectacularly from the sea.

## 2 DUNVEGAN CASTLE

Home of Clan MacLeod, Dunvegan (p216; pictured above left) claims to be the longest occupied castle in Britain, having had someone in residence since the 13th century. The castle's array of interesting artefacts, such as the Fairy Flag and Rory Mor's Drinking Horn, are enough to whet the interest of any clan aficionado. The castle sits on the shores of Loch Dunvegan, where you'll find seals frequenting the surrounding waters.

## 3 QUIRAING

This impressive rock formation (p218; pictured far left) affords superb views across a landscape where time appears to have stood still. The Jurassic scene offers careful walking out to the pillared columns of the 'Prison', which eerily protrude from the slopes. For the more agile, there's a scramble up to the 'Table' where, in days of old, the final of the annual shinty match used to take place.

## 4 FAIRY GLEN

A plethora of fairy knolls sits quietly in this peaceful and little-known glen (p219). Locals believe that the 'wee people' (*sith* in Gaelic) live here deep inside these dark caverns of the earth. Rowan trees planted to keep away evil spirits keep a close vigil. Also look out for the fairy tower and the fairy circle. This place will have you believing before you leave. Go with care!

## 5 SKYE MUSEUM OF ISLAND LIFE

Run by local Gaelic speakers, this recreation of an island township (p218;) provides an educational and informative look at Skye history and a nostalgic glimpse of daily life during the 19th century. Thatched cottages include the original croft house, the barn, the weaver's cottage, the old smithy and the ceilidh house.

# Isles of Mull & Iona

One of the most accessible of Scotland's islands (45 minutes by ferry from Oban), Mull is also one of the most beautiful. From Duart Castle perched on its dramatic headland to the holy island of Iona (p228), there are miles and miles of scenic single-track roads to explore.

Below: Tobermory, Isle of Mull; Top Right: Puffin; Bottom Right: Isle of Iona

## Need to Know

**BEST TIME TO GO** June to August for whale spotting. **BEST PHOTO OP** Summit of Dun I (Iona). **SEE WILDLIFE** View sea eagles at the Aros Experience (p213). **For more, see p222.**

2

# Isles of Mull & Iona Don't Miss List

DAVID SEXTON, RSPB MULL OFFICER &
BIRDWATCHING GUIDEBOOK AUTHOR

## 1 EAGLE HIDE

The Isle of Mull is the only place on the planet with a public viewing hide overlooking the nesting area of rare white-tailed sea eagles. The hide offers a unique and privileged view of the UK's largest bird of prey, and income goes to help local causes. Check with the visitor information centre at Craignure (p223) for the current location of the hide.

## 2 SPIRIT OF IONA

Too many visitors race through Mull. Slow down and try to spend a night on Iona (p228). On a warm, sunny day in summer you can't beat it. In the evening take a stroll or cycle along the quiet lanes and listen to the amazing call of the endangered corncrake, which the local farmers and crofters have helped recover from the brink of extinction in the UK.

## 3 STAFFA & THE TRESHNISH ISLES

A bit of puffin-spotting (p225) on these magical islands is a must. Other seabirds such as guillemots, razorbills and kittiwakes cram onto the narrow cliff ledges and their 'aroma' will stay in your nostrils for a long time. The geology of the islands, especially Staffa, is remarkable.

## 4 TOBERMORY

The colourful waterfront houses of Tobermory (p224) will be familiar to many people as the home of the popular BBC children's TV show *Balamory*. In real life it's a thriving town with a lively atmosphere, great pubs and seafood cafes. Several whale-watch boats depart from here in search of minke whales, dolphins and basking sharks. If the weather is good, get your fish and chips from the van on the pier (like Prince Charles did on a recent visit).

## 5 BEACHES

You can't come to Mull and Iona and not sample some of the beautiful white-sand beaches. Iona has many to choose from; on your way, visit Ardalanish or Uisken on the Ross of Mull (p227) for an idyllic beach experience, or head north to the stunning Calgary Bay.

## Fingal's Cave

The impressive rock architecture of Fingal's Cave on the Isle of Staffa (p230) provided the inspiration for Felix Mendelsson's famous *Hebrides Overture,* and is a don't-miss experience for anyone ticking off Scotland's west-coast sights. Weather permitting, the boat trip lands you at some rocky steps from which a walkway and natural ledge allow you to go all the way to the back of the cave.

## Whale Watching

The waters off the west coast of Scotland attract large numbers of marine mammals, from harbour porpoises and dolphins to minke whales and even – though sightings are rare – humpback and killer whales. Whale-watching boat trips (p225) from Tobermory on the Isle of Mull tend to run from April to September because of the weather (whales are easier to spot in calm conditions). Basking sharks can also often be spotted on these trips.

MARCUS MCADAM/ALAMY ©

## Eilean Donan Castle

Perched on a tiny island linked to the shore by a picturesque arched bridge, Eilean Donan (p211) is the most iconic of Scottish castles. Its image has graced everything from postcards to shortbread tins and has appeared in many movies including *Highlander* and *The World Is Not Enough*. Despite its venerable appearance, it is actually a relatively modern restoration, built in the early 20th century.

## Savouring Scottish Seafood

The waters of the west coast of Scotland are some of the most productive in Europe, yielding rich harvests of seafood. Scottish specialities to look out for in quayside restaurants such as Waterfront Fishouse Restaurant (p221) and Café Fish (p226) include juicy langoustines (also known as Dublin Bay prawns), scallops (often hand-picked by divers), razor clams (gathered on sandy beaches at low tide) and squat lobster (a smaller cousin of the common lobster).

## Hiking the Hills

The Scottish islands boast some of the finest landscapes in Europe; the best way to appreciate the view is to pull on your hiking boots and climb a hill. Skye and Mull have some truly challenging hikes, but there are many routes that can be tackled by mortals, such as the trail up to the Old Man of Storr (p218), and Dun I, the highest point on Iona.

Old Man of Storr, Isle of Skye

# Skye & the Islands' Best...

## Restaurants

- **Three Chimneys** (p217) Fine dining in a remote and beautiful corner of Skye

- **Lochbay Seafood Restaurant** (p218) One of Skye's most romantic restaurants

- **Waterfront Fishouse Restaurant** (p221) Converted seamen's mission that serves superb seafood freshly landed at the quay

- **Café Fish** (p226) Welcoming little restaurant overlooking Tobermory harbour, serving fresh shellfish straight from the boat

## Classic Views

- **Elgol** Classic panorama of the Cuillin Hills

- **Sligachan Hotel** (p214) Postcard view of the Cuillin's jagged skyline

- **Eilean Donan Castle** (p211) Set against a backdrop of sea and mountains, this castle has graced a million shortbread tins

- **McCaig's Tower** (p219) Panorama over Oban Bay to the Isles of Kerrera and Mull

- **Dun I** (p229) A 360-degree panorama of sea and islands

## Walks

- **Coire Lagan** (p214) Hike into the heart of the Cuillin Hills

- **Coral Beaches** (p216) Easy walk to unusual white-gravel beaches with views to Outer Hebrides

- **Old Man of Storr** (p218) A short uphill hike to an amazing pinnacle giving great views of mainland hills

- **Quiraing** (p218) An easy option, mostly level, amid strange and impressive rock scenery

# Boat Trips

○ **Loch Coruisk** (p213) Sail from Elgol to the mountain-ringed fastness of Coruisk

○ **Whale watching, Isle of Skye** (p212) High-speed RIB (rigid inflatable boat) takes you wildlife spotting in the waters off Skye

○ **Whale watching, Isle of Mull** (p225) Quality whale-watching cruises out of Tobermory harbour

○ **Isle of Staffa** (p230) Cruise from Iona to visit Fingal's Cave on the Isle of Staffa

# Need to Know

## ADVANCE PLANNING

○ **One month before** Reserve a table at the Three Chimneys on Skye to avoid disappointment; book accommodation on Mull and Skye

○ **Two weeks before** If travelling by car, make reservations for any ferry crossings, especially in summer

○ **One week before** Make bookings for wildlife-spotting boat trips

## RESOURCES

○ **Skye & Lochalsh** (www.skye.co.uk) Tourist information for the Isle of Skye

○ **Oban** (www.oban.org.uk) Tourist information for Oban and area

○ **Isle of Mull** (www.isle-of-mull.net) Lots of useful information, from accommodation to wildlife

○ **Isle of Iona** (www.isle-of-iona.net) Tourist information for the island of Iona

○ **Scottish Heartlands** (www.visitscottishheartlands.com) Official tourist-board website for Oban and Mull

○ **Caledonian Macbrayne** (www.calmac.co.uk) Timetables and fares for ferries to the islands

## GETTING AROUND

○ **Bus** Reasonable network of local buses on the islands

○ **Car** The most time-efficient way to get around the islands

○ **Ferry** Frequent services from Oban to Mull year-round

○ **Train** From Edinburgh or Glasgow to Oban, Mallaig or Kyle of Lochalsh

## BE FOREWARNED

○ **Midges** Tiny biting flies are a pest from June to September, especially in still weather around dawn and dusk; bring insect repellent and wear long-sleeved clothing

○ **Weather** Always unpredictable on the west coast; be prepared for wet and windy days, even in the middle of summer

**Left:** Coire Lagan (p214); **Above:** View of Oban from McCaig's Tower (p219)

(LEFT) MARK CHAPMAN/ALAMY ©;
(ABOVE) INTERNATIONAL PHOTOBANK/ALAMY ©

# Skye & the Islands Itineraries

*These itineraries take in the best of Skye and Mull. Both start and finish at a town with a railway station; you can pick up a rental car at Kyle of Lochalsh and drop it at Armadale.*

TROTTERNISH PENINSULA 5

DUNVEGAN CASTLE 6

PORTREE 4

KYLE OF LOCHALSH 1

TALISKER DISTILLERY 7

CORUISK 3

ELGOL 2

TARSKAVAIG 8

ARMADALE 9

MALLAIG 10
1

*Sea of the Hebrides*

TOBERMORY 3

CALGARY BAY 4

LOCHALINE 2

DUART CASTLE 6

CRAIGNURE 5 7

FIONNPHORT

IONA 6 5

OBAN

**KYLE OF LOCHALSH TO MALLAIG**

## Over the Sea to Skye

From **(1) Kyle of Lochalsh** the Skye Bridge leads over the water to the legendary Isle of Skye; pray for clear weather! Follow signs toward Portree, and at the far end of Broadford village detour southwest to **(2) Elgol** where a boat trip to **(3) Coruisk** awaits. It'll be afternoon by the time you return; continue north to the island capital of **(4) Portree**.

Spend your second day on a slow circuit of the **(5) Trotternish Peninsula** to visit the Old Man of Storr, Kilt Rock, the Quiraing and the Skye Museum of Island Life, returning to Portree for the night. On day three head west to **(6) Dunvegan Castle**, and afterwards take a stroll to the Coral Beaches.

Return south on the A863 via Bracadale, perhaps stopping to tour the **(7) Talisker Distillery**. Back at Broadford, you have the choice of returning to Kyle of Lochalsh, or heading south on the A851. If you're still hungry for dramatic scenery, be sure to detour west on the minor road via **(8) Tarskavaig** for stunning views of the Cuillin Hills and the Isle of Rum. Be sure to arrive at **(9) Armadale** in time for the ferry to **(10) Mallaig**.

---

**Top Left:** Loch Coruisk (p213);
**Top Right:** Cattle on a Fionnphort beach (p227)

3 DAYS

**MALLAIG TO OBAN**

## Island-Hopping to Mull

From **(1) Mallaig** a very scenic 67-mile drive (allow two hours) leads south via the A861 and A884 to **(2) Lochaline**, from where you take the ferry to Fishnish on Mull. Head north to **(3) Tobermory**, the colourful capital of the island and, after a seafood lunch, make a circuit of northern Mull, perhaps pausing for a picnic on the sandy beach at **(4) Calgary Bay**. Return to Tobermory to stay overnight.

The following day head south then west on a narrow, twisting road around the spectacular shores of Loch na Keal. Turn right on the road to **(5) Fionnphort**. It doesn't look far on the map, but Tobermory to Fionnphort will take you two to three hours, especially if you stop to soak up the magnificent scenery. Take advantage of an overnight stay in Fionnphort by exploring the holy isle of **(6) Iona** until the last ferry leaves (or you could even stay the night here), enjoying the peace after the day-trippers have departed.

In the morning, make the long drive towards Craignure (35 miles, mostly on single-track road; allow an hour and a half), stopping to visit **(7) Duart Castle**, the seat of Clan MacLean, before catching a ferry from **(8) Craignure** to Oban.

# Discover Skye & the Islands

## ISLE OF SKYE
POP 9900

The Isle of Skye (an t-Eilean Sgiatha-nach in Gaelic) takes its name from the old Norse *sky-a*, meaning 'cloud island', a Viking reference to the often mist-enshrouded Cuillin Hills. It's the largest of Scotland's islands, a 50-mile-long smorgasbord of velvet moors, jagged mountains, sparkling lochs and towering sea cliffs. The stunning scenery is the main attraction, but when the mist closes in there are plenty of castles, crofting museums and cosy pubs and restaurants in which to retire.

## 🏃 Activities

### Walking

Skye offers some of the finest – and in places, the roughest and most difficult – walking in Scotland. There are many detailed guidebooks available, including a series of four walking guides by Charles Rhodes, available from the Aros Experience (p213) and the tourist office in Portree. You'll need Ordnance Survey (OS) 1:50,000 maps 23 and 32. Don't attempt the longer walks in bad weather or in winter.

Easy, low-level routes include: through **Strath Mor** from Luib (on the Broadford–Sligachan road) and on to Torrin (on the Broadford–Elgol road; allow 1½ hours, 4 miles); from **Sligachan to Kilmarie** via Camasunary (four hours, 11 miles); and from **Elgol to Kilmarie** via Camasunary (2½ hours, 6.5 miles). The walk from **Kilmarie to Coruisk** and back via Camasunary and the 'Bad Step' is

Stone carving, Isle of Iona (p228)
CHARLES BOWMAN/GETTY IMAGES ©

superb but slightly harder (11 miles round trip, allow five hours). The Bad Step is a rocky slab poised above the sea that you have to scramble across; it's easy in fine, dry weather, but some walkers find it intimidating.

**SKYE WALKING HOLIDAYS** Walking
(☏01470-552213; www.skyewalks.co.uk; Duntulm Castle Hotel, Duntulm) Organises three-day guided walking holidays for £400 per person, including four nights of hotel accommodation.

### Sea Kayaking

The sheltered coves and sea lochs around the coast of Skye provide water lovers with magnificent sea-kayaking opportunities. The centres listed here can provide kayaking instruction, guiding and equipment hire for both beginners and experts. It costs around £35 to £40 for a half-day kayak hire with instruction.

**WHITEWAVE OUTDOOR CENTRE** Kayaking
(☏01470-542414; www.white-wave.co.uk; 19 Linicro, Kilmuir; ☺Mar-Oct) Provides kayaking instruction, guiding and equipment hire for both beginners and experts.

**SKYAK ADVENTURES** Kayaking
(☏01471-820002; www.skyakadventures.com; 29 Lower Breakish, Breakish) Expeditions and courses to take both beginners and experienced paddlers to otherwise inaccessible places.

 **Tours**

Several operators offer guided tours of Skye, covering history, culture and wildlife. Rates are from £150 to £200 for a six-hour tour for up to six people.

**SKYE TOURS** Bus Tour
(☏0800 980 4846; www.skye-tours.co.uk; adult/child £35/30; ☺Mon-Sat) Five-hour sightseeing tours of Skye in a minibus, departing from the tourist office car park in Kyle of Lochalsh (close to Kyle of Lochalsh train station).

**SKYE LIGHT IMAGES** 4WD Tour
(☏07909 706802; www.skyejeepsafaris.co.uk; ☺Oct-Easter) Offers 4WD winter safaris in the wilder areas of Skye with tuition on landscape and wildlife photography.

## ℹ Information

### Medical Services

**Portree Community Hospital** (☏01478-613200; Fancyhill) There's a casualty department and dental surgery here.

### Money

Only Portree and Broadford have banks with ATMs, and Portree's tourist office has a currency-exchange desk.

### Tourist Information

**Broadford Information Centre** (☏01471-822361; car park, Broadford; ☺9.30am-5pm Mon-Sat, 10am-4pm Sun Apr-Oct)

**Dunvegan Information Centre** (☏01470-521581; 2 Lochside, Dunvegan; ☺10am-5pm Mon-Sat Jun-Oct plus 10am-4pm Sun Jul & Aug, 10am-5pm Mon-Fri Apr & May, limited opening hrs Nov-Mar)

**Portree Information Centre** (☏01478-612137; Bayfield Rd, Portree; internet per 20min £1; ☺9am-6pm Mon-Sat, 10am-4pm Sun Jun-Aug, 9am-5pm Mon-Fri, 10am-4pm Sat Apr, May & Sep, limited opening hrs Oct-Mar)

## ℹ Getting There & Away

### Boat

Despite there being a bridge, there are still a couple of ferry links between Skye and the mainland. Ferries also operate from Uig on Skye to the Outer Hebrides.

**Mallaig to Armadale** (www.calmac.co.uk; per person/car £4.35/22.60) The Mallaig to Armadale ferry (30 minutes, eight daily Monday to Saturday, five to seven on Sunday) is very popular in July and August, so book ahead if you're travelling by car.

**Glenelg to Kylerhea** (www.skyeferry.co.uk; car with up to four passengers £14) A tiny vessel (six cars only) runs on the short Kylerhea to Glenelg crossing (five minutes, every 20 minutes).

The ferry operates from 10am to 6pm daily from Easter to October only (till 7pm June to August).

## Bus

**Glasgow to Portree** £40, seven hours, four daily

**Inverness to Portree** £23, 3½ hours, three daily

## Car & Motorcycle

The Isle of Skye became permanently tethered to the Scottish mainland when the Skye Bridge opened in 1995. The controversial bridge tolls were abolished in 2004 and the crossing is now free.

There are petrol stations at Broadford (open 24 hours), Armadale, Portree, Dunvegan and Uig.

## 🛈 Getting Around

Getting around the island by public transport can be a pain, especially if you want to explore away from the main Kyleakin–Portree–Uig road. Here, as in much of the Highlands, there are only a few buses on Saturdays, and only one Sunday service (between Kyle of Lochalsh and Portree).

## Bus

Stagecoach operates the main bus routes on the island, linking all the main villages and towns. Its **Skye Dayrider** ticket gives unlimited bus travel for one day for £7.50. For timetable info, call Traveline (☎ 0871 200 22 33).

## Taxi

Kyle Taxi Company (☎ 01599-534323) You can order a taxi or hire a car from Kyle Taxi Company. Car hire costs from around £38 a day, and you can arrange for the car to be waiting at Kyle of Lochalsh train station.

# Kyleakin (Caol Acain)
POP 100

Poor wee Kyleakin had the carpet pulled from under it when the Skye Bridge opened – it went from being the gateway to the island to a backwater bypassed by the main road. It's now a pleasant, peaceful little place, with a harbour used by yachts and fishing boats.

The community-run **Bright Water Visitor Centre** (☎ 01599-530040; www. eileanban.org; The Pier; adult/child £1/free; ⏰ 10am-4pm Mon-Fri Easter-Sep) serves as a

Sleat

DAVID C TOMLINSON/GETTY IMAGES ©

base for tours of **Eilean Ban** – the island used as a stepping stone by the Skye Bridge – where Gavin Maxwell (author of *Ring of Bright Water*) spent the last 18 months of his life in 1968–69, living in the lighthouse-keeper's cottage. The island is now a nature reserve and tours (£7 per person) are available in summer (must be booked in advance). The visitor centre also houses a child-friendly exhibition on Maxwell, the lighthouse and the island's wildlife. Tour times were uncertain at the time of research – best call ahead to check.

A shuttle bus runs half-hourly between Kyle of Lochalsh and Kyleakin (five minutes), and there are eight to 10 buses daily (except Sunday) to Broadford and Portree.

## Sleat

If you cross over the sea to Skye on the ferry from Mallaig you arrive in Armadale, at the southern end of the long, low-lying peninsula known as Sleat (pronounced 'slate'). The landscape of Sleat itself is not exceptional, but it provides a grandstand for ogling the magnificent scenery on either side – take the steep and twisting minor road that loops through **Tarskavaig** and **Tokavaig** for stunning views of the Isle of Rum, the Cuillin Hills and Bla Bheinn.

### Armadale

Armadale, where the ferry from Mallaig arrives, is little more than a store, a post office and a couple of houses. There are six or seven buses a day (Monday to Saturday) from Armadale to Broadford and Portree.

## Sights & Activities

**MUSEUM OF THE ISLES**  Museum
(☏01471-844305; www.clandonald.com; adult/child £6.95/4.95; ☽9.30am-5.30pm Apr-Oct)
Just along the road from the ferry pier is the part-ruined **Armadale Castle**, former seat of Lord MacDonald of Sleat. The neighbouring museum will tell you all you ever wanted to know about Clan Donald,

## Detour:
# Eilean Donan Castle

Photogenically sited at the entrance to Loch Duich, near Dornie village, **Eilean Donan Castle** (☏01599-555202; www.eileandonancastle.com; adult/child £6/5; ☽9.30am-6pm Mar-Oct) is one of Scotland's most evocative castles, and must be represented in millions of photo albums. It's on an offshore islet, magically linked to the mainland by an elegant, stone-arched bridge. It's very much a re-creation inside, with an excellent introductory exhibition. Keep an eye out for the photos of castle scenes from the movie *Highlander*; there's also a sword used at the battle of Culloden in 1746. The castle was bombarded into ruins by government ships in 1719 when Jacobite forces were defeated at the Battle of Glenshiel. It was rebuilt between 1912 and 1932.

Scottish Citylink buses from Fort William and Inverness to Portree, on the Isle of Skye, will stop opposite the castle.

as well as providing an easily digestible history of the Lordship of the Isles.

Prize exhibits include rare portraits of clan chiefs, and a wine glass that was once used by Bonnie Prince Charlie. The ticket also gives admission to the lovely **castle gardens**.

**FREE** AIRD OLD CHURCH
GALLERY  Gallery
(☏01471-844291; www.airdoldchurchgallery.co.uk; Aird; ☽10am-5pm Mon-Sat Easter-Sep)
At the end of the narrow road that leads southwest from Armadale through Ardvasar village, this small gallery exhibits the powerful landscape paintings of Peter McDermott.

**211**

**SEA.FARI ADVENTURES**   Boat Tour
( ☎01471-833316; www.whalespotting.co.uk; adult/child £42/34; ☯Easter-Sep) Sea.fari runs three-hour whale-watching cruises in a high-speed RIB. These trips have a high success rate for spotting minke whales in summer (an average of 180 sightings a year), with rarer sightings of bottlenose dolphins and basking sharks.

## Isleornsay

This pretty harbour, 8 miles north of Armadale, is opposite Sandaig Bay on the mainland, where Gavin Maxwell lived and wrote his much-loved memoir *Ring of Bright Water*. **Gallery An Talla Dearg** (admission free; ☯10am-6pm Mon-Fri, to 4pm Sat & Sun Apr-Oct) exhibits the works of artists who were inspired by Scottish landscapes and culture.

## Sleeping & Eating

**TORAVAIG HOUSE HOTEL**   Hotel ££
( ☎01471-820200; www.skyehotel.co.uk; d £95-120; P 🛜) This hotel, 3 miles south of Isleornsay, is one of those places where the owners know a thing or two about

hospitality – as soon as you arrive you'll feel right at home, whether relaxing on the sofas by the log fire in the lounge or admiring the view across the Sound of Sleat from the lawn chairs in the garden.

The spacious bedrooms – ask for room 1 (Eriskay), with its enormous sleigh bed – are luxuriously equipped, from the rich and heavy bed linen to the huge, high-pressure shower heads. The elegant **Islay restaurant** serves the best of local fish, game and lamb. After dinner you can retire to the lounge with a single malt and flick through the yachting magazines – you can even arrange a day trip aboard the owners' 42ft sailing yacht.

**HOTEL EILEAN IARMAIN**   Hotel £££
( ☎01471-833332; www.eilean-iarmain.co.uk; s/d from £110/170; P ) A charming old Victorian hotel with log fires, a candlelit restaurant and 12 luxurious rooms, many with sea views. The hotel's cosy, wood-panelled **An Praban Bar** (mains £9-16) serves delicious, gourmet-style bar meals – try the haddock in beer batter, venison burger or vegetable cannelloni.

Loch Slapin

# Elgol (Ealaghol)

On a clear day, the journey along the road from Broadford to Elgol is one of the most scenic on Skye. It takes in two classic postcard panoramas – the view of Bla Bheinn across **Loch Slapin** (near Torrin), and the superb view of the entire Cuillin range from **Elgol pier**.

Bus 49 runs from Broadford to Elgol (40 minutes, three daily Monday to Friday, two Saturday).

 **Activities**

**BELLA JANE**                        Boat Tour
( ☎ 0800 731 3089; www.bellajane.co.uk; ⏱ Apr-Oct) Bella Jane offers a three-hour cruise (adult/child £22/12, three daily) from Elgol harbour to the remote Loch na Cuilce, an impressive inlet surrounded by soaring peaks. On a calm day, you can clamber ashore here to make the short walk to Loch Coruisk in the heart of the Cuillin Hills. You get 1½ hours ashore and visit a seal colony en route.

**AQUAXPLORE**                        Boat Tour
( ☎ 0800 731 3089; www.aquaxplore.co.uk; ⏱ Apr-Oct) Runs 1½-hour high-speed boat trips from Elgol to an abandoned shark-hunting station on the island of **Soay** (adult/child £25/20), once owned by *Ring of Bright Water* author Gavin Maxwell. There are longer trips (adult/child £48/38, four hours) to Rum, Canna and Sanday to visit breeding colonies of puffins, with the chance of seeing minke whales on the way.

**MISTY ISLE**                        Boat Tour
( ☎ 01471-866288; www.mistyisleboattrips.co.uk; adult/child £18/7.50; ⏱ Apr-Oct) The pretty, traditional wooden launch *Misty Isle* offers cruises to Loch Coruisk with 1½ hours ashore (no Sunday service).

# Minginish

Loch Harport, to the north of the Cuillin, divides the Minginish Peninsula from the rest of Skye. On its southern shore lies the village of Carbost, home to the smooth, sweet and smoky Talisker malt whisky, produced at **Talisker Distillery** ( ☎ 01478-614308; www.discovering-distilleries.com; guided tour £6; ⏱ 9.30am-5pm Mon-Sat Apr-Oct, 11am-5pm Sun Jul & Aug, 10am-4.30pm Mon-Fri Nov-Mar). This is the only distillery on Skye; the guided tour includes a free dram. Magnificent **Talisker Bay**, 5 miles west of Carbost, has a sandy beach, sea stack and waterfall.

# Portree (Port Righ)

POP 1920

Portree is Skye's largest and liveliest town. It has a pretty harbour lined with brightly painted houses, and there are great views of the surrounding hills. Its name (from the Gaelic for King's Harbour) commemorates James V, who came here in 1540 to pacify the local clans.

## Sights & Activities

**AROS EXPERIENCE**          Visitor Centre
( ☎ 01478-613649; www.aros.co.uk; Viewfield Rd; sea-eagle exhibition £4.75; ⏱ 9am-5.30pm; 🚼)
On the southern edge of Portree, the Aros Experience is a combined visitor centre, book and gift shop, restaurant, theatre and cinema. The visitor centre offers a look at some fascinating, live CCTV images from local sea-eagle and heron nests, and a wide-screen video of Skye's impressive scenery (it's worth waiting for the aerial shots of the Cuillin).

The centre is a useful rainy-day retreat, with an indoor, soft play area for children.

**MV STARDUST**                       Boat Tour
( ☎ 07798-743858; www.skyeboat-trips.co.uk; Portree Harbour; adult/child £15/9) The MV *Stardust* offers one- to two-hour boat trips to the Sound of Raasay, with the chance to see seals, porpoises and – if you're lucky – white-tailed sea eagles. On Saturdays there are longer cruises to the Isle of Rona (£25 per person). You can also arrange to be dropped off for a hike on the Isle of Raasay and picked up again later.

MELBA/GETTY IMAGES ©

# Don't Miss Cuillin Hills

The Cuillin Hills are Britain's most spectacular mountain range (the name comes from the Old Norse *kjöllen,* meaning 'keel-shaped'). Though small in stature (**Sgurr Alasdair**, the highest summit, is only 993m), the peaks are near-alpine in character, with knife-edge ridges, jagged pinnacles, scree-filled gullies and hectares of naked rock. While they are a paradise for experienced mountaineers, the higher reaches of the Cuillin are off limits to the majority of walkers.

The good news is that there are also plenty of good low-level hikes within the ability of most walkers. One of the best (on a fine day) is the steep climb from Glenbrittle camping ground to **Coire Lagan** (6 miles round trip; allow at least three hours). The impressive upper corrie contains a lochan for bathing (for the hardy!), and the surrounding cliffs are a playground for rock climbers – bring your binoculars.

The **Sligachan Hotel**, or The Slig, is a near village in itself, encompassing a luxurious hotel, a microbrewery, self-catering cottages, a bunkhouse, a campsite, a big barn of a pub **(Seamus's Bar)** and an adventure playground. There are five buses a day on weekdays (one on Saturday) from Portree to Carbost via Sligachan.

**NEED TO KNOW**

**Sligachan Hotel** (📞01478-650204; www.sligachan.co.uk; per person £65-75; 🅿 @ 🛜)
**Seamus's Bar** (Sligachan Hotel; mains £8-10; 🕙food served 11am-11pm; 🛜 👫)

 **Sleeping**

Portree is well supplied with B&Bs, but many of them are in bland, modern bungalows that, though comfortable, often lack character. Accommodation fills up fast in July and August so be sure to book ahead.

**BEN TIANAVAIG B&B**　　　　B&B ££
(📞01478-612152; www.ben-tianavaig.co.uk; 5 Bosville Tce; r £70-80; 🅿 🛜) A warm wel-

come awaits at this appealing B&B in the centre of town. All four bedrooms have a view across the harbour to the hill that gives the house its name and breakfasts include vegetables grown in the garden.

### PEINMORE HOUSE
B&B ££

( 01478-612574; www.peinmorehouse.co.uk; r £130-140; P  ) Signposted off the main road about 2 miles south of Portree, this former manse has been converted into a guesthouse that is more luxurious than most hotels. The bedrooms and bathrooms are huge (one bathroom has an armchair in it!), as is the choice of breakfast (kippers and smoked haddock on the menu), and there are views to the Old Man of Storr.

### BOSVILLE HOTEL
Hotel ££

( 01478-612846; www.bosvillehotel.co.uk; 9-11 Bosville Tce; s/d from £130/138;  ) The Bosville brings a bit of metropolitan style to Portree with its designer fabrics and furniture, flatscreen TVs and bright, spacious bathrooms. It's worth splashing out a bit for the 'premier' rooms, with leather recliner chairs from which you can lap up the view over the town and harbour.

### ROSEDALE HOTEL
Hotel ££

( 01478-613131; www.rosedalehotelskye.co.uk; Beaumont Cres; s/d from £65/100;  Easter-Oct;  ) This cosy, old-fashioned hotel – you'll be welcomed with a glass of whisky or sherry when you check in – is situated by the waterfront. Its three converted fishermen's cottages are linked by a maze of narrow stairs and corridors, and the restaurant has a view of the harbour.

### WOODLANDS
B&B ££

( 01478-612980; www.woodlands-portree.co.uk; Viewfield Rd; r £68; P ) A great location, with views across the bay, and unstinting hospitality make this modern B&B, a half-mile south of the town centre, a good choice.

# Eating & Drinking

### CAFÉ ARRIBA
Cafe £

( 01478-611830; www.cafearriba.co.uk; Quay Brae; mains £4-8;  7am-10pm May-Sep, 8am-5.30pm Oct-Apr;  ) Arriba is a funky little cafe, brightly decked out in primary colours and offering delicious flatbread melts (bacon, leek and cheese is our favourite) and the best choice of vegetarian grub on the island, ranging from a veggie breakfast fry-up to Indian-spiced bean cakes with mint yoghurt. Also serves excellent coffee.

### HARBOUR VIEW SEAFOOD RESTAURANT
Seafood ££

( 01478-612069; www.harbourviewskye.co.uk; 7 Bosville Tce; mains £14-19;  lunch & 5.30-11pm Tue-Sun) Portree's most congenial place to eat, with a homely dining room with a log fire in winter, books on the mantelpiece and bric-a-brac on the shelves. And on the table: superb Scottish seafood, such as fresh Skye oysters, seafood chowder, king scallops, langoustines and lobster.

### SEA BREEZES
Seafood ££

( 01478-612016; www.seabreezes-skye.co.uk; 2 Marine Buildings, Quay St; mains £12-19;  lunch & dinner Apr-Oct) Sea Breezes is an informal, no-frills restaurant specialising in local fish and shellfish fresh from the boat – try the impressive seafood platter, a small mountain of langoustines, crab, oysters and lobster. Early-bird menu (5pm to 6pm) offers two courses for £17. Book early, as it's often hard to get a table.

### BISTRO AT THE BOSVILLE
Bistro ££

( 01478-612846; www.bosvillehotel.co.uk; 7 Bosville Tce; mains £9-20;  noon-2.30pm & 5.30-10pm;  ) This hotel bistro sports a relaxed atmosphere, an award-winning chef and a menu that makes the most of Skye-sourced produce – including lamb, game, seafood, cheese, organic vegetables and berries – and adds an original twist to traditional dishes. The neighbouring **Chandlery Restaurant** (three-course dinner £44) offers a more upmarket experience.

# Shopping

### SKYE BATIKS
Gifts

(www.skyebatiks.com; The Green;  9am-6pm May-Sep, to 9pm Jul & Aug, to 5pm Mon-Sat

PAUL HARRIS/GETTY IMAGES ©

# Don't Miss **Dunvegan Castle**

Skye's most famous historic building, and one of its most popular tourist attractions, is Dunvegan Castle, seat of the chief of Clan MacLeod. It has played host to Samuel Johnson, Sir Walter Scott and, most famously, Flora MacDonald. The oldest parts are the 14th-century keep and dungeon but most of it dates from the 17th to 19th centuries.

In addition to the usual castle stuff – swords, silver and family portraits – there are some interesting artefacts; the most famous is the Fairy Flag, a silk banner that dates from between the 4th and 7th centuries. Bonnie Prince Charlie's waistcoat and a lock of his hair, donated by Flora MacDonald's granddaughter, share a room with Rory Mor's Drinking Horn, a beautiful 16th-century vessel of Celtic design that could hold half a gallon of claret. Upholding the family tradition, in 1956, John MacLeod – the 29th chief, who died in 2007 – downed the contents in one minute and 57 seconds 'without setting down or falling down'.

From the end of the minor road beyond Dunvegan Castle entrance, an easy 1-mile walk leads to the **Coral Beaches** – a pair of blindingly white beaches composed of the bleached exoskeletons of coralline algae known as maerl.

On the way to Dunvegan from Portree you'll pass **Edinbane Pottery** ( 📞01470-582234; www. edinbane-pottery.co.uk; 🕙9am-6pm daily Easter-Oct, closed Sat & Sun Nov-Easter), one of the island's original craft workshops, established in 1971, where you can watch potters at work.

## NEED TO KNOW
📞01470-521206; www.dunvegancastle.com; adult/child £9.50/5; 🕙10am-5pm Apr–mid-Oct

Oct-Apr) Skye Batiks is a cut above your average gift shop, selling a range of interesting crafts such as carved wood, jewellery and batik fabrics with Celtic designs.

**ISLE OF SKYE CRAFTS@OVER THE RAINBOW** Gifts
( 📞01478-612361; www.skyeknitwear.com; Quay Brae; 🕙9am-5.30pm Mon-Sat, plus 11am-4pm

**Sun Apr-Oct)** Crammed with colourful knitwear, cross-stitch kits and lambswool and cashmere scarves, plus all kinds of interesting gifts.

**ISLE OF SKYE SOAP CO**    Cosmetics
( ☎ 01478-611350; www.skye-soap.co.uk; Somerled Sq; ⊗ 9am-5.30pm Mon-Fri, to 5pm Sat) A sweet-smelling gift shop that specialises in handmade soaps and cosmetics made using natural ingredients and aromatherapy oils.

**CARMINA GADELICA**    Music
( ☎ 01478-612585; Bank St; ⊗ 9am-5.30pm Mon-Sat, to 9pm Jun-Aug) Browse the shelves for CDs of Gaelic music and books on local subjects.

## ⓘ Getting There & Around

### Bus

The main bus stop is in Somerled Sq. There are seven Scottish Citylink buses every day, including Sundays, from Kyle of Lochalsh to Portree (£6, one hour) and on to Uig.

Local buses (Monday to Saturday only) run from Portree to Broadford (40 minutes, at least hourly) via Sligachan (15 minutes); to Armadale (1¼ hours, connecting with the ferries to Mallaig); to Carbost (40 minutes, four daily); to Uig (30 minutes, six daily) and to Dunvegan Castle (40 minutes, five daily Monday to Friday, three on Saturday). There are also five or six buses a day on a circular route around Trotternish (in both directions), taking in Flodigarry (20 minutes), Kilmuir (1¼ hours) and Uig (30 minutes). Buses from the mainland also come through Portree.

### Bicycle

Island Cycles ( ☎ 01478-613121; www.islandcycles-skye.co.uk; The Green; ⊗ 9am-5pm Mon-Sat) You can hire bikes here for £8.50/15 per half-/full day.

## Duirinish & Waternish

The Duirinish peninsula to the west of Dunvegan, and Waternish to the north, boast some of Skye's most atmospheric hotels and restaurants, plus an eclectic range of artists' studios and crafts workshops. Portree tourist office provides a free booklet listing them all.

## ⦿ Sights & Activities

The sparsely populated Duirinish Peninsula is dominated by the distinctive flat-topped peaks of Helabhal Mhor (469m) and Helabhal Bheag (488m), known locally as **MacLeod's Tables**. There are some fine walks from Orbost, including the summit of Helabhal Bheag (allow 3½ hours return) and the 5-mile trail from Orbost to **MacLeod's Maidens**, a series of pointed sea stacks at the southern tip of the peninsula.

It's worth making the long drive beyond Dunvegan to the west side of the Duirinish Peninsula to see the spectacular sea cliffs of **Waterstein Head**, and to walk down to **Neist Point lighthouse** with its views to the Outer Hebrides.

## 🛏 Sleeping & Eating

🍃 **THREE CHIMNEYS**    Modern Scottish **£££**
( ☎ 01470-511258; www.threechimneys.co.uk; Colbost; 3-course lunch/dinner £37/60; ⊗ lunch Mon-Sat mid-Mar–Oct, dinner daily year-round; Ⓟ) Halfway between Dunvegan and Waterstein, the Three Chimneys is a superb romantic retreat combining a gourmet restaurant in a candlelit crofter's cottage with sumptuous five-star rooms (double £295, dinner/B&B per couple £415) in the modern house next door. Book well in advance, and note that children are not welcome in the restaurant in the evenings.

**LOCHBAY SEAFOOD RESTAURANT**    Seafood **££**
( ☎ 01470-592235; www.lochbay-seafood-restaurant.co.uk; Stein; mains £14-23, lobster £30-42; ⊗ lunch & dinner Tue-Sat; Ⓟ)This is one of Skye's most romantic restaurants, featuring a cosy farmhouse kitchen with terracotta tiles and a wood-burning stove, and a menu that includes most things that either swim in the sea or live in a shell. Best to book ahead.

### RED ROOF CAFÉ   Cafe £
( ✆ 01470-511766; www.redroofskye.co.uk;
Glendale; mains £8-10; ⏱11am-5pm Apr-Oct;
P 🚻) Tucked away up a glen, a mile off
the main road, this restored 250-year-old
byre is a wee haven of home-grown grub.
As well as great coffee and cake, there
are lunch platters (noon to 3pm) of Skye
seafood, game or cheese served with
salad leaves and edible flowers grown
just along the road. Add in music gigs and
you can see why this place is a favourite.

### STEIN INN   Pub £
( ✆ 01470-592362; www.steininn.co.uk; Stein; bar
meals £8-12; ⏱food noon-4pm & 6-9.30pm Mon-
Sat, 12.30-4pm & 6.30-9pm Sun Easter-Oct; P )
This old country inn dates from 1790 and
has a handful of bedrooms (per person
£37 to £55), all with sea views, a lively
little bar and a delightful beer garden – a
real suntrap on warm summer afternoons – beside the loch. The bar serves
real ales from the Isle of Skye Brewery
and does an excellent crab sandwich.
Food served in winter too, but call ahead
to check.

# Trotternish

The Trotternish Peninsula to the north
of Portree has some of Skye's most
beautiful – and bizarre – scenery. A loop
road allows a circular driving tour of the
peninsula from Portree, passing through
the village of **Uig**, where the ferry to the
Outer Hebrides departs. The following
sights are described travelling anticlockwise from Portree.

## 👁 Sights & Activties

### OLD MAN OF STORR   Rock Formation
The 50m-high, pot-bellied pinnacle of
crumbling basalt known as the Old Man of
Storr is prominent above the road 6 miles
north of Portree. Walk up to its foot from
the car park in the woods at the northern
end of Loch Leathan (round trip 2 miles).
This seemingly unclimbable pinnacle was
first scaled in 1955 by English mountain-
eer Don Whillans, a feat that has been
repeated only a handful of times since.

### QUIRAING   Rock Formation
Staffin Bay is dominated by the dramatic
basalt escarpment of the Quiraing: its impressive land-slipped cliffs and pinnacles
constitute one of Skye's most remarkable landscapes. From a parking area
at the highest point of the minor
road between Staffin and Uig you
can walk north to the Quiraing
in half an hour.

### SKYE MUSEUM OF
### ISLAND LIFE   Museum
( ✆ 01470-552206; www.skye
museum.co.uk; adult/child
£2.50/50p; ⏱9.30am-5pm
Mon-Sat Easter-Oct) The
peat-reek of crofting
life in the 18th and 19th
centuries is preserved
in the thatched cottag-
es, croft houses, barns
and farm implements of
the Skye Museum of Is-
land Life in Kilmuir. Behind

Old Man of Storr
BRITAIN ONVIEW/GETTY IMAGES ©

the museum is Kilmuir Cemetery, where a tall Celtic cross marks the **grave of Flora MacDonald**; the cross was erected in 1955 to replace the original monument, of which 'every fragment was removed by tourists'.

**FAIRY GLEN**     Natural Formation
Just south of Uig, a minor road (signposted 'Sheader and Balnaknock') leads in a mile or so to the Fairy Glen, a strange and enchanting natural landscape of miniature conical hills, rocky towers, ruined cottages and a tiny roadside lochan.

# OBAN

Oban is a peaceful waterfront town on a delightful bay, with sweeping views to Kerrera and Mull. OK, that first bit about peaceful is true only in winter; in summer the town centre is a heaving mass of humanity, its streets jammed with traffic and crowded with holidaymakers, day trippers and travellers headed for the islands. But the setting is still lovely.

There's not a huge amount to see in the town itself, but it's an appealingly busy place with some excellent restaurants and lively pubs, and it's the main gateway to the islands of Mull, Iona, Colonsay, Barra, Coll and Tiree.

## 👁 Sights

**MCCAIG'S TOWER**     Historic Building
(cnr Laurel & Duncraggan Rds; ⊙24hr) Crowning the hill above the town centre is the Victorian folly known as McCaig's Tower. Its construction was commissioned in 1890 by local worthy John Stuart McCaig, an art critic, philosophical essayist and banker, with the philanthropic intention of providing work for unemployed stonemasons.

To reach it on foot, make the steep climb up Jacob's Ladder (a flight of stairs) from Argyll St and then follow the signs. The views over the bay are worth the effort.

## ♥ If You Like... Folk Museums

The history of rural communities in Scotland is preserved in a wide range of fascinating museums, often located in original farm buildings and historic houses.

1 **EASDALE ISLAND FOLK MUSEUM**
( ☎01852-300370; www.easdalemuseum.org; adult/child £2.25/50p; ⊙11am-4.30pm Apr-Oct, to 5pm Jul & Aug) Has displays about the slate industry and life on the islands in the 18th and 19th centuries; 10 miles southwest of Oban.

2 **KILMARTIN HOUSE MUSEUM**
( ☎01546-510278; www.kilmartin.org; Kilmartin; adult/child £5/2; ⊙10am-5.30pm Mar-Oct, 11am-4pm Nov-23 Dec) Exhibits of artefacts recovered from important prehistoric sites in Kilmartin Glen; 28 miles south of Oban.

3 **OLD BYRE HERITAGE CENTRE**
( ☎01688-400229; www.old-byre.co.uk; Dervaig; adult/child £4/2; ⊙10.30am-6.30pm Wed-Sun Apr-Oct) Brings Mull's heritage and natural history to life through a series of tableaux and half-hour film shows; 10 miles northwest of Tobermory.

**OBAN DISTILLERY**     Distillery
( ☎01631-572004; www.discovering-distilleries. com; Stafford St; tour £7; ⊙9.30am-5pm Mon-Sat Easter-Oct, plus noon-5pm Sun Jul-Sep, 10am-4pm Mon-Fri Nov-Dec & Feb-Easter, closed Jan) This distillery has been producing Oban single malt whisky since 1794. There are guided tours available (last tour begins one hour before closing time), but even without a tour, it's still worth a look at the small exhibition in the foyer.

FREE **WAR & PEACE MUSEUM**     Museum
( ☎01631-570007; www.obanmuseum. uk; Corran Esplanade; ⊙10am-6pm Mon-Sat, to 4pm Sun May-Sep, to 4pm daily Mar-Apr & Oct-Nov) Military buffs will enjoy the little War & Peace Museum, which chronicles Oban's role in WWII as a base for Catalina seaplanes and as a marshalling area for Atlantic convoys.

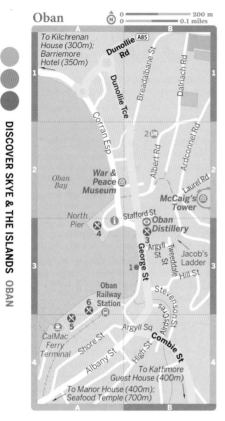

## Oban

To Kilchrenan House (300m); Barriemore Hotel (350m)

Dunollie Rd A85

Breadalbane St

Dalriach Rd

Dunollie Tce

Corran Esp

Oban Bay

Ardconnel Rd

Albert Rd

War & Peace Museum

Laurel Rd

McCaig's Tower

North Pier

Stafford St

Oban Distillery

George St

Argyll St

Tweeddale St

Jacob's Ladder

Hill St

Oban Railway Station

Stevenson St

Airds Cres

CalMac Ferry Terminal

Shore St

Argyll Sq

High St

Combie St

Albany St

To Kathmore Guest House (400m)

To Manor House (400m); Seafood Temple (700m)

looking the entrance to Oban Bay. There are 13 spacious rooms here (ask for one with a sea view), plus a guest lounge with magazines and newspapers, and plump Loch Fyne kippers on the breakfast menu.

**HEATHERFIELD HOUSE**     B&B ££
( ☏01631-562806; www.heatherfieldhouse.co.uk; Albert Rd; s/d from £38/88; **P** **@** **☎**) The welcoming Heatherfield House occupies a converted 1870s rectory set in extensive grounds and has six spacious rooms. If possible, ask for room 1, which comes complete with fireplace, sofa and a view over the garden to the harbour.

**KILCHRENAN HOUSE**     B&B ££
( ☏01631-562663; www.kilchrenanhouse.co.uk; Corran Esplanade; s/d £50/90; **P**) You'll get a warm welcome at this elegant Victorian villa built for a textile magnate in 1883. Most of the rooms have views across Oban Bay, but rooms 5 and 9 are the best: room 5 has a huge freestanding bath tub, perfect for soaking weary bones.

**MANOR HOUSE**     Hotel £££
( ☏01631-562087; www.manorhouseoban.com; Gallanach Rd; r £165-225; **P** **☎**) Built in 1780 for the Duke of Argyll as part of his Oban estates, the Manor House is now one of Oban's finest hotels. It has small but elegant Georgian-style rooms, an upmarket bar frequented by local and visiting yachties, and a fine restaurant serving

## Tours

From April to October, **Bowman's Tours** ( ☏01631-566809; www.bowmanstours.co.uk; 1 Queens Park Pl) offers a Three Isles day trip (adult/child £55/27.50, 10 hours, daily) from Oban that visits Mull, Iona and Staffa. Note that the crossing to Staffa is weather dependent. Bowman's also runs a circular coach tour around Mull (adult/child £20/10).

## Sleeping

**BARRIEMORE HOTEL**     B&B ££
( ☏01631-566356; www.barriemore-hotel.co.uk; Corran Esplanade; s/d from £70/99; **P** **☎**) The Barriemore enjoys a grand location, over-

Scottish and French cuisine. Children under 12 years are not welcome.

**KATHMORE GUEST HOUSE** B&B ££
(☏01631-562104; www.kathmore.co.uk; Soroba Rd; s £45-65, d £55-75; P 🛜) Warm and welcoming, the Kathmore combines traditional Highland hospitality and hearty breakfasts with a wee touch of boutique flair in its stylish bedspreads and colourful artwork. There's a comfortable lounge and outdoor deck where you can enjoy a pre- or post-prandial glass of wine on those long summer evenings.

 Eating

**WATERFRONT FISHOUSE RESTAURANT** Seafood ££
(☏01631-563110; www.waterfrontoban.co.uk; Railway Pier; mains £11-20; ⏰lunch & dinner; 👪) Housed on the top floor of a converted seamen's mission, the Waterfront's stylish, unfussy decor in burgundy and brown, with dark wooden furniture, does little to distract from the superb seafood freshly landed at the quay just a few metres away. The menu ranges from classic haddock and chips to fresh oysters, scallops and langoustines.

The lunch and early-evening menu (5.30pm to 6.45pm) offers two courses for £10. Best to book for dinner.

**SHELLFISH BAR** Seafood £
(Railway Pier; mains £3-13; ⏰9am-6pm) If you want to savour superb Scottish seafood without the expense of an upmarket restaurant, head for Oban's famous seafood stall – it's the green shack on the quayside near the ferry terminal. Here you can buy fresh and cooked seafood to take away – excellent prawn sandwiches (£2.95), dressed crab (£4.95), and fresh oysters for only 75p each.

**SEAFOOD TEMPLE** Seafood £££
(☏01631-566000; www.obanseafood.com; Gallanach Rd; mains £16-35; ⏰lunch & dinner) Locally sourced seafood is the god that's worshipped at this tiny temple – a former park pavilion with glorious views over bay. Oban's smallest restaurant serves up whole lobster cooked to order, baked crab with cheese and herb crust, plump langoustines, and the 'Taste of Argyll' seafood platter (£70 for two people), which offers a taste of everything. Dinner is in two sittings, at 6.15pm and 8.30pm; bookings essential.

**CUAN MOR** Bistro ££
(☏01631-565078; www.cuanmor.co.uk; 60 George St; mains £9-14; ⏰10am-midnight; 🛜🍴) This always-busy bar and bistro brews its own beer, and sports a no-nonsense menu of old favourites – from haddock and chips to homemade lasagne to sausage and mashed potatoes with onion gravy – spiced with a few more-sophisticated dishes such as squat lobster carbonara, and a decent range of vegetarian dishes. And the sticky toffee pudding is not to be missed!

**EE'USK** Seafood ££
(☏01631-565666; www.eeusk.com; North Pier; mains £13-20; ⏰lunch & dinner) Bright and modern Ee'usk (it's how you pronounce *iasg,* the Gaelic word for fish) occupies Oban's prime location on the North Pier. Floor-to-ceiling windows allow diners on two levels to enjoy views over the harbour to Kerrera and Mull, while sampling a menu of locally caught seafood ranging from fragrant Thai fish cakes to langoustines with chilli and ginger.

A little pricey, perhaps, but both food and location are first class.

ℹ️ **Information**

**Lorn & Islands District General Hospital** (☏01631-567500; Glengallan Rd) Southern end of town.

**Tourist Office** (☏01631-563122; www.oban.org. uk; 3 North Pier; ⏰9am-7pm Mon-Sat, 10am-6pm Sun May-Sep, 9am-5.30pm Mon-Sat Oct-Apr)

ℹ️ **Getting There & Away**

The bus, train and ferry terminals are all grouped conveniently together next to the harbour on the southern edge of the bay.

KATHY COLLINS/GETTY IMAGES ©

## Boat

**CalMac** (www.calmac.co.uk) ferries link Oban with the islands of **Mull**, **Coll**, **Tiree**, **Lismore**, **Colonsay**, **Barra** and **Lochboisdale** (South Uist). Information and reservations for all CalMac ferry services are available at the **ferry terminal** (☎01631-562244; Railway Pier; ⏰9am-6pm Mar-Oct) near the train station. Ferries to the **Isle of Kerrera** depart from a separate jetty, about 2 miles southwest of Oban town centre.

## Bus

**Scottish Citylink** (www.citylink.co.uk) operates intercity coaches to Oban, while **West Coast Motors** (www.westcoastmotors.co.uk) runs local and regional services. The bus terminal is outside the train station.

**Glasgow** (via Inveraray and Arrochar) £18, three hours, four daily

**Fort William** (via Appin and Ballachulish) £9.40, 1½ hours, three daily Monday to Saturday

## Train

Oban is at the terminus of a scenic route that branches off the West Highland line at Crianlarich. The train isn't much use for travelling north from Oban – to reach Fort William requires a detour via Crianlarich (3¾ hours). Take the bus instead.

**Glasgow** £22, three hours, three daily

## 🛈 Getting Around

### Car Hire

**Hazelbank Motors** (☎01631-566476; www. obancarhire.co.uk; Lynn Rd; ⏰8.30am-5.30pm Mon-Sat) hires out small cars per day/week from £40/225 including VAT, insurance and Collision Damage Waiver (CDW).

### Taxi

There's a taxi rank outside the train station. Otherwise, call **Oban Taxis** (☎01631-564666).

# ISLE OF MULL

From the rugged ridges of Ben More and the black basalt crags of Burg to the white sand, rose-pink granite and emerald waters that fringe the Ross of Mull Peninsula, Mull can lay claim to some of the finest scenery in the Inner Hebrides, while the waters to the west of the island provide some of the best whale-spotting opportunities in Scotland. Then there's two impressive castles, a narrow-gauge railway, the sacred island of Iona and easy access from Oban – no wonder Mull's so popular.

Despite the number of visitors who flock to Mull, it seems to be large enough to absorb them all; many stick to the well-worn routes from Craignure to Iona or Tobermory, returning to Oban in the evening. Besides, there are plenty of hidden corners where you can escape the crowds.

About two-thirds of Mull's population lives in and around Tobermory, the island's capital, in the north. Craignure, at the southeastern corner, has the main ferry terminal and is where most people arrive. Fionnphort is at the far-western end of the long Ross of Mull Peninsula, and is where the ferry to Iona departs.

 **Tours**

**BOWMAN'S TOURS** Tours
(☎01680-812313; www.bowmanstours.co.uk) does day trips from Oban to Mull, Staffa and Iona by ferry and bus.

**GORDON GRANT MARINE** Boat Tours
(☎01681-700388; www.staffatours.com) Runs boat trips from Fionnphort to Staffa (adult/child £25/10, 2½ hours, daily April to October), and to Staffa and the Treshnish Isles (£45/20, five hours, Sunday to Friday May to July).

**MULL MAGIC** Walking Tours
(☎01688-301245; www.mullmagic.com) Offers guided walking tours in the Mull countryside (£37.50 to £47.50 per person) to spot eagles, otters, butterfiles and other wildlife, as well as customised tours.

## ℹ Information

### Medical

**Dunaros Hospital** (☎01680-300392) Has a minor-injuries unit; the nearest casualty department is in Oban.

### Money

You can get cash using a debit card from the post offices in Salen and Craignure, or get cash back with a purchase from Co-op food stores.

### Tourist Information

**Craignure Tourist Office** (☎01680-812377; ⊙8.30am-5pm Mon-Sat, 10.30am-5pm Sun)

**Mull Visitor & Information Centre** (☎01688-302875; Ledaig, Tobermory; ⊙9am-5pm)

## ℹ Getting There & Away

There are three **CalMac** (www.calmac.co.uk) car ferries linking Mull with the mainland.

**Oban to Craignure** (passenger/car £5.25/46.50, 40 minutes, every two hours) The shortest and busiest route – booking advised for cars.

**Lochaline to Fishnish** (£3.10/13.65, 15 minutes, at least hourly) On Mull's east coast.

**Tobermory to Kilchoan** (£5/25.50, 35 minutes, seven daily Monday to Saturday) Links to the Ardnamurchan Peninsula; from May to August there are also five sailings on Sunday.

## ℹ Getting Around

### Bus

Public transport on Mull is fairly limited. Bowman's Tours is the main operator, connecting the ferry ports and the island's main villages.

**Craignure to Tobermory** (£7.30 return, one hour, four to seven daily Monday to Friday, three to five Saturday and Sunday),

**Craignure to Fionnphort** (£11 return, 1¼ hours, three daily Monday to Saturday, one Sunday).

**Tobermory to Dervaig and Calgary** (£4 return, three daily Monday to Friday, two on Saturday).

### Car

Almost all of Mull's road network consists of single-track roads. There are petrol stations at Craignure, Fionnphort, Salen and Tobermory. **Mull Self Drive** (☎01680-300402; www.mullselfdrive.co.uk) rents small cars for £45/237 per day/week.

### Taxi

**Mull Taxi** (☎07760-426351; www.mulltaxi.co.uk) is based in Tobermory, and has a vehicle that is wheelchair accessible.

## Detour:
# Kilmartin Glen

This magical glen is the focus of one of the biggest concentrations of prehistoric sites in Scotland. Burial cairns, standing stones, stone circles, hill forts and cup and ring-marked rocks litter the countryside. Within a 6-mile radius of Kilmartin village there are 25 sites with standing stones and over 100 rock carvings.

The oldest monuments at Kilmartin date from 5000 years ago and comprise a linear cemetery of burial cairns that runs south from Kilmartin village for 1.5 miles. There are also ritual monuments (two stone circles) at Temple Wood, 0.75 miles southwest of Kilmartin. The Kilmartin House Museum (p219) bookshop sells maps and guides.

The hill fort of Dunadd, 3.5 miles south of Kilmartin village, was the seat of power of the first kings of Dalriada, and may have been where the Stone of Destiny was originally located. The faint rock carvings of a wild boar and two footprints with an Ogham inscription may have been used in some kind of inauguration ceremony. A slippery path leads to the summit where you can gaze out on much the same view that the kings of Dalriada enjoyed 1300 years ago.

Bus 423 between Oban and Ardrishaig (four daily Monday to Friday, two on Saturday) stops at Kilmartin (£5, one hour and 20 minutes).

# Craignure & Around

There's not much to see at Craignure other than the ferry terminal and the hotel, so turn left and drive or cycle the 3 miles to **Duart Castle** ( 01680-812309; www.duartcastle.com; adult/child £5.50/2.75; 10.30am-5.30pm daily May–mid-Oct, 11am-4pm Sun-Thu Apr), a formidable fortress dominating the Sound of Mull (you can't miss it as you approach Craignure by ferry). The seat of the Clan Maclean, this is one of the oldest inhabited castles in Scotland – the central keep was built in 1360. It was bought and restored in 1911 by Sir Fitzroy Maclean and has damp dungeons, vast halls and bathrooms equipped with ancient fittings. A bus to the castle meets the 9.50am, 11.55am and 2pm ferries from Oban to Craignure.

On the way to Duart you'll pass **Wings Over Mull** ( 01680-812594; www.wingsovermull.com; Torosay; adult/child £4.50/1.50; 10.30am-5.30am Easter-Oct), a wildlife centre dedicated to birds of prey. The captive collection includes more than two dozen species, and there are daily displays of falconry and hawk handling.

# Tobermory

The island's main town is a picturesque little fishing port and yachting centre with brightly painted houses arranged around a sheltered harbour, with a grid-patterned 'upper town'. The village was the setting for the children's TV program *Balamory*, and while the series stopped filming in 2005, regular repeats mean that the town still swarms in summer with toddlers towing parents around looking for their favourite TV characters (frazzled parents can get a *Balamory* booklet from the tourist offices in Oban and Tobermory).

## Sights & Activities

FREE **MARINE DISCOVERY CENTRE** Wildlife Exhibition ( 01688-302620; www.whaledolphintrust.co.uk; 28 Main St; admission free; 10am-5pm Mon-Fri, 11am-4pm Sun Apr-Oct, 11am-5pm Mon-Fri Nov-Mar) The Hebridean Whale & Dolphin Trust's Marine Discovery Centre has displays, videos and interactive exhibits on whale and dolphin biology and ecology, and is a great place for kids to learn about sea mammals. It also provides information about volunteering and reporting sightings of whales and dolphins.

**MULL MUSEUM**  Museum
(☏01688-302603; www.mullmuseum.org.uk; Main St; admission by donation; ⊙10am-4pm Mon-Fri Easter-Oct) Mull Museum is a good rainy-day retreat. There are interesting exhibits on crofting and on the *Tobermory Galleon*, a ship from the Spanish Armada that sank in Tobermory Bay in 1588 and has been the objective of treasure seekers ever since.

**TOBERMORY DISTILLERY**  Distillery
(☏01688-302647; www.tobermorymalt.com; Ledaig; tour £3; ⊙10am-5pm Mon-Fri Easter-Oct) The tiny Tobermory Distillery was established in 1798.

FREE **AN TOBAR ARTS CENTRE**  Gallery
(☏01688-302211; www.antobar.co.uk; Argyll Tce; ⊙10am-5pm Mon-Sat May-Sep, plus 2-5pm Sun Jul & Aug, 10am-4pm Tue-Sat Oct-Apr) An art gallery and exhibition space with a good vegetarian-friendly cafe.

**Sleeping**

**HIGHLAND COTTAGE HOTEL**  Boutique Hotel £££
(☏01688-302030; www.highlandcottage.co.uk; Breadalbane St; d £150-165; ⊙mid-Mar–Oct; P🛜) Antique furniture, four-poster beds, embroidered bedspreads, fresh flowers and candlelight lend this small hotel (only six rooms) an appealingly old-fashioned cottage atmosphere, but with all mod

# Watching Wildlife on Mull

Mull's varied landscapes and habitats, from high mountains and wild moorland to wave-lashed sea cliffs and seaweed-fringed skerries, offer the chance to spot some of Scotland's rarest wildlife, including eagles, otters, dolphins and whales.

**Mull Wildlife Expeditions** (☏01688-500121; www.torrbuan.com;) offers full-day Land Rover tours of the island with the chance of spotting red deer, golden eagles, peregrine falcons, white-tailed sea eagles, hen harriers, otters and perhaps dolphins and porpoises. The cost (adult/child £43/40) includes pick-up from your accommodation or from any of the ferry terminals, a picnic lunch and use of binoculars. The timing of this tour makes it possible as a day-trip from Oban, with pick-up and drop-off at the Craignure ferry.

**Sea Life Surveys** (☏01688-302916; www.sealifesurveys.com; Ledaig) runs whale-watching trips from Tobermory harbour to the waters north and west of Mull. An all-day whale watch (per person £80) gives up to seven hours at sea (not recommended for kids under 14), and has a 95% success rate for sightings. The four-hour Wildlife Adventure cruise is geared more towards children (£50/40 per adult/child).

**Turus Mara** (☏08000 85 87 86; www.turusmara.com) runs boat trips from Ulva Ferry in central Mull to Staffa and the Treshnish Isles (adult/child £50/25, 6½ hours), with an hour ashore on Staffa and two hours on Lunga, where you can see seals, puffins, kittiwakes, razorbills and many other species of seabird.

**The RSPB** (☏01680-812556; www.forestry.gov.uk/mullseaeagles) runs escorted trips to a viewing hide in Glen Seilisdeir where you can watch white-tailed sea eagles. Tours (adult/child £6/3) leave at 10am and 1pm Monday to Friday, from the B8035 road about 1 mile north of Tiroran (advance booking essential, by phone or at the Craignure tourist office).

cons including cable TV, full-size baths and room service. There's also an excellent fine-dining restaurant here.

### SONAS HOUSE
B&B ££

(☎01688-302304; www.sonashouse.co.uk; The Fairways, Erray Rd; s/d £110/125, apt from £90; P 🛜 ☎) Here's a first – a B&B with a heated, indoor 10m swimming pool! Sonas is a large, modern house that offers luxury B&B in a beautiful setting with superb views over Tobermory Bay; ask for the 'Blue Poppy' bedroom, which has its own balcony. There's also a self-contained studio apartment with double bed.

### CUIDHE LEATHAIN
B&B ££

(☎01688-302504; www.cuidhe-leathain.co.uk; Salen Rd; r per person £40; 🛜) A handsome 19th-century house in the upper town, Cuidhe Leathain (coo-lane), which means Maclean's Corner, exudes a cosily cluttered Victorian atmosphere. The breakfasts will set you up for the rest of the day, and the owners are a fount of knowledge about Mull and its wildlife. Minimum two-night stay.

### HARBOUR VIEW
B&B ££

(☎01688-301111; www.tobermorybandb. com; 1 Argyll Tce; per person £40-45; 🛜) This beautifully renovated fisherman's cottage is perched on the edge of Tobermory's 'upper town'. Exposed patches of original stone walls add a touch of character, while a new extension provides the family suite (two adjoining rooms with shared bathroom, sleeps four) with an outdoor terrace that enjoys breathtaking views across the harbour.

## Eating & Drinking

### CAFÉ FISH
Seafood ££

(☎01688-301253; www.thecafefish.com; The Pier; mains £10-22; ☺lunch & dinner) Seafood doesn't come much fresher than the stuff served at this warm and welcoming little restaurant overlooking Tobermory harbour – as its motto says, 'The only thing frozen here is the fisherman'! Langoustines and squat lobsters go straight from boat to kitchen to join rich Tuscan-style seafood stew, fat scallops, fish pie and catch-of-the-day on the daily-

Glengorm Castle

changing menu. Also has freshly baked bread, homemade desserts and a range of Scottish cheeses on offer.

**FISH & CHIP VAN**  Fish & Chips £
( ☎ 01688-301109; www.tobermoryfishand chipvan.co.uk; Main St; mains £3-8; ⏱ 12.30-9pm Mon-Sat Apr-Dec, plus Sun Jun-Sep, 12.30-7pm Mon-Sat Jan-Mar) If it's a takeaway you're after, you can tuck into some of Scotland's best gourmet fish and chips down on the waterfront. And where else will you find a chip van selling freshly cooked prawns and scallops?

**MACGOCHAN'S**  Pub ££
( ☎ 01688-302350; www.macgochans-tobermory. co.uk; Ledaig; mains £9-20; ⏱ lunch & dinner) A lively pub beside the car park at the southern end of the waterfront, MacGochan's does good bar meals (haddock and chips, steak pie, vegetable lasagne), and often has outdoor barbecues on summer evenings. There's a beer garden out front, and live music in the bar on weekends.

**MISHNISH HOTEL**  Pub ££
( ☎ 01688-302009; www.mishnish.co.uk; Main St; mains £11-20; ⏱ lunch & dinner; 📶) 'The Mish' is a favourite hang-out for visiting yachties and a good place for a pint, or a meal at the pub's Mish-Dish restaurant. Wood-panelled and flag-draped, this is a good old traditional pub where you can listen to live folk music, toast your toes by the open fire or challenge the locals to a game of pool.

# North Mull

The road from Tobermory west to Calgary cuts inland, leaving most of the north coast of Mull wild and inaccessible. Just outside Tobermory a long, single-track road leads north for 4 miles to majestic **Glengorm Castle** ( ☎ 01688-302321; www. glengormcastle.co.uk; Glengorm; ⏱ 10am-5pm Easter–mid-Oct) with views across the sea to Ardnamurchan, Rum and the Outer Hebrides. The castle outbuildings house an **art gallery** featuring the work of local artists, a **farm shop** selling local produce, and an excellent **coffee shop**. The castle

itself is not open to the public, but you're free to explore the beautiful grounds.

The **Old Byre Heritage Centre** (p219) brings Mull's social and natural history to life through a series of tableaux and half-hour film shows. The prize for most bizarre exhibit goes to the 40cm-long model of a midge. The centre's tearoom serves good, inexpensive snacks, including homemade soup and clootie dumpling, and there's a kids' outdoor play area.

Mull's best (and busiest) silver-sand **beach**, flanked by cliffs and with views out to Coll and Tiree, is at **Calgary**, about 12 miles west of Tobermory. And yes – this is the place from which the more famous Calgary in Alberta, Canada, takes its name.

# South Mull

The road from Craignure to Fionnphort climbs through some wild and desolate scenery before reaching the southwestern part of the island, which consists of a long peninsula called the **Ross of Mull**. The Ross has a spectacular south coast lined with black basalt cliffs that give way further west to white-sand beaches and pink granite crags. The cliffs are highest at Malcolm's Point, near the superb **Carsaig Arches**.

The little village of **Bunessan** has a hotel, tearoom, pub and some shops, and is home to the **Ross of Mull Historical Centre** ( ☎ 01681-700659; www.romhc.org.uk; admission £2; ⏱ 10am-4pm Mon-Fri Easter-Oct), a cottage museum that houses displays on local history, geology, archaeology, genealogy and wildlife.

A minor road leads south from here to the beautiful white-sand bay of **Uisken**, with views of the Paps of Jura. You can camp beside the beach here (£1 per person; ask for permission at Uisken Croft), but there are no facilities.

At the western end of the Ross, 38 miles from Craignure, is **Fionnphort** (finn-a-fort) and the ferry to Iona. The coast here is a beautiful blend of pink granite rocks, white sandy beaches and vivid turquoise sea.

# 🛏 Sleeping & Eating

### SEAVIEW
B&B ££

(📞01681-700235; www.iona-bed-breakfast-mull.com; Fionnphort; d £70-80; 🅿🛜) Barely a minute's walk from the Iona ferry, the Seaview has five beautifully decorated bedrooms and a breakfast conservatory with grand views across to Iona. The owners – a semiretired fisherman and his wife – offer tasty three-course dinners (£23 per person, September to May only), often based around local seafood. Bike hire available for guests only.

### 🌿 STAFFA HOUSE
B&B ££

(📞01681-700677; www.staffahouse.co.uk; Fionnphort; s/d £53/76; 🅿🛜) This charming and hospitable B&B is packed with antiques and period features, and offers breakfast in a conservatory with a view of Iona. Solar panels top up the hot-water supply, and the hearty breakfasts and packed lunches (£6 to £8.50) make use of local and organic produce where possible.

### 🌿 NINTH WAVE
Seafood £££

(📞01681-700757; www.ninthwaverestaurant.co.uk; Fionnphort; 4-course dinner £48; 🕐dinner Tue-Sun May-Oct) Based in a former croft 1 mile east of Fionnphort, this restaurant is owned and operated by a lobster fisherman and his Canadian wife. The daily menu makes use of locally landed shellfish and crustaceans, and vegetables and salad grown in the croft garden, served in a stylishly converted bothy. Advance booking essential.

## ISLE OF IONA

There are few more uplifting sights on Scotland's west coast than the view of Iona from Mull on a sunny day – an emerald island set in a sparkling turquoise sea. From the moment you step off the ferry you begin to appreciate the hushed, spiritual atmosphere that pervades this sacred island. Not surprisingly, Iona attracts a lot of day trippers, so if you want to experience the island's peace and quiet, spend a night here. Once the crowds have gone for the day, you can wander in peace around the ancient graveyard where the early kings of Scotland are buried, attend an evening service at the abbey, or walk to the top of Dun I and gaze south towards Ireland, as St Columba must have done so many centuries ago.

### History

St Columba sailed from Ireland and landed on Iona in 563 before setting out to spread Christianity throughout Scotland. He established a monastery on the island and it was here that the *Book of Kells* – the prize attraction of Dublin's Trinity College – is believed to have

Iona Abbey
DANITA DELIMONT/GETTY IMAGES ©

# Thar She Blows!

The North Atlantic Drift – a swirling tendril of the Gulf Stream – carries warm water into the cold, nutrient-rich seas off the Scottish coast, resulting in huge blooms of plankton. Small fish feed on the plankton, and bigger fish feed on the smaller fish, and this huge seafood smorgasbord attracts large numbers of marine mammals, from harbour porpoises and dolphins to minke whales and even – though sightings are rare – humpback and sperm whales.

In contrast to Iceland and Norway, Scotland has cashed in on the abundance of minke whales off its coast by embracing **whale watching** rather than whaling. There are now dozens of operators around the coast offering whale-watching boat trips lasting from a couple of hours to all day; some have whale-sighting success rates of 95% in summer.

While seals, porpoises and dolphins can be seen year-round, minke whales are migratory. The best time to see them is from June to August, with August being the peak month for sightings. The website of the Hebridean Whale & Dolphin Trust (www.whaledolphintrust.co.uk) has lots of information on the species you are likely to see, and how to identify them.

A booklet titled *Is It a Whale?* is available from tourist offices and bookshops, and provides tips on identifying the various species of marine mammal that you're likely to see.

been transcribed. It was taken to Kells in Ireland when Viking raids drove the monks from Iona.

The monks returned and the monastery prospered until its destruction during the Reformation. The ruins were given to the Church of Scotland in 1899, and by 1910 a group of enthusiasts called the **Iona Community** (www.iona.org.uk) had reconstructed the abbey. It's still a flourishing spiritual community that holds regular courses and retreats.

## Sights & Activities

Head uphill from the ferry pier and turn right through the grounds of a ruined 13th-century **nunnery** with fine cloistered gardens, and exit at the far end. Across the road is the **Iona Heritage Centre** (01681-700576; adult/child £2/free; 10.30am-5pm Mon-Sat Apr-Oct), which covers the history of Iona, crofting and lighthouses; the centre's **coffee shop** serves delicious home-baked goods.

Turn right here and continue along the road to **Reilig Oran**, an ancient cemetery that holds the graves of 48 of Scotland's early kings, including Macbeth, and a tiny Romanesque chapel. Beyond rises the spiritual heart of the island – **Iona Abbey** (HS; 01681-700512; adult/child £5.50/3.30; 9.30am-5.30pm Apr-Sep, to 4.30pm Oct-Mar). The spectacular nave, dominated by Romanesque and early Gothic vaults and columns, contains the elaborate, white marble tombs of the 8th duke of Argyll and his wife. A door on the left leads to the beautiful Gothic cloister, where medieval grave slabs sit alongside modern religious sculptures. A replica of the intricately carved **St John's Cross** stands just outside the abbey – the massive 8th-century original is in the **Infirmary Museum** (around the far side of the abbey) along with many other fine examples of early Christian and medieval **carved stones**.

Continue past the abbey and look for a footpath on the left signposted **Dun I** (dun-ee). An easy walk of about 15 to 20

DANITA DELIMONT/GETTY IMAGES

# Don't Miss Isle of Staffa & the Treshnish Isles

Felix Mendelssohn, who visited the uninhabited island of Staffa in 1829, was inspired to compose his *Hebrides Overture* after hearing waves echoing in the impressive and cathedral-like **Fingal's Cave**. The cave walls and surrounding cliffs are composed of vertical, hexagonal basalt columns that look like pillars (Staffa is Norse for 'Pillar Island'). You can land on the island and walk into the cave via a causeway. Nearby **Boat Cave** can be seen from the causeway, but you can't reach it on foot. Staffa also has a sizable puffin colony, north of the landing place.

Northwest of Staffa lies a chain of uninhabited islands called the **Treshnish Isles**. The two main islands are the curiously shaped **Dutchman's Cap** and **Lunga**. You can land on Lunga, walk to the top of the hill and visit the shag, puffin and guillemot colonies on the west coast at **Harp Rock**.

Unless you have your own boat, the only way to reach Staffa and the Treshnish Isles is on an organised boat trip from Ulva, Fionnphort or Iona.

minutes leads to the highest point on Iona, with fantastic views in all directions.

### Boat Trips

**ALTERNATIVE BOAT HIRE**   Boat Tours
( ☎ 01681-700537; www.boattripsiona.com; 🕙 Mon-Thu Apr-Oct) Offers cruises in a traditional wooden sailing boat for fishing, birdwatching, picnicking or just drifting along and admiring the scenery. Three-hour afternoon trips cost £20/9 per adult/child; on Wednesday there's a full day cruise (10am to 5pm, £40/18). Booking essential.

**MV IOLAIRE**   Island Tours
( ☎ 01681-700358; www.staffatrips.co.uk) Three-hour boat trips to Staffa (adult/child £25/10), departing Iona pier at 9.45am and 1.45pm, and from Fionnphort at 10am and 2pm, with one hour ashore on Staffa.

**MV VOLANTE**    Wildlife & Fishing Tours
( 01681-700362; www.volanteiona.com;  Jun-Oct) Four-hour sea-angling trips (£50 per person including tackle and bait), as well as 1½-hour round-the-island wildlife cruises (adult/child £15/8) and 3½-hour whale-watching trips (per person £40).

 **Sleeping & Eating**

**ARGYLL HOTEL**    Hotel ££
( 01681-700334; www.argyllhoteliona.co.uk; s/d from £66/99;  Mar-Oct; @ ) This cute little hotel has 16 snug rooms (a sea view costs rather a bit more – £140 for a double) and a country-house **restaurant** (mains £12-17;  8-10am, 12.30-1.20pm & 7-8pm) with wooden fireplace and antique tables and chairs. The kitchen is supplied by a huge organic garden around the back, and the menu includes home-grown salads, local seafood and Scottish beef and lamb.

**IONA HOSTEL**    Hostel £
( 01681-700781; www.ionahostel.co.uk; dm per adult/child £20/17;  check-in 4-7pm) This hostel is set in an attractive, modern timber building on a working croft, with stunning views out to Staffa and the Treshnish Isles. Rooms are clean and functional, and the well-equipped lounge/kitchen area has an open fire. It's at the northern end of the island – to get here, continue along the road past the abbey for 1.5 miles (a 20- to 30-minute walk).

## Getting There & Away

The passenger ferry from Fionnphort to Iona (£4.80 return, five minutes, hourly) runs daily. There are also various day trips available from Oban to Iona.

# Inverness & the Highlands

From the high, subarctic plateau of the Cairngorms to the rugged, rocky peaks of Glen Coe and Ben Nevis, the mountains of the Highlands are testimony to the sculpting power of ice and weather. Here the Scottish landscape is at its grandest, with soaring hills of rock and heather bounded by wooded glens and rushing waterfalls.

Unsurprisingly, this part of the country is an adventure playground for outdoor-sports enthusiasts. Aviemore, Glen Coe and Fort William draw hordes of hill walkers and rock climbers in summer, and skiers, snowboarders and ice climbers in winter. The Highland capital Inverness provides urban relaxation, while nearby Loch Ness and its elusive monster add a hint of mystery.

From Fort William, base camp for climbing Ben Nevis, the Road to the Isles leads past the gorgeous beaches of Arisaig and Morar to Mallaig, the jumping-off point for the Isle of Skye.

Cairngorms National Park (p257)
ANDY STOTHERT/GETTY IMAGES ©

**233**

# Inverness & the Highlands

1 Loch Ness
2 Cairngorms National Park
3 Glen Coe
4 Climbing Ben Nevis
5 Glen Affric
6 The Great Outdoors
7 Watching Wildlife

North Sea

*North Harris*

● Stornoway

*The Minch*

Tarbet ○
Scourie ○
Point of Stoer
Clachtoll ○
Achmelvich ○
Lochinv
Knocka
Achiltibuie ○
*Summer Isles*

● Tarbert

Ullapool ●
Drumchork ○
Melvaig ○  Midtown  Dundonnel
Gairloch ●

● Lochmaddy

*The Little Minch*

● Uig
*Trotternish*

Kinlochewe ○
Torridon ○  Achnasheen ○
Shieldaig ○ *Loch Damh*
*Carro*
● Dunvegan  ● Portree
Inner ○ Applecross
*Sound*  Lochcarron ○  *Farrar*
Kishorn ○ *Loch Carron*
Plockton ○  *Line*
*Loch Alsh*
*Isle of Skye*
● Kyleakin
*Loch Duich*
● Glenelg  *Loch Cluanie*
Arnisdale ○  *Loch*
● Lochboisdale  *Sleat*  *Loch Hourn*  Loyne
Knoydart
*Peninsula*
Inverie ○
*Loch Nevis*
● Mallaig  Strathan
Morar ○  *Pean*
*Isle of Rum*  Arisaig ○  Achnacar
Glenfinnan
*ATLANTIC OCEAN*
*Loch Shiel*  *Cona*  ⑥
*Isle of Eigg*  Ardmolich ○  ● Fort William
*Sea of the Hebrides*
Ardnamurchan Point ○  Salen ○  Ardgour ○
Kilchoan ○  Strontian ○  Glencoe ●
● Tobermory  ○ Bonnavoulin  *Loch Linnhe*  ③
*Isle of Mull*  ○ Lochaline

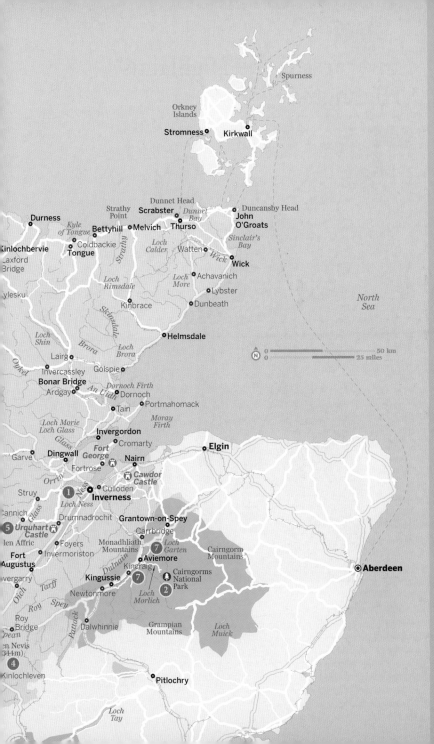

# Inverness & the Highlands' Highlights

## ① Loch Ness

Stretching along the glacier-gouged trench of the Great Glen, 23-mile-long Loch Ness contains more water than all the lakes in England and Wales combined. Its peaty depths conceal the long-standing mystery of its legendary monster, and thousands flock to its shores each year in hope of catching a glimpse. Above: Loch Ness Centre & Exhibition

### Need to Know

**BEST TIME TO GO** A calm day, for monster-spotting **TOP TIP** Avoid crowds – take the minor road on the loch's east side **BEST PHOTO OP** View from Urquhart Castle **For more: p253**

# Loch Ness Don't Miss List

ADRIAN SHINE, LEADER OF THE
LOCH NESS PROJECT

## 1 LOCH NESS CENTRE & EXHIBITION

I designed this exhibition (p253) myself, presenting the results of eight decades of research. The collection has everything from one-man submarines to the Rosetta apparatus that opened the 10,000-year-old time capsule concealed within the loch's sediment layers. The exhibition does not have all the answers and it will certainly not try to sell you a monster. Instead, it places the mystery in its proper context, which is the environment of Loch Ness.

## 2 URQUHART CASTLE

If, having learned some of the inner secrets of the loch, you want to see it through new eyes, you cannot do better than visiting Urquhart Castle (p254; pictured below left). Perched on a rocky promontory jutting into Loch Ness, its exhibits recount the castle's history, from a vitrified Pictish fort to its role in the Scottish Wars of Independence. The view from the Grant Tower is truly breathtaking.

## 3 FORT AUGUSTUS LOCKS

At the southern end of the loch is a flight of locks on the Caledonian Canal (p255; pictured above left), built by the great engineer Thomas Telford. It is always interesting to watch vessels being worked up this 'staircase' of water. British Waterways has a fascinating exhibition halfway up.

## 4 CRUISING THE LOCH

Venturing onto the water puts the seemingly tiny trunk road and Urquhart Castle into a new perspective. The Deepscan cruise boat runs from the Loch Ness Centre; I use this boat for my research and the skipper will tell you about his experiences. There are other cruise boats operating from Drumnadrochit, and the larger Jacobite vessels (p247) depart from Inverness.

## 5 WATERFALL WALKS

Starting from the car park at Invermoriston, cross the road to find the magnificent waterfall, then go back to take the path down the river through a mature beech wood to the shores of the loch. There is another famous waterfall at Foyers, on the southeastern shore of Loch Ness, as well as Divach Falls up Balmacaan Rd at Drumnadrochit.

# Cairngorms National Park

The rounded, snow-patched mountains of the Cairngorms form the largest area of high ground in Britain, with five of Scotland's six highest summits. The national park spreads out around their shoulders, encompassing pine forests, lochs, rivers and waterfalls, home to red deer, eagles, ospreys and wildcats. Below: Loch Morlich; Above Right: Lochnagar; Below Right: Scottish Crossbill

**Need to Know**

**BEST TIME TO GO** Spring for snow-patched mountains, August for purple heather. **TOP TIP** Bring waterproofs. **BEST PHOTO OP** View from top of Cairngorms. **For more, see p257.**

2

# Cairngorms National Park Don't Miss List

ERIC BAIRD, HEAD RANGER, GLEN TANAR, CAIRNGORMS NATIONAL PARK

## 1 LOCH MORLICH
Not far from Aviemore, this is a perfect loch (p262), set in a perfect forest, surrounded by perfect mountains. Go early in the morning, or out of season: you'll want to feel like the first person to discover it, and you still can.

## 2 LOCHNAGAR
Rising above Balmoral Castle (p190), Lochnagar mountain (1155m) is a serious – and massive – piece of rock, with terrific climbing on the north-facing corrie walls (summer and winter – different tools, techniques and temperatures!). But any fit person can walk up it: just be careful, stay on the path and check the weather forecast.

## 3 GLAS-ALLT WATERFALL
This comes tumbling, sometimes roaring, off Lochnagar into Loch Muick. It's the setting that makes it – you can go up from Loch Muick, past the Glas-allt Sheil house. (The building itself has a story: Queen Victoria had the place locked and unused after the death of Prince Albert. Last time I looked in the window, I saw ancient dried roses in a vase.) The path by the stream is steep, and narrow in places, but safe enough if you pay attention.

## 4 CRAIGENDARROCH
Craigendarroch (p189; 400m) – the 'rock of the oaks' – is on the edge of Ballater. You can go up after breakfast and be down for morning coffee, but you'll probably take longer. There are anthills in the spring sunshine, blueberries in late summer, turning leaves of oak and larch in autumn and terrific views up and down the River Dee all year.

## 5 FOREST OF GLEN TANAR
You can wander – for a day or a week, on foot or on a mountain bike – through the native forest of Scots pine, alongside the Water of Tanar. If it's quiet, you will see crossbills, birds of prey, red and roe deer and red squirrels. You can stay in the forest or head up onto the hill – Mt Keen, at the head of the glen, is a possibility.

239

## Glen Coe

One of Scotland's wildest, most scenic and most famous glens, the peacefulness and beauty of Glen Coe (p264) today belie the fact that it was the scene of a ruthless 17th-century massacre, in which the local MacDonalds were murdered by soldiers of the Campbell clan. Besides the history, there are many fine walks both easy and difficult, and enough photo opportunities to keep keen snappers happy.

## 4 Climbing Ben Nevis

The highest summit in all of Britain and Ireland, Ben Nevis (p272) is within reach of anyone who's reasonably fit. Don't take it lightly – it's a long, strenuous hike, and the weather can deteriorate rapidly. But treat Britain's tallest peak with respect and your reward (weather permitting) is a truly magnificent view, a great sense of achievement and a well-earned drink in the Ben Nevis Inn.

## Glen Affric

Gorgeous Glen Affric (p263) is a walkers' wonderland, a scenic extravaganza of shimmering lochs, rugged mountains, roaring waterfalls and native-pine woods. Often described as the most beautiful glen in Scotland, Affric is home to pine martens, wildcats, otters, red squirrels and golden eagles. Easily reached by car from Inverness or Loch Ness, it offers walks for all abilities, from a half-hour stroll to challenging cross-country hikes.

## The Great Outdoors

Between them, the Cairngorms and the West Highlands have the highest concentration of challenging outdoor activities in the country: Fort William (p267) calls itself the 'Outdoor Capital of the UK'. Hiking, hill walking, rock climbing, mountain biking, skiing, snowboarding, sailing, sea kayaking and canoeing, for everyone from beginners to experts – all combine to create the finest outdoor playground in Britain. Loch Lochy, Fort William

## Watching Wildlife

The Highlands are home to some of Scotland's most spectacular wildlife, including the country's largest land mammal, the red deer, and its largest native bird, the capercaillie. There are countless opportunities for spotting wildlife, from nature reserves such as Loch Garten (p263), where you can see nesting ospreys, to places like the Highland Wildlife Park (p262), which provides your best chance of seeing Scotland's most elusive creature, the wildcat. Scottish wildcat

# Inverness & the Highlands' Best...

## Historic Sites

○ **Culloden** (p251) The battlefield where Jacobite dreams were crushed

○ **Glen Coe** (p264) Site of one of Scottish history's most tragic episodes, the Glencoe Massacre

○ **Ruthven Barracks** (p263) A poignant relic of the Jacobite rebellion

○ **Fort George** (p252) One of Europe's most impressive 18th-century artillery fortresses

○ **Urquhart Castle** (p254) Impressive medieval castle, blown up to prevent Jacobite use

## Scenery

○ **Loch Ness** (p253) See classic loch views from Fort Augustus and Urquhart Castle

○ **Glen Affric** (p263) Mountains, lochs, Caledonian pine forests – sublime

○ **Glen Coe** (p264) Brooding mountain scenery looms over narrow glen

○ **Arisaig** (p273) White-sand beaches with glorious sunset views over islands

## Wildlife Experiences

○ **Loch Garten** (p263) Watch ospreys feeding and nesting in the wild.

○ **Cairngorm Reindeer Centre** (p262) Britain's only herd of reindeer will eat out of your hand

○ **Rothiemurchus Estate** (p259) Red squirrel, capercaillie and crossbill in remnant of Caledonian pine forest

○ **Moray Firth** (p265) Boat trips to see Scotland's only resident pod of bottlenose dolphins

# Need to Know

## Highland Pubs

o **Lock Inn** (p257) Cosy nook close to Loch Ness, serving real ale and fish & chips.

o **Kings House Hotel** (p265) Remote former military outpost guarding the eastern entrance to Glen Coe

o **Ben Nevis Inn** (p271) Welcoming hill-walkers' retreat at the foot of Ben Nevis

o **Clachnaharry Inn** (p250) Wonderful old real-ale pub near Caledonian Canal

## ADVANCE PLANNING

o **One month before** Reserve a table at top Inverness restaurants; book accommodation if visiting in summer

o **Two weeks before** Make bookings for any outdoor-activity instruction or hire

o **One week before** Make reservations for dolphin-spotting boat trip in Moray Firth

## RESOURCES

o **VisitHighlands** (www.visithighlands.com) Official tourist information site for the region

o **Visit Loch Ness** (www.visitlochness.com) Official tourist-board website for Loch Ness area

o **Glen Affric** (www.glenaffric.org) Loads of useful information on the Glen Affric area

o **Cairngorms National Park** (www.visitcairngorms.com) Lots of useful information, from accommodation to wildlife

o **Visit Fort William** (www.visit-fortwilliam.co.uk) Tourist information for Fort William area

o **Road to the Isles** (www.road-to-the-isles.org.uk) Useful information on the Fort William to Mallaig area

## GETTING AROUND

o **Bus** Reasonable network of local buses

o **Car** The most time-efficient way to get around the region

o **Train** Frequent services from Glasgow and Edinburgh to Inverness, Fort William and Mallaig

## BE FOREWARNED

o **Midges** Tiny biting flies are a pest from June to September, especially in still weather around dawn and dusk; bring insect repellent and wear long-sleeved clothing

o **Weather** Always unpredictable on the west coast; be prepared for wet and windy days, even in the middle of summer

**Left:** Clansman's gravestone, Culloden;
**Above:** Cairngorm Reindeer Centre

# Inverness & the Highlands Itineraries

*These two circular routes – one from Inverness (the 'Highland capital') and one from Fort William (the UK's 'outdoor capital') – showcase the superb scenery and landscapes of the Scottish Highlands.*

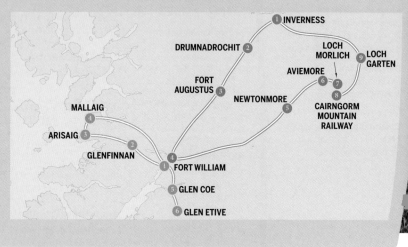

**INVERNESS TO INVERNESS**

## Monsters, Mountains and Wildlife

*3 DAYS*

Head south from **(1) Inverness** on the A82 to legendary Loch Ness, and stop at **(2) Drumnadrochit** to visit the Loch Ness monster exhibitions and Urquhart Castle, and perhaps take a cruise on the loch. In the afternoon, continue south to **(3) Fort Augustus** for a stroll beside the Caledonian Canal, then on to **(4) Fort William** – detour right on the B8004 before Spean Bridge for superb views of Ben Nevis.

Begin day two with a short side trip along beautiful Glen Nevis, which curls around the foot of Britain's highest mountain, then head east on the A86 past Loch Laggan to reach **(5) Newtonmore**. After a visit to

the Highland Folk Museum, take the quiet B9152 from Kingussie past the Highland Wildlife Park at Kincraig to reach the resort town of **(6) Aviemore**.

Spend your third day exploring the Cairngorms National Park. You can drive to **(7) Loch Morlich** for pleasant woodland walks, and continue up to the **(8) Cairngorm Mountain Railway** for a trip to the subarctic summit plateau. Stick to the B-roads as you continue north from Aviemore, stopping to see the ospreys at the **(9) Loch Garten** nature reserve. From here, the A9 leads easily back to Inverness.

**FORT WILLIAM TO FORT WILLIAM**

## Scenery Galore

**2 DAYS**

This itinerary consists of two day trips from **(1) Fort William**. On day one, head west along the A830 towards Mallaig: the famous 'Road to the Isles'. Stop at **(2) Glenfinnan**; visit the monument to Bonnie Prince Charlie before taking a walk along the glen to view the railway viaduct that features in the Harry Potter films.

Continue west through delightful scenery and leave the main road at **(3) Arisaig** for the B8008 (signposted 'Alternative Coastal Route'). This winding road leads past a series of gorgeous white-sand beaches, with stunning views to the islands of Eigg and Rum.

The road ends at **(4) Mallaig**, a less-than-pretty fishing harbour, where the ferry departs to Skye; time your trip to sample some local seafood before travelling back to Fort William.

The following day drive south to **(5) Glen Coe**, and make the most of any good weather by hiking into the hills. If a peaceful roadside picnic is more to your taste, continue through the glen and turn south along gorgeous **(6) Glen Etive**. Return to Fort William for the night, then continue towards the Cairngorms.

Glenfinnan Viaduct (p273)

# Discover Inverness & the Highlands

Victorian Market
MARTIN THOMAS PHOTOGRAPHY/ALAMY ©

## INVERNESS

POP 55,000

Inverness, the primary city and shopping centre of the Highlands, has a great location astride the River Ness at the northern end of the Great Glen. In summer it overflows with visitors intent on monster hunting at nearby Loch Ness, but it's worth a visit in its own right for a stroll along the picturesque river, a cruise on Loch Ness and a meal in one of the city's excellent restaurants.

## ◎ Sights & Activities

**NESS ISLANDS**                                  Park

The main attraction in Inverness is a leisurely stroll along the river to the Ness Islands. Planted with mature Scots pine, fir, beech and sycamore, and linked to the river banks and each other by elegant Victorian footbridges, the islands make an appealing picnic spot. They're a 20-minute walk south of the castle – head upstream on either side of the river (the start of the Great Glen Way), and return on the opposite bank. You'll pass the red-sandstone towers of St Andrew's Cathedral, dating from 1869, and the modern Eden Court Theatre (p251), which hosts art exhibits, both on the west bank.

**FREE** **INVERNESS MUSEUM & ART GALLERY**                Museum

(📞 01463-237114; www.inverness.highland.museum; Castle Wynd; ⏰ 10am-5pm Tue-Sat Apr-Oct, Thu-Sat Nov-Mar) Between the castle and the tourist office is Inverness Museum & Art Gallery, which has wildlife dioramas, geological displays, period rooms with historic weapons, Pictish stones and contemporary Highland arts and crafts.

## VICTORIAN MARKET                     Market
(www.invernessvictorianmarket.co.uk; Academy St; ⏰9am-5pm) If the rain comes down, opt for a spot of retail therapy in the Victorian Market, a shopping mall that dates from the 1890s and has rather more charm than its modern equivalents.

## INVERNESS CASTLE                     Castle
(Castle St) The hill above the city centre is topped by the Baronial turrets of Inverness Castle, a pink-sandstone confection dating from 1847 that replaced a medieval castle blown up by the Jacobites in 1746; it serves today as the Sheriff's Court. It's not open to the public, but there are good views from the surrounding gardens.

# Tours

## JACOBITE CRUISES                     Boat Tour
(📞01463-233999; www.jacobite.co.uk; Glenurquhart Rd; adult/child £29/22; ⏰twice daily Jun-Sep, once daily Apr-May) Boats depart from Tomnahurich Bridge for a 1½-hour cruise along Loch Ness, followed by a visit to Urquhart Castle and a return to Inverness by coach. You can buy tickets at the tourist office and catch a free minibus to the boat. Other cruises and combined cruise/coach tours, from one to 6½ hours, are also available.

## HAPPY TOURS                         Walking Tours
(www.happy-tours.biz) Offers 1¼-hour guided walks exploring the town's history and legends. Tours begin outside the tourist office at 11am, 1pm and 3pm daily.

## INVERNESS TAXIS                      Taxi Tours
(📞01463-222900; www.inverness-taxis.co.uk) Wide range of day tours to Urquhart Castle, Loch Ness, Culloden, and even Skye. Fares per car (up to four people) range from £60 (two hours) to £240 (all day).

# Sleeping

Inverness has a good range of backpacker accommodation, and also has several excellent boutique hotels. There are lots of guesthouses and B&Bs along Old Edinburgh Rd and Ardconnel St on the east side of the river, and on Kenneth St and Fairfield Rd on the west bank; all are within 10 minutes' walk of the city centre.

The city fills up quickly in July and August, so you should either prebook your accommodation or get an early start looking for somewhere to stay.

## TRAFFORD BANK                       B&B ££
(📞01463-241414; www.traffordbankguesthouse.co.uk; 96 Fairfield Rd; d £110-125; P 🛜) Lots of word-of-mouth rave reviews for this elegant Victorian villa that was once home to a bishop, just a mitre-toss from the Caledonian Canal and 10 minutes' walk west from the city centre. The luxurious rooms include fresh flowers and fruit, bathrobes and fluffy towels – ask for the Tartan Room, which has a wrought-iron king-size bed and Victorian roll-top bath.

## ROCPOOL RESERVE            Boutique Hotel £££
(📞01463-240089; www.rocpool.com; Culduthel Rd; s/d from £175/210; P 🛜) Boutique chic meets the Highlands in this slick and elegant little hotel, where an elegant Georgian exterior conceals an oasis of contemporary cool. A gleaming white entrance hall lined with read carpet and contemporary art leads to designer rooms in shades of chocolate, cream and gold; expect lots of high-tech gadgetry in the more expensive rooms, ranging from iPod docks to balcony hot tubs with aquavision TV. A restaurant by Albert Roux completes the luxury package.

## ARDCONNEL HOUSE                     B&B ££
(📞01463-240455; www.ardconnel-inverness.co.uk; 21 Ardconnel St; r per person £35-40; 🛜) The six-room Ardconnel is one of our favourites – a terraced Victorian house with comfortable en suite rooms, a dining room with crisp white table linen, and a breakfast menu that includes Vegemite for homesick Antipodeans. Kids under 10 not allowed.

## ACH ALUINN                         B&B ££
(📞01463-230127; www.achaluinn.com; 27 Fairfield Rd; r per person £25-35; P) This large,

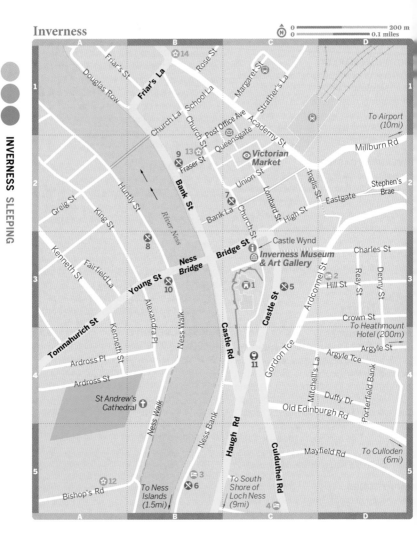

detached Victorian house is bright and homely, and offers all you might want from a B&B – private bathroom, TV, reading lights, comfy beds with two pillows each, and an excellent breakfast. Less than 10 minutes' walk west from the city centre.

### LOCH NESS COUNTRY HOUSE HOTEL
Hotel £££

(☎01463-230512; www.lochnesscountryhouse hotel.co.uk; Dunain Park, Loch Ness Rd; d from £169; P ⑤) This sumptuous country-

house hotel offers traditional decor, featuring Victorian four-poster beds, Georgian-style furniture and Italian marble bathrooms, all set in beautiful wooded grounds just five minutes' stroll from the Caledonian Canal and River Ness. The hotel is a mile southwest of Inverness on the A82 to Fort William.

### HEATHMOUNT HOTEL
Boutique Hotel ££

(☎01463-235877; www.heathmounthotel.com; Kingsmills Rd; s/d from £75/115; P ⑤) Small and friendly, the Heathmount combines

# Inverness

a popular local bar and restaurant with eight designer hotel rooms, each one different, ranging from a boldly coloured family room in purple and gold to a slinky black velvet four-poster double. Five minutes' walk southeast of the city centre.

## MACRAE GUEST HOUSE B&B ££
(☎01463-243658; joycemacrae@hotmail. com; 24 Ness Bank; s/d from £45/64; P) This pretty, flower-bedecked Victorian house on the eastern bank of the river has smart, tastefully decorated bedrooms (one is wheelchair accessible), and vegetarian breakfasts are available. Minimum two-night bookings in July and August.

## GLENMORISTON TOWN HOUSE HOTEL Boutique Hotel £££
(☎01463-223777; www.glenmoristontownhouse. com; 20 Ness Bank; s/d from £120/165; P 🛜) Luxurious boutique hotel on the banks of the River Ness. Can organise golfing and fishing for guests.

## CROWN HOTEL GUEST HOUSE B&B ££
(☎01463-231135; www.inverness-guesthouse. info; 19 Ardconnel St; s/d from £36/56; P @ 👬) Two of the six bedrooms are family rooms, and there's a spacious lounge equipped with games consoles, DVDs and board games.

 Eating

## CONTRAST BRASSERIE Brasserie ££
(☎01463-227889; www.glenmoristontownhouse. com/contrast.html; 22 Ness Bank; mains £13-20) Book early for what we think is the best restaurant in Inverness – a dining room that drips designer style, with smiling professional staff and truly delicious food. Try scallops with chorizo bolognaise, or pork belly with *mange tout* (snow pea) salad and lemongrass purée; 10 out of 10. And at £10 for a two-course lunch, or £15 for three-course early-bird dinner (5pm to 6.30pm), the value is unbeatable.

## CAFÉ 1 Bistro ££
(☎01463-226200; www.cafe1.net; 75 Castle St; mains £10-23; ⏰noon-9.30pm Mon-Fri, noon-2.30pm & 6-9.30pm Sat) Café 1 is a friendly and appealing bistro with candlelit tables amid elegant blonde-wood and wrought-iron decor. There is an international menu based on quality Scottish produce, from Aberdeen Angus steaks to crisp sea bass with velvet crab risotto and chilli jam. Early-bird menu (one/two courses for £9/12.50) is served noon to 6.45pm weekdays, and noon to 2.30pm Saturday.

## 🥖 ROCPOOL Restaurant ££
(☎01463-717274; www.rocpoolrestaurant.com; 1 Ness Walk; mains £17-24; ⏰Mon-Sat) Lots of polished wood, navy-blue leather and crisp white linen lend a nautical air to this relaxing bistro, which offers a Mediterranean-influenced menu that makes the most of quality Scottish produce, especially seafood. The two-course lunch is £14.

## 🥖 MUSTARD SEED Bistro ££
(☎01463-220220; www.mustardseedrestaurant. co.uk; 16 Fraser St; mains £11-16) The menu at this bright and bustling bistro changes

INVERNESS EATING

weekly, but focuses on Scottish and French cuisine with a modern twist. Grab a table on the upstairs balcony if you can – it's the best outdoor lunch spot in Inverness, with a great view across the river. And a two-course lunch for £7 – yes, that's right – is hard to beat.

### JOY OF TASTE                     British
( ✆ 01463-241459; www.thejoyoftaste.co.uk; 25 Church St; mains £12-17) Here's a novel concept – a restaurant run by a head chef and 25 volunteers who work a shift a week just for 'the love of creating a beautiful restaurant' (plus a share of the profits). And a very good job they're making of it, with a menu of classic British cuisine – from broccoli and stilton soup to lemon posset via Scottish sirloin – and a growing fan club of satisfied customers.

### KITCHEN                Modern Scottish ££
( ✆ 01463-259119; www.kitchenrestaurant.co.uk; 15 Huntly St; mains £11-16; 🛜 👬) This spectacular glass-fronted restaurant is under the same management as the Mustard Seed (with the same bargain lunch deal), and offers a great menu and a view of the River Ness – try to get a table upstairs.

## 🍷 Drinking

### CLACHNAHARRY INN                  Pub
( ✆ 01463-239806; www.clachnaharryinn.co.uk; 17-19 High St) Just over a mile northwest of the city centre, on the bank of the Caledonian Canal just off the A862, this is a delightful old coaching inn (with beer garden out back) serving an excellent range of real ales and good pub grub.

### CASTLE TAVERN                     Pub
( ✆ 01463-718718; www.castletavern.net; 1-2 View Pl) Under the same management as the Clachnaharry Inn and with a tasty selection of real ales, this pub has a wee suntrap of a terrace out the front. It's a great place for a pint on a summer afternoon.

## ⭐ Entertainment

### HOOTANANNY              Live Music
( ✆ 01463-233651; www.hootananny.com; 67 Church St) Hootananny is the city's best live-music venue, with traditional folk-and/or rock-music sessions nightly, including big-name bands from all over Scotland (and, indeed, the world). The bar

Old Leanach Cottage, Culloden Battlefield

s well stocked with a range of beers from the local Black Isle Brewery.

### EDEN COURT THEATRE                    Theatre
( ☑01463-234234; www.eden-court.co.uk; Bishop's Rd) The Highlands' main cultural venue – with theatre, art-house cinema and conference centre – Eden Court stages a busy program of drama, dance, comedy, music, film and children's events, and has a good bar and restaurant.

### IRONWORKS                    Live Music, Comedy
( ☑0871 789 4173; www.ironworksvenue.com; 122 Academy St) With live bands (rock, pop, tribute) and comedy shows two or three times a week, the Ironworks is the town's main venue for big-name acts.

## 🛈 Information

**Inverness tourist office** ( ☑01463-252401; www.visithighlands.com; Castle Wynd; internet access per 20min £1 ; ☺9am-6pm Mon-Sat, 9.30am-5pm Sun Jul & Aug, 9am-5pm Mon-Sat, 10am-4pm Sun Jun, Sep & Oct, 9am-5pm Mon-Sat Apr & May; @) Bureau de change and accommodation booking service; also sells tickets for tours and cruises. Opening hours limited November to March.

## 🛈 Getting There & Away

### Air

**Inverness Airport** (INV; ☑01667-464000; www.hial.co.uk) At Dalcross, 10 miles east of the city, off the A96 towards Aberdeen. There are scheduled flights to Amsterdam, Dusseldorf, London, Bristol, Manchester, Belfast, Stornoway, Benbecula, Orkney, Shetland and several other British airports.

### Bus

If you book far enough in advance, **Megabus** ( ☑0871 266 3333; www.megabus.com) offers fares from just £5.50 for buses from Inverness to Glasgow and Edinburgh, and £17 to London.

**London** £45, 13 hours, one daily; more frequent services requiring a change at Glasgow. Operated by **National Express** ( ☑08717 81 81 78; www.gobycoach.com).

**Aviemore** £5.50, 1¾ hours, three daily Monday to Friday; via Grantown-on-Spey.

**Edinburgh** £28, 3½ to 4½ hours, hourly.

**Glasgow** £28, 3½ to 4½ hours, hourly.

**Fort William** £12, two hours, five daily.

**Portree** £23, 3½ hours, four daily.

### Train

**Edinburgh** £40, 3½ hours, eight daily.

**Glasgow** £40, 3½ hours, eight daily.

## 🛈 Getting Around

### To/ From the Airport

**Stagecoach Jet** (www.stagecoachbus.com) Buses run from the airport to Inverness bus station (£3.30, 20 minutes, every 30 minutes).

### Bicycle

**Ticket to Ride** ( ☑01463-419160; www. tickettoridehighlands.co.uk; Bellfield Park; per day from £20) Hire mountain bikes, hybrids and tandems. Will deliver bikes free to local hotels and B&Bs.

### Bus

City services and buses to places around Inverness, including Nairn, Forres, the Culloden battlefield, Beauly, Dingwall and Lairg, are operated by **Stagecoach** (www.stagecoachbus. com). An Inverness City Dayrider ticket costs £3.30 and gives unlimited travel for a day on buses throughout the city.

### Car

**Focus Vehicle Rental** ( ☑01667-461212; www. focusvehiclerental.co.uk; Inverness Airport) Car rental starts at £35 per day.

### Taxi

**Highland Taxis** ( ☑01463-222222)

## Around Inverness

### Culloden Battlefield

The Battle of Culloden in 1746, the last pitched battle ever fought on British soil, saw the defeat of Bonnie Prince Charlie

and the end of the Jacobite dream when 1200 Highlanders were slaughtered by government forces in a 68-minute rout. The duke of Cumberland, son of the reigning King George II and leader of the Hanoverian army, earned the nickname 'Butcher' for his brutal treatment of the defeated Scottish forces. The battle sounded the death knell for the old clan system, and the horrors of the Clearances soon followed. The sombre moor where the conflict took place has scarcely changed in the ensuing 260 years.

Culloden is 6 miles east of Inverness. Bus No 1 runs from Queensgate in Inverness to Culloden battlefield (30 minutes, hourly).

**CULLODEN VISITOR CENTRE** Visitor Centre
(NTS; www.nts.org.uk/culloden; adult/child £10/7.50; 🕑9am-6pm Apr-Sep, 9am-5pm Oct, 10am-4pm Nov-Mar) This impressive visitor centre presents detailed information about the Battle of Culloden in 1746, including the lead-up and the aftermath,

with perspectives from both sides. An innovative film puts you on the battlefield in the middle of the mayhem, and a wealth of other audio presentations must have kept Inverness' entire acting community in business for weeks. The admission fee includes an audioguide for a self-guided tour of the battlefield itself.

## Fort George

The headland guarding the narrows in the Moray Firth opposite Fortrose is occupied by the magnificent and virtually unaltered 18th-century artillery fortification of Fort George (HS; ☎01667-462777; adult/child £6.90/4.10; 🕑9.30am-5.30pm Apr-Sep, to 4.30pm Oct-Mar).

One of the finest examples of its kind in Europe, Fort George was established in 1748 as a base for George II's army of occupation in the Highlands – by the time of its completion in 1769 it had cost the equivalent of around £1 billion in today's money.

The mile-plus walk around the ramparts offers fine views out to sea and

**Left:** A model of the Loch Ness Monster; **Below:** Cawdor Castle

(LEFT) EDUCATION IMAGES/UIG/GETTY IMAGES ©; (BELOW) BILL BACHMANN/GETTY IMAGES ©

back to the Great Glen. Given its size, you'll need at least two hours to do the place justice. The fort is off the A96 about 11 miles northeast of Inverness.

## Cawdor

**Cawdor Castle** (☎01667-404615; www.cawdorcastle.com; adult/child £9.50/6; ☺10am-5.30pm May–Sep) was the 14th-century home of the Thanes of Cawdor, one of the titles prophesied by the three witches for the eponymous character of Shakespeare's *Macbeth*. Macbeth couldn't have lived here though, since the central tower dates from the 14th century (the wings were 17th-century additions) and he died in 1057. The castle is 5 miles southwest of Nairn.

## LOCH NESS

Deep, dark and narrow, Loch Ness stretches for 23 miles between Inverness and Fort Augustus. Its waters have been extensively explored in search of Nessie, the elusive Loch Ness monster, but most visitors see her only in cardboard-cutout form at the monster exhibitions. The busy A82 road runs along the northwestern shore, while the more tranquil B862 follows the southeastern shore. A complete circuit of the loch is about 70 miles – travel anticlockwise for the best views.

## Drumnadrochit

POP 800

Seized by monster madness, its gift shops bulging with Nessie cuddly toys, Drumnadrochit is a hotbed of beastie fever, with two monster exhibitions battling it out for the tourist dollar.

 **Sights & Activities**

**LOCH NESS CENTRE & EXHIBITION**  Exhibition

(☎01456-450573; www.lochness.com; adult/child £6.95/4.95; ☺9am-6pm Jul & Aug, to 5.30pm Jun,

253

ALAN MAJCHROWICZ/GETTY IMAGES ©

# Don't Miss **Urquhart Castle**

Commanding a brilliant location 1.5 miles east of Drumnadrochit, with outstanding views (on a clear day), Urquhart Castle is a popular Nessie-watching spot. A huge visitor centre (most of which is beneath ground level) includes a video theatre (with a dramatic 'unveiling' of the castle at the end of the film) and displays of medieval items discovered in the castle.

The castle was repeatedly sacked and rebuilt (and sacked and rebuilt) over the centuries; in 1692 it was blown up to prevent the Jacobites from using it. The five-storey tower house at the northern point is the most impressive remaining fragment and offers wonderful views across the water.

**NEED TO KNOW**

HS; ☏01456-450551; adult/child £7.40/4.50; ☻9.30am-6pm Apr-Sep, to 5pm Oct, to 4.30pm Nov-Mar

9.30am-5pm Easter-May & Sep-Oct, 10am-3.30pm Nov-Easter) This Nessie-themed attraction adopts a scientific approach that allows you to weigh the evidence for yourself. Exhibits include the original equipment – sonar survey vessels, miniature submarines, cameras and sediment coring tools – used in various monster hunts, as well as original photographs and film footage of sightings. You'll find out about hoaxes and optical illusions, as well as learning a lot about the ecology of Loch Ness – is there enough food in the loch to support even one 'monster', let alone a breeding population?

**NESSIELAND CASTLE MONSTER CENTRE**   Exhibition
(www.nessieland.co.uk; adult/child £5.50/4; ☻9am-8pm Jul & Aug, 10am-5.30pm Apr-Jun & Sep-Oct, 10am-4pm Nov-Mar) More homely than the nearby Loch Ness Centre & Exhibition, this attraction is a miniature theme park aimed squarely at the kids, though we suspect its main function is to sell you Loch Ness monster souvenirs.

**NESSIE HUNTER**   Boat Trips
(☏01456-450395; www.lochness-cruises.com; adult/child £15/10; ☻Easter-Oct) One-hour

monster-hunting cruises, complete with sonar and underwater cameras. Cruises depart from Drumnadrochit hourly (except 1pm) from 9am to 6pm daily.

## 🛏 Sleeping & Eating

**LOCH NESS INN**  Inn **££**
(☎ 01456-450991; www.staylochness.co.uk; Lewiston; s/d/f £89/102/145; P 🛜) The Loch Ness Inn ticks all the weary traveller's boxes, with comfortable bedrooms (the family suite sleeps two adults and two children), a cosy bar pouring real ales from the Cairngorm and Isle of Skye breweries, and a rustic restaurant (mains £9 to £18) serving hearty, wholesome fare such as whisky-flambéed haggis, and roast rump of Scottish lamb. It's conveniently located in the quiet hamlet of Lewiston, between Drumnadrochit and Urquhart Castle.

**DRUMBUIE FARM**  B&B **££**
(☎ 01456-450634; www.loch-ness-farm.co.uk; Drumnadrochit; per person from £30; ☺ Mar-Oct; P) Drumbuie is a B&B in a modern house on a working farm – the surrounding fields are full of sheep and highland cattle – with views over Urquhart Castle and Loch Ness. Walkers and cyclists are welcome.

**FIDDLER'S COFFEE SHOP & RESTAURANT**
Cafe, Restaurant **££**
( www.fiddledrum.co.uk; mains £8-17; ☺ 11am-11pm; 🛜) The coffee shop does cappuccino and croissants, while the restaurant serves traditional Highland fare, such as venison casserole, and a wide range of bottled Scottish beers. There's also a whisky bar with a huge range of single malts.

## ℹ Getting There & Away

Scottish Citylink (www.citylink.co.uk) and Stagecoach (www.stagecoachbus.com) buses from Inverness to Fort William run along the shores of Loch Ness (six to eight daily, five on Sunday); those headed for Skye turn off at Invermoriston. There are bus stops at Drumnadrochit (£6.20, 30 minutes), Urquhart Castle car park (£6.60, 35 minutes) and Loch Ness Youth Hostel (£8.60, 45 minutes).

## Fort Augustus
POP 510

Fort Augustus, at the junction of four old military roads, was originally a government garrison and the headquarters of General George Wade's road-building operations in the 18th century. Today it's a picturesque place, often overrun by tourists in summer.

## ◎ Sights & Activities

**CALEDONIAN CANAL**  Canal
At Fort Augustus, boats using the Caledonian Canal are raised and lowered 13m by

Duncansby Stacks (p257)
RACHEL HUSBAND/ALAMY ©

a 'ladder' of five consecutive locks. It's fun to watch, and the neatly landscaped canal banks are a great place to soak up the sun or compare accents with fellow tourists. The **Caledonian Canal Heritage Centre** ( ☎ 01320-366493; admission free; ⊙ 10am-5pm Apr-Oct), beside the lowest lock, showcases the history of the canal.

**ROYAL SCOT** Boat Trips
( ☎ 01320-366277; www.cruiselochness.com; adult/child £12.50/8; ⊙ hourly 10am-4pm Apr-Oct, 1 & 2pm only Nov-Mar) One-hour cruises on Loch Ness accompanied by the latest high-tech sonar equipment so you can keep an underwater eye open for Nessie.

# Strange Spectacle on Loch Ness

Highland folklore is filled with tales of strange creatures living in lochs and rivers, notably the kelpie (water horse) that lures unwary travellers to their doom. The use of the term 'monster', however, is a relatively recent phenomenon, the origins of which lie in an article published in the *Inverness Courier* on 2 May 1933, entitled 'Strange Spectacle on Loch Ness'.

The article recounted the sighting of a disturbance in the loch by Mrs Aldie Mackay and her husband: 'There the creature disported itself, rolling and plunging for fully a minute, its body resembling that of a whale, and the water cascading and churning like a simmering cauldron.'

The story was taken up by the London press and sparked off a rash of sightings that year, including a notorious on-land encounter with London tourists Mr and Mrs Spicer on 22 July 1933, again reported in the *Inverness Courier:*

'It was horrible, an abomination. About 50 yards ahead, we saw an undulating sort of neck, and quickly followed by a large, ponderous body. I estimated the length to be 25 to 30 feet, its colour was dark elephant grey. It crossed the road in a series of jerks, but because of the slope we could not see its limbs. Although I accelerated quickly towards it, it had disappeared into the loch by the time I reached the spot. There was no sign of it in the water. I am a temperate man, but I am willing to take any oath that we saw this Loch Ness beast. I am certain that this creature was of a prehistoric species.'

The London newspapers couldn't resist. In December 1933 the *Daily Mail* sent Marmaduke Wetherall, a film director and big-game hunter, to Loch Ness to track down the beast. Within days he found 'reptilian' footprints in the shoreline mud (soon revealed to have been made with a stuffed hippopotamus foot, possibly an umbrella stand). Then in April 1934 came the famous 'long-necked monster' photograph taken by the seemingly reputable Harley St surgeon Colonel Kenneth Wilson. The press went mad and the rest, as they say, is history.

In 1994, however, Christian Spurling – Wetherall's stepson, by then 90 years old – revealed that the most famous photo of Nessie ever taken was in fact a hoax, perpetrated by his stepfather with Wilson's help. Today, of course, there are those who claim that Spurling's confession is itself a hoax. And, ironically, the researcher who exposed the surgeon's photo as a fake still believes wholeheartedly in the monster's existence.

Hoax or not, there's no denying that the bizarre mini-industry that has grown up around Loch Ness and its mysterious monster since that eventful summer 75 years ago is the strangest spectacle of all.

## Sleeping & Eating

**LOVAT**           Hotel £££

(☏01456-459250; www.thelovat.com; Main Rd; d from £121; P 🛜 👪) A boutique-style makeover has transformed this former huntin'-and-shootin' hotel into a luxurious but ecoconscious retreat set apart from the tourist crush around the canal. The bedrooms are spacious and stylishly furnished, while the lounge is equipped with a log fire, comfy armchairs and grand piano.

There's an informal brasserie and a highly acclaimed restaurant (five-course dinner £45) which serves top-quality cuisine.

**LORIEN HOUSE**      B&B ££

(☏01320-366736; www.lorien-house.co.uk; Station Rd; s/d £40/70) Lorien is a cut above your usual B&B – the bathrooms come with bidets and the breakfasts with smoked salmon, and there's a library of walking, cycling and climbing guides in the lounge.

**LOCK INN**           Pub ££

(Canal Side; mains £9-14; ⊗meals noon-8pm) A superb pub on the canal bank, the Lock Inn has a vast range of malt whiskies and a tempting menu of bar meals, which includes Orkney salmon, Highland venison and daily seafood specials; the house speciality is beer-battered haddock and chips.

## ℹ Information

There's an ATM and bureau de change in the post office beside the canal.

**Fort Augustus tourist office** (☏01320-366367; ⊗9am-6pm Mon-Sat & 9am-5pm Sun Easter-Oct) In the central car park.

## ℹ Getting There & Away

Scottish Citylink (p308) and Stagecoach (p255) buses from Inverness to Fort William stop at Fort Augustus (£10.20, one hour, six to eight daily Monday to Saturday, five on Sunday).

## THE CAIRNGORMS

The **Cairngorms National Park** (www.cairngorms.co.uk) encompasses the highest

## Detour:
# John O'Groats

Though it's not the northernmost point of the British mainland (that's Dunnet Head), John O'Groats still serves as the end point of the 874-mile trek from Land's End in Cornwall, a popular if arduous route for cyclists and walkers, many of whom raise money for charitable causes. There's a passenger ferry from here to Orkney (p262), and the settlement's spectacular setting is some consolation for the disappointment of finding that this famous destination is basically a car park surrounded by tourist shops.

Two miles east, **Duncansby Head** provides a more solemn end-of-Britain moment, with a small lighthouse and 60m-high cliffs sheltering nesting fulmars. A 15-minute walk from here through a sheep paddock yields spectacular views of the sea-surrounded monoliths known as **Duncansby Stacks**.

landmass in Britain – a broad mountain plateau, riven only by the deep valleys of the Lairig Ghru and Loch Avon, with an average altitude of over 1000m and including five of the six highest summits in the UK. This wild mountain landscape of granite and heather has a sub-Arctic climate and supports rare alpine tundra vegetation and high-altitude bird species, such as snow bunting, ptarmigan and dotterel.

The harsh mountain environment gives way lower down to scenic glens softened by beautiful open forests of native Scots pine, home to rare animals and birds such as pine martens, wildcats, red squirrels, ospreys, capercaillies and crossbills.

JOHN PETER PHOTOGRAPHY/ALAMY

## Don't Miss Cairngorm Mountain Railway

The region's most popular attraction is a funicular railway that will whisk you to the edge of the Cairngorm plateau (1085m) in just eight minutes. The bottom station is at the Coire Cas car park at the end of Ski Rd; at the top is an exhibition, a shop (of course) and a restaurant. Unfortunately, for environmental and safety reasons, you're not allowed out of the top station in summer unless you book a 90-minute guided walk to the summit of Cairn Gorm (adult/child £15.95/10.50, twice a day May to October). Check the website for details.

### NEED TO KNOW

☎01479-861261; www.cairngormmountain.org; adult/child return £9.95/6.50; ⏰10.20am-4pm May-Nov, 9am-4.30pm Dec-Apr

---

This is prime hill-walking territory, but even couch potatoes can enjoy a taste of the high life by taking the Cairngorm Mountain Railway up to the edge of the Cairngorm plateau.

## Aviemore

POP 2400

Aviemore is the gateway to the Cairngorms, the region's main centre for transport, accommodation, restaurants and shopping. It's not the prettiest town in Scotland by a long stretch – the main attractions are in the surrounding area – but when bad weather puts the hills off-limits,

Aviemore fills up with hikers, cyclists and climbers (plus skiers and snowboarders in winter) cruising the outdoor-equipment shops or recounting their latest adventures in the cafes and bars. Add in tourists and locals and the eclectic mix makes for a lively little town.

##  Sights

**STRATHSPEY STEAM
RAILWAY** Heritage Railway
(☎01479-810725; www.strathspeyrailway.
co.uk; Station Sq; return ticket per adult/child

£11.50/5.75) Strathspey Steam Railway runs steam trains on a section of restored line between Aviemore and Broomhill, 10 miles to the northeast, via Boat of Garten. There are four or five trains daily from June to September, and a more limited service in April, May, October and December.

An extension to Grantown-on-Spey is planned (see www.railstograntown.org); in the meantime, you can continue from Broomhill to Grantown-on-Spey by bus.

### ROTHIEMURCHUS ESTATE     Forest

(www.rothiemurchus.net) The Rothiemurchus Estate, which extends from the River Spey at Aviemore to the Cairngorm summit plateau, is famous for having Scotland's largest remnant of **Caledonian forest**, the ancient forest of Scots pine that once covered most of the country. The forest is home to a large population of red squirrels, and is one of the last bastions of the Scottish wildcat.

The **Rothiemurchus Estate visitor centre** ( ☎ 01479-812345; admission free; ⏰ 9am-5.30pm), a mile southeast of Aviemore along the B970, sells an *Explorer Map* detailing more than 50 miles of **footpaths** and **cycling trails**, including the wheelchair-accessible 4-mile trail around **Loch an Eilein**, with its ruined castle and peaceful pine woods.

## 🏃 Activities

### BOTHY BIKES     Mountain Biking

( ☎ 01479-810111; www.bothybikes.co.uk; Dalfaber; per half-/full day £16/20; ⏰ 9am-5.30pm) Located just outside Aviemore on the way to Cairngorm, this place rents out mountain bikes and can advise on routes and trails; a good choice for beginners is the **Old Logging Way**, which runs from the hire centre to Glenmore, where you can make a circuit of Loch Morlich. For experienced bikers, the whole of the Cairngorms is your playground. Booking recommended.

### ROTHIEMURCHUS FISHERY     Fishing

( ☎ 01479-810703; www.rothiemurchus.net; Rothiemurchus Estate; ⏰ 9am-5.30pm, to 9pm Jul & Aug) Cast for rainbow trout at this loch at the southern end of the village; buy permits (from £10 to £30 per day, plus £5 for tackle hire) at the Fish Farm Shop. If you're a fly-fishing virgin, there's a beginner's package, including tackle hire, one hour's instruction and one hour's fishing, for £39 per person.

For experienced anglers, there's also salmon and sea-trout fishing on the River Spey – a day permit costs around £20 and numbers are limited, so it's best to book in advance.

### CAIRNGORM SLED-DOG CENTRE     Dog Sledding

( ☎ 07767-270526; www.sled-dogs.co.uk; Ski Rd) This outfit will take you on a 20-minute sled tour of local forest trails in the wake of a team of huskies (adult/child £50/35), or a three-hour sled-dog safari (£150 per person). The sleds have wheels, so snow's not necessary. There are also one-hour guided tours of the kennels (adult/child £8/4). The centre is 3 miles east of Aviemore, signposted off the road to Loch Morlich.

##  Sleeping

### OLD MINISTER'S HOUSE     B&B ££

( ☎ 01479-812181; www.theoldministershouse. co.uk; Rothiemurchus; s/d £70/110; P 🛜 ) This former manse dates from 1906 and has four rooms with a homely, country-farmhouse feel. It's in a lovely setting amid Scots pines on the banks of the River Druie, just 0.75 miles southeast of Aviemore.

### ARDLOGIE GUEST HOUSE     B&B ££

( ☎ 01479-810747; www.ardlogie.co.uk; Dalfaber Rd; s/d from £40/60, Bothy per 3 nights £165; P 🛜 ) Handy for the train station, the five-room Ardlogie has great views over the River Spey towards the Cairngorms. There's also self-catering accommodation in the Bothy, a cosy, two-person timber cabin. Facilities include a boules pitch in the garden, and guests can get free use of the local country club's pool, spa and sauna.

### RAVENSCRAIG GUEST HOUSE     B&B ££

( ☎ 01479-810278; www.aviemoreonline.com; Grampian Rd; r per person £35-42; P 🛜 )

## Detour:
# Orkney's Prehistoric Sites

There's a magic to the Orkney Islands that you'll begin to feel as soon as the Scottish mainland slips away astern. It's an archipelago of old-style hospitality and Viking heritage, a spot whose ports tell of lives led with the blessings and rough moods of the sea. Above all it's famous for a series of magnificent prehistoric monuments.

**Skara Brae** (HS; www.historic-scotland.gov.uk; joint ticket with Skaill House adult/child £6.90/4.10; 9.30am-5.30pm Apr-Sep, to 4.30pm Oct-Mar) is one of Scotland's most evocative ancient sites, offering an authentic glimpse of Stone Age life. Idyllically situated by a sandy bay 8 miles north of Stromness, and predating Stonehenge and the pyramids of Giza, Skara Brae is northern Europe's best-preserved prehistoric village.

Egypt has its pyramids, Scotland has **Maes Howe** (HS; 01856-761606; www.historic-scotland.gov.uk; adult/child £5.50/3.30; tours hourly 10am-4pm). Built about 5000 years ago, it's an extraordinary place, a Stone Age tomb built from enormous sandstone blocks. Creeping down the long stone passageway to the central chamber, you feel the gulf of years that separate us from the architects of this mysterious place. Though nothing is known about who and what was interred here, the scope of the project suggests it was a structure of great significance.

Across the loch from Maes Howe is the atmospheric **Ring of Brodgar** (HS; www.historic-scotland.gov.uk; admission free; 24hr), a circle of standing stones built around 2500–2000BC. Twenty-one of the original 60 stones still stand among the heather, their curious shapes mutilated by years of climatic onslaught.

For information on tours of the Orkneys, see p262.

Ravenscraig is a large, flower-bedecked Victorian villa with six spacious en suite rooms, plus another six in a modern chalet at the back (one wheelchair accessible). It serves traditional and veggie breakfasts in an attractive conservatory dining room.

**CAIRNGORM HOTEL**  Hotel ££
( 01479-810233; www.cairngorm.com; Grampian Rd; s/d from £59/98; P ) Better known as 'the Cairn', this long-established hotel is set in the fine old granite building with the pointy turret opposite the train station. It's a welcoming place with comfortable rooms and a determinedly Scottish atmosphere, all tartan carpets and stags' antlers. There's live music on weekends, so it can get a bit noisy – not for early-to-bedders.

**HILTON COYLUMBRIDGE**  Hotel ££
( 01479-810661; www.coylumbridge.hilton. com; Coylumbridge; d from £110; P ) This modern, low-rise Hilton, set amid the pine woods just outside Aviemore, is a wonderfully family-friendly hotel, with bedrooms for up to two adults and two children, indoor and outdoor play areas, a crèche and a baby-sitting service. The hotel is 1.5 miles east of Aviemore, on the road to Loch Morlich.

 **Eating & Drinking**

**MOUNTAIN CAFE**  Cafe £
(www.mountaincafe-aviemore.co.uk; 111 Grampian Rd; mains £4-10; 8.30am-5pm Tue-Thu, to 5.30pm Fri-Mon; ) The Mountain Cafe offers freshly prepared local produce with a Kiwi twist (the owner is from NZ), such as healthy breakfasts of muesli, porridge and fresh fruit (till 11.30am), hearty lunches of seafood chowder, burgers and imaginative salads, and

homebaked breads, cakes and biscuits. Vegan, coeliac and nut-allergic diets catered for.

**SKI-ING DOO** Bistro ££
(☏ 01479-810392; 9 Grampian Rd; mains £7-12, steaks £15-17; 🛜 👶) A long-standing Aviemore institution, the child-friendly Ski-ing Doo (it's a pun...oh, ask the waiter!) is a favourite with family skiers and hikers. An informal place offering a range of hearty, homemade burgers, chilli dishes and juicy steaks; the Doo Below cafe-bar is open all day from noon.

**WINKING OWL** Pub
(Grampian Rd) Lively local pub, popular with hikers and climbers, serving a good range of real ales and malt whiskies.

**OLD BRIDGE INN** Pub
(☏ 01479-811137; www.oldbridgeinn.co.uk; 23 Dalfaber Rd; @ 🛜) The Old Bridge has a snug bar, complete with roaring log fire in winter, and a cheerful, chalet-style **restaurant** (mains £9-18; ⏲ lunch & dinner, to 10pm Fri & Sat) at the back serving quality Scottish cuisine.

## ℹ️ Information

There are ATMs outside the Tesco supermarket, and currency exchange at the post office and the tourist office, all located on Grampian Rd.

**Aviemore tourist office** (☏ 01479-810363; www.visitaviemore.com; The Mall, Grampian Rd; ⏲ 9am-6pm Mon-Sat, 9.30am-5pm Sun Jul & Aug, 9am-5pm Mon-Sat, 10am-4pm Sun Easter-Jun, Sep & Oct) Hours are limited from October to Easter.

## ℹ️ Getting There & Away

### Bus

Buses stop on Grampian Rd opposite the train station; buy tickets at the tourist office. Services include:

**Edinburgh** £24.40, 3¾ hours, three daily

**Glasgow** £24.40, 3¾ hours, three daily

**Inverness** £5.50, 1¾ hours, three daily Monday to Friday; via Grantown-on-Spey

### Train

The train station is on Grampian Rd.

**Glasgow/Edinburgh** £44, three hours, six daily

**Inverness** £11, 40 minutes, 12 daily

Skara Brae, Orkney Islands

PATRICK DIEUDONNE/GETTY IMAGES ©

## ⓘ Getting Around

### Bike

Several places in Aviemore, Rothiemurchus Estate and Glenmore have mountain bikes for hire. An off-road cycle track links Aviemore with Glenmore and Loch Morlich.

**Bothy Bikes** (☏01479-810111; www.bothybikes. co.uk; Ski Rd; ⊙9am-5.30pm) Charges £20 a day for a quality bike with front suspension and disc brakes.

### Bus

Bus 34 links Aviemore to Cairngorm car park (45 minutes, hourly) via Coylumbridge and Glenmore. A Strathspey Dayrider/Megarider ticket (£6.40/16) gives one/seven days unlimited bus travel from Aviemore as far as Cairngorm, Carrbridge and Kingussie (buy from the bus driver).

---

# Orkney Tours

**John O'Groats Ferries** (☏01955-611353; www.jogferry.co.uk; ⊙May-Sep) If you're in a hurry, this operator runs a one-day tour of the main sites for £52, including the ferry from John O'Groats. You can do the whole thing as a long day trip from Inverness.

**Wildabout Orkney** (☏01856-877737; www.wildaboutorkney.com) Operates tours covering Orkney's history, ecology, folklore and wildlife. Day trips operate year-round and cost £49, with pick-ups in Stromness and Kirkwall.

**Orkney Archaeology Tours** (☏01856-721450; www.orkneyarchaeologytours. co.uk) This company runs private half-day (£160 for up to four people) and full-day (£240) tours with an archaeologist guide.

For information on Orkney's prehistoric sites, see p260.

---

# Around Aviemore

## Loch Morlich

Six miles east of Aviemore, Loch Morlich is surrounded by some 8 sq miles of pine and spruce forest that make up the **Glenmore Forest Park**. Its attractions include a sandy beach (at the east end).

## ◉ Sights & Activities

The park's **visitor centre** at Glenmore has a small exhibition on the Caledonian forest and sells the *Glenmore Forest Park Map,* detailing local walks. The **circuit of Loch Morlich** (one hour) makes a pleasant outing; the trail is pram- and wheelchair-friendly.

**CAIRNGORM REINDEER CENTRE** 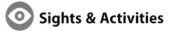 Wildlife Park
(www.cairngormreindeer.co.uk; adult/child £10/5) The warden here will take you on a tour to see and feed Britain's only herd of reindeer, who are very tame and will even eat out of your hand. Walks take place at 11am, plus another at 2.30pm from May to September, and 3.30pm Monday to Friday in July and August.

**LOCH MORLICH WATERSPORTS CENTRE** Watersports
(www.lochmorlich.com; ⊙9am-5pm May-Oct) This popular outfit rents out Canadian canoes (£19 an hour), kayaks (£7.50), windsurfers (£16.50), sailing dinghies (£23) and rowing boats (£19), and also offers instruction.

## Kincraig

The **Highland Wildlife Park** (☏01540-651270; www.highlandwildlifepark.org; adult/child £14/10; ⊙10am-5pm Apr-Oct, to 6pm Jul & Aug, to 4pm Nov-Mar) near Kincraig, 6 miles southwest of Aviemore, features a drive-through safari park and animal enclosures offering the chance to view rarely seen native wildlife, such as wildcats, capercaillies, pine martens, white-tailed sea eagles and red squirrels, as well as species that once roamed the Scottish hills but have long since disappeared, including wolf, lynx, wild boar, beaver and European bison. Visitors without cars get driven around by staff (at no extra cost). Last entry is two hours before closing.

At Kincraig the Spey widens into Loch Insh, home of the **Loch Insh Watersports Centre** (☎01540-651272; www.lochinsh. com; Kincraig; ⏰8.30am-5.30pm), which offers canoeing, windsurfing, sailing, bike hire and fishing, as well as B&B accommodation. The food here is good, especially after 6.30pm when the lochside cafe metamorphoses into a cosy restaurant.

## Boat of Garten

Boat of Garten is known as the Osprey Village because these rare and beautiful birds of prey nest nearby at the **RSPB Loch Garten Osprey Centre** (☎01479-831694; www.rspb.org.uk/lochgarten; Tulloch; adult/child £4/2.50; ⏰10am-6pm Apr-Aug). The ospreys migrate here each spring from Africa and nest in a tall pine tree – you can watch from a hide as the birds feed their young. The centre is signposted about 2 miles east of the village.

Boat of Garten is 6 miles northeast of Aviemore. The most interesting way to get here is on the Strathspey Steam Railway (p258).

## Kingussie & Newtonmore

The gracious old Speyside towns of Kingussie (kin-*yew*-see) and Newtonmore sit at the foot of the great heather-clad humps known as the Monadhliath Mountains. The towns are best known as the home of the excellent Highland Folk Museum.

## ◉ Sights & Activities

FREE **HIGHLAND FOLK**
**MUSEUM** Museum
(☎01540-673551; www.highlandfolk.museum; Kingussie Rd, Newtonmore; ⏰10.30am-5.30pm Apr-Aug, 11am-4.30pm Sep & Oct) The open-air Highland Folk Museum comprises a collection of historical buildings and

## Detour:
# Glen Affric

Glen Affric, one of the most beautiful glens in Scotland, extends deep into the hills beyond the village of Cannich. The upper reaches of the glen, now designated as **Glen Affric National Nature Reserve** (www.glenaffric.org), is a scenic wonderland of shimmering lochs, rugged mountains and native Scots pine, home to pine marten, wildcat, otter, red squirrel and golden eagle.

About 4 miles southwest of Cannich is **Dog Falls**, a scenic spot where the River Affric squeezes through a narrow, rocky gorge. A waymarked walking trail leads here easily from Dog Falls car park.

The road continues beyond Dog Falls to a parking area and picnic site at the eastern end of **Loch Affric** where there are several short walks along the river and the loch shore. The circuit of Loch Affric (10 miles, allow five hours) follows good paths right around the loch and takes you deep into the heart of some very wild scenery.

relics revealing many aspects of Highland culture and lifestyle. Laid out like a farming township, it has a community of traditional thatch-roofed cottages, a sawmill, a schoolhouse, a shepherd's bothy (hut) and a rural post office. Actors in period costume give demonstrations of woodcarving, spinning and peat-fire baking. You'll need at least two to three hours to make the most of a visit here.

**RUTHVEN BARRACKS** Ruin
(HS; ⏰24hr) Ruthven Barracks was one of four garrisons built by the British government after the first Jacobite rebellion of 1715, as part of a Hanoverian scheme to

take control of the Highlands. Ironically, the barracks were last occupied by Jacobite troops awaiting the return of Bonnie Prince Charlie after the Battle of Culloden. Learning of his defeat and subsequent flight, they set fire to the barracks before taking to the glens (the building is still roofless).

Perched dramatically on a river terrace and clearly visible from the main A9 road near Kingussie, the ruins are spectacularly floodlit at night.

# WEST HIGHLANDS

This area extends from the bleak blanket-bog of the Moor of Rannoch to the west coast beyond Glen Coe and Fort William, and includes the southern reaches of the Great Glen. The scenery is grand throughout, with high and wild mountains dominating the glens. Great expanses of moor alternate with lochs and patches of commercial forest. Fort William, at the inner end of Loch Linnhe, is the only sizable town in the area.

Since 2007 the region has been promoted as **Lochaber Geopark** (www.lochabergeopark.org.uk), an area of outstanding geology and scenery.

## Glen Coe

Scotland's most famous glen is also one of the grandest and, in bad weather, the grimmest. The approach to the glen from the east, watched over by the rocky pyramid of **Buachaille Etive Mor** – the Great Shepherd of Etive – leads over the Pass of Glencoe and into the narrow upper valley. The southern side is dominated by three massive, brooding spurs, known as the **Three Sisters**, while the northern side is enclosed by the continuous steep wall of the knife-edged Aonach Eagach ridge. The main road threads its lonely way through the middle of all this mountain grandeur, past deep gorges and crashing waterfalls, to the more pastoral lower reaches of the glen around Loch Achtriochtan and Glencoe village.

Glencoe was written into the history books in 1692 when the resident MacDonalds were murdered by Campbell soldiers in what became known as the Glencoe Massacre.

 **Activities**

There are several short, pleasant walks around **Glencoe Lochan**, near the village. To get there, turn left off the minor road to the youth hostel, just beyond the bridge over the River Coe. There are three walks (40 minutes to an hour), all detailed on a signboard at the car park. The artificial lochan was created by Lord Strathcona in 1895 for his homesick Canadian wife Isabella and is surrounded by a North American–style forest.

A more strenuous hike, but well worth the effort on a fine day, is the climb to the **Lost Valley**, a magical mountain sanctuary still haunted by the ghosts of the murdered MacDonalds (only 2.5 miles round trip, but allow three hours). A rough path from the car park at Allt na Reigh (on the A82, 6 miles east of Glencoe village) bears left down to a footbridge over the river, then climbs up the wooded valley between Beinn Fhada and Gearr Aonach (the first and second of the Three Sisters). The route leads steeply up through a maze of giant, jumbled, moss-coated boulders before emerging – unexpectedly – into a broad, open valley with an 800m-long meadow as flat as a football pitch. Back in the days of clan warfare, the valley, which is invisible from below, was used for hiding stolen cattle; its Gaelic name, Coire Gabhail, means 'corrie of capture'.

The summits of Glen Coe's mountains are for experienced mountaineers only. Details of hill-walking routes can be found in the Scottish Mountaineering Club's guidebook *Central Highlands* by Peter Hodgkiss.

### East of the Glen

**GLENCOE MOUNTAIN RESORT** Outdoors (www.glencoemountain.com) A few miles east of Glen Coe proper, on the south side of the A82, is the car park and base station for the Glencoe Mountain Resort, where commercial skiing in Scotland first began back in 1956. The **Lodge Café-Bar** has

# Detour:
## Cromarty Village

The pretty village of Cromarty at the northeastern tip of the Black Isle has lots of 18th-century red-sandstone houses, and a lovely green park beside the sea for picnics and games. An excellent walk, known as the **100 Steps**, leads from the north end of the village to the headland viewpoint of South Sutor (4 miles round trip).

The 18th-century **Cromarty Courthouse** (☎01381-600418; www.cromarty -courthouse.org.uk; Church St; admission free; ☻noon-4pm Sun-Thu Apr-Sep) details the town's history using contemporary references. Kids will love the talking mannequins.

Near the courthouse is **Hugh Miller's Cottage & Museum** (www.hughmiller. org; Church St; adult/child £5.50/4.50; ☻noon-5pm daily Apr-Sep, Tue, Thu & Fri only Oct), the thatch-roofed birthplace of Hugh Miller (1802–56), a local stonemason and amateur geologist who later moved to Edinburgh and became a famous journalist and newspaper editor. The Georgian villa next door is home to a museum celebrating his life and achievements.

From Cromarty harbour, **Ecoventures** (☎01381-600323; www.ecoventures.co.uk; Cromarty Harbour; adult/child £24/18) runs 2½-hour boat trips into the Moray Firth to see bottlenose dolphins and other wildlife.

Also at the harbour, **Sutor Creek** (☎01381-600855; www.sutorcreek.co.uk; 21 Bank St; mains £7-18; ☻11am-9pm late May-Sep) is an excellent little cafe-restaurant serving wood-fired pizzas and fresh local seafood – we can recommend the Cromarty langoustines with garlic and chilli butter.

For something lighter, there's good tea and scones at **The Pantry** (1 Church St; ☻10am-5pm Easter-Sep), or delicious filled rolls and savoury pies at the **Cromarty Bakery** (8 Bank St; ☻9am-5pm Mon-Sat).

comfy sofas where you can soak up the view through the floor-to-ceiling windows.

The **chairlift** (adult/child £10/5; ☻9.30am-4.30pm Thu-Mon) continues to operate in summer – there's a rather grand view over the Moor of Rannoch from the top station – and provides access to a downhill mountain-biking track. In winter a lift pass costs £30 a day and equipment hire is £25 a day.

Two miles west of the ski centre, a minor road leads along peaceful and beautiful **Glen Etive**, which runs southwest for 12 miles to the head of Loch Etive. On a hot summer's day the River Etive contains many tempting pools for swimming in, and there are lots of good picnic sites.

**KINGS HOUSE HOTEL**  Hotel, Pub **££**
(☎01855-851259; www.kingy.com; s/d £35/70; [P]) The remote Kings House Hotel claims to be one of Scotland's oldest licensed inns, dating from the 17th century. It has long been a favourite meeting place for climbers, skiers and hill walkers – the rustic **Climbers Bar** (bar meals £8-12; ☻11am-11pm) round the back is more relaxed than the lounge – and serves good pub grub and real ale.

The hotel lies on the old military road from Stirling to Fort William, and after the Battle of Culloden it was used as a Hanoverian garrison – hence the name.

## Glencoe Village
POP 360

The little village of Glencoe stands on the south shore of Loch Leven at the western end of the glen, 16 miles south of Fort William.

## ⊙ Sights & Activities

**GLENCOE FOLK MUSEUM**    Museum
(📞01855-811664; www.glencoemuseum.com; adult/child £3/free; ⊙10am-4.30pm Mon-Sat Easter-Oct) This small, thatched museum houses a varied collection of military memorabilia, farm equipment, and tools of the woodworking, blacksmithing and slate-quarrying trades.

**GLENCOE VISITOR CENTRE**    Visitor Centre
(NTS; 📞01855-811307; www.glencoe-nts.org.uk; adult/child £6/5; ⊙9.30am-5.30pm Easter-Oct, 10am-4pm Thu-Sun Nov-Easter) About 1.5 miles east of Glencoe village is this modern facility with an ecotourism angle. The centre provides comprehensive information on the geological, environmental and cultural history of Glencoe via high-tech interactive and audiovisual displays, charts the history of mountaineering in the glen, and tells the story of the Glencoe Massacre in all its gory detail.

**LOCHABER WATERSPORTS**    Water Sports
(📞01855-811931; www.lochaberwatersports.co.uk; Ballachulish; ⊙9.30am-5pm Apr-Oct) You can hire kayaks (£12 per hour), rowing boats (£22 per hour), motor boats (£30 per hour), and even a 10m sailing yacht complete with skipper (£150 for three hours, up to five people) here.

## ⓘ Getting There & Away

Scottish Citylink (📞0871 266 3333; www.citylink.co.uk) buses run between Fort William and Glencoe (£7.50, 30 minutes, eight daily) and from Glencoe to Glasgow (£20, 2½ hours, eight daily). Buses stop at Glencoe village, Glencoe Visitor Centre and Glencoe Mountain Resort.

Stagecoach (www.stagecoachbus.com) bus 44 links Glencoe village with Fort William (35 minutes, hourly Monday to Saturday, three on Sunday) and Kinlochleven (25 minutes).

# The Glencoe Massacre

Glen Coe is sometimes said to mean 'the glen of weeping', a romantic mistranslation that stems from the brutal murders that took place here in 1692. Following the Glorious Revolution of 1688, supporters of the exiled Roman Catholic King James – known as Jacobites – rose up against the Protestant King William. William offered the Highland clans (most of the Catholics and Jacobites) an amnesty on the condition that all clan chiefs take an oath of loyalty to him before 1 January 1692.

MacIain, the elderly chief of the MacDonalds of Glencoe, was three days late in taking the oath, and Willian's government decided to use that fact to punish the troublesome MacDonalds and set an example to other Highland clans.

A company of 120 soldiers, mainly from Campbell territory, were sent to the glen under cover of collecting taxes. It was traditional for clans to provide hospitality to travellers and so the troops were billeted in MacDonald homes.

After they'd been guests for 12 days, the government order came for the soldiers to 'fall upon the rebels the MacDonalds of Glencoe and put all to the sword under 70'. The soldiers turned on their hosts at 5am on 13 February, killing MacIain and 37 other men, women and children. Some of the soldiers alerted the MacDonalds to their intended fate, allowing them to escape; many fled into the snow-covered hills, where another 40 people died of exposure. A monument in Glencoe village commemorates the massacre.

# Fort William

POP 9910

Basking on the shores of Loch Linnhe amid magnificent mountain scenery, Fort William has one of the most enviable settings in the whole of Scotland. If it wasn't for the busy dual carriageway crammed between the town centre and the loch, and one of the highest rainfall records in the country, it would be almost idyllic. Even so, the Fort has carved out a reputation as 'Outdoor Capital of the UK' (www.outdoorcapi tal.co.uk), and its easy access by rail and bus makes it a good place to base yourself for exploring the surrounding mountains and glens.

Magical **Glen Nevis** begins near the northern end of the town and wraps itself around the southern flanks of **Ben Nevis** (1344m) – Britain's highest mountain and a magnet for hikers and climbers. The glen is also popular with movie makers – parts of *Braveheart*, *Rob Roy* and the Harry Potter movies were filmed there.

 **Sights**

## WEST HIGHLAND
## MUSEUM                          Museum

(☏ 01397-702169; www.westhighlandmuseum. org.uk; Cameron Sq; ⊙10am-5pm Mon-Sat Apr-Oct, to 4pm Mar & Oct-Dec, closed Jan & Feb) This small but fascinating museum is packed with all manner of Highland memorabilia. Look out for the secret portrait of Bonnie Prince Charlie – after the Jacobite rebellions all things Highland were banned, including pictures of the exiled leader, and this tiny painting looks like nothing more than a smear of paint until viewed in a cylindrical mirror, which reflects a credible likeness of the prince.

## BEN NEVIS DISTILLERY          Distillery

(☏ 01397-702476; www.bennevisdistillery.com; Lochy Bridge; guided tour adult/child £4/2; ⊙9am-5pm Mon-Fri year round, plus 10am-4pm Sat Easter-Sep & noon-4pm Sun Jul & Aug) A

## If You Like…
## Scenic Glens

If it's Scotland's moody lochs and epic beauty that steal your heart, you may want to set some time aside to explore these scenic glens.

○ **Glen Etive** At the eastern end of Glen Coe a minor road leads south along this peaceful and beautiful glen. The River Etive contains many tempting pools for swimming in on a hot summer day, and there are lots of good picnic sites.

○ **Glen Roy** Near Spean Bridge, 10 miles north of Fort William, this glen is noted for its intriguing, so-called 'parallel roads'. These prominent horizontal terraces are actually ancient shorelines formed during the last ice age by the waters of an ice-dammed glacial lake.

○ **Glen Feshie** Tranquil Glen Feshie extends south from Kincraig, deep into the Cairngorms, with Scots pine woods in its upper reaches surrounded by big, heathery hills. The 4WD track to the head of the glen makes a great mountain-bike excursion (25-mile round trip).

○ **Glen Lyon** This remote and stunningly beautiful glen runs for some 34 unforgettable miles of rickety stone bridges, Caledonian pine forest and sheer heather-splashed peaks poking through swirling clouds. It's reached from the A9 via Aberfeldy.

tour of this distillery makes for a warming rainy day alternative to exploring the hills.

 **Tours**

## CRANNOG CRUISES          Wildlife Cruise

(☏ 01397-700714; adult/child £10/5; ⊙four daily) Operates 1½-hour wildlife cruises on Loch Linnhe, visiting a seal colony and a salmon farm.

## AL'S TOURS                    Taxi Tour

(☏ 01397-700700; www.alstours.com) Taxi tours with driver-guide around Lochaber and Glencoe cost £80/195 for a half-/ full day.

PATRICK HORTON/GETTY IMAGES ©

# Don't Miss **Jacobite Steam Train**

The Jacobite Steam Train, hauled by a former LNER K1 or LMS Class 5MT locomotive, travels the scenic two-hour run between Fort William and Mallaig, departing from Fort William train station in the morning and returning from Mallaig in the afternoon. There's a brief stop at Glenfinnan station, and you get 1½ hours in Mallaig.

Classed as one of the great railway journeys of the world, the route crosses the historic Glenfinnan Viaduct, made famous in the Harry Potter films – the Jacobite's owners supplied the steam locomotive and rolling stock used in the film.

**NEED TO KNOW**

☏ 0844 850 4685; www.steamtrain.info; day return adult/child £32/18; ☼ daily Jul & Aug, Mon-Fri mid-May–Jun & Sep-Oct

## 🛏 Sleeping

It's best to book well ahead in summer, especially for hostels.

**LIME TREE**                Hotel ££
( ☏ 01397-701806; www.limetreefortwilliam.co.uk; Achintore Rd; s/d from £80/110; P) Much more interesting than your average guesthouse, this former Victorian manse overlooking Loch Linnhe is an 'art gallery with rooms', decorated throughout with the artist-owner's atmospheric Highland landscapes. Foodies rave about the restaurant, and the gallery space – a triumph of sensitive design – stages everything from serious exhibitions (works by David Hockney and Andy Goldsworthy have appeared) to folk concerts.

**GRANGE**                B&B ££
( ☏ 01397-705516; www.grangefortwilliam.com; Grange Rd; r per person £58-63; P) An exceptional 19th-century villa set in its own landscaped grounds, the Grange is crammed with antiques and fitted with log fires, chaise longues and Victorian

roll-top baths. The Turret Room, with its window seat in the turret overlooking Loch Linnhe, is our favourite. It's 500m southwest of the town centre.

**CROLINNHE** B&B £££
(01397-703795; www.crolinnhe.co.uk; Grange Rd; r £120-127; Easter-Oct; P @) This grand 19th-century villa has a lochside location, beautiful gardens and sumptuous accommodation. A vegetarian breakfast is provided on request.

**CALLUNA** Apartments £
(01397-700451; www.fortwilliamholiday.co.uk; Heathercroft, Connochie Rd; dm/tw £16/36, 6- to 8-person apt per week £550; P) Run by well-known mountain guide Alan Kimber and wife Sue, the Calluna offers self-catering apartments geared to groups of hikers and climbers, but also takes individual travellers prepared to share; there's a fully equipped kitchen and an excellent drying room for your soggy hiking gear.

**ST ANDREW'S GUEST HOUSE** B&B ££
(01397-703038; www.standrewsguesthouse.co.uk; Fassifern Rd; r per person £24-30; P) Set in a lovely 19th-century building that was once a rectory and choir school, St Andrew's retains period features, such as carved masonry, wood panelling and stained-glass windows. It has six spacious bedrooms, some with stunning views.

**GLENLOCHY APARTMENTS** Apartments ££
(01397-702909; www.glenlochyguesthouse.co.uk; Nevis Bridge; 2-person apt per night £65, per week £380-490; P) Convenient for Glen Nevis, Ben Nevis and the end of the West Highland Way, the Glenlochy is a sprawling modern place with five modern apartments set in a huge garden beside the River Nevis, a pleasant place to sit on summer evenings.

**FORT WILLIAM BACKPACKERS** Hostel £
(01397-700711; www.scotlands-top-hostels.com; Alma Rd; dm/tw £18/47; P @) A 10-minute walk from the bus and train stations, this lively and welcoming hostel is set in a grand Victorian villa, perched on a hillside with great views over Loch Linnhe.

**NO 6 CABERFEIDH** B&B ££
(01397-703756; www.6caberfeidh.com; Fassifern Rd, 6 Caberfeidh; r per person £30-40; ) Friendly B&B; vegetarian breakfast on request.

**ASHBURN HOUSE** B&B ££
(01397-706000; www.highland5star.co.uk; Achintore Rd; r per person £45-55; P) Grand Victorian villa south of the centre; children under 12 not welcome.

**ALEXANDRA HOTEL** Hotel £££
(01397-702241; www.strathmorehotels.com; The Parade; s/d from £110/168; P) Large, traditional, family-oriented hotel bang in the middle of town.

## Eating & Drinking

**LIME TREE** Restaurant £££
(01397-701806; www.limetreefortwilliam.co.uk; Achintore Rd; 2-/3-course dinner £28/30; dinner daily, lunch Sun) Fort William is not over-endowed with great places to eat, but the restaurant at this small hotel and art gallery has put the UK's Outdoor Capital on the gastronomic map. The chef won a Michelin star in his previous restaurant, and turns out delicious dishes built around fresh Scottish produce such as seared saddle of Glenfinnan venison with red wine and rosemary jus.

**CRANNOG SEAFOOD RESTAURANT** Restaurant ££
(01397-705589; www.crannog.net; Town Pier; mains £16-20) The Crannog wins the prize for best location in town – perched on the Town Pier, giving window-table diners an uninterrupted view down Loch Linnhe. Informal and unfussy, it specialises in fresh local seafood – there are three or four daily fish specials plus the main menu – though there are beef, poultry and vegetarian dishes, too. Two-course lunch £13.

**GROG & GRUEL**                    Restaurant ££
(www.grogandgruel.co.uk; 66 High St; mains £7-13;
🕑 bar meals noon-9pm, restaurant 5-9pm; 🛜)
Upstairs from the Grog & Gruel real-ale
pub is a lively Tex-Mex restaurant, with a
crowd-pleasing menu of tasty enchiladas,
burritos, fajitas, burgers, steaks and pizza.

**CAFÉ MANGO**                          Asian ££
( 📞01397-701367; www.thecafemango.co.uk;
24-26 High St; mains £9-14; 🕑lunch & dinner;
🛜) Bright and modern restaurant serving
fragrant Thai and spicy Indian dishes.

**SUGAR AND SPICE**                      Cafe £
( 📞01397-705005; 147 High St; mains £7-9;
🕑10am-5pm Mon-Sat, 6-9pm Thu-Sat; 🛜👶)
Enjoy what is probably the best coffee
in town at this colourful cafe, just a few
paces from the official finishing line of
the West Highland Way. In the evening
(Thursday to Saturday only) it serves
authentic Thai dishes.

**BEN NEVIS BAR**                          Pub
( 📞01397-702295; 105 High St) The lounge
here enjoys a good view over the loch, and

the bar exudes a relaxed, jovial atmosphere where climbers and tourists can
work off leftover energy jigging to live
music (Thursday and Friday nights).

## ℹ️ Information

**Belford Hospital** ( 📞01397-702481; Belford Rd)
Opposite the train station.

**Post Office** ( 📞0845 722 3344; 5 High St)

**Fort William tourist office** ( 📞01397-703781;
www.visithighlands.com; 15 High St; internet per
20min £1 ; 🕑9am-6pm Mon-Sat, 10am-5pm Sun
Apr-Sep, limited hrs Oct-Mar; @)

## ℹ️ Getting There & Away

### Bus

**Scottish Citylink** (www.citylink.co.uk) buses link
Fort William with other major towns and cities. **Shiel
Buses** (www.shielbuses.co.uk) bus route 500 runs
to Mallaig (1½ hours, three daily Monday to Friday
only) via Glenfinnan (30 minutes) and Arisaig (one
hour).

**Edinburgh** £33, 4½ hours, one daily direct,
seven with a change at Glasgow; via Glencoe
and Crianlarich.

**Glasgow** £22, three hours, eight daily.

**Inverness** £12, two hours, five daily.

**Oban** £9.40, 1½ hours, three daily.

**Portree** £28.60, three hours, four daily.

### Car

**Easydrive Car Hire** ( 📞01397-
701616; www.easydrivescotland.
co.uk; Unit 36a, Ben Nevis
Industrial Estate, Ben Nevis
Dr) Hires out small cars
from £31/195 a day/week,
including tax and unlimited
mileage, but not Collision
Damage Waiver (CDW).

### Train

The spectacular **West
Highland line** runs from
Glasgow to Mallaig via Fort

Wire bridge, Glen Nevis
CHRISTIAN HANDL/IMAGEBROKER ©

William. The overnight *Caledonian Sleeper* service connects Fort William and London Euston (£103 sharing a twin-berth cabin, 13 hours).

There's no direct rail connection between Oban and Fort William – you have to change at Crianlarich, so it's faster to use the bus.

**Edinburgh** £44, five hours; change at Glasgow's Queen St station.

**Glasgow** £26.30, 3¾ hours, three daily, two on Sunday.

**Mallaig** £11, 1½ hours, four daily, three on Sunday.

## Getting Around

### Bike

**Alpine Bikes** ( 01397-704008; www.alpinebikes.com; 117 High St; 9am-5.30pm Mon-Sat, 10am-5.30pm Sun) Rents out mountain bikes for £12/20 for a half-/full day.

### Bus

The Fort Dayrider ticket (£3) gives unlimited travel for one day on Stagecoach bus services in the Fort William area. Buy from the bus driver.

### Taxi

There's a taxi rank on the corner of High St and The Parade.

## Around Fort William

### Glen Nevis

You can walk the 3 miles from Fort William to scenic Glen Nevis in about an hour or so. The **Glen Nevis Visitor Centre** ( 01397-705922; www.bennevisweather.co.uk; 9am-5pm Apr-Oct, shorter hrs in winter) is situated 1.5 miles up the glen, and provides information on walking, weather forecasts, and specific advice on climbing Ben Nevis.

From the car park at the far end of the road along Glen Nevis, there is an excellent 1.5-mile walk through the spectacular Nevis Gorge to **Steall Meadows**, a verdant valley dominated by a 100m-high bridal-veil waterfall. You can reach the foot of the falls by crossing the river on a wobbly, three-cable wire bridge. There's one cable for your feet and one for each hand – it's a real test of balance!

# 🛏 Sleeping & Eating

**BEN NEVIS INN** Hostel £
( 01397-701227; www.ben-nevis-inn.co.uk; Achintee; dm £15.50; noon-11pm daily Apr-Oct, Thu-Sun only Nov-Mar; P ) A good alternative to the youth hostel is this great barn of a pub (real ale and tasty bar meals available; mains £9 to £16), with a comfy 24-bed hostel downstairs. It's at the Achintee start of the path up Ben Nevis, and only a mile from the end of the West Highland Way. Food served noon to 9pm.

**ACHINTEE FARM** B&B, Hostel £
( 01397-702240; www.achinteefarm.com; Achintee; B&B s/d £60/78, hostel dm/tw £17/38; P ) This attractive farmhouse offers excellent B&B accommodation and also has a small hostel attached. It's just 100m from the Ben Nevis Inn, and ideally positioned for climbing Ben Nevis.

**GLEN NEVIS SYHA** Hostel £
(SYHA; 01397-702336; www.glennevishostel.co.uk; dm £21.50; @ ) Large, impersonal and reminiscent of a school camp, this hostel is 3 miles from Fort William, right beside one of the starting points for the tourist track up Ben Nevis.

## ℹ Getting There & Away

Bus 41 runs from Fort William bus station up Glen Nevis to the Glen Nevis youth hostel (10 minutes, two daily year round, five daily Monday to Saturday June to September) and on to the Lower Falls 3 miles beyond the hostel (20 minutes). Check at the tourist office for the latest timetable, which is liable to alteration.

## Road to the Isles

The 46-mile A830 road from Fort William to Mallaig is traditionally known as the Road to the Isles, as it leads to the jumping-off point for ferries to the Small Isles and Skye, itself a stepping stone to the Outer Hebrides. This is a region steeped in Jacobite history, having witnessed both the beginning and the end of Bonnie Prince Charlie's doomed attempt to regain the British throne in 1745–46.

# Climbing Ben Nevis

As the highest peak in the British Isles, Ben Nevis (1344m) attracts many would-be ascensionists who would not normally think of climbing a Scottish mountain – a staggering (often literally) 100,000 people reach the summit each year. Although anyone who is reasonably fit should have no problem climbing Ben Nevis on a fine summer's day, an ascent should not be undertaken lightly. Every year people have to be rescued from the mountain. You will need proper walking boots (the path is rough and stony, and there may be soft, wet snowfields on the summit), warm clothing, waterproofs, a map and compass, and plenty of food and water. And don't forget to check the weather forecast (see www.bennevisweather.co.uk).

Here are a few facts to mull over before you go racing up the tourist track: the summit plateau is bounded by 700m-high cliffs and has a sub-Arctic climate; at the summit it can snow on any day of the year; the summit is wrapped in cloud nine days out of 10; in thick cloud, visibility at the summit can be 10m or less; and in such conditions the only safe way off the mountain requires careful use of a map and compass to avoid walking over those 700m cliffs.

The tourist track (the easiest route to the top) was originally called the Pony Track. It was built in the 19th century for the pack ponies that carried supplies to a meteorological observatory on the summit (now in ruins), which was manned continuously from 1883 to 1904.

There are three possible starting points for the tourist track ascent – Achintee Farm; the footbridge at Glen Nevis SYHA (p271); and, if you have a car, the car park at Glen Nevis Visitor Centre. The path climbs gradually to the shoulder at Lochan Meall an t-Suidhe (known as the Halfway Lochan), then zigzags steeply up beside the Red Burn to the summit plateau. The highest point is marked by a trig point on top of a huge cairn beside the ruins of the old observatory; the plateau is scattered with countless smaller cairns, stones arranged in the shape of people's names and, sadly, a fair bit of litter.

The total distance to the summit and back is 8 miles; allow at least four or five hours to reach the top, and another 2½ to three hours for the descent. Afterwards, as you celebrate in the pub with a pint, consider the fact that the record time for the annual Ben Nevis Hill Race is just under 1½ hours – up *and* down. Then have another pint.

The final section of this scenic route, between Arisaig and Mallaig, has been upgraded to a fast straight road. Unless you're in a hurry, opt instead for the more scenic old road (signposted Alternative Coastal Route).

## ⓘ Getting Around

### Bus

Shiel Buses (www.shielbuses.co.uk) bus 500 runs to Mallaig (1½ hours, three daily Monday to Friday, one on Saturday) via Glenfinnan (30 minutes) and Arisaig (one hour).

### Train

The Fort William–Mallaig railway line has four trains a day (three on Sunday), with stops at many points along the way, including Corpach, Glenfinnan, Lochailort, Arisaig and Morar.

## Glenfinnan

POP 100

Glenfinnan is hallowed ground for fans of Bonnie Prince Charlie; the monument here marks where he raised his Highland army. It is also a place of pilgrimage for steam train enthusiasts and Harry Potter fans – the famous railway viaduct features in the films, and is regularly traversed by the Jacobite Steam Train (p268).

## ◉ Sights & Activities

**GLENFINNAN MONUMENT**    Monument
This tall column, topped by a statue of a kilted Highlander, was erected in 1815 on the spot where the Young Pretender first raised his standard and rallied the Jacobite clans on 19 August 1745, marking the start of the ill-fated campaign that would end in disaster 14 months later. The setting, at the north end of Loch Shiel, is hauntingly beautiful.

**GLENFINNAN VISITOR
CENTRE**    Visitor Centre
(NTS; adult/child £3.50/2.50; ☺9.30am-5.30pm Jul & Aug, 10am-5pm Easter-Jun, Sep & Oct) This centre recounts the story of the '45, as the Jacobite rebellion of 1745 is known, when the prince's loyal clansmen marched and fought their way from Glenfinnan south via Edinburgh to Derby, then back north to final defeat at Culloden.

**GLENFINNAN
STATION MUSEUM**    Museum
(www.glenfinnanstationmuseum.co.uk; adult/child £1.50/75p; ☺9am-5pm Jun–mid-Oct) This museum is dedicated to the great days of steam on the West Highland line. The famous 21-arch Glenfinnan Viaduct, just east of the station, was built in 1901, and featured in the movie *Harry Potter & the Chamber of Secrets*. A pleasant walk of around 0.75 miles east from the station (signposted) leads to a viewpoint for the viaduct and for Loch Shiel.

**LOCH SHIEL CRUISES**    Boat Trips
(☎07801-537617; www.highlandcruises.co.uk; ☺Apr-Sep) Offers boat trips along Loch Shiel. There are one- to 2½-hour cruises (£10 to £18 per person) daily except Saturday and Wednesday. On Wednesday the boat goes the full length of the loch to **Acharacle** (£17/25 one way/return), calling at Polloch and Dalilea, allowing for a range of walks and bike rides using the forestry track on the eastern shore. The boat departs from a jetty near Glenfinnan House Hotel.

## Arisaig & Morar

The 5 miles of coast between Arisaig and Morar is a fretwork of rocky islets, inlets and gorgeous silver-sand beaches backed by dunes and machair, with stunning sunset views across the sea to the silhouetted peaks of Eigg and Rum. The **Silver Sands of Morar**, as they are known, draw crowds of bucket-and-spade holidaymakers in July and August.

Glenfinnan Monument
PAUL THOMPSON/GETTY IMAGES ©

The waters of Loch nan Uamh (loch nan oo-ah; 'the loch of the caves') lap at the southern shores of Arisaig; this was where Bonnie Prince Charlie first set foot on the Scottish mainland on 11 August 1745, on the shingle beach at the mouth of the Borrodale burn. Just 2 miles to the east of this bay, on a rocky point near a parking area, the Prince's Cairn marks the spot where he finally departed Scottish soil, never to return, on 19 September 1746.

## Sights

### CAMUSDARACH BEACH                Beach
Fans of the movie *Local Hero* still make pilgrimages to Camusdarach Beach, just south of Morar, which starred in the film as Ben's beach. To find it, look for the car park 800m north of Camusdarach campsite; from here, a wooden footbridge and a 400m walk through the dunes lead to the beach. (The village that featured in the film is on the other side of the country, at Pennan.)

### LAND, SEA & ISLANDS
### VISITOR CENTRE                Visitor Centre
(www.arisaigcentre.co.uk; Arisaig; ⊙10am-6pm Mon-Fri, 10-4pm Sun) This centre in Arisaig village houses exhibits on the cultural and natural history of the region, plus a small but fascinating exhibition on the part played by the local area as a base for training spies for the Special Operations Executive (SOE, forerunner of MI6) during WWII.

## Mallaig
POP 800

If you're travelling between Fort William and Skye, you may find yourself overnighting in the bustling fishing and ferry port of Mallaig. Indeed, it makes a good base for a series of day trips by ferry to the Small Isles and Knoydart.

## Sights & Activities

### LOCH MORAR                Lake
(www.lochmorar.org.uk) A minor road from Morar village, 2.5 miles south of Mallaig, leads to scenic 11-mile-long Loch Morar, which at 310m is the deepest body of

Camusdarach Beach

RICCARDO SPILA/GRAND TOUR/CORBIS ©

water in the UK. Reputed to be inhabited by its own version of Nessie – Morag, the Loch Morar monster – the loch and its surrounding hills are the haunt of otters, wildcats, red deer and golden eagles.

A 5-mile-long, signposted footpath leads along the north shore of the loch from the road-end at Bracorina, 3 miles east of Morar village, to Tarbet on Loch Nevis, from where you can catch a **passenger ferry** (☏01687-462320; www.knoydart-ferry.co.uk; one way £11) back to Mallaig (departs 3.30pm).

### MALLAIG HERITAGE CENTRE
Heritage Centre

(☏01687-462085; www.mallaigheritage.org.uk; Station Rd; adult/child £2/free; ⊙9.30am-4.30pm Mon-Fri, noon-4pm Sat & Sun) The village's rainy-day attractions are limited to this heritage centre, which covers the archaeology and history of the region, including the heart-rending tale of the Highland Clearances in Knoydart (see p284).

## 🛏 Sleeping & Eating

### SEAVIEW GUEST HOUSE
B&B ££

(☏01687-462059; www.seaviewguesthousemallaig.com; Main St; r per person £28-35; ⊙Mar-Nov; P) Just beyond the tourist office, this comfortable three-bedroom B&B has grand views over the harbour, not only from the upstairs bedrooms but also from the breakfast room. There's also a cute little cottage next door that offers self-catering accommodation (www.selfcateringmallaig.com; one double and one twin room) for £350 to £450 a week.

### SPRINGBANK GUEST HOUSE
B&B £

(☏01687-462459; www.springbank-mallaig.co.uk; East Bay; r per person £30; P 🖵) The Springbank is a traditional West Highland

house with seven homey guest bedrooms, with superb views across the harbour to the Cuillin of Skye.

### FISH MARKET RESTAURANT
Seafood ££

(☏01687-462299; Station Rd; mains £9-21) At least half-a-dozen signs in Mallaig advertise 'seafood restaurant', but this bright, modern, bistro-style place next to the harbour is our favourite, serving simply prepared scallops with smoked salmon and savoy cabbage, grilled langoustines with garlic butter, and fresh Mallaig haddock fried in breadcrumbs, as well as the tastiest Cullen skink on the west coast.

Upstairs is a **coffee shop** (mains £5-6; ⊙11am-5pm) that serves delicious, hot roast-beef rolls with horseradish sauce, and scones with clotted cream and jam.

## ℹ Information

Mallaig has a tourist office (☏01687-462170; East Bay; ⊙10am-5.30pm Mon-Fri, 10.15am-3.45pm Sat, noon-3.30pm Sun), a post office, a bank with ATM and a Co-op supermarket (⊙8.00am-10pm Mon-Sat, 9am-9pm Sun).

## ℹ Getting There & Away

### Boat

Ferries run from Mallaig to the Small Isles, the Isle of Skye and Knoydart.

### Bus

Shiel Buses (www.shielbuses.co.uk) bus 500 runs from Fort William to Mallaig (1½ hours, three daily Monday to Friday, one on Saturday) via Glenfinnan (30 minutes) and Arisaig (one hour).

### Train

The West Highland line runs between Fort William and Mallaig (£11, 1½ hours) four times a day (three on Sunday).

# Scotland
# In Focus

Edinburgh Military Tattoo (p101)
PHOTOGRAPHER: GUILLEM LOPEZ/ALAMY ©

# Scotland Today

Great Hall, Edinburgh Castle (p68)

> *Current opinion polls suggest that at least two-thirds of Scots are happy with the status quo*

## belief systems
(% of population)

| **43** | **28** | **16** | 6.8 | 6.2 |
|---|---|---|---|---|
| Church of Scotland | Non-Religious | Roman Catholic | Other Christian | Other |

## if Scotland were 100 people

98 would be white
1 would be South Asian
1 would be other

## population per sq mile

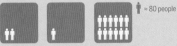

♦ ≈ 80 people

Scotland · USA · England

## Scottish Politics

Although an integral part of Great Britain since 1707, Scotland has maintained a separate and distinct identity throughout the last 300 years. The return of a devolved Scottish parliament to Edinburgh in 1999 marked a growing confidence and pride in the nation's achievements.

The first decade of devolution has seen Scottish politics diverge significantly from the Westminster way. Distinctive policies that have been applied in Scotland but not in the rest of the United Kingdom include free long-term care for the elderly, the abolition of tuition fees for university students and higher pay for teachers.

The Scottish National Party (SNP), which had led a minority government in Edinburgh since 2007, surprised the nation in the 2011 elections with a landslide victory in the Scottish parliament, winning 69 out of 129 seats. Suddenly the question of Scotland breaking away from the UK was all over the news.

SIMON BRADFIELD/GETTY IMAGES ©

becoming self-sufficient in energy by 2020, and a net exporter of 'clean' electricity.

In the first half of the 20th century the Scottish Highlands was one of the first regions in the world to develop hydroelectric power on a large scale, and in the past decade, wind turbines have sprung up all over the place. By 2009, renewables provided 27% of Scotland's energy consumption, a figure that rose to 35% in 2011; the government's target is to reach 100% by 2020.

However, the future of Scotland's energy industry lies not on land, but in the sea: Scotland has access to 25% of Europe's available tidal energy, and 10% of its wave power. The country is at the leading edge of developing wave, tidal and offshore wind power, and in 2012 the waters around Orkney and the Pentland Firth were designated as a Marine Energy Park.

The election of a Conservative/Lib Dem coalition government in Westminster in 2010 only served to heighten the political difference between Scotland and the rest of the UK – only one of Scotland's 59 constituencies returned a Conservative MP, while the Labour Party (which was defeated in Westminster) increased its share of the Scottish vote.

The SNP has pledged to hold a referendum in the autumn of 2014 on whether Scotland should have full independence. Current opinion polls suggest that at least two-thirds of Scots are happy with the status quo, but with the state of the UK economy, who knows what might happen down the line.

# Renewable Energy

One of the central planks of the SNP's vision for an independent Scotland is its energy policy. Party leader Alex Salmond has said he wants the country to be the 'Saudi Arabia of renewable energy' –

# Development vs Conservation

In 2010 the Scottish government gave the go-ahead to a 135-mile, high-voltage over-head power line from Beauly (near Inverness) to Denny in Stirlingshire, to connect wind- and marine-generated electricity from the north to the heart of the national grid. It will be carried on 600 giant pylons marching through some of the Highlands' most scenic areas, including Strathglass, Fort Augustus and Bridge of Tummel.

Supporters point out that the scheme also involves the removal of almost 60 miles of low-voltage pylons from the Cairngorms National Park; opponents claim that a seabed cable, while more expensive, would be a better alternative. The debate reflects a larger tension that exists across the Highlands and islands – between those keen to develop the region's resources and conservationists who want to keep the area unspoiled.

# History

*Since the decline of the Vikings, Scottish history has been predictably and often violently bound to that of England. Battles and border raids were common until the shared monarchy of the Stuart dynasty, then political union, drew the two together. The 18th century saw Scotland achieve international fame as the cradle of renowned philosophers, scientists and writers, and in the 19th it became a powerhouse of engineering and industry, a cornerstone of the British Empire. Even so, a lingering desire for greater independence was finally realised with the restoration of a Scottish parliament in the late 20th century.*

## Christianity & St Columba

After the Romans left Britain there were at least two indigenous peoples in the northern region of the British Isles: the Picts in the north and east, and the Britons in the southwest. The Scots probably arrived around 500AD, crossing to Argyll from Northern Ireland and establishing a kingdom called Dalriada.

In the 6th century St Columba, Scotland's most famous missionary, arrived in Scotland. According to legend,

**Early 6th century**

A Celtic tribe, the Scots, cross from Northern Ireland and establish a kingdom called Dalriada.

Columba was a scholar and a soldier-priest who fled Ireland in 563 and established a monastery on Iona. After his death he was credited with miraculous feats such as defeating what is today known as the Loch Ness monster.

## Kingdom of the Scots

The Picts and Scots were drawn together by the threat of a Norse invasion and by the combination of political and spiritual power from their common Christianity. Kenneth MacAlpin, first king of a united Scotland, achieved power using a mixture of blood ties and diplomacy. He set his capital in Pictland at Scone, and brought to it the sacred Stone of Destiny, used in the coronation of Scottish kings.

Nearly two centuries later, MacAlpin's great-great-great-grandson, Malcolm II (r 1005–18), defeated the Northumbrian Angles led by King Canute. This victory brought Edinburgh and Lothian under Scottish control and extended Scottish territory as far south as the Tweed.

With his Saxon queen, Margaret, Malcolm III Canmore (r 1058–93) – whose father Duncan was murdered by Macbeth (as described in Shakespeare's eponymous play) – founded a dynasty of able Scottish rulers. They introduced new Anglo-Norman systems of government and religious foundations.

## Robert the Bruce & William Wallace

The year 1286 saw a dispute over the succession to the Scottish throne between Robert de Brus, lord of Annandale, and John Balliol, lord of Galloway. Edward I of England, as the greatest feudal lord in Britain, was asked to arbitrate. He chose Balliol, whom he thought he could manipulate more easily.

Seeking to tighten his feudal grip on Scotland, Edward – known as the 'Hammer of the Scots' – treated the Scots king as his vassal rather than his equal. The humiliated Balliol finally turned against him and allied Scotland with France in 1295, thus beginning the enduring 'Auld Alliance' and ushering in the Wars of Independence.

Edward's response was bloody. In 1296 he invaded Scotland and Balliol was incarcerated in the Tower of London; in a final blow to Scots pride, Edward I removed the Stone of Destiny from Scone and took it back to London.

Enter arguably Scotland's most tragic hero, William Wallace. Bands of rebels were attacking the English occupiers and one such band, led by Wallace, defeated the English army at the Battle of Stirling Bridge in 1297. After Wallace was executed, Robert the Bruce, grandson of the lord of Annandale, saw his chance, defied Edward (whom he had previously aligned himself with), murdered his rival John Comyn and had himself crowned king of Scotland at Scone in 1306. Bruce mounted a campaign to drive the English out of Scotland but suffered repeated defeats.

**563**
St Columba establishes a Christian mission on Iona. By the 8th century most of Scotland is converted.

**780**
Norsemen in longboats from Scandinavia begin to pillage the Scottish coast and islands.

**1296**
King Edward I marches on Scotland with army of 30,000, butchering citizens and capturing castles.

According to legend, while Bruce was on the run he was inspired to renew his efforts by a spider's persistence in spinning its web – he went on to secure an illustrious victory over the English at Bannockburn in 1314, now enshrined in Scottish legend.

## Mary, Queen of Scots

Mary, daughter of King James V, was born at Linlithgow Palace in 1542, and inherited the throne as Queen of Scots at the tender age of six days. She was sent to France at an early age while Scotland was ruled by regents, and in 1558 she was married to the French dauphin and became queen of France as well as Scotland.

Following the death of her sickly husband, the 18-year-old Mary returned to Scotland in 1561. She was formally welcomed to her capital city and held a famous audience at Holyrood Palace with John Knox. The great reformer harangued the young queen and she later agreed to protect the budding Protestant Church in Scotland while continuing to hear Mass in private.

She married Henry Stewart, Lord Darnley, in the Chapel Royal at Holyrood and gave birth to a son (later James VI) in Edinburgh Castle in 1565. Any domestic bliss was short-lived and, in a scarcely believable train of events, Darnley was involved in the murder of Mary's Italian secretary Rizzio (rumoured to be her lover) before he himself was murdered, probably by Mary's new lover and third-husband-to-be, the Earl of Bothwell!

The Scots had had enough – Mary's enemies finally confronted her and Mary was forced to abdicate in 1567 and thrown into prison at Castle Leven. She managed to escape, and fled to England where she was imprisoned for 19 years by Queen Elizabeth I before finally being executed in 1587.

## The Declaration of Arbroath

During the Wars of Independence, Scottish nobles sent a letter to Pope John XXII requesting his support. Written by the abbot of Arbroath in 1320, it is the earliest document that seeks to place limits on royal power.

After railing against the tyranny of Edward I of England, the declaration famously states: 'For so long as a hundred of us remain alive, we will yield in no least way to English dominion. For we fight, not for glory nor for riches nor for honours, but only and alone for freedom, which no good man surrenders but with his life.'

**1298–1305**
Edward defeats the Scots at Falkirk; William Wallace resigns as guardian and is fatally betrayed.

**1314**
Robert the Bruce wins a famous victory over the English at the Battle of Bannockburn.

WILLIAM WALLACE STATUE

EPICS/GETTY IMAGES ©

## Union of the Crowns

Mary's son, the infant James VI (r 1567–1625) had meanwhile been crowned at Stirling, and a series of regents ruled in his place. In England, Elizabeth died childless, and the English, desperate for a male monarch, soon turned their attention north. In 1603 James VI of Scotland became James I of Great Britain and moved his court to London. His plan to politically unite the two countries, however, failed. For the most part, the Stewarts (now spelled Stuart) ignored Scotland from then on. Indeed, when Charles I (r 1625–49) succeeded James, he couldn't be bothered to travel north to Edinburgh to be formally crowned as king of Scotland until 1633.

## Covenanters & Civil War

Civil war strangled Scotland and England in the 17th century. Attempts by Charles I to impose episcopacy (the rule of bishops) and an English liturgy on the Presbyterian Scottish Church set off public riots in Edinburgh. The Presbyterians believed in a personal bond with God that had no need of mediation through priests, popes and kings. On 28 February 1638 hundreds gathered in Greyfriars Kirkyard to sign a National Covenant affirming their rights and beliefs. Scotland was divided between the Covenanters and those who supported the king.

After Charles II's restoration in 1660, he reneged on the Covenant; episcopacy was imposed and hardline Presbyterian ministers were deprived of their churches. Charles' brother and successor, the Catholic James VII/II (r 1685–89), made worshipping as a Covenanter a capital offence.

James had converted to Catholicism but as long as his Protestant daughter Mary was next in line a lid was kept on the simmering pot of religious conflict. When his second wife, however, gave birth to a son (a Catholic heir to the throne) in 1688, things erupted. Parliament called for James's Protestant son-in-law, William of Orange, to invade from the Netherlands, and James was forced into exile.

## Union With England

The civil wars left the country and its economy ruined. Anti-English feeling ran high: William was at war with France and was using Scottish soldiers and taxes – many Scots, sympathetic to the French, disapproved. This feeling was exacerbated by the failure of an investment venture in Panama (the so-called Darien Scheme, designed to

## The Best...
## Historic Sites

1 Bannockburn (p170)

2 Greyfriars Kirk (p76)

3 Glenfinnan (p273)

4 Culloden (p251)

5 Scottish Parliament Building (p75)

IN FOCUS HISTORY

---

**1328**
Treaty of Northampton gives Scotland independence, with Robert I, the Bruce, as king.

**1560**
Scottish parliament creates a Protestant Church that is independent of Rome and the monarchy.

**1567**
Mary Queen of Scots is deposed and thrown in prison; she is executed in 1587.

establish a Scottish colony in the Americas), which resulted in widespread bankruptcy in Scotland.

The failure of the Darien Scheme made it clear to the wealthy Scottish merchants and stockholders that the only way they could gain access to the lucrative markets of developing colonies was through union with England. The English parliament favoured union through fear of Jacobite sympathies in Scotland being exploited by its enemies, the French.

## Bonnie Prince Charlie

The Jacobite rebellions of the 18th century sought to restore a Catholic Stuart king to the British throne. James Edward Stuart (Jacobite is derived from the Latin word for James), known as the Old Pretender, was the son of James VII/II. The Old Pretender's son, Charles Edward Stuart – better known as Bonnie Prince Charlie or the Young Pretender – landed in Scotland in 1745 to lead the final Jacobite uprising. Raised in France, he had little military experience, didn't speak Gaelic and had a shaky grasp of English. Nevertheless, after rallying an army of Highlanders at Glenfinnan, he marched southwards and captured Edinburgh in September 1745. He got as far south as Derby in England, but success was short-lived; a Hanoverian army led by the duke of Cumberland harried him all the way back to the Highlands, where Jacobite dreams were finally extinguished at the Battle of Culloden in 1746.

## The Highland Clearances

In the aftermath of the Jacobite rebellions, Highland dress, the bearing of arms and the bagpipes were outlawed, and the Highlands came under military control. The clansmen, no longer of any use as soldiers and uneconomical as tenants, were evicted from their homes and farms by the Highland chieftains to make way for sheep. A few stayed to work the sheep farms; many more were forced to seek work in the cities, or to eke a living from crofts (small holdings) on poor coastal land. Men who had never seen the sea were forced to take to boats to try their luck at herring fishing, and many thousands emigrated to North America, Australia and New Zealand in the late-18th and 19th centuries.

**1603**
James VI of Scotland inherits the English throne, becoming James I of Great Britain.

**1707**
Act of Union joins England and Scotland under a single parliament, sovereign and flag.

**1745–46**
Jacobite rebellion sees Bonnie Prince Charlie invade Scotland, ends in defeat at Battle of Culloden.

## North Sea Oil & Devolution

The discovery of North Sea oil in 1970 fuelled dreams of economic self sufficiency, and led to increasing nationalist sentiment in Scotland. In 1979 a referendum was held on whether to set up a directly elected Scottish Assembly. Fifty-two per cent of those who voted said 'yes' to devolution, but the Labour prime minister decided that everyone who didn't vote should be counted as a 'no'. By this controversial reasoning, only 33% of the electorate had voted 'yes', so the Scottish Assembly was rejected.

From 1979 to 1997 Scotland was ruled by a Conservative government in London for which the majority of Scots hadn't voted. Separatist feelings, always present, grew stronger. Following the landslide victory of the Labour Party in May 1997, another referendum was held on the creation of a Scottish parliament. This time the result was overwhelmingly and unambiguously in favour. Elections to the new parliament took place on 6 May 1999 and the Scottish parliament convened for the first time on 12 May in Edinburgh.

National Museum of Scotland (p79; Architect: Gareth Hoskins)

**Late 18th–19th century**
Cultural and intellectual life flourishes; Industrial Revolution sees Scotland lead world in shipbuilding.

**1941–45**
Clydebank blitzed by German bombers in 1941; by 1945 workforce is employed in heavy industries.

**1999–2004**
Scottish parliament convened in 1999; new parliament building opened by the Queen in October 2004.

# Family Travel

Scottish Borders region

JAMES ROSS/GETTY IMA...

*Scotland is a great place for a family holiday. There are plenty of things to keep the young ones occupied, from wildlife parks and outdoor activities to top-notch museums with interactive hands-on exhibits. Many tourist towns and national parks organise events and activities for kids, and even local museums usually make an effort with an activity sheet or child-focused information panels. Tourist offices are a great source for information on child-friendly attractions.*

## Accommodation

Children are generally well received all over Scotland, but accommodation can sometimes be a headache. Not all hotels and guesthouses (especially those at the boutique end of the market) are happy to accept younger children, so check their policy before you book. Many places quote a price per person rather than per room; look for B&Bs that advertise 'family rooms' (which usually sleep two adults plus one or two children) and you'll get better value.

In places that are happy to accept children, kids under a certain age can often stay for free in their parents' room, and child-friendly facilities, including cots, are provided.

## Eating Out

Many restaurants (especially the larger ones) have highchairs and decent children's menus.

However, a lot of more upmarket places can prove distinctly chilly if you turn up with a young family.

A lot of pubs are family friendly and some have great beer gardens where kids can run around and exhaust themselves while you enjoy lunch and a quiet pint. However, be aware that many Scottish pubs, even those that serve bar meals, are forbidden by law to admit children under 14; even in family-friendly pubs (ie those in possession of a Children's Certificate), under-14s are only admitted between 11am and 8pm, and only when accompanied by an adult.

## Feeding & Changing Baby

Breastfeeding in public remains mildly controversial in the UK, but if done discreetly is usually considered OK. In 2005 the Scottish parliament passed legislation safeguarding the freedom of women to breastfeed in public, so if anyone tries to stop you, quote the law at them!

On the sticky topic of dealing with nappies (diapers) while travelling, most big museums, galleries and visitor centres have baby-changing facilities, though you probably won't be terribly impressed with the facilities in motorway service stations and city-centre public toilets.

For more advice, see www.babygoes2.com and www.travelforkids.com.

## Things To Do

The weather is usually the big deciding factor when it comes to a successful family holiday. This being Scotland, expect some rainy days. Pack waterproofs and umbrellas,

### The Best...
## Activities for Kids

1 Nessie Hunter (p254)

2 Jacobite Steam Train (p268)

3 Cairngorm Sled-Dog Centre (p259)

4 Aquaxplore (p213)

5 Sea Life Surveys (p225)

IN FOCUS FAMILY TRAVEL

## Need to Know

- **Changing facilities** Available in most shopping centres, major museums and attractions
- **Cots** Usually provided in better hotels, but rare in B&Bs
- **Health** Standards similar to most Western nations; no special innoculations needed
- **Highchairs** Common in chain restaurants and fast-food places, but ask elsewhere
- **Kids' menus** As above for highchairs
- **Nappies (diapers)** Sold in every supermarket
- **Strollers** Widely accepted on most public transport
- **Transport** Child discounts and family tickets (usually two adults plus two kids) widely available

# The Harry Potter Connection

If your kids are fans of the Harry Potter movies, then impress them with a visit to locations where many of the scenes were shot. Here are a few:

○ **Jacobite Steam Train** The locomotive that stars as the Hogwarts Express

○ **Glen Nevis** Background to the quidditch match in *Philosopher's Stone*

○ **Glenfinnan Viaduct** The railway viaduct is the setting for the flying-car sequence in *Chamber of Secrets*

○ **Glen Coe** Hagrid's Hut in *Prisoner of Azkaban* was built just outside Glencoe village

For more details check out www.scotlandthemovie.com.

and always have a 'Plan B' that involves retreating to an indoor location. Locals are well used to this, and even outdoor attractions such as national parks have visitor centres and indoor exhibitions to keep young minds occupied when it's pouring down outside.

It's well worth asking in tourist offices for local family-based publications as a source of ideas. The *List* magazine (www.list.co.uk), available at newsagents and bookshops, has a section on children's activities and events in and around Glasgow and Edinburgh. A good online resource is www.dayoutwiththekids.co.uk.

See also Lonely Planet's *Travel with Children,* by Brigitte Barta et al.

# Highland Culture

Tug-of-war at the Braemar Gathering (p191)

TIM GRAHAM/CORBIS ©

*The distinctive culture of the Scottish Highlands – from bagpipes and Highland dancing to the swing of the kilt and the spectacle of Highland games – has its origins in the clan system that was remorselessly crushed following the Jacobite rebellion of 1745. The playing of pipes and the wearing of Highland dress remained illegal until the revival of interest in all things Highland in the 19th century.*

## Highland Games

The origins of Scotland's Highland games are lost in the mists of time. It is thought that trials of strength among clansmen were staged following military musters, and these impromptu contests were formalised in the early 19th century when Highland culture was romanticised by Britain's high society.

The traditional roster of events has changed little since those days, typically including piping and dancing competitions, alongside demonstrations of physical prowess such as tossing the caber (heaving a tree trunk into the air), throwing the hammer and putting the stone. Many games also include athletic events such as running and jumping.

## The Best...
## Highland Games

1 Braemar Gathering (p191)

2 Argyllshire Gathering (www.obangames.com)

3 Isle of Skye Highland Games (www.skye-highland-games.co.uk)

4 Mull Highland Games (www.scotlandsislands.com)

5 St Andrews Highland Games (www.albagames.co.uk)

# Bagpipes

Highland soldiers were traditionally accompanied into battle by the skirl of the pipes, and the Scottish Highland bagpipe is unique in being the only musical instrument ever to be classed as a weapon of war. The playing of the pipes was banned – under pain of death – by the British government in 1747 as part of a scheme to suppress Highland culture in the wake of the Jacobite uprising of 1745. The pipes were revived when the Highland regiments were drafted into the British Army towards the end of the 18th century.

# The Kilt

The original Scottish Highland dress was not the kilt but the plaid – a long length of tartan cloth wrapped around the body and over the shoulder. The wearing of Highland dress was banned after the Jacobite rebellions but revived under royal patronage in the 19th century. George IV and his English courtiers donned kilts for their visit to Scotland in 1822.

During the same century, Sir Walter Scott – novelist, poet and dedicated patriot – did much to rekindle interest in Highland culture. By then, however, many of the old setts (the pattern for a tartan) had been forgotten, and as a result some tartans are actually Victorian creations. The modern kilt only appeared in the 18th century and was reputedly invented by Thomas Rawlinson, an Englishman!

Kilts don't have pockets, so kilted Scotsmen keep their beer money in a sporran, a pouch made of animal skin that hangs in front of the kilt, suspended from a chain around the waist.

# Exploring Your Scottish Roots

Many visitors to Scotland take the opportunity to do some detective work on their Scottish ancestry. One of the best guides is *Tracing Your Scottish Ancestry* by Kathleen B Cory.

The **Scotland's People Centre** (☎0131-314 4300; www.scotlandspeoplehub.gov.uk; 2 Princes St, Edinburgh; ⏱9am-4.30pm Mon-Fri) provides access to the main records used in Scottish genealogical research – the Statutory Registers of births, marriages and deaths (1855 to the present), the Old Parish Registers (1533–1854) and the 10-yearly census returns from 1841 to 1911. Daily search fee is £15.

The **Scotland's People Website** (www.scotlandspeople.gov.uk) allows you to search the records online (pay per view).

Sir Walter Scott's former residence, Abbotsford (p107)

DEA/W. BUSS/GETTY IMAGES ©

*In the world of literature, Scotland packs a punch well above its diminutive weight. Its national poet, Robert Burns, is known and celebrated all over the world, his works translated into dozens of languages. Walter Scott and Robert Louis Stevenson are almost as widely read, as are contemporary novelists such as Ian Rankin and Iain Banks. The Writers' Museum in Edinburgh celebrates the work of Burns, Scott and Stevenson. Scottish artists are less well known, but have carved out a niche within the British art world.*

## WRITERS
### Robert Burns
Best remembered for penning the words of 'Auld Lang Syne', Robert Burns (1759–96) is Scotland's most famous poet and a popular hero whose birthday (25 January) is celebrated as Burns Night by Scots around the world.

Burns was born in 1759 in Alloway to a poor family who scraped together a living by gardening and farming. At school he soon showed an aptitude for literature and a fondness for the folk song. He later began to write his own songs and satires. When the problems of his arduous farming life were compounded by the threat of prosecution from the father of Jean Armour, with whom he'd had an affair, he decided to emigrate to Jamaica. He gave up his share of the family farm and published his poems to raise money for the journey.

The poems were so well reviewed in Edinburgh that Burns decided to remain in Scotland and devote himself to writing. He went to Edinburgh in 1787 to publish a second edition, but the financial rewards were not enough to live on and he had to take a job as an excise man in Dumfriesshire. Though he worked well, he wasn't a taxman by nature, and described his job as 'the execrable office of whip-person to the blood-hounds of justice'. He contributed many songs to collections published by Johnson and Thomson in Edinburgh, and a 3rd edition of his poems was published in 1793. To give an idea of the prodigious writings of the man, Robert Burns composed more than 28,000 lines of verse over 22 years. Burns died of rheumatic fever in Dumfries in 1796, aged 37.

Burns wrote in Lallans, the Scottish Lowland dialect of English that is not very accessible to the Sassenach (Englishman), or foreigner; perhaps this is part of his appeal. He was also very much a man of the people, satirising the upper classes and the church for their hypocrisy.

Many of the local landmarks mentioned in the verse-tale 'Tam o'Shanter' can still be visited. Farmer Tam, riding home after a hard night's drinking in a pub in Ayr, sees witches dancing in Alloway churchyard. He calls out to the one pretty witch, but is pursued by them all and has to reach the other side of the River Doon to be safe. He just manages to cross the Brig o'Doon, but his mare loses her tail to the witches.

## Sir Walter Scott

In 1787 Robert Burns was introduced to a 16-year-old boy at a social gathering in the house of an Edinburgh professor. The boy grew up to be Sir Walter Scott (1771–1832), Scotland's greatest and most prolific novelist. The son of an Edinburgh lawyer, Scott lived at various New Town addresses before moving to his country house at Abbotsford, south of Edinburgh.

Scott's early works were rhyming ballads, such as *The Lady of the Lake,* while his first historical novels – Scott effectively invented the genre – were published anonymously. He almost singlehandedly revived interest in Scottish history and legend in the early 19th century, and was largely responsible for organising King George IV's visit to Scotland in 1822. Plagued by debt in later life, he wrote obsessively – to the detriment of his health – in order to make money, but will always be best remembered for classic tales such as *Waverley, The Antiquary, The Heart of Midlothian, Ivanhoe, Redgauntlet* and *Castle Dangerous*.

## Robert Louis Stevenson

Along with Scott, Robert Louis Stevenson (1850–94) ranks as Scotland's best-known novelist. Born at 8 Howard Pl in Edinburgh into a family of famous lighthouse engineers, Stevenson studied law at Edinburgh University but was always intent on pursuing the life of a writer. An inveterate traveller, but dogged by ill health, he finally settled in Samoa in 1889, where he was revered by the natives as 'Tusitala' – the teller of tales. Stevenson is known and loved around the world for those tales: *Kidnapped, Catriona, Treasure Island, The Master of Ballantrae* and *The Strange Case of Dr Jekyll and Mr Hyde*.

## Sir Arthur Conan Doyle

Sir Arthur Conan Doyle (1859–1930), the creator of Sherlock Holmes, was born in Edinburgh and studied medicine at Edinburgh University. He based the character of Holmes on one of his lecturers, the surgeon Dr Joseph Bell, who had employed his forensic skills and powers of deduction on several murder cases in Edinburgh. There's a fascinating exhibit on Dr Bell in Edinburgh's Surgeons' Hall Museums.

# Iain Banks

One of Scotland's most successful contemporary authors, Iain Banks (1954–) is also one of its most prolific. His most enjoyable books include Complicity (1993), a gruesome and often hilarious thriller, and The Crow Road (1992), a warm, witty and moving family saga. The latter provides one of Scottish fiction's most memorable opening sentences: 'It was the day my grandmother exploded.'

# Ian Rankin

The Edinburgh-based crime novels of Ian Rankin (1960–), featuring the hard-drinking, introspective detective inspector John Rebus, are sinister, engrossing mysteries that explore the darker side of Scotland's capital city. Rankin's novels are filled with sharp dialogue, telling detail and three-dimensional characters, and his books have been translated into 22 languages.

# ARTISTS

## The Scottish Colourists

In the early 20th century the Scottish painters most widely acclaimed outside of the country were the group known as the Scottish Colourists – SJ Peploe, Francis Cadell, Leslie Hunter and JD Fergusson – whose striking paintings drew on French post-impressionist and Fauvist influences. Peploe and Cadell, active in the 1920s and '30s, often spent the summer painting together on the Isle of Iona, and reproductions of their beautiful landscapes and seascapes appear on many a print and postcard.

## The Edinburgh School

In the 1930s a group of modernist landscape artists called themselves the Edinburgh School. Chief among them were William Gillies (1898–1978), Sir William MacTaggart (1903–81) and Anne Redpath (1895–1965). Following WWII, artists such as Alan Davie (1920–) and Sir Eduardo Paolozzi (1924–2005) gained international reputations in abstract expressionism and pop art.

## Contemporary Artists

Among contemporary Scottish artists the most famous – or rather notorious – are Peter Howson and Jack Vettriano. Howson (1958–) hit the headlines when he went to Bosnia as an official war artist in 1993 and produced some controversial works. *Croatian and Muslim*, an uncompromising rape scene, sparked a debate about what was acceptable in a public exhibition of art.

Jack Vettriano (1954–), a self-taught painter, ranks as one of Scotland's most commercially successful artists. His work – realistic, voyeuristic, occasionally sinister and often carrying a powerful erotic charge – has been compared to that of the American painters Edward Hopper and Walter Sickert.

## The Best...
## Art Galleries

1 Scottish National Gallery (p78)

2 Royal Scottish Academy (p80)

3 Scottish National Gallery of Modern Art (p65)

4 Gallery of Modern Art, Glasgow (p125)

5 Kelvingrove Art Gallery & Museum (p132)

6 Burrell Collection (p136)

IN FOCUS WRITERS & ARTISTS

# Flavours of Scotland

Haggis, Scotland's national dish

FOODFOLIO/THE FOOD PASSIONATES/CO

*Traditional Scottish cookery is all about comfort food: solid, nourishing fare, often high in fat and carbohydrates, that would keep you warm on a winter's day spent in the fields or out fishing, and sweet treats to come home to in the evening. Scotland's traditional drinks – whisky and beer – have found a new lease of life in recent years, with single malts being marketed like fine wines, and a new breed of microbreweries springing up all over the country.*

## Scotch Whisky

'Love makes the world go round? Not at all! Whisky makes it go round twice as fast.'

*Whisky Galore*, Compton Mackenzie (1883–1972)

Scotch whisky (always spelt without an 'e' – whiskey with an 'e' is Irish or American) is Scotland's best-known product and biggest export. The spirit has been distilled in Scotland at least since the 15th century.

Malt whisky is distilled from malted barley – that is, barley that has been soaked in water, then allowed to germinate for around 10 days until the starch has turned into sugar – while grain whiskies are made from other cereals, usually wheat, corn or unmalted barley.

A single malt is a whisky that has been made with malted barley and is the product of a single distillery. A pure (vatted) malt is a mixture of single malts from several distilleries, and a blended whisky is a mixture of various grain whiskies (about 60%) and malt whiskies (about 40%) from many different distilleries.

A single malt, like a fine wine, somehow captures the essence of the place where it was made and matured – a combination of the water, the barley, the peat smoke, the oak barrels in which it was aged, and (in the case of certain coastal distilleries) the sea air and salt spray. Each distillation varies from the one before, like different vintages from the same vineyard.

A good malt whisky can be drunk neat, or preferably with a little water added. To appreciate the aroma and flavour to the utmost, a measure of malt whisky should be cut (diluted) with one-third to two-thirds as much spring water (still, bottled spring water will do). Ice, tap water and (God forbid) mixers are for philistines. Would you add lemonade or ice to a glass of Chablis?

**The Best...**
# Single Malt Whiskies

1 Bowmore (Islay)

2 Macallan (Speyside)

3 Highland Park (Orkney)

4 Bruichladdich (Islay)

5 Springbank (Campbeltown)

6 Talisker (Skye)

IN FOCUS FLAVOURS OF SCOTLAND

## Haggis

Scotland's national dish is often ridiculed because of its ingredients, which admittedly don't sound promising – the finely chopped lungs, heart and liver of a sheep, mixed with oatmeal and onion and stuffed into a sheep's stomach. However, it tastes surprisingly good.

Haggis should be served with *champit tatties* and *bashed neeps* (mashed potatoes and turnips), with a generous dollop of butter and a good sprinkling of black pepper.

Although it's eaten year-round, haggis is central to the celebrations of 25 January, in honour of Scotland's national poet, Robert Burns. Scots worldwide unite on Burns Night to revel in their Scottishness. A piper announces the arrival of the haggis and Burns' poem 'Address to a Haggis' is recited to this 'Great chieftan o' the puddin-race'. The bulging haggis is then lanced with a dirk (dagger) to reveal the steaming offal within, 'warm, reekin, rich'.

Vegetarians (and quite a few carnivores, no doubt) will be relieved to know that veggie haggis is available in some restaurants.

## Smoked Fish

Scotland is famous for its smoked salmon, but there are many other varieties of smoked fish – plus smoked meats and cheeses – to enjoy. Smoking food to preserve it is an ancient art that has recently undergone a revival, but this time it's more about flavour than preservation.

There are two parts to the process– first the cure, which involves covering the fish in a mixture of salt and molasses sugar, or soaking it in brine; and then the smoke, which can be either cold smoking (at less than 34°C), which results in a raw product, or hot smoking (at more than 60°C), which cooks it. Cold-smoked products include traditional smoked salmon, kippers and Finnan haddies. Hot-smoked products include *bradan rost* ('flaky' smoked salmon) and Arbroath smokies.

# Scottish Ales

The increasing popularity of real ales (traditionally brewed beers) has seen a huge rise in the number of specialist brewers and microbreweries springing up all over Scotland. They take pride in using only natural ingredients, and many try to revive ancient recipes, such as heather- and seaweed-flavoured ales. Here are a few of our favourites:

**Cairngorm Brewery** Creator of multi-award-winning Trade Winds ale.

**Islay Ales** Refreshing and citrusy Saligo Ale.

**Orkney Brewery** Famous for itsrich, chocolatey Dark Island ale, and the dangerously strong Skull Splitter.

**Williams Bros** Produces historic beers flavoured with heather flowers, seaweed, Scots pine and elderberries.

Arbroath smokies are haddock that have been gutted, beheaded and cleaned, then salted and dried overnight, tied together at the tail in pairs, and hot-smoked over oak or beech chippings for 45 to 90 minutes. Finnan haddies (named after the fishing village of Findon in Aberdeenshire) are also haddock, but these are split down the middle like kippers, and cold-smoked.

Kippers (smoked herring) were invented in Northumberland, in northern England, in the mid-19th century, but Scotland soon picked up the technique, and both Loch Fyne and Mallaig are famous for their kippers.

## Oat Cuisine

The most distinctive feature of traditional Scottish cookery is the abundant use of oatmeal. Oats (Avena sativa) grow well in the cool, wet climate of Scotland and have been cultivated here for at least 2000 years. Up to the 19th century, oatmeal was the main source of calories for the rural Scottish population. The farmer in his field, the cattle drover on the road to the market, the soldier on the march, all would carry with them a bag of meal that could be mixed with water and baked on a griddle or on hot stones beside a fire.

Long despised as an inferior foodstuff, oatmeal is enjoying a return to popularity as recent research has proved it to be highly nutritious (high in iron, calcium and B vitamins) and healthy (rich in soluble fibre, which helps to reduce cholesterol).

The best-known Scottish oatmeal dish is, of course, porridge, which is simply rolled oatmeal boiled with water. A lot of nonsense has been written about porridge and whether it should be eaten with salt or sugar. It should be eaten however you like it – as a child in the 1850s, Robert Louis Stevenson had golden syrup with his.

Oatcakes are another traditional dish that you will certainly come across during a visit to Edinburgh, usually as an accompaniment to cheese at the end of a meal.

A mealie pudding is a sausage-skin stuffed with oatmeal and onion and boiled for an hour or so. Add blood to the mixture and you have a black pudding.

Skirlie is simply chopped onions and oatmeal fried in beef dripping and seasoned with salt and pepper; it's usually served as a side dish.

Trout and herring can be dipped in oatmeal before frying, and it can be added to soups and stews as a thickening agent. It's even used in desserts – toasted oatmeal is a vital flavouring in cranachan, a delicious mixture of whipped cream, whisky and raspberries.

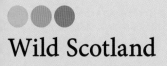

# Wild Scotland

Ospreys (p298)

MARK HAMBLIN/GETTY IMAGES ©

*Scotland can boast the best wildlife watching in Britain – from the majestic sea eagle to the iconic red deer, its roar reverberating among the hills during the autumn rut. The countless islands moored offshore, pounded by the raging North Atlantic Ocean, are havens for species hunted to extinction centuries ago in habitats further south. Whales and dolphins patrol the seas, and the remote archipelagos of the northeast are sanctuaries for seabird breeding colonies of extraordinary magnitude.*

## The Land

Scotland's mainland can be neatly divided into three. The southern Uplands, ranges of rounded hills bounded by fertile coastal plains, extend south from Girvan in Ayrshire to Dunbar in East Lothian.

The central Lowlands stretch from Glasgow and Ayr in the west to Edinburgh and Dundee in the east. This area is underlaid by the beds of coal and oil shale that fuelled Scotland's industrial revolution. Though it's only a fifth of the nation by land area, most of the country's industry, its two largest cities and 80% of the population are here.

Another great geological divide – the Highland Boundary Fault – runs from Helensburgh in the west to Stonehaven on the east coast, and marks the southern edge of the Scottish Highlands.

## The Best...
# Wildlife Encounters

1 Ospreys, Loch Garten (p263)

2 Sea eagles, Skye (p213)

3 Minke whales, Mull (p225)

4 Bottlenose dolphins, Moray Firth (p265)

5 Reindeer, Aviemore (p262)

Offshore, some 800 islands are concentrated in four main groups: Shetlands, Orkneys, Outer Hebrides and Inner Hebrides.

## The Water

It rains a lot in Scotland – some parts of the western Highlands get over 4.5m of it a year – so it's not surprising that about 3% of Scotland's land surface is fresh water. Lochs, rivers and burns form the majority of this, but about a third is wetlands: the peat bogs that form so much of the Highland and island landscape.

## Mammals

Britain's largest land animal, the red deer, is present in large numbers, as is the more common roe deer. You'll see them in the Highlands.

Otters are found in most parts of Scotland, around the coast and along salmon and trout rivers. The best places to spot them are in the northwest, especially on Skye.

Scotland is home to 75% of Britain's red squirrel population; they've been pushed out in most of the rest of the country by the dominant grey squirrels, introduced from North America.

The waters off Scotland's north and west coasts are rich in marine mammals. Dolphins and porpoises are fairly common, and in summer, minke whales are regular visitors. Orcas are occasionally sighted, and seals are widespread.

## Birds

Scotland has an immense variety of birds, including the mighty white-tailed sea eagle, Britain's biggest bird of prey. Reintroduced to the western seaboard after having been hunted almost to extinction, they once again patrol the skies above Skye and Mull.

The majestic osprey (also absent for most of the 20th century) nests in Scotland from mid-March through to September, after migrating from West Africa. There are around 200 breeding pairs; you can see nesting sites throughout the country. Other birds of prey, such as the golden eagle, buzzards, peregrine falcon and hen harrier, are also protected.

## National Parks

Scotland has two national parks – **Loch Lomond & the Trossachs** (p257) and the Cairngorms (p257). There's also a huge range of protected areas. Forty-seven **National Nature Reserves** (www.nnr-scotland. org.uk) span the country, and there are also marine areas under various levels of protection.

## The Salmon's Journey

One of Scotland's most thrilling sights is the flash of rippling silver as a salmon leaps up a fast-flowing cascade. The salmon's life begins in early spring, hatching in a gravel stream bed in a remote Scottish glen. The salmon fry stay in the river for a couple of years until they are big enough to head downstream and out to sea. After several years in the North Atlantic, they return home to reproduce, unerringly finding the river of their birth.

# Golf

Old Course (p180), St Andrews

NEIL SETCHFIELD/GETTY IMAGES ©

*Scotland is the home of golf. There are more than 550 golf courses here – that's more per capita than in any other country. The sport is hugely popular and much more egalitarian than in other countries, with lots of affordable, council-owned courses. There are many world-famous champion-ship courses too, of course, from Muirfield in East Lothian, and Turnberry and Troon in Ayrshire, to Carnoustie in Angus and St Andrews Old Course in Fife.*

## Origins of the Game

The oldest documented evidence of a game of golf being played dates from 1456, referring to Bruntsfield Links in Edinburgh. The game itself is much older – depending on which version you believe, it may have its origins in Roman times, or in medieval China, or it may have been invented in Scotland in the 12th century; some sources claim it was introduced to Scotland from the Low Countries.

Whatever its origins, there is no denying that golf was first systematised and given a set of official rules in Scotland in the 18th century. The country is home to the world's oldest golf course, its oldest golf club and the sport's governing body (except for the USA and Mexico, where the PGA holds sway), the Royal and Ancient Golf Club of St Andrews.

# Leith Links

Although St Andrews claims seniority in having the oldest golf course in the world, it was at Leith Links in 1744 that the first official rules of the game were formulated by the Honorable Company of Edinburgh Golfers – these 13 rules formed the basis of the modern game. Back then, the game was played over five holes, each being around 400 yards. Rule No 9 gives some insight into the 18th-century sport – 'If a ball be stop'd by any person, Horse, Dog or anything else, the Ball so stop'd must be played where it lyes'. The original document is in the National Library of Scotland and the Honorable Company is now the famous Muirfield Golf Club.

# St Andrews

St Andrews is the headquarters of the game's governing body, the Royal and Ancient, and the location of the world's oldest and most famous golf course, the Old Course. The earliest written evidence of golf being played on the links at St Andrews dates from 1552, but the present course layout took form in the 1860s when Old Tom Morris had a hand in its design. One of the course's many unusual features is its double greens: seven of the greens have two holes each. And then there's the Road Hole, the 17th – probably the most famous golf hole in the world – where the hazards include a hotel, a stone dyke and a tarmac road (all of which are in play).

# Playing Golf in Scotland

VisitScotland publishes the *Official Guide to Golf in Scotland*, a free annual brochure listing course details, costs and clubs, with information on where to stay. Some regions offer a Golf Pass (http://golf.visitscotland.com), costing between £40 and £120 for five days (Monday to Friday), which allows play on a range of courses. Most clubs, be they obscurely local or internationally famous, are open to visitors – details can be found at www.scotlands-golf-courses.com.

# Survival
# Guide

River Muick, Cairngorms National Park (p257)
PHOTOGRAPHER: RADIUS IMAGES/CORBIS ©

# Directory

●●●

# Accommodation

Scotland provides a comprehensive choice of accommodation to suit all visitors.

For budget travel, the options are campsites, hostels and cheap B&Bs. Above this price level is a plethora of comfortable B&Bs and guesthouses (£25 to £40 per person per night). Midrange hotels are present in most places, while for high-end lodgings (£65-plus per person a night) there are some superb hotels, the most interesting being converted castles and mansions, or chic designer options in cities.

If you're travelling solo, expect to pay a supplement in hotels and B&Bs, meaning you'll often be forking over 75% of the price of a double for your single room.

Almost all B&Bs, guesthouses and hotels (and even some hostels) include breakfast in the room price.

Prices increase over the peak tourist season (June to September) and are at their highest in July and August. Outside of these months, and particularly in winter, special deals are often available at guesthouses and hotels.

If you're going to be in Edinburgh in the festival month of August or at Hogmanay (New Year), book as far in advance as you can – a year if possible – as the city will be packed.

Tourist offices have an accommodation booking service (£4), which can be handy over summer. However, note that they can only book the ever-decreasing number of places that are registered with **VisitScotland** (☎ 0845 859 1006; www.visitscotland.com/accommodation). There are many other fine accommodation options which, mostly due to the hefty registration fee, choose not to register with the tourist board. Registered places tend to be a little pricier than nonregistered ones. VisitScotland's star system is based on a rather arbitrary set of criteria, so don't set too much store by it.

## ACCOMMODATION PRICE INDICATORS

Accommodation choices are flagged with price indicators, based on the cheapest accommodation for two people in high season:

| £ | up to £50 |
|---|---|
| ££ | from £50 to £130 |
| £££ | £130 and over |

## B&BS & GUESTHOUSES

B&Bs are a Scottish institution. At the bottom end you get a bedroom in a private house, a shared bathroom and a fry-up (juice, coffee or tea, cereal and cooked breakfast – bacon, eggs, sausage, baked beans and toast). Midrange B&Bs have en suite bathrooms, TVs in each room and more variety (and healthier options) for breakfast. Almost all B&Bs provide hospitality trays (tea- and coffee-making facilities) in bedrooms. B&B options range from urban houses to pubs to rural farms.

Guesthouses, often large converted private houses, are an extension of the B&B concept. They are normally larger and less personal than B&Bs.

## HOTELS

There are some wonderfully luxurious places, including rustic countryhouse hotels in fabulous settings, and castles complete with crenellated battlements, grand staircases and the obligatory rows of stag heads. Expect all the perks at these places, often including a gym, a sauna, a pool and first-class service. Even if you're on a budget, it's worth splashing out for a night at one of the classic Highland hotels, which also function as community centres, including the local pub and restaurant.

In the cities, dullish chain options dominate the midrange category, though there are some quirkier options to be found in Glasgow and Edinburgh.

Increasingly, hotels use an airline-style pricing system, so it's worth booking well ahead to take advantage of the cheapest rates. The website www.moneysavingexpert.com has a good guide to finding cheap hotel rooms.

Try these online discount sites:

o www.hotels.com

o www.booking.com

o www.lastminute.com

o www.laterooms.com

●●●
# Activities

Scotland is a brilliant place for outdoor recreation and has something to offer everyone, from those who enjoy a short stroll to full-on adrenalin junkies. Although hiking, golf, fishing and cycling are the most popular activities, there is an astonishing variety of things to do.

Most activities are well organised and have clubs and associations that can give visitors invaluable information and, sometimes, substantial discounts. **Visit Scotland** (www.visitscotland.com) has information on most activities. Its website

## Practicalities

o Leaf through Edinburgh's *Scotsman* newspaper or Glasgow's *Herald*; the latter is over 225 years old.

o Have a giggle at the popular Labour-influenced tabloid, the *Daily Record,* or try the *Sunday Post* for rose-tinted nostalgia.

o BBC Radio Scotland (AM 810kHz, FM 92.4–94.7MHz) provides a Scottish point of view.

o Watch BBC1 Scotland, BBC2 Scotland and ITV stations STV or Border. Channels Four and Five are nationwide channels with unchanged content for Scotland.

o Use the metric system for weights and measures, with the exception of road distances (in miles) and beer (in pints). The pint is 570mL, more than the US version.

o In Scotland you can't smoke in any public place with a roof and that is at least half enclosed. That means pubs, bus shelters, restaurants and hotels – basically, anywhere you might want to.

has useful pages on walking, fishing, golf, skiing, cycling and adventure sports. They also produce a good booklet, *Active in Scotland*, available at tourist offices.

●●●
# Business Hours

In the Highlands and islands Sunday opening is restricted, and it's common for there to be little or no public transport.

Opening hours are as follows:

**Banks** 9.30am to 4pm or 5pm Monday to Friday, plus some are open 9.30am to 1pm Saturday.

**Nightclubs** 9pm or 10pm to 1am, 2am or later. Often only open Thursday to Saturday.

**Post offices** 9am to 6pm Monday to Friday, 9am to 12.30pm Saturday (main branches to 5pm Saturday).

**Pubs & Bars** 11am to 11pm Monday to Thursday, 11am to 1am Friday and Saturday, 12.30pm to 11pm Sunday; lunch is served noon to 2.30pm, dinner 6pm to 9pm daily.

**Shops** 9am to 5.30pm (or 6pm in cities) Monday to Saturday, and often 11am to 5pm Sunday.

**Restaurants** Lunch noon to 2.30pm, dinner 6pm to 9pm or 10pm; in small towns and villages the chippy (fish-and-chip shop) is often the only place to buy cooked food after 8pm.

# Climate

### Edinburgh

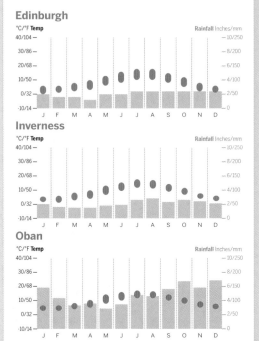

### Inverness

### Oban

## HISTORIC SCOTLAND
Heritage Organisation

(HS; 0131-668 8999; www.
historic-scotland.gov.uk)
A non-profit organisation that
cares for hundreds of sites
of historical importance. A
year's membership costs
£46.50/86.50 per adult/fam-
ily, and gives free entry to HS
sites (half-price entry to sites
in England and Wales). Also
offers a short-term Explorer
membership – three days out
of five for £28, seven days out
of 14 for £37.

## NATIONAL TRUST FOR
SCOTLAND
Heritage Organisation

(NTS; 0844-493 2100; www.
nts.org.uk)
NTS looks after hundreds of
sites of historical, architectural or environmental importance. A year's membership,
costing £49/84 for an adult/
family, offers free access to all
NTS and National Trust properties (in the rest of the UK).

## Customs Regulations

Travellers from outside the EU
can bring in, duty-free:
- 200 cigarettes or 100
cigarillos or 50 cigars or 250g
of tobacco
- 16L of beer
- 4L of non-sparkling wine
- 1L of spirits or 2L of fortified
wine or sparkling wine
- £390 worth of all other
goods, including perfume, gifts
and souvenirs.

Anything over this limit must
be declared to customs officers on arrival.

For details of restrictions
and quarantine regulations,
see the customs website
(www.hmrc.gov.uk/customs).

## Discount Cards

Membership of **Historic
Scotland** (HS) and the
**National Trust for Scotland**
(NTS) is worth considering,
especially if you're going to be
in Scotland for a while. Both
are nonprofit organisations
dedicated to the preservation
of the environment, and both
care for hundreds of spectacular sites. You can join up
at any of their properties.

## Electricity

230V/50Hz

304

# Food

In this guide eating choices are flagged with price indicators, based on the cost of an average main course from the dinner menu:

EATING PRICE INDICATORS

| £ | up to £9 |
| £££ | from £9 to £18 |
| £££ | £18 and over |

Note though that lunch mains are often cheaper than dinner mains, and many places offer an 'early bird' special with lower prices (usually available between 5pm and 7pm).

# Gay & Lesbian Travellers

Although many Scots are fairly tolerant of homosexuality, overt displays of affection aren't wise if conducted away from acknowledged 'gay' venues or districts – hostility may be encountered.

Edinburgh and Glasgow have small but flourishing gay scenes. The website and monthly magazine *Scotsgay* (www.scotsgay.co.uk) keep gays, lesbians and bisexuals informed about gay-scene issues.

# Health

◦ If you're an EU citizen, a European Health Insurance Card (EHIC) – available from health centres or, in the UK, post offices – covers you for most medical care. An EHIC will not cover you for non-urgent cases, or emergency repatriation.

◦ Citizens from non-EU countries should find out if there is a reciprocal arrangement for free medical care between their country and the UK.

◦ If you do need health insurance, make sure you get a policy that covers you for the worst possible case, such as an accident requiring an emergency flight home.

◦ No jabs are required to travel to Scotland.

◦ The most painful problems facing visitors to the Highlands and islands are midges.

# Insurance

This not only covers you for medical expenses, theft or loss, but also for cancellation of, or delays in, any of your travel arrangements.

Lots of bank accounts give their clients automatic travel insurance – check if this is the case for you.

Always read the small print carefully. Some policies specifically exclude 'dangerous activities', such as scuba diving, motorcycling, skiing, mountaineering and even trekking.

There's a variety of policies and your travel agent can give recommendations. Make sure the policy includes health care and medication in the countries you may visit on your way to/from Scotland.

You may prefer a policy that pays doctors or hospitals directly rather than forcing you to pay on the spot and claim the money back later. If you have to claim later, make sure you keep all documentation. Some policies ask you to call back (reverse charges) to a centre in your home country where an immediate assessment of your problem is made.

Not all policies cover ambulances, helicopter rescue or emergency flights home. Most policies exclude cover for pre-existing illnesses.

Worldwide travel insurance is available at www.lonelyplanet.com/travel_services. You can buy, extend and claim online anytime – even if you're already on the road.

# Internet Access

If you're travelling with a laptop, you'll find a wide range of places offering a wi-fi connection. These range from cafes to B&Bs and public spaces.

We've indicated accommodation and eating and drinking options that have wi-fi with the 🛜 symbol in the text. Wi-fi is often free, but some places (typically, upmarket hotels) charge.

If you don't have a laptop, the best places to surf the internet are public libraries – nearly all of which have a couple of computer terminals devoted to internet use, and they are free to use, though there's often a time limit.

Internet cafes also exist in the cities and larger towns and generally charge about £2 to £3 per hour.

Many of the larger tourist offices across the country also have internet access.

## Legal Matters

Police have the power to detain, for up to six hours, anyone suspected of having committed an offence punishable by imprisonment (including drug offences).

If you need legal assistance, contact the **Scottish Legal Aid Board** (☏ 0845 122 8686; www.slab.org.uk; 44 Drumsheugh Gardens, Edinburgh).

## Money

The British currency is the pound sterling (£), with 100 pence (p) to a pound. 'Quid' is the slang term for pound.

Three Scottish banks issue their own banknotes, meaning there's quite a variety of different notes in circulation. They are legal currency in England too, but you'll sometimes run into problems changing them. They are also harder to exchange once you get outside the UK.

### ATMS

ATMs (called cashpoints in Scotland) are widespread and you'll usually find at least one in small towns and villages. You can use Visa, MasterCard, Amex, Cirrus, Plus and Maestro to withdraw cash from ATMs belonging to most banks and building societies in Scotland.

Cash withdrawals from some ATMs may be subject to a small charge, but most are free. If you're not from the UK, your home bank will likely charge you for withdrawing money overseas; it pays to be aware of how much, as it may be much better to withdraw larger amounts less often.

### CREDIT CARDS

Visa and MasterCard cards are widely recognised, although many places will charge a small amount for accepting them. Charge cards such as Amex and Diners Club may not be accepted in smaller establishments. Many smaller B&Bs do not take cards.

### MONEYCHANGERS

Be careful using bureaux de change; they may offer good exchange rates but frequently levy outrageous commissions and fees. The best-value place to change money in the UK is at post offices, but only the ones in larger towns and cities offer this service. Larger tourist offices also have exchange facilities.

### TIPPING

Tip 10% in sit-down restaurants, but not if there's already a service charge on the bill.

In very classy places they may expect closer to 15%.

Service is at your discretion: even if the charge is added to the bill, you don't have to pay it if you feel service has been poor.

Don't tip in pubs: if the service has been exceptional over the course of an evening, you can say 'have one for yourself'.

Tip taxi drivers in cities about 10%, or just round up.

## Public Holidays

Although bank holidays are general public holidays in the rest of the UK, in Scotland they only apply to banks and some other commercial offices.

Scottish towns normally have four days of public holiday, which they allocate themselves; dates vary from year to year and from town to town. Most places celebrate St Andrew's Day (30 November) as a public holiday.

General public holidays:

**New Year** 1 & 2 January

**Good Friday** March or April

**Christmas Day** 25 December

**Boxing Day** 26 December

## Telephone

The famous red telephone boxes are a dying breed now, surviving mainly in conservation areas. You'll mainly see two types of phone booths in Scotland: one takes money (and doesn't give change), while the other uses prepaid phonecards and credit cards. Some phones accept both coins and cards. Payphone cards are widely available.

The cheapest way of calling internationally is via the internet, or by buying a discount call card; you'll see these in newsagents, along with tables of countries and the number of minutes you'll get for your money.

### MOBILE PHONES

Codes for mobile phones usually begin with 07. The UK uses the GSM 900/1800 network, which covers the rest of Europe, Australia and New Zealand, but isn't compatible with the North American GSM

1900. Most modern mobiles, however, can function on both networks – check before you leave home.

## PHONE CODES & USEFUL NUMBERS

**Dialling the UK** Dial your country's international access code then ☎44 (the UK country code), then the area code (dropping the first 0) followed by the phone number.

**Dialling out of the UK** The international access code is ☎00; dial this, then add the code of the country you wish to call.

**Making a reverse-charge (collect) international call** Dial ☎155 for the operator. It's an expensive option, but not for the caller.

**Area codes in Scotland** Begin with ☎01, eg Edinburgh ☎0131, Wick ☎01955.

**Directory Assistance** There are several numbers; ☎118500 is one.

**Mobile phones** Codes usually begin with ☎07.

**Free calls** Numbers starting with ☎0800 are free; calls to ☎0845 numbers are charged at local rates.

### TIME DIFFERENCE BETWEEN SCOTLAND & MAJOR CITIES

|  |  |
| --- | --- |
| Paris, Berlin, Rome | 1hr ahead |
| New York | 5hr behind |
| Sydney | 9hr ahead Apr-Sep, 10hr Oct, 11hr Nov-Mar. |
| Los Angeles | 8hr behind |
| Mumbai | 5½hr ahead, 4½hr Mar-Oct |
| Tokyo | 9hr ahead, 8hr Mar-Oct |

# Tourist Information

The Scottish Tourist Board, known as **VisitScotland** (☎ 0845 225 5121; www.visitscotland.com; Ocean Point One, 94 Ocean Dr), deals with inquiries made by post, email and telephone. You can ask for regional brochures to be posted to you.

Most larger towns have tourist offices ('information centres') that open 9am or 10am to 5pm Monday to Friday, and on weekends in summer. In small places, particularly in the Highlands, tourist offices only open from Easter to September.

To email a tourist office, use townname@visitscotland.com.

# Travellers with Disabilities

Travellers with disabilities will find Scotland a strange mix of user-friendliness and unfriendliness. Most new buildings are accessible to wheelchair users, so modern hotels and tourist attractions are fine. However, most B&Bs and guesthouses are in hard-to-adapt older buildings, which means that travellers with mobility problems may pay more for accommodation. Things are constantly improving, though.

It's a similar story with public transport. Newer buses have steps that lower for easier access, as do trains, but it's wise to check before setting out. Tourist attractions usually reserve parking spaces near the entrance for drivers with disabilities.

Many places such as ticket offices and banks are fitted with hearing loops to assist the hearing-impaired; look for a posted symbol of a large ear.

A few tourist attractions, such as Glasgow Cathedral, have Braille guides or scented gardens for the visually impaired.

VisitScotland produces the guide *Accessible Scotland* for wheelchair-bound travellers, and many tourist offices have leaflets with accessibility details for their area. Regional accommodation guides have a wheelchair-accessible criterion.

Many regions have organisations that hire out wheelchairs; contact the local tourist office for details. Many nature trails have been adapted for wheelchair use.

# Time

Scotland is on GMT/UTC. The clocks go forward for 'summer time' one hour at the end of March, and go back at the end of October. The 24-hour clock is used for transport timetables.

# Visas

○ If you're a citizen of the EEA (European Economic Area) nations or Switzerland, you don't need a visa to enter or work in Britain – enter using your national identity card.

307

- Visa regulations are always subject to change, so it's essential to check with your local British embassy, high commission or consulate before leaving home.

- Currently, if you're a citizen of Australia, Canada, New Zealand, Japan, Israel, the USA and several other countries, you can stay for up to six months (no visa required), but are not allowed to work.

- Nationals of many countries, including South Africa, will need to obtain a visa: for more info, see www.ukvisas.gov.uk.

# Transport

●●●
# Getting There & Away

Flights, tours and rail tickets can be booked online at lonely planet.com/bookings.

## ✈ AIR

There are direct flights to Scottish airports from England, Wales, Ireland, the USA, Canada, Scandinavia and several countries in western and central Europe. From elsewhere, you'll probably have to fly into a European hub and catch a connecting flight

to a Scottish airport – London, Amsterdam, Frankfurt and Paris have the best connections. If flying from North America, it's worth looking at Icelandair, which often has good deals to Glasgow via Reykjavik.

## AIRPORTS

Scotland has four main international airports: Aberdeen, Edinburgh, Glasgow and Glasgow Prestwick. A few short-haul international flights land at Inverness and Sumburgh, while London is the main UK gateway for long-haul flights.

## 🚗 LAND

### BUS

Buses are usually the cheapest way to get to Scotland from other parts of the UK. The main operators:

#### MEGABUS

( ☏ 0871 266 3333; www.megabus.com) One-way fares from London to Glasgow from as little as £5 if you book well in advance (up to 12 weeks).

#### NATIONAL EXPRESS

( ☏ 08717 818178; www.nationalexpress.com) Regular services from London and other cities in England and Wales to Glasgow and Edinburgh.

#### SCOTTISH CITYLINK

( ☏ 0871 266 3333; www.citylink.co.uk) Daily service between Belfast and Glasgow and Edinburgh via Cairnryan ferry.

### CAR & MOTORCYCLE

Drivers of EU-registered vehicles will find bringing a car or motorcycle into Scotland fairly easy. The vehicle must

have registration papers and a nationality plate, and you must have insurance. The International Insurance Certificate (Green Card) isn't compulsory, but it is excellent proof that you're covered. If driving from mainland Europe via the Channel Tunnel or ferry ports, head for London and follow the M25 orbital road to the M1 motorway, then follow the M1 and M6 north.

### TRAIN

Travelling to Scotland by train is faster and usually more comfortable than the bus, but more expensive. Taking into account check-ins and travel time between city centre and airport, the train is a competitive alternative, timewise, to air travel on the London to Edinburgh route.

#### NATIONAL RAIL ENQUIRY SERVICE

( ☏ 08457 48 49 50; www.nationalrail.co.uk) Timetable and fare info for all UK trains.

●●●
# Getting Around

Public transport in Scotland is generally good, but it can be costly compared with other European countries. Buses are usually the cheapest way to get around, but also the slowest. With a discount pass, trains can be competitive; they're also quicker and often take you through beautiful scenery.

**Traveline** ( ☏ 0871 200 2233; www.travelinescotland.com) provides timetable info for all public-transport services in Scotland, but can't provide fare information or book tickets.

## ✈ AIR

Most domestic air services are geared to business needs, or are lifelines for remote island communities. Flying is a pricey way to cover relatively short distances, and only worth considering if you're short of time and want to visit the Hebrides, Orkney or Shetland.

## 🚢 BOAT

**CALEDONIAN MACBRAYNE**
(CalMac; ☎ 0800 066 5000; www.calmac.co.uk) Serves the west coast and islands. Comprehensive timetable booklet available from tourist offices. **CalMac Island Hopscotch** offers more than two dozen tickets, giving reduced fares for various combinations of crossings; these are listed on the website and in the CalMac timetables booklet. **Island Rover** tickets allow unlimited ferry travel for £55/79 for a foot passenger for eight/15 days, plus £259/388 for a car or £130/195 for a motorbike. Bicycles travel free with a foot passenger's ticket.

## 🚌 BUS

Scotland is served by an extensive bus network that covers most of the country. In remote rural areas, however, services are more geared to the needs of locals (getting to school or the shops in the nearest large town) and may not be conveniently timed for visitors.

## BUS PASSES

The **Scottish Citylink Explorer Pass** offers unlimited travel on Scottish Citylink (and other selected bus routes)

services within Scotland for any three days out of five (£39), any five days out of 10 (£59) or any eight days out of 16 (£79). It also gives discounts on various regional bus services, on Northlink and CalMac ferries, and in SYHA hostels. The pass can be bought in the UK by both UK and overseas citizens.

## 🚗 CAR & MOTORCYCLE

Scotland's roads are generally good and far less busy than in England, so driving's more enjoyable. However, cars are nearly always inconvenient in city centres.

Motorways (designated 'M') are toll-free dual carriageways, limited mainly to central Scotland. Main roads ('A') are dual or single carriageways and are sometimes clogged with slow-moving trucks or caravans; the A9 from Perth to Inverness is notoriously busy.

Life on the road is more relaxed and interesting on the secondary roads (designated 'B') and minor roads (undesignated), although in the Highlands and islands there's the added hazard of suicidal sheep wandering onto the road (be particularly wary of lambs in spring).

At around £1.45 per litre (equivalent to around US$9 per US gallon), petrol's expensive by American or Australian standards; diesel is about 3p per litre more expensive. Prices tend to rise as you get further from the main centres and are over 10% higher in the Outer Hebrides. In remote areas

petrol stations are widely spaced and sometimes closed on Sunday.

## DRIVING LICENCE

A non-EU licence is valid in Britain for up to 12 months from time of entry into the country. If bringing a car from Europe, make sure you're adequately insured.

## HIRE

Car hire in the UK is competitively priced by European standards, and shopping around online can unearth some great deals, which can drop as low as £12 per day for an extended hire period. Hit comparison sites like **Kayak**

## Track Roads

...ntry areas, and especially in the ...d islands, you will find single-...hat are only wide enough for one ...g places (usually marked with a ...d sign, or a black-and-white striped pole) are used to allow oncoming traffic to pass. Remember that passing places are also for overtaking – pull over to let faster vehicles pass if necessary. Be aware that it's illegal to park in passing places.

(www.kayak.com) or **Kelkoo** (www.kelkoo.com) to find some of the best prices.

The minimum legal age for driving is 17 but to rent a car, drivers must usually be aged 23 to 65 – outside these limits special conditions or insurance requirements may apply.

### ROAD RULES

The *Highway Code,* widely available in bookshops, details all UK road regulations. Vehicles drive on the left. Front seatbelts are compulsory; if the back seat has belts, they must be worn too. The speed limit is 30mph in built-up areas, 60mph on single carriageways and 70mph on dual carriageways. Give way to your right at roundabouts (traffic already on the roundabout has right of way). Motorcyclists must wear helmets.

It is a criminal offence to use a hand-held mobile phone or similar device while driving; this includes while you are stopped at traffic lights, or stuck in traffic, when you can expect to be moving again at any moment.

The maximum permitted blood-alcohol level when driving is 80mg/100mL

(35mg per 100mL of breath); this is slightly higher than in many other countries.

Traffic offences (illegal parking, speeding etc) usually incur a fine for which you're allowed 30 to 60 days to pay. In Glasgow and Edinburgh the parking inspectors are numerous and without mercy – never leave your car around the city centres without a valid parking ticket, as you risk a hefty fine.

### TOURS

There are lots of companies in Scotland offering all kinds of tours, including historical, activity-based and backpacker tours. It's a question of picking the tour that suits your requirements and budget.

### HEART OF SCOTLAND TOURS

( 01828-627799; www.heart ofscotlandtours.co.uk) Specialises in mini-coach day tours of central Scotland and the Highlands, departing from Edinburgh.

### RABBIE'S

( 0131-226 3133; www. rabbies.com) One- to five-day tours of the Highlands in 16-seat minibuses with professional driver/guide.

### TIMBERBUSH TOURS

( 0131-226 6066; www. timberbush-tours.co.uk) Comfortable small-group minibus tours around Scotland, with Glasgow and Edinburgh departures.

### TRAIN

Scotland's train network extends to all major cities and towns, but the railway

## Road Distances (miles)

| | Aberdeen | Dundee | Edinburgh | Fort William | Glasgow | Inverness | Kyle of Lochalsh | Mallaig | Oban | Scrabster | Stranraer |
|---|---|---|---|---|---|---|---|---|---|---|---|
| Dundee | 70 | | | | | | | | | | |
| Edinburgh | 129 | 62 | | | | | | | | | |
| Fort William | 165 | 121 | 146 | | | | | | | | |
| Glasgow | 145 | 84 | 42 | 104 | | | | | | | |
| Inverness | 105 | 131 | 155 | 66 | 166 | | | | | | |
| Kyle of Lochalsh | 188 | 177 | 206 | 76 | 181 | 82 | | | | | |
| Mallaig | 189 | 161 | 180 | 44 | 150 | 106 | 34 | | | | |
| Oban | 180 | 118 | 123 | 45 | 94 | 110 | 120 | 85 | | | |
| Scrabster | 218 | 250 | 279 | 185 | 286 | 119 | 214 | 238 | 230 | | |
| Stranraer | 233 | 171 | 120 | 184 | 80 | 250 | 265 | 232 | 178 | 374 | |
| Ullapool | 150 | 189 | 215 | 90 | 225 | 135 | 88 | 166 | 161 | 125 | 158 |

map has a lot of large, blank areas in the Highlands and the Southern Uplands where you'll need to switch to bus or car. The West Highland line from Glasgow to Fort William and Mallaig, and the Inverness to Kyle of Lochalsh line, offer two of the world's most scenic rail journeys.

## NATIONAL RAIL ENQUIRY SERVICE

(☎ 08457 48 49 50; www.nationalrail.co.uk) Timetable and fare info for all UK trains.

## COSTS & RESERVATIONS

Train travel is more expensive than the bus, but usually more comfortable: a standard return from Edinburgh to Inverness is about £62 compared with £28 on the bus.

Reservations are recommended for intercity trips, especially on Fridays and public holidays. For shorter journeys, just buy a ticket at the station before you go. On certain routes, including the Glasgow–Edinburgh express, and in places where there's no ticket office at the station, you can buy tickets on the train.

Children under five travel free; those five to 15 usually pay half-fare.

There are several types of ticket; in general, the further ahead you can book the cheaper your ticket will be:

**Advance Purchase** Book by 6pm on the day before travel; cheaper than Anytime.

**Anytime** Buy any time and travel any time, with no restrictions.

**Off Peak** There are time restrictions (you're not usually allowed to travel on a train that leaves before 9.15am); relatively cheap.

## TRAIN PASSES

ScotRail has a range of good-value passes for train travel. You can buy them online or by phone or at train stations throughout Britain. Note that Travelpass and Rover tickets are not valid for travel on certain (eg commuter) services before 9.15am weekdays.

**Central Scotland Rover** Covers train travel between Glasgow, Edinburgh, North Berwick, Stirling and Fife; costs £35 for three days' travel out of seven.

**Freedom of Scotland Travelpass** Gives unlimited travel on all Scottish train services (some restrictions), all CalMac ferry services and on certain Scottish Citylink coach services (on routes not covered by rail). It's available for four days' travel out of eight (£129) or eight days out of 15 (£173).

**Highland Rover** Allows unlimited train travel from Glasgow to Oban, Fort William and Mallaig, and from Inverness to Kyle of Lochalsh, Aviemore, Aberdeen and Thurso. It also gives free travel on the Oban/Fort William to Inverness bus, on the Oban–Mull and Mallaig–Skye ferries, and on buses on Mull and Skye. It's valid for four days' travel out of eight (£79).

# Behind the Scenes

## Our Readers

Many thanks to the travellers who used the last edition and wrote to us with helpful hints, useful advice and interesting anecdotes: Liisa Macnaughton, Arlette McDaniel and Nickos Yoldassis.

## Author Thanks

### NEIL WILSON

Many thanks to all the helpful and enthusiastic staff at TICs throughout the country, and to the many travellers I met on the road who chipped in with advice and recommendations. Thanks also to Carol Downie and Peter Yeoman, Fiona Maxwell, Neil Ballantyne, Jason McInally, Ian Logan, Suu Ramsay, David Sexton, Adrian Shine and Eric Baird. Finally, thanks to coauthor Andy and to the ever-helpful and patient editors and cartographers at Lonely Planet.

## Acknowledgments

Climate map data adapted from Peel MC, Finlayson BL & McMahon TA (2007) 'Updated World Map of the Köppen-Geiger Climate Classification', Hydrology and Earth System Sciences, 11, 1633–44.

Illustrations p70-71, p92-93 and p166-67 by Javier Zarracina.

Cover photographs: Front: Eilean Donan Castle, Britain on View / Getty Images. Back: Dugald Stewart Memorial, Calton Hill, Edinburgh, Karl Blackwell / Getty Images.

## This Book

This guidebook was commissioned in Lonely Planet's London office, and produced by the following:

**Commissioning Editors** Katie O'Connell, Clifton Wilkinson

**Coordinating Editor** Luna Soo

**Coordinating Cartographer** Brendan Streager

**Coordinating Layout Designer** Nicholas Colicchia

**Managing Editor** Angela Tinson

**Managing Cartographers** Alison Lyall, Anthony Phelan

**Managing Layout Designer** Chris Girdler

**Assisting Editors** Samantha Forge, Anne Mason, Fionnuala Twomey

**Assisting Layout Designer** Wibowo Rusli

**Cover Research** Naomi Parker

**Internal Image Research** Barbara Di Castro

**Thanks to** Brigitte Ellemor, Ryan Evans, Larissa Frost, Jouve India, Kate McDonell, Trent Paton, Raphael Richards, Dianne Schallmeiner, Joseph Spanti, Gerard Walker

### SEND US YOUR FEEDBACK

We love to hear from travellers – your comments keep us on our toes and help make our books better. Our well-travelled team reads every word on what you loved or loathed about this book. Although we cannot reply individually to postal submissions, we always guarantee that your feedback goes straight to the appropriate authors, in time for the next edition. Each person who sends us information is thanked in the next edition, the most useful submissions are rewarded with a selection of digital PDF chapters.

Visit **lonelyplanet.com/contact** to submit your updates and suggestions or to ask for help. Our award-winning website also features inspirational travel stories, news and discussions.

Note: We may edit, reproduce and incorporate your comments in Lonely Planet products such as guidebooks, websites and digital products, so let us know if you don't want your comments reproduced or your name acknowledged. For a copy of our privacy policy visit lonelyplanet.com/privacy.

# Index

**000** Map pages